The TRAGIC HISTORY of the SEA

The TRAGIC HISTORY *of the* SEA

SHIPWRECKS FROM THE BIBLE TO TITANIC

ANTHONY BRANDT

NATIONAL GEOGRAPHIC

WASHINGTON, D.C.

Library of Congress Cataloging-in-Publication Data

The tragic history of the sea : shipwrecks from the Bible to Titanic / edited by Anthony Brandt.
p. cm.
Includes bibliographical references.
ISBN 0-7922-5908-4
1. Shipwrecks--History. I. Brandt, Anthony. II. National Geographic Society (U.S.)
G525.T663 2006
910.4'52--dc22
2006010749

ISBN-10: 0-7922-5908-4
ISBN-13: 978-0-7922-5908-4

One of the world's largest nonprofit scientific and educational organizations, the National Geographic Society was founded in 1888 "for the increase and diffusion of geographic knowledge." Fulfilling this mission, the Society educates and inspires millions every day through its magazines, books, television programs, videos, maps and atlases, research grants, the National Geographic Bee, teacher workshops, and innovative classroom materials. The Society is supported through membership dues, charitable gifts, and income from the sale of its educational products. This support is vital to National Geographic's mission to increase global understanding and promote conservation of our planet through exploration, research, and education.

For more information, please call 1-800-NGS LINE (647-5463) or write to the following address:

National Geographic Society
1145 17th Street N.W.
Washington, D.C. 20036-4688 U.S.A.

Visit the Society's Web site at www.nationalgeographic.com.

Inerior Design by Cameron Zotter

For Dylan and Eli, some rip-roaring tales

My visions were of shipwrecks, famines, of death and captivity among barbarian hordes, of a lifetime dragged out in sorrow and tears upon some gray and desolate wreck, in an ocean unfathomable and unknown.

—Edgar Allan Poe, *The Narrative of Arthur Gordon Pym*

If you want to learn how to pray, go to sea.

—*Old Portuguese proverb*

TABLE OF CONTENTS

Introduction by Anthony Brandt xiii

Chapter 1 The Shipwreck of Apostle Paul 1
From "The Acts of the Apostles," The New Testament, Chapter 27
CA 60 C.E.

Chapter 2 New World Tempests 5
From *History of the Life of the Admiral Christopher Columbus*
by Ferdinand Columbus, CA 1502

Chapter 3 The Story of Pedro Serrano 11
From *Royal Commentaries of the Incas* by Garcilaso de la Vega, CA 1550S

Chapter 4 The Shipwreck of a Portuguese Vessel 16
From *The Mariner's Chronicle* by Bernardo Gomes de Brito, 1552–1553

Chapter 5 The Wreck of the *Delight* 24
From *A Relation of Richard Clarke of Weymouth, Master of the Ship Called The* Delight, *Going for the Discovery of Norembega, with Sir Humphrey Gilbert,* 1583
[from *Richard Hakluyt's Principall Navigations,* 1589]

Chapter 6 The Last Voyage of Thomas Cavendish 29
From *The Last Voyage of the Worshipful M. Thomas Cavendish Esquire, Intended for the South Sea, the Phillipines, and the Coast of China, with 3 Tall Ships, and Two Barks*
by M. John Jane, 1591

Chapter 7 The Wreck and Redemption of Sir Thomas Gates 43
From *A True Reportory of the Wreck and Redemption of Sir Thomas Gates, Knight*
by William Strachey, 1609

Chapter 8 A Most Dangerous Voyage 51
From *A Most Dangerous Voyage*
by Captain John Monck, 1619

Chapter 9 Letter of James Pierpont 59
From *Magnalia Christi Americana* by Cotton Mather, 1647

Chapter 10 God's Protecting Providence 63
From *God's Protecting Providence, ... Evidenced in the Remarkable Deliverance of Divers Persons from the Devouring Waves of the Sea...and Also from the More Cruelly Devouring Jaws of the Inhumane Cannibals of Florida*
by Jonathan Dickinson, 1696-1697

Chapter 11 The Loss of the *Nottingham Galley* 76
From "The Preservation of John Dean" by John Dean, 1710

Chapter 12 Alexander Selkirk: Castaway 87
Various Sources, CA 1712

Chapter 13 The Wreck of the *Wager* 99
From *The Narrative of the Honourable John Byron*
by John Byron, 1740

Chapter 14 The Ordeal of the *Peggy* 122
From *An Extraordinary Famine in the American Ship* Peggy, 1765

Chapter 15 The Loss of the *Halsewell* 127
From *The Loss of the Halsewell East Indiaman,* 1786

Chapter 16 Loss of the *Lady Hobart* 137
From *Perils of the Sea*, 1803

Chapter 17 The Loss of the *Polly* 147
From R. Thomas, ed., *Interesting and authentic narratives of the most remarkable shipwrecks, fires, famines, calamites, presidential delicrances, and disasters in the seas in most parts of the world,* 1811

Chapter 18 The Treachery 152
From *A Narrative of the Sufferings and Adventures of Capt. Charles H. Barnard*
by Charles H. Barnard, 1813

Chapter 19 The Raft of the *Medusa* 171
From *Narrative of a Voyage to Senegal*
J.–B. Henry Savigny and Alexander Correard, 1816

Chapter 20 The Loss of the *Essex* 205
From *Captain Pollard's Narrative,* 1820

Chapter 21 The Loss of the *Kent* 216
From *Perils of the Sea,* 1825

Chapter 22 The Sufferings of Miss Ann Saunders 242
From *Narrative of the Shipwreck and Sufferings of Miss Ann Saunders,* 1826

Chapter 23 Narrative of a Shipwreck, Captivity & Sufferings 251
From *Narrative of the Shipwreck, Captivity & Sufferings of Horace Holden & Benj. H. Nute* by Horace Holden, 1832

Chapter 24 The Shipwreck 267
From *Cape Cod* by Henry David Thoreau, 1855

Chapter 25 The Runaways 277
From *Arctic Researches, and Life Among the Esquimaux* by Charles Francis Hall, 1865

Chapter 26 The Burning of the Clipper Ship *Hornet* at Sea 287
From *The Sacramento Daily Union* by Mark Twain, July 19, 1866

Chapter 27 A Report of Events on the Coast of Peru 304
From *Reports of the USS* Powhatan *and USS* Wateree *Concerning the Earthquake and Tidal Wave of 13 August 1868 at Arica, Peru* U.S. Navy, 1868

Chapter 28 Story of a Hoodoo Ship, 310
From *The New York Times,* June 24, 1900

Chapter 29 Unsinkable 313
From Titanic *Disaster: Hearings Before a Subcommittee of the Committee on Commerce, United States Senate* April 19–May 25, 1912

INTRODUCTION

The oldest account of a shipwreck we have dates from the Middle Kingdom in Egypt, around 2000 B.C.E., when a storm destroyed a ship off the east coast of Africa below the Red Sea, and all aboard, save one, drowned. This nameless sailor "was cast on to an island by a wave of the sea," he reports, where he found food and water and a great bearded serpent whose body seemed overlaid with gold and lapis lazuli and who spoke to him—serpents who spoke existed long before the Bible, evidently—and asked him what he was doing there. "I was going to the mines of Pharaoh," he replied, "and I went down to the sea in a ship of one hundred and fifty cubits long and forty cubits wide, with one hundred and fifty sailors of the best of Egypt who had seen heaven and earth, and whose hearts were stronger than lions. They had said that the wind would not be contrary, or that there would be none. But as we approached the land, the wind arose, and threw up waves eight cubits high." A cubit was about 18 inches long. His ship was huge, then, over 200 feet long and 60 wide. And of its crew of 150, 149 died.

"And I only," as it says in the Book of Job, "am escaped alone to tell thee."

ALREADY, 4,000 YEARS AGO, SHIPWRECK AND CASTAWAY STORIES WERE *popular. This one hovers halfway between reality and folktale, and the same is true of shipwreck stories even now; a great many seem to have, not speaking serpents, to be sure, but an element of the fictional about them, an air of the marvelous, miraculous deliveries, extraordinary heroics, boundless despair, life driven to its extremes. "And I only am escaped alone to tell thee." You will find the same quotation from the* Book of Job *on the last page of* Moby Dick, *when the* Pequod *has sunk with all hands but one, the narrator, who survives by using an empty coffin as a flotation device. Even when they do not seem in some sense fictional, shipwrecks have inspired countless works of fiction.* Moby Dick *is based on accounts of the destruction of the whaleship* Essex *in 1820 by a sperm whale that stove it in—deliberately—it would seem. The English poet Gerard Manley Hopkins made his name with a long poem called* The Wreck of the Deutschland, *based on the actual wreck of the* Deutschland *in 1875, when, rather than saving lives, rescuers stole clothing off the bodies of the dead—clothing and wedding rings. Stephen Crane was himself a shipwreck survivor, reaching shore in a dinghy holding three other men, one of whom died in the surf when the overturned dinghy struck him on the head, after the ship he was taking to Cuba, the* Commodore, *filled and sank. Out of that experience came his great story* "The Open Boat." *Shakespeare's last play,* The Tempest, *takes the germ of its plot, and perhaps some of its inspiration, from the pamphlets circulating at the time describing the shipwreck of Sir George Somers in 1609 in the Bermudas, which "were never inhabited by any Christian or heathen people, but ever esteemed and reputed a most prodigious and inchanted place." Coleridge's "The Ancient Mariner," all death and transfiguration, assigned reading once upon a time in grammar schools all over the English-speaking world, came not only from Coleridge's imagination, but also his large reading in voyages and travels. The most famous castaway story of all, Daniel Defoe's* Robinson Crusoe, *moralizes upon the story of the very real Alexander Selkirk, abandoned on the island of Juan Fernandez off the coast of Chile in the early 1700s.*

This marriage of literature and shipwreck dates in Western civilization from The Odyssey *and it extends into the present. Nobel Prize winner Gabriel Garcia Marquez has written a story called* "The Shipwrecked Sailor." *James Cameron's movie* Titanic *is half shipwreck, half dramatic fiction. It was inevitable that the marriage should have lasted, for in shipwrecks the drama is built in. The stories tend always toward the amazing, the tragic, the redemptive. What could be more dramatic than the tale of Jonah, thrown overboard as a sacrifice to the great storm that was about to destroy the ship he was taking to Tarshish, only to be swallowed by a whale? In 1891 James Bartley, sailor on the whaling ship* Star of the East, *was aboard a small whaleboat when a wounded whale took it in its jaws and crushed it, throwing him into the sea, whereupon he vanished. Later the same day the ship killed the same whale and brought it alongside the ship. Two days after that, while processing the carcass, they discovered Bartley in the whale's stomach, still alive.*

Those who believe in the literal truth of the Bible still accept Bartley's story and have made much of it, but alas, investigation has revealed that it is not true. It could not be true. But we are all half ready to believe in these wonderful deliverances, these tales of courage and despair, the unsinkable ocean liner sinking and the women who would not leave their husbands, choosing to die beside them, all the heartbreaking losses and the astonishing survivals. Edward Snow tells the story of the Polly, *fishing out of Cape Cod in 1803 with a crew of ten, including the captain's nephew, a boy named Ned Rider. On their way home they came near St. Paul's Island, off the coast of Cape Breton, and as the boat drifted in the calm, young Ned heard in the distance the cry of a child, which seemed to be coming from a rock, a pinnacle sticking up out of the sea some ways off shore. The captain heard it too and sent two men, with Ned as the third, in a rowboat to investigate. Ned scrambled over the rock and there she was, a little girl, crying pitifully, standing in water up to her waist, with the tide rising. No other person was in sight.*

Years later, Ned and the little girl were married and lived happily ever after. No one ever found out how she came to be on that rock. Or so the story goes.

AND IS THE STORY TRUE? AND DO WE CARE? HALFWAY THROUGH THE *research for this anthology I entertained the idea of printing fiction as well as fact, the two seemed so intertwined, but then decided no, the factual accounts were literature of a kind all by themselves. It is a literature very much of the people. It has never achieved academic respectability. Almost no one has studied the accounts of shipwrecks, despite their obvious status as a genre. Their heyday came in the 17th through 19th centuries, during the age of sail, when the world was being explored and thousands of merchant ships were plowing the ocean. At their most dignified they were printed as pamphlets, sold for a penny or two, and wound up, if they were good enough, being collected in anthologies like this one, of which there were a myriad. They are still a popular subject of anthologies. Many of the accounts they contain, indeed, have achieved canonical status, and we see them again and again: "*The Loss of the Ship Betsy*"; "Loss of the* Halsewell *East Indiaman; "Narrative of the Loss of the* Kent.*" Keith Huntress, in his own such collection,* Narratives of Shipwrecks and Disasters, *published in 1974, dates the first such anthology to 1675, but the real mother of all later anthologies is Archibald Duncan's six-volume* The Mariner's Chronicle, *the first volume of which appeared in 1804. Most subsequent anthologies have been based on Duncan's book, or at least derive from it, adding stories to Duncan's core collection as they occurred.*

But these are only the anthologies devoted exclusively to shipwrecks and other disasters at sea. Hakluyt's Principall Navigations *of 1589, expanded ten years later, his great collection of voyages and travels, is dotted with shipwreck and disaster tales. So are the other great voyage collections that preceded and succeeded* Hakluyt. *Whenever people take to the sea there will be shipwrecks, and the losses during the age of sail, although we have no accurate figures, were prodigious.* Hakluyt *took note of the Spanish losses in 1591, when, "of this whole fleete that should have come into Spaine this yeere, being one hundred twentie and three sayle, there are arrived as yet but five and twentie." The great Spanish fleets sailed from the* West Indies, *typically, in summer and fall, the season of hurricanes. In* George P. Landow's *book* Images of Crisis, *whose subject is the literary and iconological representations of shipwrecks and other disasters, he quotes "*The Wreck Register *of 1859" from the* Illustrated London News: *"A terrible record of shipwreck and loss of life will be found in the '*Board of Trade Wreck Register.*' This states that the increase in these disasters is mainly to be traced to the very heavy storms of* October *25 and 26, and of* October *31 and* November *1 and 2 last. In the former gale there were 133 total wrecks and 90 casualties, resulting in serious damage, and 798 lives were lost."* Most *of these were from the wreck of the* Royal Charter, *but that's still a lot of lives.* Keith Huntress *quotes an account of major wrecks in the* Royal Navy *over a period of 13 years at the turn of the 19th century, and the deaths involved, ship by ship: 290 men out of 294; 300 of 491; 673 of 859; 400 of 590; 731 of 738; 587 of 593.* In *1782, just after the end of the* American Revolution, *a* Royal Navy *fleet ran into a gale on the* Grand Banks *off* Newfoundland. *There were nine ships all told; only one reached* England. *"The total loss of life from that equinoctial gale off* Newfoundland," Huntress *says, "was more than 3,500—exceeding the total number killed in the* Navy *during the whole war."*

In the same year, Huntress *goes on to point out, the* Royal George, *lying at anchor at* Spithead, *heeled over to do some work on the hull, sank when an officer had a few hogshead of rum put on board on the lower side. That sufficiently unbalanced the ship that when a slight breeze sprang up, the ship heeled a bit more and the sea rushed into the open gun ports.* Almost *900 men drowned.*

There are so many ways to die. Ships burn at sea; they get hung up on uncharted reefs and rocks; masts and rigging get swept overboard and the ship drifts and the crew starves. No *one would have predicted in 1819 that a whale could sink a ship.* I *print here an account of a ship taken a third of a mile inland on the west coast of* Chile *by a tsunami. (All hands, amazingly, survived.)* Storms *large and small sink ships; so do mistakes large and small.* The Grosvenor, *an* East Indiaman, *sailed straight into the coast of* South Africa *on the fourth of* August *1782, in the dead of a moonless night, because the captain was sure that he was still 300 miles from land and would not be persuaded otherwise, even though members of the watch had seen lights dead ahead. Many of those on board survived the wreck, but not the long walk toward civilization. One or two of the women passengers, it was rumored, eventually married the chiefs of local tribes.*

A surprising number of ships collide, if not with continents, then with other things. A 1906 study by the federal government of shipwrecks along the Atlantic and Gulf Coasts for that year found that out of 398 wrecks, collisions had caused close to half. Ships run into other ships, into the land, into floating debris. It is extraordinary, given the vastness, the emptiness of the oceans, that so many ships should collide with each other. Six years after this study, the Titanic *would collide with an iceberg. Death ranges the sea. One of the most dangerous jobs in the world is commercial fishing. Waves can sometimes reach 100 feet high. Laperouse, looking for the Northwest Passage in 1786 on the wild coast of southern Alaska, came to a bay now known as Lituya Bay, its narrow entrance hiding a great expanse of deep water, which the French explorer thought might be what he was looking for—the route into the interior of North America. He and his ships sailed in and mapped the bay, which was a cul de sac. To finish the mapping he sent three small boats into the narrow entrance gap to take soundings. The ebb tide caught them and drove them to the breakers. No matter how hard they rowed, they could make no headway. The tide had them in its grip. One boat managed to pull to shore. The other two capsized in the surf and were destroyed. Twenty-one men died.*

Two years later, having explored much of the Pacific, Laperouse and his two ships left Australia for Tonga. They were never seen again.

Lituya Bay was the site of the largest wave ever recorded, a wave nearly 100 yards high, a splash wave caused when a piece of a mountain dropped into the bay.

I have not even mentioned scurvy, which probably took the lives of more seamen during the age of sail than all its shipwrecks put together.

The sea is full of death, of ghosts, of mysteries. The *Mary Celeste* *is only the best known of the ships found adrift, sails rigged, food on the table, but with no captain, no crew. The* Flying Dutchman, *it is said, still appears, luminous, aglow, off the coast of South Africa. King George VI of England, then a young midshipman, claimed to have seen it. In 1754 several men fishing for menhaden in the gap between Plum Island and Gardiner's Bay off the northern tip of Long Island watched a naval battle involving three fully rigged ships that lasted 15 minutes before it faded back into whatever realm of the mysterious it emerged from.*

Grist for a children's tale. But we have already seen how many serious writers have turned shipwreck and castaway stories into literature. This anthology lays some stress on the literary leanings of the genre. Wherever possible, I have reprinted material that a major writer subsequently used as the basis for a poem or a work of fiction. The genre has always worked its magic somewhere between the boy's adventure story and serious tragedy. The shipwreck story is, after all, a hubris machine; it demonstrates in the most graphic ways the folly and carelessness of overweening humankind caught in the grip of immense natural forces. We are 300 miles from land, the captain said. Stay on course. Within an hour they had crashed into South Africa.

For centuries, moralizing religious writers have also used the genre, with its frequent extravagant deliverances, as an antidote to tragedy and an illustration of God's providence. I own a little volume from 1833 called *The Perils of the Sea*, from Harper's School District Library series; in it the loss of the *Lady Hobart* (among this book's many other losses), we are told, illustrates "the benefit of religion and the consolation of prayer under the pressure of calamity."

This sort of thing is common in these stories. Prayer is always available. People are always thanking God for surviving. Despair is common, too. Actual shipwreck tends to be arbitrary in its choice of who lives, who dies. The shipwreck story may be a hubris machine; it is not necessarily a justice machine. When the *Titanic* sank, not all the women and children made it into the lifeboats. The wealthy survived in far greater proportion to their numbers aboard than the poor. In what George P. Landow calls the "post-Christian" period, beginning in the 19th century, the serious literature derived from shipwrecks starts to lose its center. It becomes harder and harder to find transcendent meanings in the doom of ships. Landow quotes Edmund Burke: "When ancient opinions and rules of life are taken away, the loss cannot possibly be estimated. From that moment we have no compass to govern us; nor can we know distinctly to what port we steer." And here is the English poet Shelley, who was an atheist:

We, the weak mariners of that wide lake
Where'er its shores extend or billows roll,
Our course unpiloted and starless make
O'er its wild surface to an unknown goal.

Shelley, of course, died when his sailboat, which he had taken out in the face of a rising storm, capsized in the Mediterranean. His friends cremated him on the beach. Byron was present. Byron's grandfather, John Byron, had been shipwrecked as a midshipman on the western coast of Patagonia, just north of the Strait of Magellan, and survived with a bare handful of men who made it to a Spanish settlement up the coast. It's a famous story: the wreck of the *Wager*. Byron used the story in his epic poem *Don Juan*. I print it here.

I print stories that are centuries old, and as fresh as the Titanic. In a sense they are all fresh, or rather timeless. Call them ahistorical. Men have been sailing for thousands of years now, and foundering, and those who survive have stories to tell, all of which are oddly the same. The same things always happen. Men break on the rocks, drown, starve, while a few live to tell the tale. And we are never not interested. It is a peculiar sort of entertainment, when you think about it, this endless fascination with other people's disasters, tragedies, loss. Aristotle explained it as catharsis, a human need to arouse in ourselves, then purge, the twin emotions of pity and fear. It is so sad. And it could happen to us. It also poses a basic, inescapable question: What would we do in similar circumstances? Would we have the presence of mind in a crisis to do what might save us? Would we have the character to meet death bravely? That's part of it too. Many do meet death bravely in these stories; others do not. It is an ancient metaphor that life is a voyage. In shipwreck we come to its limits, to the most critical of test cases. Who could not be interested in the outcome?

We shall never get enough of reading these tales, so I offer no apologies for yet another shipwreck anthology. Life in crisis, at its extreme, is always fascinating.

1

The SHIPWRECK *of* APOSTLE PAUL

From *The Acts of the Apostles, Chapter 27 1–44*

CA 60 C.E.

Underwater archaeology dates from around 1960, not too long after the invention of scuba gear, and since that time hundreds of ancient wrecks have been identified and excavated, mostly in the Mediterranean, where civilization got its start. But because the discipline is so recent, the history of ancient ships is still being written. We know that the Mesopotamians built boats out of saplings and animal skins that must have resembled the so-called bull boats Plains Indians made in this country, or the skin boats, called corracks or curraughs, that Celtic tribes built in Wales and Ireland. English and Continental bogs have yielded Stone Age dugouts, one of them a remarkable 48 feet long and 4½ feet wide. It was probably the Egyptians who invented the planked ship, and possibly the sail as well; one source dates the invention of the latter to 3100 B.C.E. As early as 2600 B.C.E. an Egyptian scribe records the shipment of cedar logs from what is now Lebanon in a convoy of 40 ships. By this time, merchants in Babylon were crossing the Arabian Sea and trading in India.

All of this is older than the first shipwreck found, which dates to about 1350 B.C.E. This ship, evidently Canaanite, was discovered just off the rocky coast of Turkey in a place called Ulu Burun. It was full of trade goods, and its excavation has had a decided impact on the history of seaborne trade in the Mediterranean. Underwater archaeology in general promises to deepen greatly our knowledge of ancient trade, but it has the disadvantage of being expensive. It took ten years and more than 20,000 individual dives to finish the work on this particular wreck. And, like almost all such ancient wrecks, it comes without a story. We can only speculate where it was going and why it sits where it sits.

With Paul's shipwreck we have the opposite situation—no physical evidence but a definite story, even a route map—if we cared to make one. Acts of the Apostles, *or* Acts, *as it is usually known, the fifth book of the* New Testament, *is a continuation of the* Gospel According to St. Luke, *written by the same author, and describing the growth and spread of the early* Christian Church. *It ends with Paul being sent to Rome as a prisoner after an inconclusive hearing in Jerusalem before the Roman magistrate. He had been accused by the Jewish priests of fomenting discontent with his preaching, but he had committed no crime and they had no other evidence against him, and he insisted on appealing his imprisonment before Caesar himself, which was his right as a Roman citizen. He sailed under the charge of a Roman centurion named Julius, and the text describes the route and the events that happened.*

The text dates, most biblical scholars agree, to about 75–80 C.E., *while the date for the shipwreck itself would probably date to around or shortly after 60* C.E. *The chapter we are printing is written as if Luke were on board the ship, which was a large one, with Paul, and some scholars think it is based on Luke's travel diary. It reads like a factual account, except, perhaps, for the angel who appears to Paul and tells him that all the hundreds of people on board will survive if they just stick with him and do what he says, and for the miraculous cures that follow in Malta, which is where the ship is wrecked.*

It's hardly necessary to add that Paul's shipwreck, with the unlikely deliverance of its crew and passengers, the reliance on prayer and revelation, the Christian promise it embodies, has drawn a great deal of exegesis for the past 2,000 years, and that it became something of a model for later shipwreck accounts.

AND WHEN IT WAS DETERMINED THAT WE SHOULD SAIL INTO ITALY, THEY delivered Paul and certain other prisoners unto *one* named Julius; a centurion of Augustus' band. And entering into a ship of Adramyttium, we launched, meaning to sail by the coasts of Asia; *one* Aristarchus, a Macedonian of Thessalonica, being with us. And the next *day* we touched at Sidon. And Julius courteously entreated Paul, and gave *him* liberty to go unto his friends to refresh himself. And when we had launched from thence, we sailed under Cyprus, because the winds were contrary. And when we had sailed over the sea of Cilicia and Pamphylia, we came to Myra, *a city* of Lycia. And there the centurion found a ship of Alexandria sailing into Italy; and he put us therein. And when we had sailed slowly many days, and scarce were come over against Cnidus, the wind not suffering us, we sailed under Crete, over against Salmone; And, hardly passing it, came unto a place which is called The fair havens; nigh whereunto was the city *of* Lasea.

Now when much time was spent, and when sailing was now dangerous, because the fast was now already past, Paul admonished *them*, And said unto them, Sirs, I perceive that this voyage will be with hurt and much damage, not only of the lading and ship, but also of our lives. Nevertheless the centurion believed the master and the owner of the ship, more than those things which were spoken by Paul. And because the haven was not commodious to winter in, the more part advised to depart thence also, if by any means they might attain to Phenice, *and there* to winter; *which is* an haven of Crete, and lieth toward the south west and north west. And when the south wind blew softly, supposing that they had obtained *their* purpose, loosing *thence*, they sailed close by Crete.

But not long after there arose against it a tempestuous wind, called Euroclydon.

And when the ship was caught, and could not bear up into the wind, we let *her* drive.

And running under a certain island which is called Clauda, we had much work to come by the boat: Which when they had taken up, they used helps, undergirding the ship; and, fearing lest they should fall into the quicksands, strake sail, and so were driven.

And we being exceedingly tossed with a tempest, the next *day* they lightened the ship;

And the third *day* we cast out with our own hands the tackling of the ship.

And when neither sun nor stars in many days appeared, and no small tempest lay on *us*, all hope that we should be saved was then taken away.

But after long abstinence Paul stood forth in the midst of them, and said, Sirs, ye should have hearkened unto me, and not have loosed from Crete, and to have gained this harm and loss. And now I exhort you to be of good cheer: for there shall be no loss of *any man's* life among you, but of the ship. For there stood by me this night the angel of God, whose I am, and whom I serve, Saying, Fear not, Paul; thou must be brought before Cæsar: and, lo, God hath given thee all them that sail with thee. Wherefore, sirs, be of good cheer: for I believe God, that it shall be even as it was told me. Howbeit we must be cast upon a certain island.

But when the fourteenth night was come, as we were driven up and down in Adria, about midnight the shipmen deemed that they drew near to some country;

And sounded, and found *it* twenty fathoms: and when they had gone a little further, they sounded again, and found *it* fifteen fathoms. Then fearing lest we should have fallen upon rocks, they cast four anchors out of the stern, and wished for the day. And as the shipmen were about to flee out of the ship, when they had let down the boat into the sea, under colour as though they would have cast anchors out of the foreship, Paul said to the centurion and to the soldiers, Except these abide in the ship, ye cannot be saved.

Then the soldiers cut off the ropes of the boat, and let her fall off. And while the day was coming on, Paul besought *them* all to take meat, saying, This day is the fourteenth day that ye have tarried and continued fasting, having taken nothing. Wherefore I pray you to take *some* meat: for this is for your health: for there shall not an hair fall from the head of any of you. And when he had thus spoken, he took bread, and gave thanks to God in presence of them all: and when he had broken *it*, he began to eat. Then were they all of good cheer, and they also took *some* meat. And we were in all in the ship two hundred threescore and sixteen souls. And when they had eaten enough, they lightened the ship, and cast out the wheat into the sea. And when it was day, they knew not the land: but they discovered a certain creek with a shore, into the which they were minded, if it were possible, to thrust in the ship. And when they had taken up the anchors, they committed *themselves* unto the sea, and loosed the rudder bands, and hoisted up the mainsail to the wind, and made toward shore. And falling into a place where two seas met, they ran the ship aground; and the forepart stuck fast, and remained unmoveable, but the hinder part was broken with the violence of the waves. And the soldiers' counsel was to kill the prisoners, lest any of them should swim out, and escape. But the centurion, willing to save Paul, kept them from *their* purpose; and commanded that they which could swim should cast *themselves* first *into the sea*, and get to land: And the rest, some on boards, and some on *broken pieces* of the ship. And so it came to pass, that they escaped all safe to land.

2

NEW WORLD TEMPESTS

From *History of the Life of the Admiral Christopher Columbus*—"How, Forced by Tempests, the Admiral returned Westward to Inquire about the Mines and get Information about Veragua."

BY FERDINAND COLUMBUS

CA 1502

If there are accounts of shipwrecks before the age of discovery, they are extremely rare. During the Middle Ages ships sailed all over the Mediterranean and coasted the Atlantic shores of Europe. A number of medieval wrecks have been found, both in the Mediterranean and especially in the Dutch lowlands, where ships that sank in water have been dug up on what is now land, the Dutch having reclaimed sea bottom with their amazing dikes. But no significant literature of travel emerged from the medieval period except for the work of Marco Polo and the Travels *of Sir John Mandeville, both of which were highly colored by tales of men with faces in their chests, or who were dog-headed, or who were born with only one leg and shaded themselves from the hot sun by lying on their backs underneath their one foot, which was the size of an umbrella.*

But the age of discovery generated something new: an accompanying fact-based literature of travel, narratives of voyages, "a new kind of prose writing," says David B. Quinn, "practical, objective, clear, exciting." And real. The fantasies of dog-faced men and the like could not compete in the end with the actual human oddness found beyond the seas. What could be more interesting, for example, than cannibals? The works of art in solid gold of the Aztecs and Incas? The giants of Patagonia? The real world turned out to be just as amazing as anything Mandeville could have imagined, and you could, thanks to these accounts, which multiplied rapidly as more and more of the world was explored, experience vicariously what the explorers experienced, see in crude woodcuts or in your mind's eye the wonders they had found. The literature of exploration rapidly became extremely popular. Sir Thomas More wrote his Utopia based upon it. Shakespeare clearly knew it well. Christopher Columbus's first Letter describing his discoveries was reprinted all over Europe. The New World was the biggest news in the Renaissance. The reading public, limited as it was then, devoured it.

With this literature, inevitably, came shipwreck accounts; for shipwrecks were almost routinely part of the experience of exploration. When Magellan left Spain in 1519 to sail around the world, he had five ships with him. Only one returned. Christopher Columbus lost a total of nine ships during his four voyages to the New World. Shipwreck stories were not yet a separate genre, but the ships were small and frail, the dangers of the sea and the weather great, and it was not long before a growing pamphlet literature began to seize on them to satisfy the curiosity of a fascinated public. By the middle of the 16th century pamphlets describing shipwrecks were common in Portugal, a pioneer of the age of discovery, and most of the seafaring countries of Europe followed suit with their own pamphlet literature. By the middle of the 17th century shipwreck lit had become its own genre, written often by hack writers who put their material together from evidence supplied by survivors and were not afraid to embellish it.

Whether Christopher Columbus embellished his account of his fourth voyage is hard to say, but his losses were so severe it seems doubtful. He had four ships with him; all of them were so damaged by storms and hard use that they had to be abandoned and Columbus had to hitch a ride on someone else's ship to get back to Spain. When he wrote his Letter to the King and Queen describing his voyage he is only half coherent about the sequence of events, but there can be no question that he was badly beset by storms: "The tempest was terrible throughout the night," he writes, "all the ships were separated, and each one driven to the last extremity, without hope of anything but death; each of them also looked upon the loss of the rest as a certainty. What man was ever born, not even excepting Job, who would not have been ready to die of despair at finding himself as I then was, in anxious fear for my own safety, and that of my son, my brother and my friends..." The other three ships reappeared the next day, but storms continued as they beat toward Jamaica—endless storms, he says; "Eighty-eight days did this fearful tempest continue, during which I was at sea, and saw neither sun nor stars; my ships lay exposed, with sails torn, and anchors, rigging, cables, boats and a great quantity of provisions lost; my people were very weak and humbled in spirit, many of them promising to lead a religious life, and all making vows and promising to perform pilgrimages, while some of them would frequently go to their messmates to make confession. Other tempests have been experienced, but never of so long a duration or so fearful as this: many whom we looked upon as brave men, on *several occasions showed considerable trepidation; but the distress of my son who was with me grieved me to the soul, and the more when I considered his tender age, for he was but thirteen years old, and he enduring so much toil for so long a time."*

The son in question was Ferdinand Columbus, and he wrote his own account of this voyage in his biography of his father sometime before 1539. We print here Chapter 94 of his book.

On Monday 5 December the Admiral, seeing that the violent E and NE winds did not abate and that he could not trade with those people, resolved to turn back to ascertain the truth of what the Indians said concerning the mines of Veragua. Therefore that day he proceeded to sleep at Puerto Bello, 10 leagues westward. Continuing his course next day he was assaulted by a W wind, which was contrary to his new plan, but favorable to what he had had for the past three months. However, he did not believe that this wind would last long, so he decided not to change his plan but beat against the wind for a few days because the weather was unsettled. When a little fair weather came, fair for going to Veragua, a new contrary wind arose and drove us back to Puerto Bello. But just when we were most hopeful of making the harbor the wind changed again, against our plan, and with so much thunder and lightning that the people did not dare to open their eyes; and it seemed as if the ships were sinking and the sky coming down on them. Sometimes the thunder was so long drawn out that we thought certain that some ship of the fleet was firing guns in distress. Another time the weather would turn to such heavy rain that for two or three days it poured incessantly so that it seemed like a new universal deluge. As a consequence everyone on board was in terrible distress and almost desperate, since one could not rest even for half an hour and was continually drenched, tacking sometimes one way, sometimes another, struggling against all the elements and dreading them all. For in such dreadful storms one dreads the fire for lightning and thunderbolts, the air because of its fury, the water for the waves, and the earth for the rocks and shoals of that unknown coast. Such rocks and shoals are sometimes found near the harbor where one hopes to find refuge, but one is not acquainted and does not know the entrance well enough, and therefore prefers to fight with the other elements with which he is less familiar. And besides all these various terrors there occurred another no less dangerous and astonishing, a waterspout which on Tuesday 13 December passed among the ships, which, had they not cut by saying the Gospel according to St. John, there is no doubt that whomsoever it fell upon would have been drowned. For it draws the water up to the clouds in the form of a pillar thicker than a hogshead, twisting it about like a whirlwind.

That same night we lost sight of the vessel *Vizcaína*, but fortunately, at the end of three very dark days she saw us again although she had lost her boat. She had been in great danger because near the shore she let go her anchor, which was lost as they were forced to cut the cable. And then we understood that the currents of that coast conformed to the storms, which then were going eastward following the wind, and turned the contrary way toward the west when the easterly winds prevailed; because the water seems to follow in that part the course of the wind which blows the strongest.

When the contrariety of wind and sea had battered the fleet so violently that it had almost come apart, and nobody could bear a hand from exhaustion, one or two days of light airs gave us some respite. At the same time so many sharks came about the ships, that we were frightened, especially those among us who pay attention to signs and omens; for some believe it to be true of the sharks what they say of the ravens, that they foretell when there is a dead body and can detect it by the odor at a distance of several leagues. They get a hold of the leg or arm of a person with their teeth and cut it like a razor, as they have two rows of teeth in the shape of a saw. We made such a slaughter of these sharks with hook and chain that we were unable to kill any more, and they went floating upon the water. They are so voracious that not only they bite at carrion but they may be taken with a red rag on the hook. And I have seen taken from the belly of one of these sharks a turtle which afterwards lived aboard the ship; and from another was taken the whole head of one of his fellows which we had cut off and thrown into the water as not good to eat (no more than they are themselves) and which that shark had swallowed; and to us it seemed beyond reason that one creature should swallow the head of another of its own size. However, it is not to be wondered at, since they have a mouth extending almost up to the belly, and their heads are shaped like an olive. Now, although some of the crew looked upon them as a bad omen, and others as a bad fish, yet all of us made much of them because we were short of provisions, having by that time been 8 months at sea, so that we had consumed all the meat and fish we had brought from Spain. What with the heat and the damp sea, the biscuit had become so full of maggots that, God help me, I saw many men wait until nightfall to eat their porridge so as not to see the maggots in it; others were so used to it that they did not even take the trouble to throw the maggots away when they saw them since in so doing they might have lost their supper.

On Saturday the 17th of the month, the Admiral put into a harbor three leagues east of Peñon, which the Indians called *Huiva*. It was like a great channel, where we rested three days. Going ashore we saw the inhabitants living in the tops of trees like birds. They had laid sticks across from branch to branch and there built cabins, a name more appropriate than houses. Although we did not know the reason for this strange custom, yet we guessed that it was done out of fear of the griffons that are in that country, or of enemies; because all along that coast the people at a distance of a league are great enemies to one another.

We sailed from this harbor on the 20th of the same month [December] with fair but unsettled weather. In fact, as soon as were out to sea, the winds and the tempest began to harass us again so that we were forced into another harbor, whence we departed on the third day, with weather that seemed to be on the mend, but which, like an enemy that lies in wait for a man, assaulted us again, and forced us to Peñon. There, when we were hoping to enter the harbor where we had first found refuge, and right at the entrance of the same port, the wind, as if it were tormenting us, started up so violently that it was a favor that it permitted us to make that same harbor where we had been on Thursday the 12th of the same month, out of whose mouth it had first pulled us. There we remained from the second day of the Nativity to 3 January the following year 1503; when having repaired the vessel Gallego and taken on a large quantity of maize, water and wood, we turned back again towards Veragua with very wretched and foul weather, which in fact had so changed just as the Admiral altered his course. And this was so unusual and unheard of a thing that I would not have related so many changes if not only I had been present, but I have also seen it written by Diego Mendez, who sailed with the Jamaican canoes, of which I shall speak later. He also wrote an account of this voyage. And in the letter which the Admiral sent through him to the Catholic Sovereigns, which has been printed, the reader may learn our sufferings and how ill fortune persecutes him whom she should favor most.

To return to the changes and contrarieties of the weather and of the course, which put us to so much trouble between Veragua and Puerto Bello that this coast was called *La Costa de los Contrastes,* I say that on Thursday, being the day of Epiphany we anchored near a river which the Indians call *Gieura* and the Admiral named Belén, because we reached that place on the day of the Three Magi. He immediately ordered the mouth of that river to be sounded, and that of another river more to the westward, which the Indians call Veragua, and he found that the entrance was very shoal and that in the Rio Belén there were four *braccia* of water with high tide. Our boats entered this river of Belén and up-stream reached a village where they were told that the gold mines were in Veragua. At the beginning not only did the Indians not want to talk, but they gathered together under arms to prevent the Christians from landing. The following day our boats going to the Rio de Veragua, the Indians of that village did exactly what the others had done; and not only on land but on water also prepared for defense with their canoes. But there had come with the Christians one Indian of that coast, who could make himself understood a little, and he told them that we were good people and that we did not want anything we would not pay for. So they quieted down somewhat, and exchanged 20 gold mirrors and some bracelets and some nuggets of gold never melted, the which to value the more highly they said had been collected afar off in rough mountains; and that when they collected it they would not eat or take women along. This was also said by the people of Hispaniola when it was first discovered.

3

The STORY *of* PEDRO SERRANO

From *Royal Commentaries of the Incas* by Garcilaso de la Vega

CA 1550s

The beginning of the age of exploration is also the beginning of castaway stories. The most famous by far is that of Alexander Selkirk, marooned on the Juan Fernandez islands in the early 18th century, which Daniel Defoe so memorably fictionalized as Robinson Crusoe. *But it is not the first. That honor belongs to a Spaniard named Pedro Serrano, who was cast away on an island off the coast of Peru, or conversely on a small set of cays in the Caribbean. Two versions of this story exist—take your pick. Ours comes from the history of the Inca empire and its conquest by Pizarro written by the son of an Incan woman and a Spanish conquistador. He was educated and lived in Spain for most of his life but felt great pride in his Incan origins and wrote this long and invaluable account of the Incas partly to recover the reputation of his mother's people. Toward the beginning, just a couple of dozen pages into the book, he inserted the Pedro Serrano story, which has little to do with his subject but proved, evidently, irresistible.*

The other version I have not seen. Robert F. Marx, who in his search for treasure ships has done a good deal of underwater archaeology and written extensively about shipwrecks, discovered it when he was poking through manuscript records in the Archive of the Indies in Seville. He subsequently translated and published it in the journal Oceans *in 1974. Here Serrano is marooned for eight years on what became known as the Serrano Bank, and the details of the story are apparently so different that they bear no relation to each other except for Serrano's name.*

Which version is the true one? No one has any idea.

BEFORE GOING FURTHER, IT WOULD BE AS WELL TO TELL HERE THE STORY of Pedro Serrano mentioned above, so that it is not too far from its place, and in order that this chapter may not be too short. Pedro Serrano swam to the hitherto unnamed desert island, which, as he said, would be about two leagues in circumference. The chart shows this to be so: it gives three small islets with a great many banks round about, and the same appearance is given to the one called Serranilla, which is five islets with more shoals than Serrana: there are many banks in all these parts, and ships avoid them so as not to fall into danger.

It was Pedro Serrano's fate to be wrecked among them and to reach the island swimming. He was in a state of despair, for he found no water nor fuel nor even grass he could graze on, nor anything else to maintain life till some ship might pass to rescue him before he perished from hunger and thirst; this seemed to him a harder fate than death by drowning, which is quicker. So he spent the first night bewailing his misfortune, and was as cast down as one would suppose a man to be in such a plight. As soon as dawn came, he again walked round the island, and found some shellfish from the sea, crabs, shrimps, and other creatures. He caught what he could and ate them raw, having no flame to roast or boil them with. Thus he kept himself going until he saw turtles come forth. Seeing them some distance from the sea, he seized one and turned it over, and did the same to as many as he could, for they are clumsy in righting themselves when on their backs. Drawing a knife he used to wear in his belt, and which saved his life, he beheaded one and drank its blood instead of water. He did the same with the rest, and laid out their flesh in the sun to make dried meat and cleaned out the shells to catch rainwater, for the whole region is, of course, very rainy. Thus he sustained himself during the first days by killing all the turtles he could. Some were as big as and bigger than the biggest shields, and others like smaller shields and targes. They were in fact of all sizes. The largest of them he could not contrive to turn over on their backs, because they were stronger than he, and though he climbed on them to subdue them by tiring them, it was no use because they could make their way to the sea with him astraddle. So experience taught him which turtles he could attack and which to abandon. In their shells he collected a great deal of water, for some could hold two arrobas, and others less. Finding himself adequately supplied with food and drink, Pedro Serrano thought that if he could make fire so as to be able to roast his food and produce smoke in case a ship should pass, he could lack nothing. With this idea, being a man with long experience of the sea (and they certainly have a great advantage over other men in any sort of task), he looked for a pair of pebbles that he could use as flint, hoping to use his knife to strike fire from them. But not finding any such stones on the island, which was covered with bare sand, he swam into the sea and dived, carefully searching the sea bottom in all directions, and persisting in his labors until he found pebbles and collected what he could, picking out the best and breaking them on one another so as to make edges to strike the knife on. He then tried out his idea, and seeing that he could strike fire, made shreds of a piece of his shirt, torn very small like carded cotton. This served as tinder, and by dint of industry and skill, after great perseverance, he made himself a fire. Having got it, he counted himself fortunate and sustained it by collecting the jetsam thrown up by the sea. He spent hours collecting weeds called sea-pods, timber from ships lost at sea, shells, fish bones, and other material to feed his fire. So that the showers should not extinguish it, he made a hut with the biggest shells from the turtles he had killed, and tended the fire with great diligence lest it should slip from his hands. Within two months or less, he was as naked as when he was born, for the great rain, the heat, and the humidity of the region rotted the few clothes he had. The sun wearied him with its great heat, for he had no clothes to protect himself nor any shade. When he was very extenuated, he entered the water and submerged himself. He lived three years amidst these hardships and cares, and though he saw several ships pass in that time, and made smoke (the usual signal for people lost at sea), they did not see him, or else feared the shoals and did not dare to approach, but passed well out to sea, all of which left Pedro Serrano so discouraged that he had resigned himself to dying and ending his misery. Owing to the harshness of the climate hair grew all over his body till it was like an animal's pelt, and not just any animal's, but a wild boar's. His hair and beard fell below his waist.

After three years, one afternoon when he was not expecting anything, he saw a man on the island. This man had been wrecked on the shoals the night before and had saved himself on a ship's plank. As soon as dawn appeared, he saw the smoke of Pedro Serrano's fire, and guessing what it was, made for it, aided by the plank and his good swimming. When they saw one another, it would be hard to say which was the more surprised. Serrano thought it was the Devil come in human form to tempt him to some desperate act. His guest thought Serrano was the Devil in his true form, he was so coated with hair, beard, and hide. Each fled from the other, and Pedro Serrano went off crying: "Jesus! Jesus! Oh Lord, deliver me from the demon!"

Hearing this, the other was reassured, and turned towards him saying: "Flee me not, brother, for I am a Christian too," and to prove it, as he still ran away, shouted the Credo. Pedro Serrano heard it, turned back, and they advanced with the greatest tenderness and many tears and groans, seeing that they were both in the same plight with no hope of escape. Each briefly told the other the story of his past life. Pedro Serrano, realizing his guest's need, gave him some of his food and drink, which comforted him a little, and they again discussed their plight. They arranged their life as best they could, dividing the hours of the day and night between the duties of collecting shellfish to eat and sea-pods and wood and fish bones and anything else thrown up by the sea to sustain the fire, and especially the perpetual vigil they had to keep on it, hour by hour, lest it go out. They lived in this way for some days, but it was not long before they quarreled, and so violently that they lived apart and nearly came to blows (which shows how great is the misery of human passions). The cause of the strife was that one accused the other of not doing the necessary duties properly. This accusation and the words they exchanged were enough to destroy their harmony and divide them. But they themselves soon realized their folly, asked one another's forgiveness, made friends, and lived together again. Thus they continued for four years. During this time they saw some ships pass and made their smoke signals, but in vain, and this so depressed them that they all but died.

At the end of this long time, a ship chanced to pass so near that their smoke was sighted and a boat put out to pick them up. Pedro Serrano and his companion, who had grown a similar pelt, seeing the boat approach, fell to saying the Credo and calling on the name of our Redeemer aloud, so that the sailors should not think they were demons and flee from them. This availed them, for otherwise the mariners would doubtless have fled: they no longer looked like human beings. So they were carried to the ship, where they astounded all who saw them and heard about their labors. The companion died at sea returning to Spain. Pedro Serrano reached here and went on to Germany where the emperor then was. He kept his pelt as it was, as a proof of his wreck and all he had gone through. In every village he passed through on the way he earned much money whenever he chose to exhibit himself. Some of the lords and principal knights who liked to see his figure contributed toward the cost of the journey, and his imperial majesty, having seen and heard him, gave him a reward of 4,000 pesos in income, or 4,800 ducats, in Peru. On the way to enjoy this, he died at Panama, and never saw it. All this story, as I have repeated it, is told by a gentleman called Sánchez de Figueroa, from whom I heard it. He knew Pedro Serrano and warrants that he had heard it from him, and that after seeing the emperor, Pedro Serrano cut his hair and beard to just above the waist; and to enable him to sleep at night, he plaited it, for otherwise it spread out over the bed and disturbed his rest.

4

The SHIPWRECK *of a* PORTUGUESE VESSEL

From *The Mariner's Chronicle*

BY BERNARDO GOMES DE BRITO

1552–1553

The Portuguese invented the shipwreck genre in the 16th century, and this particular account is one of the first to appear in the genre and the first in point of date to be collected in the two-volume text of pamphlet narratives, put together by Bernardo Gomes de Brito and published in 1735, known in English as The Tragic History of the Sea. This and most of the later Portuguese shipwreck narratives grew out of the trade between Lisbon and Goa (called here Cochin), the Portuguese colony on the west coast of India, a round-trip known to the Portuguese as the "carreira da India" that took some six to eight months each way. These trips were made in huge carracks, ships that might carry 600 or 700 people, a significant portion of whom would normally die on the way, sometimes of scurvy, more often of disease. The conditions were horrendous. C. R. Boxer, who translated the Gomes de Brito collection for the Hakluyt Society in 1959, writes that "by the time the carracks reached the equator they were often floating pest-houses, and their occupants died like flies. They had to endure extreme heat in the Gulf of Guinea, where they were sometimes becalmed for weeks together, and bitter cold off the Cape of Good Hope. Tropical rain and seasonal storms wetted or chilled them to the bone, especially the large numbers who had no place to sleep but on the upper decks...The chronic overcrowding naturally facilitated the spread of dysentery and infectious diseases, while the rancid or salty nature of much of the rations fostered the ravages of scurvy." Sanitary conditions were truly awful, he goes on, "and the stench between decks was so foul that anyone coming down the *hatchway was liable to swoon." Cockroaches and rats reached the proportions of a plague.*

But it was on the trips back, from India to Portugal, that most of the shipwrecks took place. On the voyages out the ships tended to be lightly loaded; coming back they jammed their holds full of spices, lumber, furniture, saltpeter, cotton goods, then piled more things on the deck, so much that it was impossible to pass from one end of the ship to the other without climbing over crates of goods piled everywhere. Overloading made the ships, awkward and top-heavy to begin with, much more difficult to manage. One source estimates the losses on this route over a period of a hundred years, 1550–1650, the heyday of the Portuguese overseas empire, to be 130 ships—more than one a year. Timing was everything in making these voyages. Ships had to leave Goa by the end of February at the latest to avoid the worst of the Southern Hemisphere winter and the storms that raged in the Indian Ocean east of Africa. Immanuel (or Manuel; his name is spelled in various ways at various times) de Sosa (or Sousa) left Goa on February 3, 1552, which should have given him plenty of time to double the Cape before the worst of the storms struck. Luck would not have it so.

The shipwreck accounts included in The Tragic History of the Sea, *especially this particular account, had an impact on Portuguese literature that is unique to Portugal. This particular account was important because Luis de Camoens made it a central episode in his poem* The Lusiads, *first published in 1572, which became the great epic poem of the Portuguese empire—great and tragic, because Camoens saw the empire as doomed, as indeed it was, too demanding a responsibility for such a small country as Portugal to maintain. Thus shipwreck became a controlling image of Portuguese history, and the accounts of them reached something like canonical status in the long decline of the empire. Now they are taught in schools as prime examples of Portuguese prose.*

Our version comes from Archibald Duncan's 1806 collection of shipwreck tales, The Mariner's Chronicle. *It is shorter than other versions but not necessarily less reliable. Given that this was pamphlet literature to begin with, in fact, reliability is not that big an issue. Shipwreck accounts were often written not only to tell the story, but to draw morals from it. In this case the moral to be drawn was quite practical: Don't be so stupid as to give up your only bargaining tool, your weapons.*

EMMANUEL SOSA DE SEPULVEDA, DESCENDED FROM ONE OF THE MOST ancient and distinguished families of Portugal, obtained great reputation in the Indies by his courage and talents. About the middle of the sixteenth century he obtained the government of the citadel of Diu, a post given only to officers of merit and tried valour. This situation he held several years, till conceiving an irresistible desire to revisit his native land, he embarked at the port of Cochin. The vessel in which he sailed had on board the wealth he had amassed, together with the property of the officers and passengers who accompanied him. Sosa likewise took with him his wife, Eleonora Garcia, the Daughter of Sala, at that time general of the Portuguese in the Indies; his children; his brother-in-law Pantaleon Sala; together with several officers and gentlemen. The number of sailors, servants and slaves was very great; the whole of the crew and passengers amounting to about six hundred persons.

An acquaintance with the sea and winds has proved that the month of January is the most favourable season for the passage from India to Europe. Sala stopped to make some purchases at Coulan, by which he was detained till February. On the 13th of April they discovered the coast of Caffraria; from thence they proceeded without accident to the Cape of Good Hope, when a north wind that arose produced the most tremendous hurricane that had ever been experienced in those seas. The sky was suddenly overcast; the waves, rising to the clouds, threatened every moment to engulf the vessel: the darkness was interrupted only by the lightning's blaze and the pealing thunder, which struck terror into the hearts of the most resolute. The pilot and sailors deliberated whether they should strike the yards and wait at sea till the tempest was over; but being terrifled by its continuing with redoubled fury and deprived of all hope of being able to double the Cape, on account of the season, they unanimously agreed to steer their course back to India. In this design they were not more fortunate than in the other, and the unrelenting winds seemed to have conspired the destruction of the wretched vessel, which was already considerably injured; in vain the pilot and sailors employed their utmost efforts to save her from their fury. The sides were so rudely shaken by the waves, that at length the planks gave way and the ship made more water than the pumps were able to discharge. The goods were thrown overboard to lighten the vessel, but this measure did not lessen the danger. Their condition was hopeless and every wave threatened them with inevitable destruction; but after the tempest had continued several days, without intermission, a south wind decided their fate and drove the ship aground, which was the least misfortune that could happen to them.

The anchor was immediately thrown out and the boats, which were their last resource, were hoisted overboard. Sosa, his wife, and children, and the principal persons of his suite, snatching up in haste their most valuable effects, threw themselves into the boats. New dangers attended them; the waves impelled by the force of the wind, dashed against the shore and formed mountains that appeared ready to overwhelm their feeble bark. At length, after much difficulty and danger, they reached the shore. All could not effect their escape in the boats, for after the second or third voyage they were dashed to pieces upon hidden rocks; at the same time the cable parted, and those who remained in the vessel had no other method of saving their lives than to throw themselves overboard and endeavour to gain the shore. Some seized hold of casks or boxes while others trusted to their strength and their expertness in swimming. Very few, however, were so fortunate as to arrive without accident, and by this disaster three hundred men, Portuguese and foreigners, lost their lives. Those who escaped had scarcely reached the shore when the vessel foundered. This loss overwhelmed the Portuguese with despair; from the fragments of the ship they might have constructed a brigantine and have gone to seek some relief at Sofala and Mozambique; but from this hope they were now completely cut off.

The country on which they were wrecked was in the latitude of 31° south. Sosa directed large fires to be made, in order to dry and warm his people, who suffered exceedingly from cold and hunger and their wounds. He distributed among them, with the greatest economy, a small quantity of flour picked up from the wreck, but half spoiled by the salt water. Their situation was dreadful. The shore presented to their view nothing but desert sands and arid rocks. After a long search they discovered some springs of fresh water, which were extremely serviceable, and then began to form an entrenchment of boxes and large stones that they might pass the night in safety. Sosa, on this occasion, forgot none of the duties of a good citizen and a benevolent master. Here he remained with his people till they had recovered from the fatigues of the sea, and as long as he entertained any hope of being able to subsist upon the provisions thrown on shore from the vessel. It became necessary, however, to think of removing and they deliberated upon the course that ought to be pursued: all were in favour of proceeding along the coast till they found the river to which Marchesez had given the name of Santo Spiritu and where the Portuguese of Sofala and Mozambique carried on a considerable traffic.

That river was about one hundred and eighty leagues distant from their post. Sosa, after adopting the resolution, encouraged his troop and exhorted them, by his words and example, not to lose their courage. "Before a person exposes himself," said he, "to the dangers of the sea, he ought to be resolved to bear thirst, hunger, hardships and inconvenience of every kind. Far from being dejected at their approach he ought to meet them as if he had expected them, and substitute those transient evils instead of the eternal misery due to the crimes he has committed. In our present misfortune (added he) we ought less to consider what we have lost than what we have saved; the loss of our property is a small object when compared with the preservation of our lives. I can give you no better advice than to resign all private claims and relinquish all personal and individual interest in favour of the public welfare. If we are split into parties we can never be secure; but while united we have nothing to fear!" He concluded with a prayer, extorted by love, on behalf of his wife and children, and entreated his companions in misfortune to pay some respect on the way to the sex of the one and the age of the others. All replied, it was but just that the strongest and most robust should assist the weakest, that he might lead them wherever he pleased, and that they would never withdraw themselves from his command.

They immediately set off. This caravan was composed of Sosa, his wife, Eleonora, a woman of a masculine courage, their children, as yet too young to know the dangers of their situation, Andrew Vasez, the master of the vessel, and eighty Portuguese. This first troop was followed by about one hundred servants, who alternately carried the children on their backs and their mistress on a rude kind of chair. These were succeeded by the sailors and the female servants; and Pantaleon, with a number of Portuguese and slaves, closed the rear.

After proceeding several days through a very dangerous country, they were stopped by inaccessible rocks and torrents, swelled by the rains that had recently fallen. By endeavouring to discover the easiest roads, they had made a circuit of above one hundred leagues, while they would have had to go about thirty if they had kept along the seacoast. Their provisions were soon consumed and they were obliged to live upon apples and wild fruits and even upon certain herbs, of which the animals of that country are very fond.

After a progress of four months they at length arrived at the river Santo Spirito, but without recognizing it, for the country is traversed by three different branches, which unite before they discharge themselves into the sea.

Their doubts were removed by the king of the district, who was the more favourably disposed towards the Portuguese, because he had, some time before, traded peaceably with Lorenzo Marchesez and Antonio Caldera. That prince gave a kind of reception to Sosa and his people and informed them that the king of the country contiguous to his dominions was a crafty and rapacious man, of whom they ought to beware. The desire of speedily reaching some place inhabited by Europeans rendered them blind to the misfortunes that were predicted; but they soon had reason to repent having passed the second arm of the river.

The following day they perceived two hundred Caffres coming towards them. Though exhausted with hardships and fatigue they prepared their arms and put themselves in a posture of defence; but seeing that the Caffres approached them peaceably and rather shewed a desire of forming an acquaintance with them than of doing them an injury, their fears were dissipated and they endeavoured to obtain provisions, either for money or in exchange for implements of iron, which those people highly value. A mutual confidence appeared to be established and the wants of the Portuguese encouraged their good opinion of the natives, but the opportunity of stripping the strangers of all they possessed was too favourable for the barbarians to be neglected. In order to accomplish their design with the greater facility, they gave the Portuguese to understand that if they would proceed to the habitation of their king they would experience a gracious reception. Their excessive weariness, their joy at having found the river they were in search of, and a still more powerful motive, the want of provisions, induced them to embrace the proposal of the Caffres. They followed them towards the habitation of their chief; but the latter directed them to stop on the way, in a place shaded by trees. Here they remained several days, during which they purchased various kinds of coarse provisions with the effects they had saved from the wreck. Deceived by the air of sincerity of those people, Sosa conceived that he might wait at this place for the arrival of some merchants from Sofala and demanded permission of the king to erect huts for himself, his wife, and all his people, whose number had been much diminished by the fatigues of their long peregrination.

The king, with more artifice than he could be suspected of, told Sosa that two circumstances retarded the favourable reception which he wished to give them; the first was the dearness and scarcity of provisions; and the second, the fear which his subjects entertained of the swords and fire-arms of the Portuguese; that if these were sent to him as a pledge of their peaceable and tranquil disposition, he would agree to their request.

The hope of arriving at the end of their hardships induced the Portuguese to comply with these conditions, to which prudence ought to have dictated a refusal. In vain Eleonora reminded Sosa of the unfavourable account given of this sovereign by the other king; deaf to the intreaties and admonitions of his wife he accepted, with fatal credulity, the subtle offers of this prince. The rest of the troop followed their captain's example and the arms were delivered to the perfidious monarch. They, however, soon repented of this step, for the Caffres immediately seized upon the treasures they had brought with them with such fatigue and stripped them of all their clothes. Those who attempted to make any resistance were massacred without mercy by the unrelenting barbarians.

Eleonora alone resisted with courage; but of what avails are the efforts of a female against men of a disposition so ferocious! They stripped her likewise of all her clothes. Ashamed to be exposed stark naked to the view of those wretches and of her own servants, she threw herself into a ditch a few paces distant and buried herself, as it were, in the sand, resolving not to leave that situation. Overwhelmed with fatigue and chagrin she could not forbear saying to Andrew Vasez, and others of the Portuguese who would not leave her, "There, my friends, you see the consequence of your silly confidence. Go: I want nothing more; think only of yourselves; and should heaven permit you to revisit your native land, tell those who enquire after the unfortunate Eleonora and her husband, that our sins have drawn upon us the indignation of heaven and have precipitated us into this abyss of misery." Here sighs choked her utterance, but she cast a tender look at her children and her husband. The latter, overcome with grief for his imprudence and its fatal consequences, remained motionless. The Caffres had by this time retired with all their booty; his companions had dispersed to avoid the fate that impended over them and not one was to be seen. At length the sentiments of tenderness were again excited in his breast and he ran about in every direction, in quest of fruit of any kind, by which he might prolong the existence of his wife and his wretched infants. But naked and unarmed, Sosa was unable to find any thing in a country ravaged by barbarians and burned up by the sun. He frequently returned exhausted with fatigue, and the last time he returned he found that his wife and children had expired with hunger and thirst. He had sufficient strength to perform the rites of interment, after which, fleeing from this scene of horror, he roved about in the deserts where doubtless he died, as he was never heard of afterwards.

Such was the fatal issue of Sosa's voyage in the year 1553. The miserable remains of this troop, reduced in number to twenty-six persons, by the fatigues and miseries they endured, wandered about a long time, and were, at length, treated as slaves. They would all have finished their career in this state of hardship and humiliation, had not a Portuguese merchant, who repaired from Mozambique to this part of the country to purchase ivory, ransomed them for four piastres apiece. Of these Pantaleon Sala was one; he died at Lisbon of an apoplexy, at a very advanced age.

The disaster of Sosa excited great compassion among his countrymen but did not correct their imprudence. The following year five more vessels sailed from the port of Cochin for Portugal, under the command of Fernand Alvarez Capral. Only one of these ships arrived at Lisbon, after encountering a thousand dangers. It is not known what became of any of the others, excepting the *St. Benedict*, which was so deeply laden that the sailors could scarcely work her. A violent tempest overtook her in the middle of her course, near the Cape of Good Hope; a gale of wind drove her ashore and destroyed her on the desert coast called Natal. Two hundred men, who endeavoured to save themselves by swimming, perished on this occasion.

Mesquita Perestrella, who survived this disaster, and has left a very accurate account of it, exaggerates the terrors which his companions underwent by the apparition of demons in the air, and the noise of the wandering spirits of the sailors, which he declares that he both saw and heard. The unfortunate wretches who escaped from the wreck experienced the same hardships as Sosa and his company for having pursued almost the same course, they had to endure the greatest extremity of hunger and thirst. In short, from three hundred they were reduced in number to twenty-three, who, half dead with famine and fatigue, were at length made slaves. A few months afterward some merchants, who visited that part of the country for the purposes of trade, ransomed and conveyed them to Sofala and Mozambique, where they arrived after suffering almost incredible misery.

5

The WRECK *of the* DELIGHT

From *A Relation of* Richard Clarke *of* Weymouth, *Master of the Ship Called* The Delight, *Going for the Discovery of* Norumbega, *with* Sir Humphrey Gilbert, 1583 [*from* Richard Hakluyt's Principall Navigations, 1589]

1583

The back story to Clarke's account of his shipwreck on the shoals of Sable Island, *east of* Cape Breton, *is as interesting as his account is brief. Clarke's ship, the* Delight, *was one of five under* Sir Humphrey Gilbert *that sailed from* England *to establish the first* English *colony in* North America. Gilbert *was* Sir Walter Raleigh's *half-brother and a great promoter of* English *overseas colonies, a subject he had first written about in 1566. He had a patent for his colony from the queen. In 1578 he made a preliminary voyage, possibly to* Florida, *about which little is known. The voyage of 1583 was headed for* Norumbega, *a region of indeterminate width and breadth named after an* Indian *village located somewhere around the mouth of the* Penobscot River *in* Maine *that was thought to be the capital of an extensive* Indian *nation. Since nobody knew much about the size of* North America, *the geographers of the time found it difficult to set limits to their notions of what prospective colonists like* Gilbert *might find there, but evidently* Gilbert *thought that the nation of* Norumbega, *which did not exist, corresponded to what we now call* New England.

Gilbert *might actually have succeeded in establishing a colony if he had not been such a fool. The queen, no fool herself, said of* Gilbert *that he was "a man noted of not good hap by sea," and did not invest in his voyage. She had invested heavily in* Martin Frobisher's *fruitless attempts of a few years before to find the* Northwest Passage; *perhaps she didn't want to see good money go the way of bad. But* Gilbert *was able to interest a good many other prominent people in his project, among them* Sir Philip

Sidney, who almost went with Gilbert on this voyage, and to whom, in recompense for his backing, Gilbert assigned no less than three million acres of America, should he wish to take possession of them. It is worth noting that Sidney, when he came to write his great romance, The Countess of Pembroke's Arcadia, *began the narrative with a shipwreck.*

With his little flotilla Gilbert sailed straight to Newfoundland and claimed it for England with all the proper ceremonies, including the erection of a wooden pillar with the arms of England engraved on a lead plaque nailed to it. St. John's harbor, where the ceremony took place, was full of fishing boats from other nations, but no one objected; it had not occurred to anyone yet that Newfoundland was worth owning. Walter Raleigh had come with him; he was in charge of one of the ships. Raleigh would shortly inherit Gilbert's plans for English colonies, but he had the wisdom to try farther south, where the weather was more agreeable.

By the time he reached Newfoundland Gilbert was down to four ships, one having returned to England after only two days. He lost another in St. John's, where they spent two weeks feasting with the sailors from other countries, when he punished the captain of one ship for piratical acts against innocent fishermen and left his ship behind, annexing the crew. Then he set sail for Sable Island, which earlier fishermen had stocked with cattle and pigs, leaving them to breed. It is here that Richard Clarke's narrative of the loss of the Delight *begins. Gilbert spent two days searching for the survivors; then he gave up and turned for home. Some ten days later his ship vanished in a major storm north of the Azores, all hands lost. Only one of the four ships that made it to the New World returned home*

Richard Hakluyt was himself a great promoter of English colonization schemes and knew Gilbert, knew Raleigh, knew all the major players. His collection of voyages, the Principall Navigations, *is a wonderfully indiscriminate book that prints everything he could find on English exploration and trading enterprises. Clarke's brief story is among the most poignant. I have modernized the spelling to make it easier to read.*

DEPARTING OUT OF SAINT JOHN'S HARBOR IN NEWFOUNDLAND THE 20th of August unto Cape Race, from thence we directed our course unto the Isle of Sable or the Isle of Sand, which the General Sir Humphrey Gilbert would willingly have seen. But when we came within twenty leagues of the Isle of Sable, we fell to controversy of our course. The General came up in his frigate and demanded of me, Richard Clarke, master of the *Admiral* [*another name for the* Delight; *it was also called the* George], what course was best to keep. I said that Westsouthwest was best, because the wind was at South and night at hand and unknown sands lay off a great way from the land. The General commanded me to go Westnorthwest. I told him again that the Isle of Sable was Westnorthwest and but 15 leagues off, and that he should be upon the Island before day, if he went that course. The General said, my reckoning was untrue, and charged me in her Majesty's name, and as I would show myself in her country, to follow him that night. I, fearing his threatenings, because he [*re*]presented her Majesty's person, did follow his commandment, and about seven of the clock in the morning the ship struck on ground, where she was cast away. Then the General went off to sea, the course that I would have had them go before, and saw the ship cast away men and all, and was not able to save a man, for there was not water upon the sand for either of them much less for the Admiral, that drew fourteen foot. Now as God would, the day before it was very calm, and a soldier of the ship had killed some fowl with his piece, and some of the company desired me that they might hoist out the boat [*the ship's pinnace*] to recover the fowl, which I granted them: and when they came aboard they did not hoist it in again that night. And when the ship was cast away the boat was astern being in burden one ton and a half: there was left in the boat one oar and nothing else. Some of the company could swim, and recovered the boat and did haul in out of the water as many men as they could: among the rest they had a care to watch for the Captain or the Master. They happened on myself being the master, but could never see the captain [*in those days the captain had overall command of the ship but the master had the sailing of the ship in his charge*]. Then they hauled into the boat as many men as they cold, in number 16, whose names hereafter I will rehearse. And when the 16 were in the boat, some had small remembrance and some had none, for they did not make account to live, but to prolong their lives as long as it pleased God, and looked every moment of an hour when the sea would eat them up, the boat being so little and so many men in her, and so foul weather, that it was not possible for a ship to brook half a course of sail. Thus while we remained two days and two nights, and that we saw it pleased God our boat lived in the sea (although we had nothing to help us withal but one oar, which we kept up the boat withal upon the sea, and so went even as the sea would drive us) there was in our company one master Headly that put forth this question to me the master. I do see that it doth please God, that our boat liveth in the sea, and it may please God that some of us may come to the land if our boat were not overladen. Let us make sixteen lots, and those four that have the four shortest lots we will cast overboard, preserving the master among us all. I replied unto him, saying, no, we will live and die together. Master Headly asked me if my remembrance were good. I answered I gave God praise it was good, and knew how far I was off the land, and was in hope to come to the land within two or three days, and said they were but threescore leagues from the land, (when they were seventy) all to put them in comfort. Thus we continued the third and fourth day without any sustenance, save only the weeds that swam in the sea, and salt water to drink. The fifth day Headly died and another moreover. Then we desired all to die, for in all these five days and five nights we saw the sun but once and the stars but none night, it was so foul weather.

Thus we did remain the sixth day. Then we were very weak and wished all to die saving only myself which did comfort them and promised they should come soon to land by the help of God. But the company were very importunate, and were in doubt they should never come to land, but that I promised them the seventh day they should come to shore, or else they should cast me overboard. Which did happen true the seventh day, for at eleven of the clock we had sight of the land, and at 3 of the clock at afternoon we came on land. All these seven days and seven nights, the wind kept continually South. If the wind had in the meantime shifted upon any other point, we had never come to land. We were no sooner come to the land, but the wind came clean contrary at North within half an hour after our arrival. But we were so weak that one could scarcely help another of us out of the boat, yet with much ado being come all on shore we kneeled down upon our knees and gave God praise that he had dealt so mercifully with us. Afterwards those which were strongest helped their fellows unto a fresh brook, where we satisfied ourselves with water and berries very well. There were of all sorts of berries plenty, & as goodly a country as ever I saw. We found a very fair plain champion [*i.e., level, open ground, a champaign*] ground that a man might see very far every way. By the seaside was here and there a little wood with goodly trees as good as ever I saw any in Norway, able to mast any ship, of pine trees, spruce trees, fir, and very great birch trees. Where we came on land we made a little house with boughs, where we rested all that night. In the morning I divided the company three and three to go every way to see what food they could find to sustain themselves, and appointed them to meet there all again at noon with such food as they could get. As we went abroad we found great store of wild peas as good as any we have in England. A man would think they had been sown there. We rested there three days and three nights and lived very well with peas and berries, we named the place Saint Laurence, because it was a very goodly river like the river of S. Laurence in Canada, and we found it very full of salmon. When we had well rested ourselves we rowed our boat along the shore [*they knew they were in* Newfoundland], thinking to have gone to the Grand Bay to have come home with some Spaniards which are yearly there to kill the whale. And when we were hungry or athirst we put our boat on land and gathered peas and berries. Thus we rowed our boat along the shore five days, about which time we came to a very goodly river that ran far up into the country and saw very goodly grown trees of all sorts. There we happened upon a ship of Saint John de Luz, which ship brought us into Biscay to a harbor called The Passage. The master of the ship was our great friend, or else we had been put to death if he had not kept our counsel. For when the visitors came aboard, as it is the order in Spain, they demanding what we were, he said we were poor fishermen that had cast away our ship in Newfoundland, and so the visitors inquired no more of the matter at that time. As soon as night was come he put us on land and bade us shift for ourselves. Then had we but ten or twelve miles into France, which we went that night, and then cared not for the Spaniard. And so shortly after we came into England toward the end of the year 1583.

6

The LAST VOYAGE *of* THOMAS CAVENDISH

From *The Last Voyage of the Worshipful M. Thomas Cavendish Esquire, Intended for the South Sea, the Phillipines, and the Coast of China, with 3 Tall Ships, and Two Barks*

BY M. JOHN JANE, A MAN OF GOOD OBSERVATION, EMPLOYED IN THE SAME AND MANY OTHER VOYAGES

1591

This is another from Hakluyt's great collection, the second edition of 1600, and it tells what happened to some of the men involved in the disastrous attempt of Thomas Cavendish to repeat his voyage around the world of 1586–88, which itself repeated Sir Francis Drake's circumnavigation of 1579, to the same purpose—to destroy Spanish towns on the west coast of South America and intercept the great Spanish treasure galleons that sailed back and forth between the Philippines and Vera Cruz. Cavendish died on this voyage (at the age of 32) just off Ascension Island in the South Atlantic. The fleet had separated in a storm and the ships remaining became stranded in and around the Strait of Magellan for what amounted to a full year, never able to make it through the Strait far enough to get clear of the terrible weather that part of the world is subject to. It is amazing that any of these people survived to tell the tale. Starvation, shipwreck, the threat of murder: It is a harrowing story and a prime example of what mariners faced in the relatively primitive sailing ships of the time. I have again modernized the spelling and abridged the story somewhat.

THE 26 OF AUGUST 1591, WE DEPARTED FROM PLYMOUTH WITH 3 TALL ships and two barks, the Galleon wherein Mr. Cavendish went himself being Admiral, the Roebuck, Vice-Admiral whereof M. Cocke was Captain, the Desire, Rear-Admiral whereof was Captain John Davis (with whom and for whose sake I went this voyage) the Black, pinnace, and a bark of M. Adrian Gilbert, whereof M. Randolf Cotton was Captain.

The 29 of November we fell with the bay of Salvador upon the coast of Brazil 12 leagues on this side Cabo Frio, where we were becalmed until the second of December, at which time we took a small bark bound for the River of Plate with sugar, haberdash wares, and Negroes. The Master of this bark brought us unto an isle called Placencia thirty leagues west from Cabo Frio, where we arrived the fifth of December, and rifled six or seven houses inhabited by Portuguese. The 11th we departed from this place, and the fourteenth we arrived at the isle of S. Sebastian, from whence M. Cocke and Captain Davis presently departed with the Desire and the Black pinnace for the taking of the town of Santos. The 15 at evening we anchored at the bar of Santos, from whence we departed with out boats to the towns, and the next morning about nine of the clock we came to Santos, where being discovered, we were enforced to land with 24 gentlemen, our long boat being far astern, by which expedition we took all the people the town at Mass both men and women, whom we kept all that day in the Church as prisoners. The cause why master Cavendish desired to take this town was to supply his great wants, for being in Santos, and having it in quiet possession, we stood in assurance to supply all our needs in great abundance. But such was the negligence of our governor master Cocke, that the Indians were suffered to carry out of the town whatsoever they would in open view, and no man did control them. And the next day after we had won the town, our prisoners were all set at liberty; only four poor old men were kept as pawns to supply our wants. Thus in three days the town that was able to furnish such another fleet with all kind of necessaries, was left unto us nakedly bare, without people or provision.

They stayed nevertheless until January 22, when they left Santos and burned Saint Vincent, nearby, to the ground. Two days later they set sail for the Strait of Magellan. On February 7 a great storm separated the ships and the ship James *was on made for Port Desire, not a town but a harbor, now* Puerto Deseado, *where they all eventually converged, except for the ship belonging to Adrian Gilbert, which set sail back to England without the ship's captain, who was sailing on board the* Roebuck. *He was left without his personal belongings; he had only the clothes on his back. They stayed at* Port Desire *well into March, by which time the southern winter was beginning. It was not time to attempt the Strait. Nevertheless they did.*

The 20 of March we departed from Port Desire, master Cavendish being in the Desire with us. The eighth of April 1592 we fell with the Straits of Magellan, enduring many furious storms between Port Desire and the Straits. The 16 we passed the second Strait being ten leagues distant from the first. The 18 we doubled Cape Forward, which Cape lies in 53 degrees [*south latitude*]. The 21 we were enforced by the fury of the weather to put into a small cove with our ships, 4 leagues from the said Cape, upon the south shore, where we remained until the 15 of May. In the which time we endured extreme storms, with perpetual snow, where many of our men died with cursed famine and miserable cold, not having wherewith to cover their bodies, nor to fill their bellies, but living by mussels, water, and weeds of the sea, with a small relief of the ships store in meal sometimes. And all the sick men in the Galleon were most uncharitably put ashore into the woods in the snow, rain and cold, when men of good health could scarcely endure it, where they ended their lives in the highest degree of misery, master Cavendish all this while being aboard the Desire. In these great extremities of snow and cold, doubting what the end would be, he asked our Captain's opinion, because he was a man that had good experience of the Northwest parts [*this would be John Davis, who had made three voyages to find the Northwest Passage and for whom Davis Strait between Greenland and Baffin Island is named*], in his 3 several discoveries that way, employed by the merchants of London. Our Captain told him that this snow was a matter of no long continuance, and gave him sufficient reason for it, and that thereby he could not much be prejudiced or hindered in his proceeding. Notwithstanding he called together all the company, and told them that he purposed not to stay in the Straits, but to depart upon some other voyage, or else to return again for Brazil. But his resolution was to go for the Cape of Buena Esperanza [*Cape of Good Hope*]. The company answered, that if it pleased him, they did desire to stay God's favor for a wind, and to endure all hardness whatsoever, rather than to give over the voyage, considering they had been here but a small time, and because they were within forty leagues of the South Sea, it grieved them now to return, notwithstanding what he purposed that they would perform. So he concluded to go for the Cape of Buena Esperanza and to give over this voyage. Then our Captain, after master Cavendish was come aboard the *Desire* from talking with the company, told him, that if it pleased him to consider the great extremity of his estate, the slenderness of his provisions, with the weakness of his men, it was no course for him to proceed in that new enterprise; for if the rest of your ships (said he) be answerable to this, it is impossible to perform your determination. For we have no more sails than masts, no victuals, no ground tackling, no cordage more than is overhead, and among seventy and five persons, there is but the Master alone that can order the ship, and but fourteen sailors. The rest are gentlemen, serving men, and artificers. Therefore it will be a desperate case to take so hard an enterprise in hand. These persuasions did our Captain not only use to Master Cavendish, but also to Master Cocke. In fine upon a petition delivered in writing by the chief of the whole company, the General [*i.e., Cavendish*] determined to depart out of the Straits of Magellan, and to return again for Santos in Brazil.

In mid-May, then, the fleet sailed for Santos, but difficulties still attended them. The Desire *lost its ship's boat when it sank during the night and was split apart, and they lost all their oars, and within a week the fleet split up without warning. At dusk one day they could still see the ship, the* Galleon, *that Cavendish was sailing. The next day it was gone. They made their way back then to* Port Desire *in hopes of finding him there. He never showed up. They found the* Black, *the pinnace there, but not Cavendish. Thinking that he might have returned to the Strait, Capt. Davis decided to take the pinnace and return to the Strait to look for him, leaving the* Desire, *which was in very poor shape, at* Port Desire *to refit as best they could. This aroused the suspicion among certain members of the crew that they would be abandoned there.*

But the General having in our ship two most pestilent fellows, when they heard of this determination they utterly misliked it, and in secret dealt with the company of both ships, vehemently persuading them that our Captain and Master would leave them in the country to be devoured of the cannibals, and that they were merciless and without charity, whereupon the whole company joined in secret with them in a night to murder our Captain and Master, with myself, and all those which they thought were their friends. There were marks taken in his cabin how to kill him with muskets through the ship's side, and bullets made of silver for the execution, if their other purposes should fail. All agreed hereunto, except it were the boatswain of our ship, who when he knew the matter, and the slender ground thereof, revealed it unto our Master, and so to the Captain. Then the matter being called in question, those two most murderous fellows were found out, whose names were Charles Parker and Edward Smith.

The Captain being thus hardly beset in peril of famine, and in danger of murdering, was constrained to use lenity, and by courteous means to pacify this fury, showing that to do the General service, unto whom he had vowed faith in this action, was the cause why he purposed to go unto him in the pinnace, considering that the pinnace was so necessary a thing for him, as that he could not be without her, because he was fearful of the shore in so great ships. Whereupon all cried out with cursing and swearing that the pinnace should not go unless the ship went. Then the Captain desired them to show themselves Christians, and not so blasphemously to behave themselves, without regard or thanksgiving to God for their great deliverance and present sustenance bestowed upon them, alleging many examples of God's sharp punishment for such ingratitude, and withal promised to do anything that might stand with their good liking. By which gentle speeches the matter was pacified, and the Captain and Master at the request of the company were content to forgive this great treachery of Parker and Smith, who after many admonitions concluded in these words: The Lord judge between you and me; which after came to a most sharp revenge even by the punishment of the Almighty. Thus by a general consent it was concluded not to depart, but there to stay for the General's return.

Captain Davis then had someone write up an account of what had happened to them since leaving the Strait and why they had not gone to look for Cavendish, and everyone signed it. They then spent the next few months setting up a forge to make nails, bolts, and spikes, hunting seals at an island some ten miles distant where they abounded, and hoping for Cavendish to return. They left in August to head for the Strait again, thinking that was the best place to find Cavendish or to intercept him, should he be trying once again to complete his mission.

The sixth of August we set sail, and went to Penguin Island, and the next day we salted twenty hogsheads of seals, which was as much as our salt could possibly do, and so we departed for the Straits the poorest wretches that ever were created. The seventh of August toward night we departed from Penguin Island, shaping our course for the Straits, where we had full confidence to meet with our General. The ninth we had a sore storm, so that we were constrained to hull [*i.e., lower all sails*], for our sails were not to endure any force. The 14 we were driven in among certain isles never before discovered by any known relation, lying fifty leagues or better from the shore east and northerly from the Straits, in which place, unless it had pleased God of his wonderful mercy to have ceased the wind, we must of necessity have perished. [*These were the Falklands and this discovery is the basis for the British claim to them.*] But the wind shifting to the east, we directed our course for the Straits, and the 18 of August we fell with the Cape in a very thick fog; and the same night we anchored ten leagues within the Cape. The 19 day we passed the first and the second Straits. The 21 we doubled Cape Forward. The 22 we anchored in Savage Cove, so named because we found many savages there. Notwithstanding the extreme cold of this place, yet do all these wild people go naked, and live in the woods like satyrs, painted and disguised, and flee from you like wild deer. They are very strong and threw stones at us of three or four pounds weight an incredible distance. The 24 in the morning we departed from this cove, and the same day we came into the Northwest Reach, which is the last reach of the Straits. The 25 we anchored in a good cove, within fourteen leagues of the South Sea. In this place we purposed to stay for the General, for the strait in this place is scarce three miles broad, so that he could not pass but we must see him. After we had stayed here a fortnight in the deep of winter, our victuals consuming, (for our seals stunk most vilely, and our men died pitifully through cold and famine, for the greatest part of them had not clothes to defend the extremity of the winter's cold) being in this heavy distress, our Captain and Master thought it the best course to depart from the Straits into the South Sea and to go for the Isle of Santa Maria, which is to the northward of Baldivia in 37 degrees & a quarter, where we might have relief, and be in a temperate clime, and there stay for the General, for of necessity he must come by that isle. So we departed the 13 of September, & came in sight of the South Sea. The 14 we were forced back again, and recovered a cove 3 leagues within the Straits from the South Sea. Again we put forth, & being 8 or 10 leagues free of the land, the wind rising furiously at Westnorthwest, we were enforced again into the Straits only for want of sails; for we never dared bear sail in any stress of weather, they were so weak. So again we recovered the cove three leagues within the Straits, where we endured most furious weather, so that one of our two cables broke whereby we were hopeless of life. Yet it pleased God to calm the storm and we unrived [*untangled, played out*] our sheets, tackles, halyards and other ropes, and moored our ship to the trees close by the rocks. We labored to recover our anchor again, but could not by any means, it lay so deep in the water, and as we think clean covered with ooze. Now had we but one anchor which had but one whole fluke, a cable spliced in two places, and a piece of an old cable. In the midst of these our troubles it pleased God that the wind came fair the first of October, whereupon with all expedition we loosed our moorings and weighed our anchor, and so towed off into the channel; for we had mended our boat in Port Desire, and had five oars of the pinnace. When we had weighed our anchor we found our cable broken, only one strand held. Then we praised God, for we saw apparently his mercies in preserving us. Being in the channel, we rived our ropes, & again rigged our ship, no man's hand was idle, but all labored even for the last gasp of life.

Once in the channel, ready to proceed, the question arose—where? Cavendish had not shown up as they had hoped, the weather had beaten them out of the Pacific whenever they tried to proceed, the ship was in terrible condition, the sails rotting, the anchor cable hardly usable and one anchor lost, and they were constantly hungry and cold. Davis did not know what to do or which way lay the best chance of not dying. In the end they decided to try once more for the Isle of Santa Maria, where they hoped to find food and a milder, less stormy climate, and on October 2 they sailed once more into the Pacific.

This night the wind began to blow very much at Westnorthwest, and still increased in fury, so that we were in great doubt what course to take. To put into the Straits we durst not for lack of ground tackle; to bear sail we doubted, the tempest was so furious and our sails so bad. The pinnace came room with us and told us that she had received many grievous seas, and that her ropes did every hour fail her, so as they could not tell what shift to make. We being unable in any sort to help them, stood under our courses in view of the lee shore, still expecting our ruinous end.

The fourth of October the storm growing beyond all reason furious, the pinnace being in the wind of us, struck suddenly ahull, so that we thought she had received some grievous sea, or sprung a leak, or that her sails failed her, because she came not with us. But we durst not hull in that unmerciful storm, but sometimes tried our main course, sometimes with a haddock of our sail, for our ship was very leeward, and most laborsome in the sea. This night we lost the pinnace and never saw her again.

The fifth, our foresail was split and all torn; then our Master took the mizzen and brought it to the foremast, to make our ship work, and with our sprit sail we mended our foresail, the storm continuing without all reason in fury, with hail, snow, rain and wind such and so mighty as that in nature it could not possibly be more, the seas such and so lofty, with continual breach, that many times we were doubtful whether our ship did sink or swim.

The tenth of October being by the account of our Captain and Master very near the shore, the weather dark, the storm furious, and most of our men having given over to travail, we yielded ourselves to death, without further hope of succor. Our Captain sitting in the gallery very pensive, I came and brought him some *rosa solis* to comfort him, for he was so cold, that he was scarce able to move a joint. After he had drunk, and was comforted in heart, he began for the ease of his conscience to make a large repetition of his forepassed time, and with many grievous sighs he concluded in these words: "Oh most glorious God, with whose power the mightiest things among men are matters of no moment, I most humbly beseech thee, that the intolerable burden of my sins may through the blood of Jesus Christ be taken from me; and end our days with speed, or show us some merciful sign of thy love and our preservation." Having thus ended, he desired me not to make known to any of the company his intolerable grief and anguish of mind, because they should not thereby be dismayed. And so suddenly, before I went from him, the sun shined clear; so that he and the aster both observed the true elevation of the Pole, whereby they knew by what course to recover the Straits. Wherewithal our Captain and Master were so revived, & gave such comfortable speeches to the company, that every man rejoiced, as though we had received a present deliverance. The next day being the 11 of October, we saw Cabo Deseado being the cape on the south shore (the north shore is nothing but a company of dangerous rocks, isles, and shoals.) This cape being within two leagues to leeward of us, our master greatly doubted that we could not double the same; whereupon the captain told him, "You see there is no remedy, either we must double it or before noon we must die; therefore loose your sails, and let us put it to God's mercy." The master being a man of good spirit resolutely made quick dispatch & set sails. Our sails had not been half an hour aboard, but the footrope of our foresail broke, so that nothing held but the owlet holes. The seas continually broke over the ship's poop and flew into the sails with such violence that we still expected the tearing of our sails or oversetting of the ship, and withal to our utter discomfort, we perceived that we fell still more and more to leeward, so that we could not double the cape. We were now come within half a mile of the cape and so near the shore that the counter surf of the sea would rebound against the ship's side, so that were much dismayed with the horror of our present end. Being thus at the very pinch of death, the wind and seas raging beyond measure, our Master veered some of the main sheet; and whether it was by that occasion or by some current, or by the wonderful power of God, as we verily think it was, the ship quickened her way and shot past that rock, where we thought she would have shored. Then between the cape and the point there was a little bay, so that we were somewhat farther from the shore; and when we were come so far as the cape, we yielded to death, yet our good God the Father of all mercies delivered us, and we doubled the cape about the length of our ship, or very little more. Being shot past the cape, we presently took in our sails, which only God had preserved unto us; and when we were shot in between the high lands, the wind blowing trade, without any inch of sail, we spooned before the sea, three men being not able to guide the helm, and in six hours we were put five and twenty leagues within the Straits, where we found a sea answerable to the Ocean.

In this time we freed our ship from water, and after we had rested a little, our men were not able to move; their sinews were stiff and their flesh dead, and many of them (which is most lamentable to be reported) were so eaten with lice, as that in their flesh did lie clusters of lice as big as peas, yea and some as big as beans. Being in this misery we were constrained to put into a cove for the refreshing of our men. Our Master knowing the shore and every cove very perfectly, put in with the shore, and moored to the trees, as beforetime we had done, laying our anchor to the seaward. Here we continued until the twentieth of October, but not being able any longer to stay through extremity of famine, the one and twentieth we put off into the channel, the weather being reasonably calm. But before night it blew most extremely at Westnorthwest. The storm growing outrageous, our men could scarcely stand by their labor, and the Straits being full of turning reaches we were constrained by discretion of the Captain and Master in their accounts to guide the ship in the hell-dark night, when we could not see any shore, the channel being in some places scarce three miles broad. But our captain as we first passed through the Straits drew such an exquisite plat of the same, as I am assured it cannot in any sort be bettered, which plat he and the master so often perused, and so carefully regarded, as that in memory they had every turning and crick, and in the deep dark night without any doubting they conveyed the ship through that crooked channel. So that I conclude, the world has not any so skillful pilots for that place, as they are; for otherwise we could never have passed in such sort as we did.

After this the ship left the Strait, though not without further hardships, and made for Port Desire, restocking with provisions at Penguin Island on the way, where, the men said, they could not walk without stepping on the birds; and at Port Desire they ran the ship aground to make repairs, and to prepare for the trip back to England. But their troubles were hardly over.

The third of November our boat with water, wood, and as many as she could carry, went for the Isle of Penguins, but being deep [*i.e., overladen*], she dared not proceed, but returned again the same night. Then Parker, Smith, Townsend, Purpet, with five others, desired that they might go by land, and that the boat might fetch them when they were against the Isle, it being scarce a mile from the shore. The captain bade them do what they thought best, advising them to take weapons with them, for, said he, although we have not at any time seen people in this place, yet in the country there may be savages. They answered that here were great store of deer and ostriches; but if there were savages, they would devour them [*i.e. the deer and ostriches*]. Notwithstanding the captain caused them to carry weapons, so the sixth of November they departed by land and the boat by sea; but from that day to this day we never heard of our men. The 11 while most of our men were at the Isle, only the Captain and Master with six others being left in the ship, there came a great multitude of savages to the ship, throwing dust in the air, leaping and running like brute beasts, having vizards on their faces like dogs' faces, or else their faces are dogs' faces indeed. We greatly feared lest they would set our ship on fire, for they would suddenly make fire, whereat we much marveled. They came to windward of our ship and set the bushes on fire, so that we were in a very stinking smoke; but as soon as they came within our shot, we shot at them, & striking one of them in the thigh they all presently fled, so that we never heard nor saw more of them. Hereby we judged that these cannibals had slain our 9 men. When we considered what they were that thus were slain, and found that they were the principal men that would have murdered our Captain and Master, with the rest of their friends, we saw the just judgment of God and made supplication to his divine Majesty to be merciful to us. While we were in this harbor, our Captain and Master went with the boat to discover how far this river did run, that if need should enforce us to leave our ship, we might know how far we might go by water. So they found that farther than 20 miles we could not go with the boat. At their return they sent the boat to the Isle of Penguins, whereby we understood that the penguins dried to our heart's content, and that the multitude of them was infinite. This penguin has the shape of a bird, but has no wings, only two stumps in the place of wings, by which he swims under water with as great swiftness as any fish. They live upon smelts, whereof there is great abundance upon this coast. In eating they be neither fish nor flesh; they lay great eggs, and the bird is of a reasonable bigness, very near twice so big as a duck. All the time that we were in this place, we fared passing well with eggs, penguins, young seals, young gulls, besides other birds, such as I know not, of all which we had great abundance. In this place we found an herb called scurvy grass, which we fried with eggs, using train oil [*fish oil*] instead of butter. This herb did so purge the blood that it took away all kinds of swellings, of which many died, & restored us to perfect health of body, so that we were in as good case as when we came first out of England. We stayed in this harbor until the 22 of December, in which time we had dried 20,000 penguins; & the Captain, the Master, and myself had made some salt, by laying salt water upon the rocks in holes, which in 6 days would be kerned. Thus God did feed us even as it were with manna from heaven.

The 22 of December we departed with our ship for the Isle, where with great difficulty, by the skillful industry of our Master we got 14,000 of our birds, and had almost lost our captain in laboring to bring the birds aboard; & had not our Master been very expert in the set of those wicked tides, which run after many fashions, we had also lost our ship in the same place. But God in his goodness has in all our extremities been our protector. So the 22 at night we departed with 14,000 dried penguins, not being able to fetch the rest, and shaped our course for Brazil. Now our captain rated our victuals and brought us to such allowance, as that our victuals might last six months; for our hope was that within six months we might recover our country, though our sails were very bad. So the allowance was two ounces & a half of meal for a man a day, and to have so twice a week, so that 5 ounces did serve for a week. Three days a week we had oil, three spoonfuls for a man a day; and 2 days in a week peas, a pint between 4 men a day, and every day 5 penguins for 4 men, and 6 quarts of water for 4 men a day. This was our allowance, wherewith (we praise God) we lived, though weakly, and very feeble. The 30 of January we arrived at the Isle of Placencia in Brazil, the first place that outward bound we were at, and have made the shoals, our ship lying off at sea, the Captain with 24 of the company went with the boat on shore, being a whole night before they could recover it. The last of January at sunrising they suddenly landed, hoping to take the Portuguese in their houses, & by that means to recover some cassava meal, or other victuals for our relief. But when they came to the houses they were all razed, and burnt to the ground, so that we thought no man had remained on the island. Then the Captain went to the gardens, & brought from thence fruits & roots for the company, and came aboard the ship, and brought her into a fine creek which he had found out, where we might moor her by the trees, and where there was water, and hoops to trim our cask. Our case being very desperate, we presently labored for dispatch away; some cut hoops, which the coopers made, other labored upon the sails and ship, every man working for his life, & still a guard was kept on shore to defend those that labored, every man having his weapon likewise by him. The 3 of February our men with 23 shot went again to the gardens, being 3 miles from us on the north shore, and fetched cassava roots out of the ground, to relieve our company instead of bread; for we spent not of our meal while we stayed there. The 5 of February being Monday, our captain and master hastened the company to their labor; so some went with the coopers to gather hoops, and the rest labored aboard. This night many of our men in the ship dreamed of murder & slaughter. In the morning they reported their dreams, one saying to another, this night I dreamed that thou were slain, another answered, and I dreamed that thou were slain; and this was general through the ship. The captain hearing this, who likewise had dreamed very strangely himself, gave very straight charge that those which went on shore should take weapons with them and saw them himself delivered into the boat, & sent some on purpose to guard the laborers. All the forenoon they labored in quietness, & when it was ten of the clock, the heat being extreme, they came to a rock near the woods side (for all this country is nothing but thick woods) and there they boiled cassava roots, & dined. After dinner some slept, some washed themselves in the sea, all being stripped to their shirts, & no man keeping watch, no match lighted, not a piece charged. Suddenly as they were thus sleeping & sporting, having gotten themselves into a corner out of sight of the ship, there came a multitude of Indians & Portuguese upon them, and slew them sleeping. Only two escaped, one very sorely hurt, the other not touched, by whom we understood of this miserable massacre. With all speed we manned our boat, & landed to succor our men, but we found them slain, & laid naked on a rank one by another, with their faces upward, and a cross set by them. And withal we saw two very great pinnaces come from the river of Janeiro very full of men, whom we mistrusted came from thence to take us, because there came from Janeiro soldiers to Santos when the General had taken the town and was strong in it. Of 76 persons which departed in our ship out of England, we were now left but 27, having lost 13 in this place, with their chief furniture, as muskets, calivers [*a light musket*], powder, & shot. Our cask was all in decay, so that we could not take in more water than was in our ship, for want of cask, and that which we had was marvelous ill conditioned; and being there moored by trees for want of cables and anchors, we still expected the cutting of our moorings, to be beaten from our decks with our own furniture, & to be assailed by them of Janeiro. What distress we were now driven into, I am not able to express. To depart with 8 tuns of water in such bad cask was to starve at sea, & in staying our case was ruinous. These were hard choices; but being thus perplexed, we made choice rather to fall into the hands of the Lord, than into the hands of men. For his exceeding mercies we had tasted, & of the others' cruelty we were not ignorant. So concluding to depart, the 6 of February we were off in the channel, with out ordnance & small shot in readiness for any assault that should come, & having a small gale of wind we recovered the sea in most deep distress. Then bemoaning our estate to one another and recounting over all our extremities, nothing grieved us more than the loss of our men twice, first by the slaughter of the cannibals at Port Desire, and at this Isle of Placencia by the Indians and Portuguese. And considering what they were that were lost, we found that all those that conspired the murdering of our captain & master were now slain by savages, the gunner only excepted. Being thus at sea, when we came to Cape Frio the wind was contrary; so that 3 weeks we were grievously vexed with cross winds, & our water consuming, our hope of life was very small. Some desired to go to Bahia & to submit themselves to the Portuguese, rather than to die for thirst; but the captain with fair persuasions altered their purpose of yielding to the Portuguese. In this distress it pleased God to send us rain in such plenty, as that we were well watered, & in good comfort to return. But after we came near unto the sun, our dried penguins began to corrupt, and there bred in them a most loathsome & ugly worm of an inch long. This worm did so mightily increase and devour our victuals that there was in reason no hope how we should avoid famine, but be devoured of these wicked creatures. There was nothing that they did not devour, only iron excepted—our clothes, boots, shoes, hats, shirts, stockings. And for the ship they did so eat the timbers, as that we greatly feared they would undo us, by gnawing through the ship's side. Great was the care and diligence of our captain, master, and company to consume these vermin, but the more we labored to kill them, the more they increased, so that at the last we could not sleep for them, but they would eat our flesh, and bite like mosquitoes. In this woeful case, after we had passed the equinoctial toward the north, our men began to fall sick of such a monstrous disease, as I think the like was never heard of. For in their ankles it began to swell; from thence in two days it would be in their breasts, so that they could not draw their breath, and then fell into their cods; and their cods and yards did swell most grievously, and most dreadfully to behold, so that they could neither stand, lie, nor go. Whereupon our men grew mad with grief. Our captain with extreme anguish of his soul was in such woeful case that he desired only a speedy end, and though he were scarce able to speak for sorrow, yet he persuaded them to patience and to give God thanks, & like dutiful children to accept of his chastisement. For all this diverse grew raging mad, & some died in most loathsome & furious pain. It were incredible to write our misery as it was. There was no man in perfect health, but the captain & one boy. The master being a man of good spirit with extreme labor bore out his grief, so that it grew not upon him. To be short, all our men died except 16, of which there were but 5 able to move. The captain was in good health, the master indifferent, captain Cotton and myself swollen and short-winded, yet better than the rest that were sick, and one boy in health; upon us 5 only the labor of the ship did stand. The captain and master, as occasion served, would take in and heave out the top-sails, the master only attended on the sprit-sail, and all of us at the capstan without sheets and tacks. In fine our misery and weakness was so great that we could not take in, nor heave out a sail; so our top-sail and sprit-sails were torn all in pieces by the weather. The master and captain taking their turns at the helm were mightily distressed and monstrously grieved with the most woeful lamentation of our sick men. Thus as lost wanderers upon the sea, the 11 of June 1593, it pleased God that we arrived at Bearhaven in Ireland, and there ran the ship on shore, where the Irish men helped us to take in our sails, and to moor our ship for floating, which slender pains of theirs cost the captain some ten pounds before he could have the ship in safety. Thus without victuals, sails, men, or any furniture God only guided us into Ireland, where the captain left the master and three or four of the company to keep the ship. And within 5 days after he and certain others had passage in an English fisher-boat to Padstow in Cornwall. In this manner our small remnant by God's only mercy were preserved, and restored to our country, to Whom be all honor and glory world without end.

7

The WRECK *and* REDEMPTION *of* SIR THOMAS GATES

From A True Reportory of the Wreck and Redemption of Sir Thomas Gates, Knight

BY WILLIAM STRACHEY

1609

If the previous story be one of the most relentlessly desperate of all the stories in this book, this one is the happiest. Strachey was on board the Sea Venture, *the flagship of an eight-ship fleet that was en route to the newly fledged colony of Jamestown in Virginia with supplies and colonists. The storm that he here describes scattered the fleet, but all the other ships survived, regrouped, and reached Virginia. Only the* Sea Venture *was wrecked, in the Bermudas, as it turned out. But all the people on board escaped to shore, the climate was mild, and the islands, which had a vicious reputation as being full of devils and exceedingly treacherous to mariners, were in fact nothing of the sort. They found wild pigs on the island, no doubt from a previous wreck, birds of various kinds were incredibly easy to take, fish were abundant, and they were able not only to live but to store up provisions for their escape to Virginia, which they effected nine months later after building two smaller boats out of the ruins of the* Sea Venture.

The real interest in the wreck is not the wreck itself, then, although Strachey describes it quite vividly, but the outcome. William Shakespeare was acquainted with some of the factors in the Virginia Company; he had opportunity to meet Strachey and may well have known him, and he certainly read the pamphlet before it was published, because Strachey's account is all over his last play, The Tempest. *The St. Elmo's fire that Strachey describes playing about the masts of the ship, the word "Bermoothes" or Bermudas in the play, the fact that the islands were supposed to be full of spirits—all this, and a number of other verbal parallels, testify to his familiarity with Strachey's account. Shakespeare's works as a whole, for that matter, are shot through with echoes from the writings of explorers, but this pamphlet in particular has attracted attention because the parallels are so obvious.*

It was on the basis of the shipwrecked company's occupation of Bermuda that Britain lay claim to the islands, which became known in England as the Somers Islands, and then, over time, the Summer Islands, Sir George Somers having been admiral of the fleet that was on its way to Virginia and on the Sea Venture *when it was wrecked. Once the shipwrecked colonists landed in Virginia and discovered the desperate straits of the colony, Somers volunteered to return to Bermuda in one of the pinnaces they had built to escape in and there collect hogs and fish and other supplies to feed them. He was a man in his 60s, but vigorous, according to one source, and he had built the boat himself, "all with cedar, with little or no ironwork at all, having in her but one bolt, which was in the keelson. Notwithstanding," says our source, "thanks be to God, she brought us in safety to Virginia, and so I trust He will protect him and send him well back again, to his heart's desire and the great comfort of all the company there." Somers and his little ship were never seen again.*

EXCELLENT LADY, KNOW THAT UPON FRIDAY LATE IN THE EVENING WE brake ground out of the sound of Plymouth, our whole fleet then consisting of seven good ships and two pinnaces, all which from the said second of June unto the twenty-third of July kept in friendly consort together, not a whole watch at any time losing the sight each of other. Our course, when we came about the height of between 26 and 27 degrees, we declined to the northward and, according to our governor's instructions, altered the trade and ordinary way used heretofore by Dominica and Nevis in the West Indies and found the wind to this course indeed as friendly as in the judgment of all seamen it is upon a more direct line and by Sir George Somers our admiral had been likewise in former time sailed, being a gentleman of approved assuredness and ready knowledge in seafaring actions, having often carried command and chief charge in many ships royal of Her Majesty's and in sundry voyages made many defeats and attempts in the time of the Spaniard's quarreling with us upon the islands and Indies, etc.

We had followed this course so long as now we were within seven or eight days at the most, by Captain Newport's reckoning, of making Cape Henry upon the coast of Virginia, when on St. James his day, July 24, being Monday (preparing for no less all the black night before), the clouds gathering thick upon us and the winds singing and whistling most unusually (which made us to cast off our pinnace, towing the same until then astern), a dreadful storm and hideous began to blow from out the northeast, which, swelling and roaring as it were by fits, some hours with more violence than others, at length did beat all light from Heaven; which, like an hell of darkness, turned black upon us, so much the more fuller of horror as in such cases horror and fear use to overrun the troubled and overmastered senses of all, which taken up with amazement, the ears lay so sensible to the terrible cries and murmurs of the winds and distraction of our company as who was most armed and best prepared was not a little shaken.

For surely, noble Lady, as death comes not so sudden nor apparent, so he comes not so elvish and painful (to men, especially, even then in health and perfect habitudes of body) as at sea; who comes at no time so welcome but our frailty (so weak is the hold of hope in miserable demonstrations of danger) it makes guilty of many contrary changes and conflicts. For, indeed, death is accompanied at no time nor place with circumstances every way so uncapable of particularities of goodness and inward comforts as at sea. For it is most true, there ariseth commonly no such unmerciful tempest, compound of so many contrary and divers nations, but that it worketh upon the whole frame of the body and most loathsomely affecteth all the powers thereof. And the manner of the sickness it lays upon the body, being so unsufferable, gives not the mind any free and quiet time to use her judgment and empire; which made the poet say:

Hostium uxores, puerique caecos
Sentiant motus orientis Haedi, *et*
Aequoris nigri fremitum, et trementes
Verbere ripas.

For four-and-twenty hours the storm in a restless tumult had blown so exceedingly as we could not apprehend in our imaginations any possibility of greater violence; yet did we still find it not only more terrible but more constant, fury added to fury, and one storm urging a second more outrageous than the former, whether it so wrought upon our fears or indeed met with new forces. Sometimes strikes [? shrieks] in our ship amongst women and passengers not used to such hurly and discomforts made us look one upon the other with troubled hearts and panting bosoms, our clamors drowned in the winds and the winds in thunder. Prayers might well be in the heart and lips but drowned in the outcries of the officers: nothing heard that could give comfort, nothing seen that might encourage hope. It is impossible for me, had I the voice of Stentor and expression of as many tongues as his throat of voices, to express the outcries and miseries, not languishing but wasting his spirits, and art constant to his own principles but not prevailing.

Our sails wound up lay without their use, and if at any time we bore but a hullock, or half forecourse, to guide her before the sea, six and sometimes eight men were not enough to hold the whipstaff in the steerage and the tiller below in the gunner room: by which may be imagined the strength of the storm, in which the sea swelled above the clouds and gave battle unto Heaven. It could not be said to rain: the waters like whole rivers did flood in the air. And this I did still observe: that whereas upon the land when a storm hath poured itself forth once in drifts of rain, the wind, as beaten down and vanquished therewith, not long after endureth; here the glut of water (as if throttling the wind erewhile) was no sooner a little emptied and qualified but instantly the winds (as having gotten their mouths now free and at liberty) spake more loud and grew more tumultuous and malignant. What shall I say? Winds and seas were as mad as fury and rage could make them. For my own part, I had been in some storms before, as well upon the coast of Barbary and Algiers, in the Levant, and once, more distressful, in the Adriatic gulf in a bottom of Candy, so as I may well say: *Ego quid sit ater Hadriae novi sinus, et quid albus peccet Iapyx.* Yet all that I had ever suffered gathered together might not hold comparison with this: there was not a moment in which the sudden splitting or instant oversetting of the ship was not expected.

Howbeit this was not all. It pleased God to bring a greater affliction yet upon us; for in the beginning of the storm we had received likewise a mighty leak. And the ship, in every joint almost having spewed out her oakum before we were aware (a casualty more desperate than any other that a voyage by sea draweth with it), was grown five foot suddenly deep with water above her ballast, and we almost drowned within whilst we sat looking when to perish from above. This, imparting no less terror than danger, ran through the whole ship with much fright and amazement, startled and turned the blood and took down the braves of the most hardy mariner of them all, insomuch as he that before happily felt not the sorrow of others now began to sorrow for himself, when he saw such a pond of water so suddenly broken in and which he knew could not (without present avoiding) but instantly sink him. So as joining (only for his own sake, not yet worth the saving) in the public safety there might be seen master, master's mate, boatswain, quartermaster, coopers, carpenters, and who not, with candles in their hands, creeping along the ribs viewing the sides, searching every corner, and listening in every place if they could hear the water run. Many a weeping leak was this way found and hastily stopped, and at length one in the gunner room made up with I know not how many pieces of beef. But all was to no purpose; the leak (if it were but one) which drunk in our greatest seas and took in our destruction fastest could not then be found, nor ever was, by any labor, counsel, or search. The waters still increasing and the pumps going, which at length choked with bringing up whole and continual biscuit (and indeed all we had, ten thousandweight), it was conceived as most likely that the leak might be sprung in the bread room; whereupon the carpenter went down and ripped up all the room but could not find it so.

I am not able to give unto Your Ladyship every man's thought in this perplexity to which we were now brought; but to me this leakage appeared as a wound given to men that were before dead. The Lord knoweth, I had as little hope as desire of life in the storm, and in this: it went beyond my will because beyond my reason why we should labor to preserve life. Yet we did, eitherbecause so dear are a few lingering hours of life in all mankind, or that our Christian knowledges taught us how much we owed to the rites of nature, as bound not to be false to ourselves or to neglect the means of our own preservation, the most despairful things amongst men being matters of no wonder nor moment with Him Who is the rich fountain and admirable essence of all mercy.

Our governor, upon the Tuesday morning (at what time, by such who had been below in the hold, the leak was first discovered) had caused the whole company, about 140, besides women, to be equally divided into three parts and, opening the ship in three places (under the forecastle, in the waist, and hard by the bittacle), appointed each man where to attend; and thereunto every man came duly upon his watch, took the bucket or pump for one hour, and rested another. Then men might be seen to labor, I may well say, for life; and the better sort, even our governor and admiral themselves, not refusing their turn and to spell each the other, to give example to other. The common sort, stripped naked as men in galleys, the easier both to hold out and to shrink from under the salt water which continually leapt in among them, kept their eyes waking and their thoughts and hands working with tired bodies and wasted spirits three days and four nights, destitute of outward comfort and desperate of any deliverance, testifying how mutually willing they were yet by labor to keep each other from drowning, albeit each one drowned whilst he labored.

Once so huge a sea brake upon the poop and quarter upon us as it covered our ship from stern to stem like a garment or a vast cloud; it filled her brim full for a while within, from the hatches up to the spardeck. The source or confluence of water was so violent as it rushed and carried the helm-man from the helm and wrested the whipstaff out of his hand, which so flew from side to side that when he would have seized the same again it so tossed him from starboard to larboard as it was God's mercy it had not split him. It so beat him from his hold and so bruised him as a fresh man hazarding in by chance fell fair with it and, by main strength bearing somewhat up, made good his place and with much clamor encouraged and called upon others, who gave her now up, rent in pieces and absolutely lost. Our governor was at this time below at the capstan, both by his speech and authority heartening every man unto his labor. It struck him from the place where he sat and groveled him and all us about him on our faces, beating together with our breaths all thoughts from our bosoms else than that we were now sinking. For my part, I thought her already in the bottom of the sea; and I have heard him say, wading out of the flood thereof, all his ambition was but to climb up above-hatches to die in *aperto coelo* and in the company of his old friends. It so stunned the ship in her full pace that she stirred no more than if she had been caught in a net, or than as if the fabulous remora had struck her forecastle. Yet, without bearing one inch of sail, even then she was making her way nine or ten leagues in a watch. One thing it is not without his wonder (whether it were the fear of death in so great a storm, or that it pleased God to be gracious unto us), there was not a passenger, gentleman or other, after he began to stir and labor, but was able to relieve his fellow and make good his course. And it is most true, such as in all their lifetimes had never done hour's work before (their minds now helping their bodies) were able twice forty-eight hours together to toil with the best.

During all this time the heavens looked so black upon us that it was not possible the elevation of the Pole might be observed; nor a star by night nor sunbeam by day was to be seen. Only upon the Thursday night Sir George Somers, being upon the watch, had an apparition of a little, round light, like a faint star, trembling and streaming along with a sparkling blaze, half the height upon the main mast and shooting sometimes from shroud to shroud, 'tempting to settle, as it were, upon any of the four shrouds. And for three or four hours together, or rather more, half the night, it kept with us, running sometimes along the main yard to the very end and then returning; at which Sir George Somers called divers about him and showed them the same, who observed it with much wonder and carefulness. But upon a sudden, toward the morning watch, they lost the sight of it and knew not what way it made.

The superstitious seamen make many constructions of this sea fire, which nevertheless is usual in storms, the same (it may be) which the

Grecians were wont in the Mediterranean to call Castor and Pollux, of which if one only appeared without the other they took it for an evil sign of great tempest. The Italians and such who lie open to the Adriatic and Tyrrhenian Sea call it (a sacred body) *corpo sancto;* the Spaniards call it St. Elmo and have an authentic and miraculous legend for it. Be it what it will, we laid other foundations of safety or ruin than in the rising or falling of it. Could it have served us now miraculously to have taken our height by, it might have strucken amazement and a reverence in our devotions according to the due of a miracle. But it did not light us any whit the more to our known way, who ran now (as do hoodwinked men) at all adventures, sometimes north and northeast, then north and by west, and in an instant again varying two or three points, and sometimes half the compass. East and by south we steered away as much as we could to bear upright, which was no small carefulness nor pain to do, albeit we much unrigged our ship, threw overboard much luggage, many a trunk and chest (in which I suffered no mean loss), and staved many a butt of beer, hogsheads of oil, cider, wine, and vinegar, and heaved away all our ordnance on the starboard side, and had now purposed to have cut down the main mast the more to lighten her, for we were much spent and our men so weary as their strengths together failed them with their hearts, having travailed now from Tuesday till Friday morning, day and night, without either sleep or food; for, the leakage taking up all the hold, we could neither come by beer nor fresh water; fire we could keep none in the cook room to dress any meat; and carefulness, grief, and our turn at the pump or bucket were sufficient to hold sleep from our eyes.

And surely, madam, it is most true, there was not any hour (a matter of admiration) all these days in which we freed not twelve hundred barricos of water, the least whereof contained six gallons, and some eight; besides three deep pumps continually going, two beneath at the capstan and the other above in the half deck, and at each pump four thousand strokes at the least in a watch. So as I may well say, every four hours we quitted one hundred tons of water. And from Tuesday noon till Friday noon we bailed and pumped two thousand ton; and yet, do what we could, when our ship held least in her (after Tuesday night second watch), she bore ten foot deep; at which stay our extreme working kept her one eight glasses, forbearance whereof had instantly sunk us. And it being now Friday, the fourth morning, it wanted little but that there had been a general determination to have shut up hatches and, commending our sinful souls to God, committed the ship to the mercy of the gale. Surely, that night we must have done it, and that night had we then perished. But see the goodness and sweet introduction of better hope by our merciful God given unto us: Sir George Somers, when no man dreamed of such happiness, had discovered and cried land.

Indeed the morning, now three-quarters spent, had won a little clearness from the days before, and it being better surveyed, the very trees were seen to move with the wind upon the shoreside; whereupon our governor commanded the helm-man to bear up. The boatswain, sounding at the first, found it thirteen fathom, and when we stood [in] a little, in seven fathom; and presently, heaving his lead the third time, had ground at four fathom; and by this we had got her within a mile under the southeast point of the land, where we had somewhat smooth water. But having no hope to save her by coming to an anchor in the same, we were enforced to run her ashore as near the land as we could, which brought us within three-quarters of a mile of shore; and by the mercy of God unto us, making out our boats, we had ere night brought all our men, women, and children, about the number of 150, safe into the island.

We found it to be the dangerous and dreaded island, or rather islands, of the Bermuda; whereof let me give Your Ladyship a brief description before I proceed to my narration. And that the rather because they be so terrible to all that ever touched on them, and such tempests, thunders, and other fearful objects are seen and heard about them, that they be called commonly the Devil's Islands and are feared and avoided of all sea travelers alive above any other place in the world. Yet it pleased our merciful God to make even this hideous and hated place both the place of our safety and means of our deliverance.

And hereby, also, I hope to deliver the world from a foul and general error, it being counted of most that they can be no habitation for men but rather given over to devils and wicked spirits; whereas indeed we find them now by experience to be as habitable and commodious as most countries of the same climate and situation, insomuch as, if the entrance into them were as easy as the place itself is contenting, it had long ere this been inhabited as well as other islands. Thus shall we make it appear that Truth is the daughter of Time, and that men ought not to deny everything which is not subject to their own sense.

8

A MOST DANGEROUS VOYAGE

BY CAPTAIN JOHN MONCK

1619

This tale comes without an author—it was probably a hack writer—from the two-volume collection of voyages and travels published by A. and J. Churchill in 1732, which by then was but one more in a long series of such collections dating from Hakluyt, and in Europe from well before. There can be no doubt about how popular travel literature had become. John Monck is an Anglicization of the name of Jens Munk, an experienced Danish ship's captain who knew something about the English attempts at finding a Northwest Passage and persuaded the Danish king, Christian IV, to sponsor one of his own. Two ships, the Unicorn *and the* Lamprey, *left Denmark with an English pilot who had sailed into the area with William Baffin four years before. Only three men returned alive. Munk was one of them.*

Munk's own account of the journey, published in 1624, is surely the ultimate source for what we have here, although the additional business about his own death must have come from the writer's imagination. Munk did not die in the fashion our writer would have it. He did try to persuade the king to sponsor another expedition, but when the king refused, he took other commissions from the king and served as an admiral in the Danish Navy during the Thirty Years' War. He was also responsible for inaugurating the Danish whaling industry. It's a poignant little tale nevertheless, not least for the helplessness with which these mariners had to endure scurvy, a disease whose cause was not finally discovered until the discovery of vitamin C in the 1920s. Munk was the first European to spend the winter at what is now the town of Churchill in Canada, on Hudson Bay. Jens Munk's name lives on as a variety of rose.

CHRISTIAN IV, KING OF DENMARK, BEING DESIROUS TO FIND OUT A passage betwixt Greenland and America to facilitate the voyage to the East Indies, did order one Captain Monck, a person of great bravery, to sail with two stout ships to the Straits which were not many years before discovered by one Mr. Hudson, an Englishman.

This Mr. Hudson, having been several times before on the northern coasts, was at last prevailed upon by some English merchants to try his fortune whether he could find out a passage betwixt Greenland and America to the East Indies. Accordingly, he set sail from England with one ship only in the year 1610 and, passing along the coast of Greenland, was, what with the fogs and what with storms, forced into a strait passage, which at last brought him into an open sea; which made him begin to conceive certain hopes that he had been so fortunate as to be the discoverer of the said passage.

But after he had for a considerable time cruised up and down this sea without being able to discover the desired passage, he resolved (contrary to the opinion of the rest) to pass the winter thereabouts, though he was not sufficiently stored with provisions for so long a time. And they must infallibly have perished for want of food if they had not met with several sorts of birds and among the rest with white partridges, of whom they catched about a hundred dozen. And these leaving that part of the country towards the Spring, they were in their stead supplied with swans, ducks, geese and other such like water fowl which were easily catched. Besides, they met with a certain tree there of a most miraculous nature, its leaves being green inclining to yellow, had a strong taste of spice and, being boiled, afforded a balsamic oil, the decoction itself being a present remedy against the scurvy, the sciatica and other distempers occasioned by cold and vicious humors.

The approaching spring furnished them with such store of fish as would be sufficient to freight their whole ship if Mr. Hudson had not been more intent upon his intended discovery than anything else. Which, however, being not able to effect, he saw himself under a necessity of bending his course back to England. In the meanwhile there happened a mutiny against the captain, carried on by one Green, his clerk, who did force his cabin, from whence they took him and his son and, putting them with seven more in a shallop, committed them to the mercy of the sea.

But we must return to Captain Monck, who set sail from the Sound with two ships, one manned with forty-eight men, the other with sixteen, on the 16th day of May in the year 1619. He arrived on the 20th of June near Cape Farewell, being very rocky, covered with ice and snow, and situated under 62 1/2 degrees. From thence steering his course to the northwest towards Hudson's Straits, he was much incommoded by the ice, which however did him no considerable damage, he having sea-room enough. Among other accidents that befell him, it froze so violently on the 18th of June at night, and the winds blew so hard and cold, that his sails were rendered useless by reason of the ice that adhered to them; yet the next following day proved so excessive hot in the afternoon that they were forced to lay by their clothes and to go in their shirts only.

He did not arrive at Hudson's Straits till the 17th of July, which he called, after the King of Denmark, Christian's Straits. His first landing was in an island directly opposite to Greenland; and, having sent some of his people to take a view of the country, they found no men, but by their footsteps were convinced there were some in this island. The next following day they saw some of the savages, who, seeming to be surprised at the sight of the Danes, hid their arms behind a great stone heap and then advanced toward them in a friendly posture, but kept continually a watchful eye upon their arms for fear the Danes should come too near them. Notwithstanding which, they found means to get betwixt them and their arms, which they seized. The savages seemed to be exceedingly troubled at this loss and in an humble posture begged the Danes to have them restored, without which they were not able to subsist, hunting being their only livelihood. They offered to exchange their clothes for them, which moved the Danes at last to compassion; so that they not only gave them back their arms but also presented them with several toys, which they received very thankfully, and in lieu of them brought the Danes several sorts of fowl and fish.

One among them having got a small looking-glass, and seeing himself in it, was so overjoyed that he put it into his bosom and did run away as fast as his legs could carry him. The Danes laughed heartily at his simplicity; but what diverted them more than all the rest was that they perceived some of these savages to make their courtship, after their way, to one of the ship's crew, who having long black hair and being of a swarthy complexion, with a flattish nose, they took him for one of their countrymen who perhaps had been carried away from Greenland some time before; which often furnished them afterwards with matter of laughter, so that the poor fellow was always jeered as long as the voyage lasted.

On the 19th of the same month Captain Monck ordered the sails to be hoisted up in order to leave this island, but was forced to return into the same harbor by reason of the ice, which obstructed his passage. In the meanwhile they left no stone unturned to find out some of the inhabitants, but in vain. They found some nets spread near the seashore, on which they hung knives, looking-glasses and other such-like toys, in hopes to allure them to the seaside. But nobody appeared, whether out of fear of the Danes or because they were commanded to the contrary by their superiors is uncertain.

Captain Monck, being disappointed in his hopes of meeting with the inhabitants, ordered a wild reindeer to be shot, of which there were great numbers there; wherefore he gave the name of Reensund to the island, and to the harbor that of the Monckepes, being situated under 64 degrees and 20 minutes. And after he had planted the Danish arms there he once more left the said island on the 22nd of July but met with such bad weather and so many vast ice shoals at sea that on the 28th of the same month he was forced to seek for shelter betwixt two islands, near one of which he came to an anchor. But, finding it unsafe to continue thus, he brought his ships as near the shore as possible he could, so that at low water they lay upon the sand; and the high tide carried such a prodigious quantity of ice to the shore that they were in no small danger if by their industry they had not prevented it. There was a great ice shoal, near fifty-foot thick, which, being loosened by the violence of the sea, carried all before it, and among the rest their shallops, which narrowly escaped sinking.

Ashore they saw several footsteps of men, a sign that the place was not destitute of inhabitants; but whatever care they took, they could not get sight of any. They also found there some mineral stones and a very good talc, of which they carried off several ton-weight. There were several other small islands thereabouts but the sea did run so high near the shore that the Danes durst not venture to land. These islands are situated under 62 degrees, 20 minutes, about fifty leagues within Hudson's, or as Monck calls it, Christian's Straits. The bay where he came to an anchor he called Hareford, from the great number of hares they met with there. He again set up the arms of Denmark and the initial letter of his royal master, viz. C. IV, signifying Christian IV.

On the 9th of August he set sail again from this place with a northwest wind, steering his course west-southwest, and on the 10th came to the south of the straits of America and cast his anchor near a large island, unto which he gave the name of Snow Island because it was all covered with snow.

On the 20th of August he directed his course to the northwest, being then (as his own diary testifies) exactly under the elevation of 62 degrees, 20 minutes; but there fell so much snow, and the wind did blow so violently, that they could see no land, though the straits were not above sixteen leagues over thereabouts, which shows that they are broader in some other places. After having past these straits, he got into Hudson's sea, which he furnished with another name, or rather gave it two names instead of one. For that part of it which washes the American shore he called Mare Novum, or the New Sea. To the other part, which extends to Greenland (if it be really Greenland), he gave the name of Mare Christianum, or Christian's Sea. He continued his course west-northwest till he came to 63 degrees, 20 minutes, when, finding himself surrounded on all sides by the ice, he resolved to pass the winter there. The harbor he called Monck's Winter Harbor and the country New Denmark. In his relation he makes mention only of two islands in the Christian Sea, which he styles "the two sisters"; and in the New Sea, but one, called Dichles Oeland. He advises those who undertake the voyage through these straits to keep as much as possibly they can in the middle to avoid being carried away by the stormy tides and the great ice shoals which are of such a thickness there that if a ship happen to get betwixt them it seldom escapes. He says that it flows exactly five hours in the Christian Sea, the tide being regulated by the moon.

On the 7th of September Captain Monck cast anchor there, and after his people had refreshed themselves for some days he ordered them to bring the ships into a little creek, where they were sheltered against the violence of the winds and ice. The next thing they had to do was to provide themselves good huts against the approaching winter season. This harbor lay near the entrance of a river, which was not frozen up in October, though the sea was full of ice all round about.

On the 7th day of the same month Captain Monck had a mind to go up the river in a boat, but could not go further than about a league and a half by reason of the cataracts or rocky waterfalls that opposed his passage. He then marched with some of his men about four leagues deep into the country to see whether he could meet with any of the inhabitants; but, nobody appearing, he resolved to return another way. Here he met with a certain stone raised above the ground, upon which was painted an image resembling the Devil with claws and horns. Near this stone was a place of about eight foot square, enclosed with lesser stones. On one side of this enclosure there lay a heap of small flat stones intermixt with moss of trees. On the opposite side was a large flat stone laid upon two others in the shape of an altar, upon which they found three coals laid across. They saw several more of those altars as they were walking about, and some footsteps of men near each of them, though they did not come in sight at that time. It is very likely that the inhabitants used to sacrifice upon those altars, either with fire, or perhaps offer their sacrifices to the fire itself, for round about them they saw abundance of bones, which probably were the bones of the sacrificed beasts, whose flesh the savages had devoured raw, according to their custom. They met also with many trees, cut down to the roots with iron instruments; and with dogs that were muzzled. But what most confirmed them in their opinion that this isle was not destitute of inhabitants was that in many places they could discover the holes where they had fixed the poles belonging to their tents, and found many pieces of skins of bears, wolves, dogs and sea calves wherewith they used to cover them; which seemed to intimate that the inhabitants here did lead a vagabond life like the Tartars and Lapponians.

After the Danes had planted their huts they cut good store of wood to be laid up for the winter and killed abundance of wild fowl. Captain Monck killed a white bear with his own hands, which they ate, and he says expressly that it agreed very well with them. They catched abundance of hares, partridges and other fowl, besides four black foxes and some sables.

On the 27th of November there appeared three suns to them and on the next following 24th of January two. On the 10th of December (old style) there happened an eclipse of the moon, which they saw about eight o'clock at night; after which they saw the same night the moon surrounded with a very bright circle, through the middle of which was a cross which divided the moon in two. This seemed to be the forerunner of those evils which these poor wretches were to suffer hereafter, as will appear out of the following account.

The cold began to increase with the winter season to such a degree that they saw ice of three hundred, nay three hundred and sixty, foot thick. No beer, no wine or brandy was strong enough to be proof against it but froze to the bottom and the vessels split in pieces, so that they cut the frozen liquor with hatchets and melted it before the fire before they could drink it. If they happened to leave any quantity of water in their copper or tin vessels they found them all in pieces the next morning. Neither were the poor Danes able to resist so excessive a frost which mastered the metals, for they all fell sick and their sickness increased with the cold; they were generally seized with a griping looseness which did not leave them till it put an end to their days. Thus they dropped away one after another, so that about the beginning of March the Captain was fain to do duty as a sentry for want of others. The worst was that the Spring did augment their distemper, for their teeth were ready to fall out and their gums swelled to that degree that they could not take any other nourishment but bread soaked in water. The poor remnants of these unfortunate wretches were in the next following May seized with another looseness, with such violent pricking pains in their limbs as made them look like mere shadows, their arms and legs being quite lame and full of blue spots, as if they had been beaten, being a distemper not unknown to seamen, by whom it is commonly called the scurvy. So many of them died that there were not enough left to bury them, the rest being likewise sick and very weak. And to complete their misery they began to want bread, instead of which they made use of raspberries which they digged out from under the snow, which supplied the defect of bread. But they were fain to eat them as soon as they were taken from under the snow, where they kept fresh, but soon grew useless afterwards.

On the 12th day of April it rained the fifth time after seven months; and towards the end of May there appeared again all sorts of fowl, such as wild geese and ducks, swans, swallows, partridges, ravens, snipes, falcons and eagles; but they were too weak to catch them.

On the 4th of June Captain Monck himself fell down so dangerously ill that he did take no food for four days together; and expecting nothing else but present death, he made his last will, in which he desired those that might by chance come to this place to bury his corpse and to send the diary of his voyage to the King of Denmark. After four days were past he began however to recover a little and with much ado got out of his hut to see whether there were any of his ship's crew left alive, of whom he found no more than two of sixty-four persons he brought along with him. These two being overjoyed to see their captain in a condition to stir abroad, took him in their arms and carried him to a fire to refresh his spirits. They now began to encourage one another, promising to stand by one another to the last gasp. They digged everywhere among the snow till at last they met with a certain root, which being both restorative and food to them, they were restored in a few days. The ice began now to melt apace, so that on the 18th of June they catched some salmon and other fish, which with what exercise they used in hunting, so strengthened them in a little time that they resolved to return to Denmark.

The summer season approaching, they were extremely pestered with gnats, which made them hasten their departure. So that on the 16th of July they went aboard their lesser ship (leaving the biggest behind) and steered their course toward Monck's harbor. They were much incommoded by the ice and lost their boat and rudder. Whilst they were busy in making a new one they fastened their ship to an ice-rock, which being loosened by the tide, their ship was carried away with it. But the ice being melted soon after, they got clear again and met with their boat, which they had lost ten days before. It was not long before they got fast within the ice once more. But the weather changing almost every day, they were soon released again. Having at last repassed the Straits, they sailed by Cape Farewell into the ocean but were on the 8th of September overtaken by a most terrible tempest, which threatened no less than their total destruction, they being quite tired out, and not able to manage the ship. So that, leaving themselves to the mercy of the winds, they lost their mast, and the sails blew overboard, which however they made shift to save.

In this condition they were forced upon the coast of Norway, where they cast a piece of an anchor (the only one they had left) in a small creek, where they hoped to shelter themselves against the storm; but found themselves deceived in their hopes, for they were in most imminent danger of being dashed to pieces against the rocks, if by good fortune they had not got betwixt them and the shore; where after they had refreshed themselves for some days they pursued their voyage and arrived at last in Denmark.

Captain Monck had no sooner set foot ashore but he went to Copenhagen to give the king an account of his unfortunate voyage; who, not imagining him to be still among the living, received him with all imaginable marks of his favor. Thus we have seen the brave Captain Monck return to the Danish shore, which, as might reasonably be supposed, would put an end to all his sufferings. But it seems his ill destiny had preserved him for more, which was to put an unhappy period to the life of this brave man.

For whilst he was in Denmark he used often to ruminate upon his past adventures; and, being by degrees convinced of what had been the chief cause of his miscarriage in his voyage through the Straits, he took a resolution to try his fortune once more, in which he hoped to supply the defects of the former, arising from the want of knowledge of those seas and some other circumstances. Accordingly he proposed his design to some persons of quality, who, approving of it, equipped two ships which he was to command in chief.

Having provided himself with all necessaries for such a voyage, he was ready to set sail, when (as his ill fortune would have it) the king sent for him, and happening, among other things, to speak of his former unfortunate voyage, told him that he had lost two ships by his want of conduct. Which the captain answering somewhat briskly, the king took his cane and pushed it in anger against his breast. The captain took this affront so heinously that he immediately went home to bed and would not be persuaded to take the least nourishment. So that in ten days after he died for melancholy and want of food.

9

LETTER OF JAMES PIERPONT

From: *Magnalia Christi Americana*

BY COTTON MATHER

1647

If ever there was a writer disposed to draw Christian *morals from disaster tales, it was* Cotton Mather, *the great preacherman from colonial* Boston, *who with his father,* Increase Mather, *is perhaps most famous today for his involvement in the witch trials in* Salem *in 1692, where the two men played a role in bringing the trials to an end. ("I had rather judge a* Witch *to be an honest woman,"* Increase Mather *wrote, "than judge an honest woman as a* Witch.") *The title of this, among his dozens of works probably his magnum opus, is in* English *translation* The Great Deeds of Christ in America *and it was intended as an ecclesiastical history of* New England. *He based the story below on an unpublished history on the same subject written some years earlier by another minister of the gospel,* Thomas Hubbard, *which covered the first 60 years of* English *occupation of* New England.

The story is straightforward enough and needs little comment, except to note that, in what was becoming a growing tradition in shipwreck accounts, this one also led to a work of literature, a poem in this case by Henry Wadsworth Longfellow, *"*The Phantom Ship,*" which follows the story exactly and even attributes it to its source in* Mather's *book.* Phantom *ships might be said to constitute a sub-genre of shipwreck literature. The* Flying Dutchman *is the best known, but there have been modern ships as well that were sighted long after they had been lost. The most intriguing example is the* Kobenhaven, *a* Danish *ship built shortly after* World War I *and the only five-masted sailing ship in existence at the time. Sailing out of* Argentina, *it vanished* *in 1928. On three separate occasions in 1930 a five-masted sailing ship was seen in the Pacific. It was unmistakably the* Kobenhaven.

In Mather's story the word "walty" means unsteady, having a tendency to roll easily.

BUT THERE WAS ONE THING THAT MADE THIS COLONY TO BECOME VERY considerable; which thing remains now to be considered. The well-known Mr. *Davenport*, and Mr. *Eaton*, and several Eminent Persons that came over to the *Massachuset-Bay*, among some of the First Planters, were strongly urged, that they would have settled in this *Bay*; but hearing of another *Bay* to the South-West of *Connecticut*, which might be more capable to entertain those that were to follow them, they desired that their Friends at *Connecticut* would purchase of the Native Proprietors for *them*, all the Land that lay between themselves and *Hudson's* River, which was in part effected. Accordingly removing thither in the Year 1637, they seated themselves in a pleasant *Bay*, where they spread themselves along the *Sea-Coasts*; and one might have been suddenly, as it were surprized with the sight of such notable Towns, as first *New-Haven*; then *Guilford*; then *Milford*; then *Stamford*; and then *Brainford*, where our Lord Jesus Christ is Worshipped in *Churches* of an Evangelical Constitution; and from thence, if the Enquirer made a Salley over to *Long Island*, he might there also have seen the Churches of our Lord beginning to take root in the Eastern Parts of that Island. All this while this *Fourth Colony* wanted the legal *Basis* of a *Charter* to build upon; but they did by mutual Agreement form them selves into a *Body-Politick*, as like as they judg'd fit unto the other Colonies in their Neighbourhood; and as for their *Church-Order*, it was generally, *Secundum Usum Massachusettensem*.

Behold, a Fourth Colony of *New-English* Christians, in a manner *stoln* into the World, and a Colony, indeed, *constellated* with many Stars of the *First Magnitude*. The Colony was under the Conduct of as Holy, and as Prudent, and as Genteel Persons as most that ever visited these Nooks of *America*; and yet *these* too were Try'd with very humbling Circumstances.

Being *Londoners*, or Merchants, and Men of Traffick and Business, their Design was in a manner wholly to apply themselves unto *Trade*; but the Design failing, they found their great Estates to sink so fast, that they must quickly *do something*. Whereupon in the Year 1646. gathering together almost all the Strength which was left 'em, they Built one Ship more, which they fraighted for *England* with the best part of their Tradable Estates; and sundry of their Eminent Persons Embarked themselves in her for the Voyage. But, alas, the Ship was never after heard of! She foundred in the Sea; and in her were lost, not only the *Hopes* of their future Trade, but also the *Lives* of several Excellent Persons, as well as divers *Manuscripts* of some great Men in the Country, sent over for the Service of the Church, which were now buried in the Ocean. The *fuller Story* of that *grievous Matter*, let the Reader with a just Astonishment accept from the Pen of the Reverend Person, who is now the Pastor of *New-Haven*. I wrote unto him for it, and was thus Answered.

Reverend and Dear Sir,

'In Compliance with your Desires, I now give you the Relation of that *Apparition* of a *Ship in the Air*, which I have received from the most Credible, Judicious and Curious Surviving Observers of it.

'In the Year 1647. besides much other Lading, a far more Rich Treasure of Passengers, (Five or Six of which were Persons of chief Note and Worth in *New-Haven*) put themselves on Board a *New Ship*, built at *Rhode-Island*, of about 150 Tuns; but so walty, that the Master, (*Lamberton*) often said she would prove their Grave. In the Month of *January*, cutting their way thro' much Ice, on which they were accompanied with the Reverend Mr. *Davenport*, besides many other Friends, with many Fears, as well as Prayers and Tears, they set Sail. Mr. *Davenport* in Prayer with an observable *Emphasis* used these Words, *Lord, if it be thy pleasure to bury these our Friends in the bottom of the Sea, they are thine; save them!* The Spring following no Tidings of these Friends arrived with the Ships from *England*: *New-Haven's* Heart began to fail her: This put the Godly People on much *Prayer*, both Publick and Private, *That the Lord would (if it was his Pleasure) let them hear what he had done with their dear Friends, and prepare them with a suitable Submission to his Holy Will*. In *June* next ensuing, a great *Thunder-storm* arose out of the *North-West*: after which, (the *Hemisphere* being serene) about an Hour before Sunset a SHIP of like Dimensions with the aforesaid, with her Canvas and Colours abroad (tho' the Wind Northernly) appeared in the Air coming up from our Harbour's Mouth, which lyes Southward from the Town, seemingly with her *Sails* filled under a fresh Gale, holding her Course North, and continuing under Observation, Sailing against the Wind for the space of half an Hour. *Many* were drawn to behold this great Work of God; yea, the very *Children* cry'd out, *There's a Brave Ship!* At length, crouding up as far as there is usually *Water* sufficient for such a Vessel, and so near some of the Spectators, as that they imagined a Man might hurl a Stone on Board her, her *Maintop* seem'd to be blown off, but left hanging in the Shrouds; then her *Missen-top*; then all her *Masting* seemed blown away by the Board: Quickly after the *Hull* brought unto a

Careen, she overset, and so vanished into a smoaky Cloud, which in some time dissipated, leaving, as everywhere else, a clear Air. The admiring Spectators could distinguish the several Colours of each Part, the Principal Riging, and such Proportions, as caused not only the generality of Persons to say, *This was the Mould of their Ship, and thus was her Tragick End:* But Mr. *Davenport* also in publick declared to this Effect, *That God had condescended, for the quieting of their afflicted Spirits, this Extraordinary Account of his Soveraign Disposal of those for whom so many Fervent Prayers were made continually.* Thus I am, Sir,'

Your Humble Servant,
James Pierpont.

Reader, There being yet living so many Credible Gentlemen, that were Eye-Witnesses of this *Wonderful* Thing, I venture to Publish it for a thing as *undoubted*, as 'tis *wonderful.*

10

GOD'S PROTECTING PROVIDENCE

From *God's Protecting Providence, ... Evidenced in the Remarkable Deliverance of Divers Persons from the Devouring Waves of the Sea ... and Also from the More Cruelly Devouring Jaws of the Inhumane Cannibals of Florida*

BY JONATHAN DICKINSON

1696–1697

Jonathan Dickinson was a Quaker on his way from Jamaica to Philadelphia in August 1696, with his wife, his infant child, and a group of other people, including some of Dickinson's slaves, when a storm drove their ship ashore on the coast of Florida at about the site of present-day Hobe Sound. The ship was a total loss and they landed just north of an Indian village whose inhabitants immediately took them captive, stole their goods and almost all their clothing, and would, they thought, have killed and eaten them if the local cacique had not prevented it. But they were not cannibals; the Indians fed them, and in a few days they were released, minus the things the Indians had taken, and started north toward St. Augustine, partly on foot and partly in the ship's boat, which was intact.

Indians continued to harass them as they moved north. At the next village to the north Indians stripped them of all that remained of their clothing, threatened them, then took them to their cacique, who was kinder and gave them some small things to cover their nakedness, and fed them. Dickinson's description of the Indian villages and the conditions in them is sometimes quite vivid. "In a little time," he writes, "some raw deer skins were brought in and given to my wife and Negro women, and to us men such as the Indian men wear, being a piece of platwork of straws wrought of divers colors and of a triangular figure, with a belt of four fingers broad of the same wrought together, which goeth about the waist and the angle of the other having a thing to it, coming between the legs, and strings to the end of the belt; all three meeting together are fastened behind with a horsetail, or a bunch of silk-grass exactly resembling it, of a flaxen color, this being all the apparel or covering that the men wear; and thus they clothed us. A place was appointed for us, mats being laid on the floor of the house, where we were ordered to lie down. But the place was extremely nasty; for all the stones of the berries which they eat and all the nastiness that's made amongst them lay on their floor, that the place swarmed with abundance of many sorts of creeping things; as a large black hairy spider, which hath two claws like a crab; scorpions; and a numberless number of small bugs. On these mats we lay, these vermin crawling over our naked bodies. To brush them off was like driving off mosquitoes from one where they are extreme thick."

They continued north, now mostly naked, enduring storms and delay, trying to persuade the Indians they encountered that they were not English but Spanish, to whom the Indians were loyal. They were detained nearly a month at one village, with little food and almost no clothing. It was nearly 200 miles to St. Augustine. Then Spanish soldiers came with instructions to lead them north, but they were little help. It was getting into November. The party once more had to split up, some going on foot, some in the two small boats they now had. They were now somewhere above Daytona Beach, and it is here we pick up the narrative. We think of northern Florida as being warm, but this was the beginning of winter and these people were more or less naked, and starving. Then they began to die.

Dickinson's journal of their trek north, which he published in 1700, was quite popular for its time. It appeared in Dutch and German translations three times each, and there were 17 printings in England and America to 1859. It is largely forgotten now except among specialists in colonial Americana, but it's a fine story, told in plain and powerful prose.

THE 9 MONTH, 8; THE 1 OF THE WEEK.

This morning we set forward; but the water was so low that we were forced to wade and thrust the boat along for some miles. At length we got into a deep channel, where was nothing to be seen but marsh and water, and no fast land, nor trees.

About ten o'clock we heard three or four muskets fired a little ahead of us in the channel we were in. Our Spaniards presently answered them with the like, and in a little time we met. This was a piragua to join with that came for us, having order to go to the place where we were cast away, and to get what was to be had from the Indians: but this other boat turned back, for there was no place to go on shore; and in an hour or two's time we got into the other sound where the land was not to be seen from side to side in some places.

The like was in the other we came through. About an hour before sunset we got to an Indian plantation (this was the first place we saw anything planted) being full of pumpion vines and some small pumpions on them but the Spaniards were too quick for us and got all before us: some of us got a few as big as one's fist. We had a fire there, yet had not patience to dress them as they should be, but put them into the fire, roasted them and eat them. The Spaniards used a great deal of cookery with their pumpions, and the piragua that came last from Augustine had brought bread, corn and strung beef; but it was kept from us, except a piece of strung beef the captain of the Spaniards gave my wife as big as a stick of sealing-wax; which we treasured up, expecting it must be harder with us when we left these people. Here Captain Sebastian Lopez drew up a writing, and would have had me and Joseph Kirle to sign it; which we refused: for we perceived he had a design especially against me, to oblige me to give him some of my Negroes. We answered him short; that I reckoned myself and Negroes at the Governor of Augustine's disposal; and we would sign no writing. We borrowed a pot and boiled pumpion leaves, having nothing to put to them but water, which was satisfactory; but this night was more terrible than the last, the wind being at northwest; it did not blow hard, yet it was very cold, we lieing in an open field without any shelter; one side of us would scorch while the other was freezing. Our Negro woman Hagar's little boy named Cajoe was seized with convulsion fits about two in the morning which was chiefly occasioned by the cold and want of food: but help there was not from us. The Spanish captain came to see the child, and supposing that it would die, asked if the child was a Christian? He was answered, as good a one as he could make it; but he called for some water, putting some of it on the crown of the child's head, and crossing it, called him Francisco. This action pacified its mother and father.

The 9 month, 9; the 2 of the week.

This morning we were to go forward and the Spaniards were to return to the place where we were cast away: but our two boats would not carry us all; therefore we had the Spaniards great piragua to carry us one day's journey further to an Indian town, and four Spaniards with us, three of which were to bring the piragua back, the other was to be our guide for Augustine. We departed and met with intricate passage; for sometimes we should be aground on oyster banks, or shoals, and almost out of sight of land. About two or three in the afternoon we had not water to go any further: the wind being northwesterly drove the water out of the sound: but being nigh the shore where had been an Indian town: we went on shore and found some ripe berries on the palm shrubs, which we were very earnest after till such time as a storm of wind with rain began to come upon us and night nigh at hand; whereupon we all got together, considering what we should do, since there was no possibility of getting shelter here. Our Indian guide said, we might get to a town about two leagues off; which we were glad to hear, for it rained hard so we with our guide set forward and walked over a parcel of scraggy shrubby hills to the seashore, along which we traveled till we got to the Indian town, where we got plenty of berries for our supper. It rained much till towards morning.

The 9 month. 10.

This morning the Indians were not willing to stay any longer; and we were by our guide required to depart; which we did, and a great many young Indian men followed us some miles along the bay, and offered violence to Robert Barrow and several others; but were easily stopped by showing them a rusty musket presented towards them, and so they left us. We had an untoward passage from the seashore athwart the land to the Indian town, the ground being swampy, and scraggy hills, which to our bare feet was very troublesome. This was a large town, and there was another large town about a mile distant in sight, thither part of our company was sent to be quartered: at which town about a twelvemonth since a parcel of Dutchmen were killed who, having been cast away on the Bohemia shoals, in a flat which they built escaped hither, and were here devoured by these cannibals, as we understood by the Spaniards. The flat or boat our people saw: but they seemed kind to them, giving them fish and berries to eat. We remained at these two towns till next morning. The Indians of the town I was at, were not so kind as those at the other town had been: some of our people were for selling their rags to the Indians for fish; but we thought 'twas most necessary, of the two extremes, to defend against the cold: for every day grew colder than other; and we feared that if we were much longer exposed to it, we should not live it out.

The 9 month, 11; the 4 of the week.

This morning leaving this town, we embarked in our two boats, and those of our people that were at the other town were to have a large canoe to carry them thence, and were to meet us in the sound. We rowed several leagues and did not meet them; it being then about ten o'clock; the Spaniard would go on shore and travel back by land to see after them. We being by an inlet of the sea which was a mile over, the Spaniard ordered us to go on the other side, and there stay for him; which we did many hours. At this place we all went upon the search to see if anything was to be had for the belly, some on the land, some in the water. The land yielded nothing; but in the water we got a sort of shellfish called Water-Soldiers, which we eat: at length the canoe with our people came, but our Spaniard was not come; but in about half an hour's time he came with a small canoe. This was the place where Solomon met the Spaniards. The canoes had each two Indians to set them along: and we had one Indian for our guide named Wan-Antonia who the Spaniard said was a Christian, but an inhabitant of that town where the Dutchmen were killed. We set forward in our two boats and the two canoes, and rowed till night, being nigh a place of thickety wood, which we made choice of to lodge at for this night: here was wood enough. We made large fires, were pleased with the place, and lay down to rest. About midnight I had a great loss; having about a quart of berries whole, and as much pounded to mix with water to feed our child with; the fire being disturbed, the cloth which we had our food in was burnt. All was lost, and nothing to be had until we could get to the Spaniards, which was two days' march at least. About an hour after this the wind rose at northwest, and it began to rain; but having small palmetto which grew nigh, Joseph Kirle and I set to work and made a shelter which would keep ten or more of us from the weather. We had no sooner completed our work, but it rained hard. In this shower of rain the four Indians got from amongst us, took their canoes, and away they went back again. When day appeared, we missed them, upon which we went to the waterside, where we found the two canoes gone. And now we were in a great strait. But the Spaniard said those that could travel best must go by land. The persons pitched upon were Richard Limpeney, Andrew Murray, Cornelius Toker, Joseph Kirle's boy, John Hilliard, and Penelope with seven Negroes named Peter, Jack, Caesar, Sarah, Bell, Susanna and Quenza. The Spaniards and the Indian Wan-Antonia went with them to direct them the way carrying them over land to the seashore, and then directing to keep the seashore along to the northward.

They returned to us, and we with our two boats rowed all day without ceasing till sunsetting: and when we put on shore, the place was an old Indian field on a high bleak hill where had been a large Indian house, but it was tumbled down. Of the ruins of this house we made a shelter against the northwest wind, which began to blow very bleak. The Spaniard went to the sea, which was not two miles off, to see if our people had passed, and at his return he said, they were gone by. We asked if they could reach to any house or Indian town for shelter? For we supposed, should they be without fire this night, they could not live. He said, they must travel all night. Night came on: We had fire and wood enough, and had gathered a great heap of grass to lie in, hoping to have got some rest. But the northwest increased, and the cold was so violent, that we were in a lamentable condition, not able to rest, for as we lay or stood so close to the fire that it would scorch us, that side from it was ready to freeze: we had no other way, but to stand and keep turning for the most part of the night. We all thought that we never felt the like. The Spaniard that was clothed was as bad to bear it as we that were naked. At length day appeared and we must go.

The 9 month, 13; the 6 of the week.

This morning, we were loath to part with our fires, but to stay here it could not be: so we went to our boats; wading in the water was ready to benumb us. But we put forward, and rowing about 2 leagues came to an old house, where the Spaniard told us we must leave the boats and travel by land; we had a boggy marsh to wade through for a mile to get to the seashore, and had about five or six leagues along the bay or strand to the Spanish sentinel's house. The northwest wind was violent, and the cold such that the strongest of us thought we should not out-live that day. Having got through the boggy marsh and on the seashore, our people, black and white, made all speed, one not staying for another that could not travel so fast; none but I with my wife and child, Robert Barrow, my kinsman Benjamin Allen and my Negro London, whom I kept to help carry my child, keeping together. The rest of our company had left us, expecting not to see some of us again; especially Robert Barrow, my wife and child. We traveled after as well as we could having gone about two miles the cold so seized on my kinsman Benjamin Allen that he began to be stiff in his limbs, and staggered and fell, grievously complaining that the cold would kill him. Our Negro having our young child I and my wife took our kinsman under each arm and helped him along; but at length his limbs were quite stiff, his speech almost gone, and he began to foam at [the] mouth. In this strait we knew not what to do; to stay with him we must perish also, and we were willing to strive as long as we could. We carried our kinsman and laid him under the bank, not being dead. I resolved to run after our people, some of them not being out of sight; which I did and left my wife and child with the Negro to follow as fast as they could. I run about two miles, making signs to them, thinking if they should look behind them and see me running, they would stop till I got up with them. I was in hopes that if I could have accomplished this my design, to have got help to have carried my kinsman along; but they stopped not, and I run until the wind pierced me so that my limbs failed and I fell; yet still I strove, and getting up walked backwards to meet my wife. As I was going I met with the Spaniard coming out of the sand-hills and Joseph Kirle's Negro Ben. I made my complaint to the Spaniard, but he not being able to understand me well, went forward. I then applied myself to the Negro, making large promises if he would fetch my kinsman; he offered to go back and use his endeavor, which he did. At length my wife and child came up with me; she was almost overcome with grief, expressing in what manner we were forced to part with our kinsman, and expecting that she and the child should go next.

Poor Robert Barrow was a great way behind us: I feared we should never see him again. I used my endeavor to comfort and cheer my wife, entreating her, not to let grief overcome her; I had hopes that the Lord would help us in this strait, as He hath done in many since we were in this land. And if it pleased God that we might lay down our lives in this wilderness, that we might beseech Him to enable us to do it willingly. Thus striving in a deep exercise of body and mind we traveled on, admiring God's goodness in preserving us thus far through so many eminent dangers. In the sense of which a secret hope would arise (though involved with human doubts and fear) that the Lord would yet preserve us. I took my child from the Negro and carried him. I had an Indian mat with a split in it, through which I put my head, hanging over my breast unto my waist: under this I carried my child, which helped to break the wind off; but the poor babe was black with cold from head to foot, and its flesh as cold as a stone; yet it was not froward. Its mother would take it now and then and give it the breast, but little could it get at it; besides we dared not stop in the least, for if we did, we should perceive our limbs to fail. About two o'clock in the afternoon we came up with our Negro woman Hagar with her child at her back almost dead: and a little further we came up with our Negro girl Quenza, being dead, as we thought, for she was as stiff as a dead body could be, and her eyes set; but at length we perceived her breathe; but she had no sense, nor motion. We carried her from the waterside under the bank. This increased my wife's sorrow; and she began to doubt she should not be able to travel much further: but I endeavored to encourage her not to leave striving as long as any ability was left. All our people were out of sight except four, and those we had gained upon. I sent my Negro to overtake them, and to desire them to slacken their pace till we got up with them; being in hopes that gaining their company would [help] to cheer up my wife: but they would not; so the Negro stopped for us. We had lost sight of Robert Barrow by this time. Soon after we overtook John Smith who was one of the four: he began to fail, and his companions left him; whereupon he made grievous complaints which I reproved him for, lest he should discourage my wife. The sun was nigh setting; and we began to look out for the sentinel's post; and my Negro at times got upon several of the highest sand hills to look out, but could not see any house, nor the smoke of fire. This was terrible to us all, for the day being so cold, the night much more, and we not able to travel without rest, being a starved people both within our bodies and without, and if we ceased from traveling, we should instantly be numbed and move no further. In the midst of these reasonings and doubtings we were got into, I espied a man as I thought, standing on the bank but at great distance; I was afraid to speak lest it should prove otherwise, but he was soon seen by the whole company, and at length we espied him walking towards the land; this confirmed us, and so we took to the hills again to look out, yet could not see the house from thence, but on the next hill we saw it. This was joy unto us, though we began to have a sense of our tiredness, for our resolution abated after we had got sight of the house.

When we got to the house, we found four sentinels and the Spaniards our guide with three of our men; viz Joseph Buckley, Nathaniel Randall, and John Shears. The Spaniard bid us welcome, and made room for us to sit down by the fire. The chiefest man of the sentinel took a kersey coat and gave my wife to cover her, and gave each of us a piece of bread made of Indian corn, which was pleasant unto us: after it we had plenty of hot casseena drink. It was dark and we endeavored to prevail with the Spaniards to go seek for Robert Barrow and my kinsman, offering them considerable, but they seemed not fully to understand me, yet I could make them sensible that my kinsman was almost dead, if not quite; and that the old man was in a bad condition. They made me to understand that the weather was not fit to go out, but they would watch if Robert should pass by. About an hour or two after one of the Spaniards being walking out of the bay met with Robert and brought him into the house. We rejoiced to see him, and inquired concerning our kinsman and Negro Ben. He said our kinsman was striving to get up and could not; he came to him and spake unto him; he could not answer but cried, and he could not help him; but coming along at some considerable distance met Negro Ben; who said he was going for Benjamin Allen, so he passed him; and some miles further he saw Negro Jack drawing himself down from the bank, his lower parts being dead, and crying out for some fire that he might save his life; but he did not see the Negro girl whom we hauled out of the way. We were under a great concern for our kinsman; the Spaniards we could not prevail upon to go and fetch him, or go and carry wherewith to make a fire: which had they done and found them living, it might have preserved them. But we hoped Negro Ben would bring our kinsman. The Spaniards would have had most of us to have gone to the next sentinel's house; which was a league further; but we all begged hard of them to let us lie in their house in any place on the ground, for we were not able to travel further: besides the cold would kill us; for we were in such a trembling shaking condition, and so full of pain from head to foot, that it's not to be expressed. At length the Spaniards consented that Robert Barrow, I, my wife and child, and John Smith should lie in the house; but to Joseph Buckley, Nathaniel Randall, John Shears, and my Negro London, they would not grant that favor: so one of the Spaniards taking a fire-brand bid those four go with him. He directed them to a small thicket of trees and showed them to gather wood and make large fires and sleep there. These poor creatures lay out, and it proved a hard frosty night. The Spaniard returned and said they were got into a wood, and had fire enough. We were silent, but feared they would hardly live till morning.

After they were gone, the Spaniards took a pint of Indian corn and parched it and gave part to us, which we accepted cheerfully; also they gave us some casseena drink. We were in extraordinary pain, so that we could not rest; and our feet were extremely bruised, the skin was off and the sand caked with the blood that we could hardly set our feet to the ground after we had been some time in the house. The night was extreme cold though we were in the house; and by the fire we could not be warm, for one side did scorch whilst the other was ready to freeze: and thus we passed the night.

The 9 month, 14; the 7 of the week.

This morning we looked out, and there was a very hard frost on the ground, so it was terrible to go out of doors. Our people returned from the wood, but complained heavily of their hardship in the night. They had not been an hour in the house before the Spaniards gave us all a charge to be gone to the next sentinel's house: this was grievous to us all, but more especially to my wife, who could not raise herself when down; but go we must, for though we entreated hard for my wife and Robert Barrow, we could not prevail that they might stay until we could get a canoe. As we were all going one Spaniard made a sign for me and my wife to stay, which we did; and it was to have a handful of parched corn. As soon as we had received it they bid us be gone to the next sentinel's, where was victuals enough for us. The sun was a great height, but we could not feel any warmth it gave, the northwester beginning to blow as hard as it did the day before. And having deep sand to travel through, which made our traveling this one league very hard, especially to my wife and Robert. The Spaniards sent my wife a blanket to be left at the next sentinel's house.

At length we came to an inlet of the sea; on the other side was the lookout and sentinel's house: here were all our people sitting waiting to be carried over and in a little time came one of the sentinels, with a canoe and carried us over.

This sentinel would not suffer us to come into his house, but caused us to kindle a fire under the lee of his house and there sit down: about half an hour after he bid us be gone to the next sentinel's, which was a league further, giving us a cup of casseena and two quarts of Indian corn for us all, bidding us go to our company at next house and [get] our corn dressed there.

I understood that our Negro woman Hagar got hither late last night having her child dead at her back, which the Spaniards buried.

One of the Spaniards went with us to the next inlet carrying a stick of fire to set fire of some trash to make a signal for them on the other side to fetch us over, the inlet being very wide. When the canoe came over for us, our guide took the blanket from my wife; but the Negro which brought over the canoe lent my wife one of his coats, so we got over, but before we got to the house we had a shower of hail. At this house we were kindly received, having such a mess of victuals as we had not had in a long time before, which was very pleasant to our hunger-starved stomachs. Our people went hence, this morning, for Augustine, having a guide with them: but John Hosler and Penelope were left here, not being able to travel. We remained here till the morrow, but the night was so extreme cold that we could not rest.

The 9 month, 15; the 1 of the week.

This morning the Spaniards bid us prepare to travel for they were not able to maintain us. We understood that it was five or six leagues to Augustine, and we could not travel so far, being all of us lamed and stiff: we entreated them to let us go in a canoe, but they denied us: we entreated for the two women and Robert Barrow; at length we prevailed that they should go up in a canoe, for the canoe was to go whether we went or not.

While all this discourse was, came in a couple of Spaniards, one being the sentinel that went with our people the day before, the other was a person the governor had sent with a canoe and four Spaniards to fetch us. This was cheerful news; for had we gone to have traveled without a guide, we should have perished. The man that came for us brought two blankets, one for my wife, the other for Penelope: he desired us to be going. About a league distance from the place he left the canoe, which we parted with very unwillingly; for some of our people, had they had a mile further to have gone, could not have gone it. The wind still continued at northwest and blowed very fiercely; and extreme cold it was. We had such a continual shivering and pain in our bones that we were in violent anguish.

Our poor child was quiet, but so black with cold and shaking that it was admirable how it lived. We got to Augustine about two hours before night; being put on shore, we were directed to the governor's house: being got thither we were got up a pair of stairs, at the head whereof stood the governor, who ordered my wife to be conducted to his wife's apartment. I and John Smith went into a room where the governor asked us a few questions; but seeing how extreme cold we were, he gave us a cup of Spanish wine and sent us into his kitchen to warm ourselves at the fire. About half an hour afterwards the governor sent for John Smith and me and gave us a shirt and sliders, a hat and a pair of silk stockings, telling us he had no woollen clothes as yet, but would have some made. We put on the linen and made all haste into the kitchen to the fire. Robert Barrow was quartered at another house. The persons came to the governor's house and took such as they were minded to quarter in their houses; so that Joseph Kirle, John Smith, I, my wife and child lodged at the governor's house. All our people that came up with Joseph Kirle came to see us. We perceived the people's great kindness; for they were all well clothed from head to foot with the best the people had. Joseph Kirle began to tell us of his travail after he had left us on the bay, and how that they all concluded that they should never see my wife and child and Robert Barrow any more, if they did my kinsman and me. Richard Limpeney and those that went with him had a hard travel for thirty-six hours without ceasing, in which travel three of our Negroes that went with them were lost (viz Jack, Caesar, and Quenza), by sitting down to rest themselves they were in a little time so numbed that they could not go, and there perished. So that we lost five in that day's travel, and began to doubt that Negro Ben perished also. Joseph Kirle said that he thought he should have lost some of our people in their travel from the last sentinel's hither, for they were much tired, and the cold violent and the latter part of that day's journey they wading for many miles through much water, and deep sand-hills, and when they came in sight of Augustine they stayed for boats to fetch them, in which time some were numbed with the cold. Joseph Kirle applied himself to the governor on our behalfs to send us help, for he doubted whether we were all living; the governor readily assented and forthwith sent for a person fit for his purpose; charging him to get a piragua and men, and go forthwith and fetch us, but the tide fell out, so that we could not go till midnight. The governor was so concerned that he would not go to bed till they were gone; when the tide served he went to the waterside and saw the men put off, giving them a strict charge.

Solomon Cresson began to tell us of his travels from Jece, having most part of the way much rain. The Indians were very kind unto him until they came to the Indian town where the Dutchmen were killed; at which place some of those Indians made a discovery of him to be no Spaniard. They said nothing to him thereof, but were very dogged to him, giving him no food, and causing him to lie on the ground amongst vermin. On the morrow he was to go with his former company; who were grown so extremely bitter and envious to him that when they did but look upon him, they were ready to smite him; having gone until about mid-day, passing an inlet, the weather being extreme bad with wind, rain and much cold, they put on shore; (this was the place where we put on shore and got water-soldiers and stayed for the Spaniard when he went back to look for our people that were to follow us in a canoe). But the rage of these bloody people was such that he expected to die; being on shore they readily kindled a fire, about which time he heard a noise of a boat and oars, and presently the Spanish piragua put on shore upon them. The Indians were extraordinarily surprised and stood amazed but Solomon was glad to see them, and they him: the Spaniards took the Old Casseekey's chest and whatever he had from him, commanding them to return to the Indian towns from which they came. Staying all night the next morning the Spaniards sent Solomon under the conduct of two Indians belonging to these towns who were commanded by the Spaniards to carry Solomon unto the sentinel's house, but these two Indians carried him a little beyond the place where we put on shore to travel, and they seemed as though they had mischief in their hearts against him: he asked if they would go forward? But they looking untowardly on him, answered him not: so he went himself and was glad when he saw they did not follow him.

But we were desirous to know how the Spaniards had knowledge of us which it seems was thus.

When we got to Jece where Smith and his company were, and we going under the denomination of Spaniards and the other English, the report of us run from Indian town to Indian town to the northward unto the northernmost town, at which town were two or more Indians that were converted to the Romish faith. These or one of these went to the next Spanish sentinel's and gave an account that he heard that there were two vessels cast away to the southward of Jece, one being a Spaniard and the other an English vessel. The Spaniards having two vessels gone for the Havana to seek for supplies, feared it was those vessels. And the same day as this news came to the governor of Augustine came also news of one of their friars being murdered by some of the Cape Indians. After this manner we understood it; viz. three friars being under a vow to go amongst the Indians on the Cape to convert them, they went to a certain town to the northward of where we were cast away, but it lay within the sound. The Casseekey of this town they gained on to embrace the Roman faith, but all his people were much incensed against the friars, and therefore would have their Casseekey renounce his faith, and put the friars to death; but he would assent to neither: therefore they killed him and one friar; the other two escaped. Herewith was a piragua forthwith sent for us of what nation soever we might be, also a party of Spaniards and Indians were sent against that town where the friar was killed. We had a plentiful supper, and we fed like people that had been half starved, for we eat not knowing when we had enough: and we found our palates so changed by eating of berries that we could not relish the taste of salt any more than if it had no saltness in it. We had lodging provided, but few beds.

11

The LOSS *of the* NOTTINGHAM GALLEY

From "*The Preservation of John Dean*"

BY JOHN DEAN

1710

This account enjoys canonical status among shipwreck stories. It's hardly possible to pick up an anthology like this one without finding it reprinted. The reason is clear enough—cannibalism. The ship came to grief on Boon Island, east of Portsmouth, New Hampshire, in December 1710, and for 24 days the survivors were stuck there in winter weather that frustrated all attempts to escape. In the end they resorted to eating their carpenter.

But the story is interesting for other reasons as well. Other survivors protested Dean's version of it, blaming him for the accident in the first place (he had been ordered, they said, to wreck the ship so the owners could collect the insurance money; conversely he was supposed to be trying to betray the ship to the French, for the same reason), he had been below when it happened, not on deck giving orders, and it was his idea to flay and eat the carpenter. It must be added that they had no fire; eating the carpenter meant eating him raw. Dean responded to this attack by publishing another version of the wreck under his brother's name, and finally a third, 15 years later. In each version John Dean comes out smelling better and better. The tale ended its life finally as a piece of outright fiction: Kenneth Roberts wrote a novel called Boon Island *based on the conflict between Dean and the authors of the pamphlet attacking him. Sadly, it is not one of his best.*

THE *NOTTINGHAM GALLEY*, OF AND FROM LONDON, 120 TONS, 10 GUNS and 14 men, John Dean, Commander, having taken in cordage in England

and butter and cheese, etc., in Ireland, sailed for Boston in New England the 25th of September, 1710. But meeting with contrary winds and bad weather, 'twas the beginning of December when first made land to the eastward of Piscataqua and hailing southerly for the Massachusetts Bay, under a hard gale of wind at northeast, accompanied with rain, hail and snow, having no observation for ten or twelve days. We on the eleventh handed all our sails except our foresail and main topsail double reefed, ordering one hand forward to look out. Between eight and nine, going forward myself, I saw the breakers ahead, whereupon I called out to put the helm hard a starboard, but ere the ship could veer we struck upon the east end of the rock called Boon Island, four leagues to the eastward of Piscataqua.

The second or third sea heaved the ship alongside it, running likewise so very high and the ship laboring so excessively that we were not able to stand upon deck, and notwithstanding it was not above thirty or forty yards, yet the weather was so thick and dark we could not see the rock, so that we were justly thrown into a consternation at the sad prospect of immediately perishing in the sea. I presently called down all hands to the cabin, where we continued a few minutes earnestly supplicating mercy; but, knowing prayers without endeavors are vain, I ordered all up again to cut the masts by the board; but several sunk so under racks of conscience that they were not able to stir. However, we upon deck cut the weather-most shrouds, and the ship heeling towards the rock, the force of the sea soon broke the masts so that they fell right towards the shore.

One of the men went out on the boltspright and, returning, told me he saw something black ahead and would adventure to get on shore, accompanied with any other person; upon which I desired some of the best swimmers (my mate and one more) to go with him, and if they recovered the rock to give notice by their calls and direct us to the most secure place. And remembering some money and papers that might be of use, also ammunition, brandy, etc., I went down and opened the place in which they were; but the ship bulging, her decks opening, her back broke, and beams giving way, so that the stern sunk almost under water, I was obliged to hasten forward to prevent immediate perishing. And, having heard nothing of the men gone before, concluded them lost; yet, notwithstanding, I was under a necessity to make the same adventure upon the foremast, moving gradually forward betwixt every sea till, at last quitting it, I cast myself with all my strength I had toward the rock, and it being dead low water and the rock exceeding slippery I could get no hold but tore my fingers, hands and arms in a most lamentable manner, every wash of the sea fetching me off again, so that it was with the utmost peril and difficulty that I got safe on shore at last. The rest of the men ran the same hazard yet through mercy we all escaped with our lives.

After endeavoring to discharge the salt water, and creeping a little way up the rock, I heard the three men mentioned before, and by ten all met together; where with joyful hearts we returned humble thanks to Providence for our deliverance from so eminent a danger. We then endeavored to gain shelter to the leeward of the rock but found it so small and inconsiderable that it would afford none (being but about a hundred yards long and fifty broad) and so very craggy that we could not walk to keep ourselves warm, the weather still continuing extreme cold, with snow and rain.

As soon as daylight appeared I went towards the place where we came on shore, not questioning but we should meet with provisions enough from the wreck for our support; but found only some pieces of the masts and yards amongst some old junk and cables congered together, which the anchors had prevented from being carried away and kept moving about the rock at some distance. Part of the ship's stores, with some pieces of plank and timber, old sails and canvas, etc., drove on shore, but nothing to eat except some small pieces of cheese we picked up from the rockweed (in the whole to the quantity of three small cheeses).

We used our utmost endeavor to get fire (having a steel and flint with us, also by a drill with a very swift motion); but, having nothing but what had been long water-soaked, we could not effect it.

At night we stowed one upon another under our canvas in the best manner possible to keep each other warm; and the next day, the weather a little clearing and inclining to frost, I went out; and, seeing the mainland, knew where we was, therefore encouraged my men with hopes of being discovered by fishing shallops, requiring them to go about and fetch up what planks they could get, as also carpenter's tools and stores, in order to build a tent and a boat. The cook then complaining he was almost starved, and his countenance discovering his illness, I ordered him to remain with two or three more the frost had seized. About noon the men acquainted me that he was dead, so laid him in a convenient place for the sea to carry him away, none mentioning eating of him, though several with myself afterwards acknowledged had thoughts of it.

After we had been there two or three days the frost being very severe and the weather extremely cold, it seized most of our hands and feet to such a degree as to take away the sense of feeling and render them almost useless; so benumbing and discoloring them as gave us just reason to fear mortifications. We pulled off our shoes and cut off our boots, but in getting off our stockings many whose legs were blistered pulled off skin and all and some the nails of their toes. We wrapped up our legs and feet as warm as we could in oakum and canvas.

We now began to build our tent in a triangular form, each angle about eight foot, covered with what sails and old canvas came on shore, having just room for all to lie down each on one side, so that none could turn except all turned, which was about every two hours, upon notice given. We also fixed a staff to the top of our tent, upon which (as often as weather would permit) we hoisted a piece of cloth in the form of a flag in order to discover ourselves to any vessels that might come near.

We began now to build our boat of plank and timber belonging to the wreck, our tools the blade of a cutlass (made into a saw with our knives), a hammer and a caulking mallet. Some nails we found in the clefts of the rock, others we got from the sheathing. We laid three planks flat for the bottom and two up each side fixed to stanchions and let into the bottom timbers, with two short pieces at each end, also one breadth of new Holland duck round the sides to keep out the spray of the sea. We corked all we could with oakum drawn from the old junk and in other places, filled up the distances with long pieces of canvas, all which we secured in the best manner possible. We found also some sheet lead and pump leather, which proved of use. We fixed a short mast and square sail, with seven paddles to row, and another longer to steer. But our carpenter, who now should have been of most use to us, was by reason of illness scarce able to afford us either assistance or advice; and all the rest benumbed and feeble as not able to stir, except myself and two more, also the weather so extreme cold that we could seldom stay out of the tent above four hours in the day, and some days do nothing at all.

When we had been there about a week without any manner of provisions except the cheese before-mentioned and some beef bones, which we eat (first beating them to pieces), we saw three boats about five leagues from us, which may be easily imagined rejoiced us not a little, believing our deliverance was now come. I made all creep out of the tent and hollo together so well as our strength would allow, making also all the signals we could; but alas, all in vain, they neither hearing nor otherwise discovering us. However, we received no small encouragement from the sight of 'em; they coming from southwest, and the wind at northeast when we were cast away, gave us reason to conclude our distress might be known by the wreck driving on shore, and to presume were come out in search of us and that they would daily do so when weather would permit. Thus we flattered ourselves in hopes of deliverance though in vain.

Just before we finished our boat, Providence so ordered it that the carpenter's ax was cast on the rock to us, whereby we were enabled to complete our work. But then we had scarce strength enough to get her into the water.

About the 21st December, the boat just perfected, a fine day, and the water smoother than I had ever yet seen it since we came there, we consulted who should attempt getting on shore, I offering myself as one to adventure, which they agreed to because I was the strongest and therefore fittest to undergo the extremities we might be reduced to. My mate also offering himself and desiring to accompany me, I was allowed him with my brother and four more. So, committing our enterprise to Divine Providence, all that were able came out and with much difficulty we got our poor patched-up boat to the water's side. And the surf running very high, was obliged to wade very deep to launch her, which being done and myself and one more got into her, the swell of the sea heaved her alongshore and overset her upon us, whereby we again narrowly escaped drowning, and staved our poor boat all to pieces, totally disappointing our enterprise and destroying all our hopes at once.

We lost with our boat our ax and hammer, which would have been of great use to us if we should hereafter attempt to build a raft, yet had we reason to admire the goodness of God in overruling our disappointment for our safety, for that afternoon the wind, springing up, it blew very hard, so that had we been at sea in that imitation of a boat, in all probability we must have perished and the rest left behind had no better fare because unable to help themselves.

We were now reduced to the most deplorable and melancholy circumstance imaginable, almost every man but myself weak to an extremity and near starved with hunger and cold, their hands and feet frozen and mortified, with large and deep ulcers in their legs, the very smell offensive, and nothing to dress them with but a piece of linen that was cast on the shore. No fire, and the weather extreme cold; our small stock of cheese spent and nothing to support our feeble bodies but rockweed and a few mussels, scarce and difficult to get (at most not above two or three for each man a day). So that we had our miserable bodies perishing and our poor disconsolate spirits overpowered with the deplorable prospect of starving, without any appearance of relief. Besides, to heighten if possible the aggravation, we had to apprehend lest the approaching spring tide (if accompanied with high winds) should totally overflow us. How dismal such a circumstance must be is impossible to express: the pinching cold and hunger, extremity of weakness and pain, racks and horror of conscience (to many) and foresight of certain and painful but lingering death, without any (even the most remote) views of deliverance.

The last method of safety we could possibly propose was the fixing a raft that might carry two men, which was mightily urged by one of our men, a Swede, a stout brave fellow, but had since lost both his feet by the frost. He frequently importuned me to attempt our deliverance in that way, offering himself to accompany me, or if I refused him to go alone. After deliberate thoughts and consideration we resolved upon a raft but found abundance of labor and difficulty in clearing the foreyard (of which it was chiefly to be made) from the junk, by reason our working hands were so few and weak.

That done, we split the yard and with the two parts made side pieces, fixing others and adding some of the lightest plank we could get, first spiking and afterwards seizing them firm, in breadth four foot. We likewise fixed a mast, and of two hammocks that were drove on shore we made a sail, with a paddle for each man and a spare one in case of necessity. This difficulty thus surmounted and brought to a period, he would frequently ask me whether I designed to accompany him, giving me also to understand that if I declined there was another ready to embrace the offer.

About this time we saw a sail come out of Piscataqua River, about seven leagues to the westward. We again made all the signal we could, but the wind being at northwest and the ship standing to the eastward, was presently out of sight without ever coming near us, which proved a very great mortification to our hopes. But the next day being moderate, and in the afternoon a small breeze right on shore, also the raft finished, the two men were very solicitous to have it launched, and the mate as strenuously opposed it on account 'twas so late (being two in the afternoon); but they, urging the light nights, begged of me to have it done, to which at last I agreed, first committing the enterprise to God's blessing. They both got upon it and, the swell rolling very high, soon overset them as it did our boat. The Swede, not minding it, swam on shore, but the other (being no swimmer) continued some time under water, and as soon as he appeared, I caught hold of him and saved him but he was so discouraged that he was afraid to make a second attempt.

I desired the Swede to wait a more favorable opportunity, but he, continuing resolute, begged of me to go with him or help him to turn the raft and would go himself alone.

By this time another man came down and offered to adventure; so, getting upon the raft, I launched 'em off, they desiring us to go to prayers, also to watch what became of them. I did so, and by sunset judged them half way to the main, and that they might reach the shore by two in the morning. But I suppose they fell in with some breakers, or the violence of the sea overset them and they perished; for, two days after, the raft was found on shore and one man dead about a mile from it, with a paddle fastened to his wrist; but the Swede who was so very forward to adventure was never heard of more.

At our first coming, saw several seals upon the rock and, supposing they might harbor there in the night, I walked round at midnight but could never get anything. We also saw a great many fowls, but they perceiving us daily there would never come on the rock to lodge, so that we caught none.

Which disappointment was very grievous and still served to irritate our miseries, but it was more especially afflicting to a brother I had with me and another young gentleman, who had never either of 'em been at sea or endured any severities before, but were now reduced to the last extremities, having no assistance but what they received from me.

Part of a green hide being thrown up by the sea, fastened to a piece of the mainyard, the men importuned me to bring it to the tent, which being done we minced it small and swallowed it down.

About this time I set the men to open junk, and with the rope-yarn (when weather would permit) I thatched the tent in the best manner my strength would allow, that it might the better shelter us from extremities of weather.

About the latter end of this month our carpenter (a fat man and naturally of a dull, heavy, phlegmatic constitution and disposition, aged about 47) who from our first coming on shore had been always very ill and lost the use of his feet, complained of an excessive pain in his back and stiffness in his neck; being likewise almost choked with phlegm for want of strength to discharge it, so that to our apprehension he drew near his end. We prayed over him and used our utmost endeavors to be serviceable to him in his last moments. He showed himself sensible though speechless and that night died. We suffered the body to remain with us till morning, when I desired them who were best able to remove it, creeping out myself to see if Providence had yet sent us anything to satisfy our extremely craving appetites. Before noon, returning and not seeing the dead body without, I asked why they had not removed it. And received for answer, they were not all of them able. Whereupon fastening a rope to the body, I gave the utmost of my assistance, and with some difficulty we got it out of the tent. But the fatigue and consideration of our misery together so overcame my spirits that, being ready to faint, I crept into the tent and was no sooner got in there but (as the highest addition of trouble) the men began to request of me the dead body to eat, the better to support their lives.

This, of all I had met with, was the most grievous and shocking to me, to see myself and company, who came thither laden with provisions but three weeks before, now reduced to such a deplorable circumstance as to have two of us absolutely starved to death, other two we knew not what was become of, and the rest of us at the last extremity and though still living yet requiring to eat the dead for support.

After abundance of mature thought and consultation about the lawfulness or sinfulness on the one hand and absolute necessity on the other, judgment, conscience, etc., were obliged to submit to the more prevailing arguments of our craving appetites, so that at last we determined to satisfy our hunger and support our feeble bodies with the carcass in possession. First I ordered his skin, head, hands, feet and bowels to be buried in the sea and the body to be quartered for convenience of drying and carriage, to which I again received for answer that they were not all of them able but entreated I would perform it for them. A task very grievous, and not readily complied with, but their incessant prayers and entreaties at last prevailed and by night I had performed my labor.

I then cut part of the flesh in thin slices and, washing it in salt water, brought it to the tent and obliged the men to eat rockweed along with it, to serve instead of bread.

My mate and two others refused to eat any that night, but next morning complied and earnestly desired to partake with the rest.

I found they all eat abundance and with the utmost greediness, so that I was constrained to carry the quarters farther from the tent, quite out of their reach, lest they should prejudice themselves by overmuch eating, as also expend our small stock too soon.

I also limited each man to an equal proportion, that none might quarrel or entertain hard thoughts of myself or one another, and I was the more obliged to this method because I found in a few days their very natural dispositions changed, and that affectionate, peacable temper they had all along discovered totally lost, their eyes staring and looking wild, their countenances fierce and barbarous, and instead of obeying my commands as they had universally and readily done before, I found all I could say, even prayers and entreaties, vain and fruitless, nothing now being to be heard but brutish quarrels, with horrid oaths and imprecations, instead of that quiet submissive spirit of prayer and supplication we had before enjoyed.

This, together with the dismal prospect of future want, obliged me to keep a strict watch over the rest of the body, lest any of 'em should if able get to it, and this being spent we be forced to feed upon the living, which we must certainly have done had we stayed a few days longer.

But now the goodness of God began to appear and make provision for our deliverance by putting it in the hearts of the good people on shore, where our raft drove, to come out in search of us; which they did the 2nd of January in the morning.

Just as I was creeping out of the tent I saw a shallop halfway from shore, standing directly towards us, which may be easily imagined was life from the dead. How great our joys and satisfactions were at the prospect of so speedy and unexpected deliverance no tongue is able to express nor thoughts to conceive.

Our good and welcome friends came to an anchor to the southwest at about 100 yards distance, the swell not suffering them to come nearer. But their anchor coming home, obliged them to stand off till about noon, waiting for smoother water upon the flood. Meantime our passions were differently moved, our expectations of deliverance and fears of miscarriage hurried our weak and disordered spirits strangely.

I gave them account of our miseries in every respect except the want of provisions (which I did not mention, lest I should not get them on shore for fear of being constrained by the weather to tarry with us). I earnestly entreated them to attempt our immediate deliverance, or at least if possible to furnish us with fire, which with the utmost hazard and difficulty they at last accomplished, by sending a small canoe with one man, who with abundance of labor got on shore.

After helping him up with his canoe and seeing nothing to eat I asked him if he could give us fire. He answered in the affirmative but was so affrighted, seeing me look so thin and meager that could hardly at first return me an answer. But recollecting himself, after several questions asked on both sides, he went with me to the tent, where was surprised to see so many of us in so deplorable condition, our flesh so wasted and our looks so ghastly and frightful that it was really a very dismal prospect.

With some difficulty we made a fire, determining to go myself with the man on board and after to send for the rest, one or two at a time, and accordingly got both into the canoe, but the sea immediately drove it with such violence against the rock, that overset us into the water; and I being very weak, 'twas a great while before I could recover myself, so that I had a very narrow escape from drowning.

The good man with very great difficulty got on board himself without me, designing to return the next day with better conveniences if weather would permit.

'Twas a very uncomfortable sight to see our worthy friends in the shallop stand away from the shore without us. But God, who orders all our affairs by unseen movements for the best, had doubtless designs of preservation towards us in denying us that appearance of present deliverance. For that night the wind coming about to southeast, blowing hard and being dark weather, our good friends lost their shallop and with extreme difficulty saved their lives. But, in all probability, had we been with them we must have perished, not having strength sufficient to help ourselves.

Immediately after their getting on shore they sent an express to Portsmouth in Piscataqua, where the good people made no delay in hastening to our deliverance as soon as weather would allow. But to our great sorrow and for further trial of our patience, the next day continued very stormy, so that though we doubted not but the people on shore knew our condition and would assist us as soon as possible, yet our flesh being near spent, no fresh water, nor any certainty how long the weather might continue thus, rendered our circumstance still miserable though much advanced by the fire, for now we could both warm ourselves and broil our meat.

The next day, our men urging me vehemently for flesh, I gave them a little more than usual, but not to their satisfaction, for they would certainly have eat up the whole at once had I not carefully watched 'em, designing to share the rest next morning if the weather continued bad. But it pleased God that night the wind abated, and early next morning a shallop came for us, with my much esteemed friends Captain Longland and Captain Purver and three more men who brought a large canoe; and in two hours' time got us all on board to their satisfaction and our great comfort, being forced to carry almost all the men on their backs from the tent to the canoe and fetch us off by two or three at a time.

When we first came on board the shallop each of us eat a bit of bread and drank a dram of rum, and most of us were extremely seasick; but after we had cleansed our stomachs and tasted warm nourishing food we became so exceeding hungry and ravenous that had not our worthy friends dieted us and limited the quantity for about two or three days we should certainly have destroyed ourselves with eating.

We had also two other vessels come off for our assistance if there had been any necessity (so generous and charitable were the good people of New England in our distress); but, seeing us all on board the shallop, made the best of their way home again.

At eight at night we came on shore, where we were kindly entertained myself and another at a private house (having credit sufficient to help us), all the rest at the charge of the government, who took such care that the poor men knew not the least want of anything their necessities called for or the kind and generous gentlemen could furnish them with (the care, industry and generosity of my much honored friends John Plaisted, Esq., and Captain John Wentworth, in serving both myself and these poor men being particularly eminent), providing them a good surgeon and nurses till well, bearing the charge and afterwards allowing each man sufficient clothing; behaving themselves in the whole with so much freedom, generosity and Christian temper that was no small addition to their other services, and rendered the whole worthy both of admiration and imitation; and likewise was of the last consequence to the poor men in their distress.

Two days after we came on shore my apprentice lost a great part of one foot; the rest all recovered their limbs but not their perfect life, very few besides myself escaping without losing the benefit of fingers or toes, though thank God all otherwise in perfect health.

12

ALEXANDER SELKIRK: CASTAWAY

Various Sources
CA 1712

Selkirk's story is famous for having inspired Daniel Defoe's Robinson Crusoe, *one of the first true adventure novels and still probably the best known. But it is an interesting story in its own right, and it has a nice roundness to it. The same privateer under whose command he was marooned on Juan Fernandez Island in the first place was present when he was picked up four years and four months later. His name was William Dampier, he was well known in England for his prowess as a privateer and also for his scientific interests, and he knew Selkirk personally to be an accomplished mariner and ship's quartermaster.*

Dampier drank too much, however, he did not command well, and his expeditions were always troubled with the threat of mutiny. In 1703 he sailed with two ships, his own and another, the Cinque Ports, *to capture the Spanish treasure galleon from Manila—the grail of English privateers—on its approach to Acapulco. Selkirk, 23, was quartermaster on the* Cinque Ports, *which had a new captain, untried 21-year-old Thomas Stradling.*

Both Selkirk and Stradling were cranky and difficult to get along with, and the voyage went poorly. The two ships failed to capture the galleon, the two captains were suspicious of each other, and eventually, after months of desultory raiding along the Pacific Coast of South America and the fortuitous capture of a minor treasure ship, they parted. The Cinque Ports *was leaking badly by this time. On the way back to Cape Horn and thence to England the ship stopped at Juan Fernandez Island for provisions and water—earlier mariners had planted turnips there; they throve in the fertile soil—and Selkirk refused to go any farther. The ship was unsafe, he said. Stradling left him there, at his own request. Not long after, the* Cinque Ports *went down. Only eight men survived.*

Four years later it was another privateering expedition, with William Dampier on board as navigator, still hoping to capture that Spanish treasure ship, that found Selkirk alive and established on Juan Fernandez. Because Dampier knew his abilities, Selkirk was made mate of one of the ships and participated in the raiding, and this time the expedition did go well, capturing one of the treasure ships off the coast of Baja California before Dampier sailed west, around the world, to England.

We print here excerpts from three separate accounts of Selkirk's great adventure, along with another written by William Dampier that describes an earlier voyage in which yet another castaway had been found on Juan Fernandez Island, this time a Moskito Indian from the east coast of Nicaragua. This puts to rest Defoe's idea that only an Englishman would be resourceful enough to survive if cast away on an island. Defoe probably knew of this account as well. He was an inveterate reader of travel literature and voyages and owned 49 such books, quite a collection at the time; indeed, he was an expert on the subject and wrote the text for a major maritime atlas. But it is Robinson Crusoe *we remember him for, and why we remember Alexander Selkirk, too. There's a statue of Selkirk in his hometown, Fife, in Scotland. He is dressed in animal skins. He holds a rifle. He gazes into the distance. He is master of all he surveys.*

Edward Cooke, *A Voyage to the South Sea, and around the World*

February 1. In the Morning tack'd and stood to the Westward; but the Wind shrinking, and blowing off the Island in Squals, could not get in 'till Eight in the Evening, when having little Wind, we row'd and tow'd into the great Bay, and came to an Anchor in 50 Fathom Water with our best Bower, carrying our Stream-Anchor in with the Shore. All this Day had a clear Ship, hoping to get some Purchase, but saw no Vessel, only one Man ashore, with a white Ensign, which made us conclude, that some Men had been left there by some Ship, because the Island is not inhabited. The Duke's Boat went ashore, and found one Alexander Selkirk, who had been formerly Master of the Cinque Ports Galley, an English Privateer in those Parts; and having some Difference with the Captain of the said Ship, and she being leaky, he left the said Capt. Stradling, going ashore on this Island, where he continu'd four Years and four Months, living on Goats and Cabbages that grow on Trees, Turnips, Parsnips, &c. He told us a Spanish Ship or two which touch'd there, had like to have taken him, and fir'd some Shot at him. He was cloath'd in a Goat's Skin jacket, Breeches, and Cap, sew'd together with Thongs of the same. He tam'd some wild Goats and Cats, whereof there are great Numbers.

Woodes Rogers, A *Cruising Voyage round the World*

Febr. 2...Immediately our Pinnace return'd from the shore, and brought abundance of Craw-fish, with a Man cloth'd in Goat-Skins, who look'd wilder than the first Owners of them. He had been on the Island four Years and four Months, being left there by Capt. Stradling in the Cinque-Ports; his Name was Alexander Selkirk a Scotch Man, who had been Master of the Cinque-Ports, a Ship that came here last with Capt. Dampier, who told me that this was the best Man in her; so I immediately agreed with him to be a Mate on board our Ship. 'Twas he that made the Fire last night when he saw our Ships, which he judg'd to be English. During his stay here, he saw several Ships pass by, but only two came in to anchor. As he went to view them, he found 'em to be Spaniards, and retir'd from 'em; upon which they shot at him. Had they been French, he would have submitted; but chose to risque his dying alone on the Island, rather than fall into the hands of the Spaniards in these parts, because he apprehended they would murder him, or make a Slave of him in the Mines, for he fear'd they would spare no Stranger that might be capable of discovering the South-Sea. The Spaniards had landed, before he knew what they were, and they came so near him that he had much ado to escape; for they not only shot at him but pursu'd him into the Woods, where he climb'd to the top of a Tree, at the foot of which they made water, and kill'd several Goats just by, but went off again without discovering him. He told us that he was born at Largo in the County of Fife in Scotland, and was bred a Sailor from his Youth. The reason of his being left here was a difference betwixt him and his Captain; which, together with the Ships being leaky, made him willing rather to stay here, than go along with him at first; and when he was at last willing, the Captain would not receive him. He had been in the Island before to wood and water, when two of the Ships Company were left upon it for six Months till the Ship return'd, being chas'd thence by two French South-Sea Ships.

He had with him his Clothes and Bedding, with a Firelock, some Powder, Bullets, and Tobacco, a Hatchet, a Knife, a Kettle, a Bible, some practical Pieces, and his Mathematical Instruments and Books. He diverted and provided for himself as well as he could; but for the first eight months had much ado to bear up against Melancholy, and the Terror of being left alone in such a desolate place. He built two Hutts with Piemento Trees, cover'd them with long Grass, and lin'd them with the Skins of Goats, which he kill'd with his Gun as he wanted, so long as his Powder lasted, which was but a pound; and that being near spent, he got fire by rubbing two sticks of Piemento Wood together upon his knee. In the lesser Hutt, at some distance from the other, he dress'd his Victuals, and in the larger he slept, and employ'd himself in reading, singing Psalms, and praying; so that he said he was a better Christian while in this Solitude than ever he was before, or than, he was afraid, he should ever be again. At first he never eat any thing till Hunger constrain'd him, partly for grief and partly for want of Bread and Salt; nor did he go to bed till he could watch no longer: the Piemento Wood, which burnt very clear, serv'd him both for Firing and Candle, and refresh'd him with its fragrant Smell.

He might have had Fish enough, but could not eat 'em for want of Salt, because they occasion'd a Looseness; except Crawfish, which are there as large as our Lobsters, and very good: These he sometimes boil'd, and at other times broil'd, as he did his Goats Flesh, of which he made very good Broth, for they are not so rank as ours: he kept an Account of 500 that he kill'd while there, and caught as many more, which he mark'd on the Ear and let go. When his Powder fail'd, he took them by speed of foot; for his way of living and continual Exercise of walking and running, clear'd him of all gross Humours, so that he ran with wonderful Swiftness thro the Woods and up the Rocks and Hills, as we perceiv'd when we employ'd him to catch Goats for us. We had a Bull-Dog, which we sent with several of our nimblest Runners, to help him in catching Goats; but he distane'd and tir'd both the Dog and the Men, catch'd the Goats, and brought 'em to us on his back. He told us that his Agility in pursuing a Goat had once like to have cost him his Life; he pursu'd it with so much Eagerness that he catch'd hold of it on the brink of a Precipice, of which he was not aware, the Bushes having hid it from him; so that he fell with the Goat down the said Precipice a great height, and was so stun'd and bruis'd with the Fall, that he narrowly escap'd with his Life, and when he came to his Senses, found the Goat dead under him. He lay there about

24 hours, and was scarce able to crawl to his Hutt, which was about a mile distant, or to stir abroad again in ten days.

He came at last to relish his Meat well enough without Salt or Bread, and in the Season had plenty of good Turnips, which had been sow'd there by Capt. Dampier's Men, and have now overspread some Acres of Ground. He had enough of good Cabbage from the Cabbage-Trees, and season'd his Meat with the Fruit of the Piemento Trees, which is the same as the Jamaica Pepper, and smells deliciously. He found there also a black Pepper call'd Malagita, which was very good to expel Wind, and against Griping of the Guts.

He soon wore out all his Shoes and Clothes by running thro the Woods; and at last being forc'd to shift without them, his Feet became so hard, that he run every where without Annoyance: and it was some time before he could wear Shoes after we found him; for not being us'd to any so long, his Feet swell'd when he came first to wear 'em again.

After he had conquer'd his Melancholy, he diverted himself sometimes by cutting his Name on the Trees, and the Time of his being left and Continuance there. He was at first much pester'd with Cats and Rats, that had bred in great numbers from some of each Species which had got ashore from Ships that put in there to wood and water. The Rats gnaw'd his Feet and Clothes while asleep, which oblig'd him to cherish the Cats with his Goats-flesh; by which many of them became so tame, that they would lie about him in hundreds, and soon deliver'd him from the Rats. He likewise tam'd some Kids, and to divert himself would now and then sing and dance with them and his Cats: so that by the Care of Providence and Vigour of his Youth, being now but about 30 years old, he came at last to conquer all the Inconveniences of his Solitude, and to be very easy. When his Clothes wore out, he made himself a Coat and Cap of Goat-Skins, which he stitch'd together with little Thongs of the same, that he cut with his Knife. He had no other Needle but a Nail; and when his Knife was wore to the back, he made others as well as he could of some Iron Hoops that were left ashore, which he beat thin and ground upon Stones. Having some Linen Cloth by him, he sow'd himself Shirts with a Nail, and stitch'd 'em with the Worsted of his old Stockings, which he pull'd out on purpose. He had his last Shirt on when we found him in the Island.

At his first coming on board us, he had so much forgot his Language for want of Use, that we could scarce understand him, for he seem'd to speak his words by halves. We offer'd him a Dram, but he would not touch it, having drank nothing but Water since his being there, and 'twas some time before he could relish our Victuals.

He could give us an account of no other Product of the Island than what we have mention'd, except small black Plums, which are very good, but hard to come at, the Trees which bear 'em growing on high Mountains and Rocks. Piemento Trees are plenty here, and we saw some of 60 foot high, and about two yards thick; and Cotton Trees higher, and near four fathom round in the Stock.

The Climate is so good, that the Trees and Grass are verdant all the Year. The Winter lasts no longer than June and July, and is not then severe, there being only a small Frost and a little Hail, but sometimes great Rains. The Heat of the Summer is equally moderate, and there's not much Thunder or tempestuous Weather of any sort. He saw no venomous or savage Creature on the Island, nor any other sort of Beast but Goats, &c. as above-mention'd; the first of which had been put ashore here on purpose for a Breed by Juan Fernando, a Spaniard who settled there with some Families for a time, till the Continent of Chili began to submit to the Spaniards; which being more profitable, tempted them to quit this Island, which is capable of maintaining a good number of People, and of being made so strong that they could not be easily dislodg'd.

Ringrose in his Account of Capt. Sharp's Voyage and other Buccaneers, mentions one who had escap'd ashore here out of a Ship which was cast away with all the rest of the Company, and says he liv'd five years alone before he had the opportunity of another Ship to carry him off. Capt. Dampier talks of a Moskito Indian that belong'd to Capt. Watlin, who being a hunting in the Woods when the Captain left the Island, liv'd here three years alone, shifted much in the same manner as Mr. Selkirk did, till Capt. Dampier came hither in 1684, and carry'd him off. The first that went ashore was one of his Countrymen, and they saluted one another first by prostrating themselves by turns on the ground, and then embracing. But whatever there is in these Stories, this of Mr. Selkirk I know to be true; and his Behaviour afterwards gives me reason to believe the Account he gave me how he spent his time, and bore up under such an Affliction, in which nothing but the Divine Providence could have supported any Man. By this one may see that Solitude and Retirement from the World is not such an unsufferable State of Life as most Men imagine, especially when People are fairly call'd or thrown into it unavoidably, as this Man was; who in all probability must otherwise have perish'd in the Seas, the Ship which left him being cast away not long after, and few of the Company escap'd. We may perceive by this Story the Truth of the Maxim, That Necessity is the Mother of Invention, since he found means to supply his Wants in a very natural manner, so as to maintain his Life, tho not so conveniently, yet as effectually as we are able to do with the help of all our Arts and Society. It may likewise instruct us, how much a plain and temperate way of living conduces to the Health of the Body and the Vigour of the Mind, both which we are apt to destroy by Excess and Plenty, especially of strong Liquor, and the Variety as well as the Nature of our Meat and Drink: for this Man, when he came to our ordinary method of Diet and Life, tho he was sober enough, lost much of his Strength and Agility. But I must quit these Reflections, which are more proper for a Philosopher and Divine than a Mariner, and return to my own Subject.

Richard Steele, "Alexander Selkirk," *The Englishman*

Under the Title of this Paper, I do not think it foreign to my Design, to speak of a Man born in Her majesty's Dominions, and relate an Adventure in his Life so uncommon, that it's doubtful whether the like has happen'd to any other of human Race. The Person I speak of is Alexander Selkirk, whose Name is familiar to Men of Curiosity, from the Fame of his having lived four years and four Months alone in the Island of Juan Fernandez. I had the pleasure frequently to converse with the Man soon after his Arrival in England, in the Year 1711. It was matter of great Curiosity to hear him, as he is a Man of good Sense, give an Account of the different Revolutions in his own Mind in that long Solitude. When we consider how painful Absence from Company for the space of but one Evening, is to the generality of Mankind, we may have a sense how painful this necessary and constant Solitude was to a Man bred a Sailor, and ever accustomed to enjoy and suffer, eat, drink, and sleep, and perform all Offices of Life, in Fellowship and Company. He was put ashore from a leaky Vessel, with the Captain of which he had had an irreconcileable difference; and he chose rather to take his Fate in this place, than in a crazy Vessel, under a disagreeable Commander. His Portion were a Sea-Chest, his wearing Cloaths and Bedding, a Fire-lock, a Pound of Gun-powder, a large quantity of Bullets, a Flint and Steel, a few Pounds of Tobacco, an Hatchet, a Knife, a Kettle, a Bible, and other Books of Devotion, together with Pieces that concerned Navigation, and his Mathematical Instruments. Resentment against his Officer, who had ill used him, made him look forward on this Change of Life, as the more eligible one, till the Instant in which he saw the Vessel put off; at which moment, his Heart yearned within him, and melted at the parting with his Comrades and all Human Society at once. He had in Provisions for the Sustenance of Life but the quantity of two Meals, the Island abounding only with wild Goats, Cats and Rats. He judged it most probable that he should find more immediate and easy Relief, by finding Shell-fish on the Shore, than seeking Game with his Gun. He accordingly found great quantities of Turtles, whose Flesh is extreamly delicious, and of which he frequently eat very plentifully on his first Arrival, till it grew disagreeable to his Stomach, except in Jellies. The Necessities of Hunger and Thirst, were his greatest Diversions from the Reflection on his lonely Condition. When those Appetites were satisfied, the Desire of Society was as strong a Call upon him, and he appeared to himself least necessitious when he wanted every thing; for the Supports of his Body were easily attained, but the eager Longings for seeing again the Face of Man during the Interval of craving bodily Appetites, were hardly supportable. He grew dejected, languid, and melancholy, scarce able to refrain from doing himself Violence, till by Degrees, by the Force of Reason, and frequent reading of the Scriptures, and turning his Thoughts upon the Study of Navigation, after the Space of eighteen Months, he grew thoroughly reconciled to his Condition. When he had made this Conquest, the Vigour of his Health, Disengagement from the World, a constant, chearful, serene Sky, and a temperate Air, made his Life one continual Feast, and his Being much more joyful than it had before been irksome. He now taking Delight in every thing, made the Hutt in which he lay, by Ornaments which he cut down from a spacious Wood, on the side of which it was situated, the most delicious Bower, fann'd with continual Breezes, and gentle Aspirations of Wind, that made his Repose after the Chase equal to the most sensual Pleasures.

I forgot to observe, that during the Time of his Dissatisfaction, Monsters of the Deep, which frequently lay on the Shore, added to the Terrors of his Solitude; the dreadful Howlings and Voices seemed too terrible to be made for human Ears; but upon the Recovery of his Temper, he could with Pleasure not only hear their Voices, but approach the Monsters themselves with great Intrepidity. He speaks of Sea-Lions, whose Jaws and Tails were capable of seizing or breaking the Limbs of a Man, if he approached them: But at that Time his Spirits and Life were so high, and he could act so regularly and unconcerned, that meerly from being unruffled in himself, he killed them with the greatest Ease imaginable: For observing, that though their Jaws and Tails were so terrible, yet the Animals being mighty slow in working themselves round, he had nothing to do but place himself exactly opposite their Middle, and as close to them as possible, and he dispatched them with his Hatchet at Will.

The Precaution which he took against Want, in case of Sickness, was to lame Kids when very young, so as that they might recover their Health, but never be capable of Speed. These he had in great Numbers about his Hutt; and when he was himself in full Vigour, he could take at full Speed the swiftest Goat running up a Promontory, and never failed of catching them but on a Descent.

His Habitation was extremely pester'd with Rats, which gnaw'd his Cloaths and Feet when sleeping. To defend him against them, he fed and tamed Numbers of young Kitlings, who lay about his Bed, and preserved him from the Enemy. When his Cloaths were quite worn out, he dried and tacked together the skins of Goats, with which he cloathed himself, and was enured to pass through Woods, Bushes, and Brambles with as much Carelessness and Precipitance as any other Animal. It happened once to him, that running on the Summit of a Hill, he made a Stretch to seize a Goat, with which under him, he fell down a Precipice, and lay sensless for the Space of three Days, the Length of which Time he Measured by the Moon's Growth since his last Observation. This manner of life grew so exquisitely pleasant, that he never had a Moment heavy upon his Hands; his Nights were untroubled, and his Days joyous, from the Practice of Temperance and Exercise. It was his Manner to use stated Hours and Places for Exercises of Devotion, which he performed aloud, in order to keep up the Faculties of Speech, and to utter himself with greater Energy.

When I first saw him, I thought, if I had not been let into his Character and Story, I could have discerned that he had been much separated from Company, from his Aspect and Gesture; there was a strong but chearful Seriousness in his Look, and a certain Disregard to the ordinary things about him, as if he had been sunk in Thought. When the Ship which brought him off the Island came in, he received them with the greatest Indifference, with relation to the Prospect of going off with them, but with great Satisfaction in an Opportunity to refresh and help them. The Man frequently bewailed his Return to the World, which could not, he said, with all its Enjoyments, restore him to the Tranquility of his Solitude. Though I had frequently conversed with him, after a few Months Absence he met me in the Street, and though he spoke to me, I could not recollect that I had seen him; familiar Converse in this Town had taken off the Loneliness of his Aspect, and quite altered the Air of his Face.

This plain Man's Story is a memorable Example, that he is happiest who confines his Wants to natural Necessities; and he that goes further in his Desires, increases his Wants in Proportion to his Acquisitions; or to use his own Expression, I am now worth 800 Pounds, but shall never be so happy, as when I was not worth a Farthing.

William Dampier, A *New Voyage round the World*

March 22, 1684.

We presently got out our Canoa, and went ashore to see for a Moskito Indian, whom we left here when we were chased hence by 3 Spanish Ships in the year 1681, a little before we went to Africa; Capt. Watlin being then our Commander, after Capt. Sharp, was turn'd out.

This Indian lived here alone above 3 years, and altho' he was several time sought after by the Spaniards, who knew he was left on the Island, yet they could never find him. He was in the Woods, hunting for Goats, when Capt. Watlin drew off his Men, and the Ship was under sail before he came back to shore. He had with him his Gun and a Knife, with a small Horn of Powder, and a few Shot; which being spent, he contrived a way by notching his Knife, to saw the Barrel of his Gun into small Pieces, wherewith he made Harpoons, Lances, Hooks and a long Knife; heating the pieces first in the fire, which he struck with his Gunflint, and a piece of the Barrel of his Gun, which he hardned; having learnt to do that among the English. The hot pieces of Iron he would hammer out and bend as he pleased with Stones, and saw them with his jagged Knife, or grind them to an Edge by long labour, and harden them to a good temper as there was occasion. All this may seem strange to those that are not acquainted with the sagacity of the Indians; but it is no more than these Moskito Men are accustomed to in their own Country, where they make their own Fishing and striking Instruments, without either Forge or Anvil; tho' they spend a great deal of time about them.

...With such Instruments as he made in that manner, he got such Provision as the Island afforded; either Goats or Fish. He told us that at first he was forced to eat Seal, which is very ordinary Meat, before he had made hooks: but afterwards he never killed any Seals but to make Lines, cutting their Skins into Thongs. He had a little House or Hut half a mile from the Sea, which was lined with Goats Skin; his Couch or Barbecu of Sticks lying along about 2 foot distant from the Ground, was spread with the same, and was all his Bedding. He had no Cloaths left, having worn out those he brought from Watlin's Ship, but only a Skin about his Waste. He saw our Ship the day before we came to an Anchor, and did believe we were English, and therefore kill'd 3 Goats in the Morning, before we came to an Anchor, and drest them with Cabbage, to treat us when we came ashore. He came then to the Sea side to congratulate our safe arrival. And when we landed, a Moskito Indian, named Robin, first leap'd ashore, and running to his Brother Moskito Man, threw himself flat on his face at his feet, who helping him up, and embracing him, fell flat with his face on the Ground at Robin's feet, and was by him taken up also. We stood with pleasure to behold the suprize and tenderness, and solemnity of this interview, which was exceedingly affectionate on both sides; and when their Ceremonies of Civility were over, we also that stood gazing at them drew near, each of us embracing him we had found here, who was overjoyed to see so many of his old Friends come hither as he thought purposely to fetch him. He was named Will, as the other was Robin. These were names given them by the English, for they have no Names among themselves; and they take it as a great favour to be named by any of us; and will complain for want of it, if we do not appoint them some name when they are with us: saying of themselves they are poor Men, and have no Name.

This Island is in lat. 34 d. 15 m. and about 120 leagues from the Main. It is about 12 leagues round, full of high Hills, and small pleasant Valleys, which if manured, would probably produce any thing proper for the Climate. The sides of the Mountains are part Savannahs, part Wood-land. Savannahs' are clear pieces of Land without Woods; not because more barren than the Wood-land, for they are frequently spots of as good Land as any, and often are intermixt with Wood-land. In the Bay of Campeachy are very large Savannahs, which I have seen full of Cattle: But about the River of Plate are the largest that ever I heard of, 50 60 or 100 Miles. in length; and Jamaica, Cuba and Hispaniola have many Savannahs intermixt with Woods. Places cleared of Wood by Art and Labour do not go by this Name, but those only which are found so in the uninhabited parts of America, such as this Isle of John Fernando's; or which were originally clear in other parts.

The Grass in these Savannahs at John Fernando's is not a long flaggy Grass, such as is usually in the Savannahs in the West-Indies, but a sort of kindly Grass, both thick and flourishing the biggest part of the year. The Woods afford divers sorts of Trees; some large and good Timber for Building, but none fit for Masts. The Cabbage Trees of this Isle are but small and low; yet afford a good head, and the Cabbage very sweet....

The Savannahs are stocked with Goats in great Herds: but those that live on the East end of the Island are not so fat as those on the West end; for though there is much more Grass, and plenty of Water in every Valley, nevertheless they thrive not so well here as on the West end, where there is less Food; and yet there are found greater Flocks, and those too fatter and sweeter.

That West end of the Island is all high Champion Ground without any Valley, and but one place to land; there is neither Wood nor any fresh Water, and the Grass short and dry.

Goats were first put on the Island by John Fernando, who first discovered it in his Voyage from Lima to Baldivia; (and discovered also another Island about the same bigness, 20 leagues to the Westward of this.) From those Goats these were propagated, and the Island hath taken its Name from this its first Discoverer; who, when he returned to Lima, desired a Patent for it, designing to settle here; and it was in his second Voyage hither that he set ashore 3 or 4 Goats, which have since, by their increase, so well stock'd the whole Island. But he could never get a Patent for it, therefore it lies still destitute of Inhabitants, tho' doubtless capable of maintaining 4 or 500 Families, by what may be produced off the Land only. I speak much within compass; for the Savannahs would at present feed 1000 Head of Cattle besides Goats, and the Land being cultivated would probably bear Corn, or Wheat, and good Pease, Yams, or Potatoes; for the Land in their Valleys and sides of the Mountains, is of a good black fruitful Mould. The Sea about it is likewise very productive of its Inhabitants. Seals swarm as thick about this Island, as if they had no other place in the World to live in; for there is not a Bay nor Rock that one can get ashoar on, but is full of them. Sea Lyons are here in great Companies, and Fish, particularly Snappers and Rockfish, are so plentiful, that two Men in an hours time will take with Hook and Line, as many as will serve 100 Men.

13

The WRECK *of the* WAGER

From *The Narrative of the Honourable John Byron*

BY JOHN BYRON

1740

It was once again the Spanish treasure galleon, making its annual run from Manila to Acapulco and back, that occasioned our next entry, John Byron's vivid tale of what happened to the Wager *and its crew on the rugged, storm-wracked coast of Patagonia when it came to grief on the rocks and was lost. The* Wager *was one of the ships in the seven-ship squadron that George Anson was leading to the Pacific, like Dampier before him, to capture the galleon and return rich beyond his wildest dreams. This was what the English did when England was at war with Spain, not an infrequent event in the 17th and 18th centuries. In 1740 it was the War of Jenkin's Ear, as it was popularly known, declared in 1739 after centuries of mutual hatred between the English and the Spanish and years of mutual resentments generated by depredations by both sides on the other's shipping in the Caribbean. The English had safe harbor in Jamaica, the Spanish had ports all over the Caribbean, and they were continually getting in each other's way. In the summer of 1739 an English merchant captain named Jenkins showed up on the floor of Parliament with his ear in a bottle. The Spanish coast guard, he said, had cut it off. Thus the name of this particular war.*

George Anson is an interesting character in his own right. He was a captain in the Royal Navy who had served in South Carolina, chasing smugglers and protecting the coast from Spanish raiders; stationed in Charleston, he liked to gamble and used his winnings to buy land. A suburb of Charleston was for a time named Ansonburg after him. He was a survivor. In the expedition he led, seven ships sailed from

England; only one returned, Anson's flagship, the Centurion. *Of the more than 1,900 men who had sailed, 188 came back. Four had died in an enemy action. The rest died primarily from scurvy. But George Anson had survived, and he brought with him treasure worth probably about a million English pounds. It took 32 wagons to carry it from the docks to the Tower of London. Anson wound up richer than he could have hoped, and an English Lord.*

John Byron was 16 years old and a midshipman on the Wager *when it was wrecked on the coast of Patagonia. He would go on to fame of his own as "Foul-Weather Jack" and lead yet another voyage around the world, this time in 1764, more or less in Anson's wake and to a similar, anti-Spanish purpose—to lay claim to the Falkland Islands and to explore the possibility of an English presence in the western Pacific. He did not write his account of the* Wager *wreck until 1768, long after the event, and it is still not clear why he waited so long. He wanted, he said, to correct the record. After the wreck, as was well known, the majority of the men mutinied and took the ship's longboat back through the Strait of Magellan and reached England before any other survivors had returned. Trying to justify their actions, two of them wrote their own account of the wreck, and that was the only account of it there was. Byron wrote, presumably, in defense of the truth.*

And his grandson, George Gordon, Lord Byron, the great Romantic poet? In the second canto of Don Juan, *the epic satiric poem that crowned his career, he drew upon his grandfather's narrative, along with other shipwreck stories, for his own parodic version of a longboat filled with shipwrecked men who eat each other to survive. The story in* Don Juan *of survivors drawing lots to see who would die and feed the others comes from the story of the* Peggy, *which is our next selection after the* Wager. *Once more shipwreck finds its way into literature.*

THE EQUIPMENT AND DESTINATION OF THE SQUADRON FITTED OUT IN the year 1740, of which Commodore Anson had the command, being sufficiently known from the ample and well-penned relation of it, under his direction, I shall recite no particulars that are to be found in that work. But it may be necessary, for better understanding the disastrous fate of the *Wager,* the subject of the following sheets, to repeat the remark, that a strange infatuation seemed to prevail in the whole conduct of this embarkation. For though it was unaccountably detained, till the season for its sailing was past, no proper use was made of that time, which should have been employed in providing a suitable force of sailors and soldiery; nor was there a due attention given to other requisites for so peculiar and extensive a destination.

This neglect not only rendered the expedition abortive in its principal object, but most materially affected the condition of each particular ship; and none so fatally as the *Wager*, who being an old Indiaman brought into the service upon this occasion, was now fitted out as a man of war, but being made to serve as a store-ship, was deeply laden with all kinds of careening geer, military, and other stores, for the use of the other ships; and, what is more, crowded with bale goods, and encumbered with merchandise. A ship of this quality and condition could not be expected to work with that readiness and ease which was necessary for her security and preservation in those heavy seas which she was to encounter. Her crew consisted of men pressed from long voyages to be sent upon a distant and hazardous service: on the other hand, all her land forces were no more than a poor detachment of infirm and decrepid invalids from Chelsea Hospital, desponding under the apprehensions of a long voyage. It is not then to be wondered that Captain Kid, under whose command this ship sailed out of the port, should, in his last moments, presage her ill success, though nothing very material happened during his command.

At his death, he was succeeded by Captain Cheap, who still, without any accident, kept company with the squadron, till we had almost gained the southernmost mouth of Straits Le Maire; when, being the sternmost ship, we were, by the sudden shifting of the wind to the southward, and the turn of the tide, very near being wrecked upon the rocks of Staten Land; which notwithstanding, having weathered, contrary to the expectation of the rest of the squadron, we endeavoured all in our power to make up our lost way, and regain our station. This we effected, and proceeded in our voyage, keeping company with the rest of the ships for some time; when, by a great roll of a hollow sea, we carried away our mizen-mast, all the chain-plates to windward being broken. Soon after, hard gales at west coming on with a prodigious swell, there broke a heavy sea in upon the ship, which stove our boats, and filled us for some time.

These accidents were the most disheartening, as our carpenter was on board the *Gloucester*, and detained there by the incessant tempestuous weather, and sea impracticable for boats. In a few days he returned, and supplied the loss of a mizen-mast by a lower studding-sail boom; but this expedient, together with the patching up of our rigging, was a poor temporary relief to us. We were soon obliged to cut away our best bower anchor to ease the foremast, the shrouds and chain-plates of which were all broken, and the ship in all parts in a most crazy condition.

Thus shattered and disabled, and a single ship (for we had now lost sight of our squadron) we had the additional mortification to find ourselves bearing for the land on a lee-shore; having thus far persevered in the course we held, from an error in conjecture: for the weather was unfavourable for observation, and there are no charts of that part of the coast. When those officers who first perceived their mistake, endeavoured to persuade the captain to alter his course, and bear away for the greater surety, to the westward, he persisted in making directly, as he thought, for the island of Socoro; and to such as dared from time to time to deliver their doubts of being entangled with the land stretching to the westward, he replied, that he thought himself in no case at liberty to deviate from his orders; and that the absence of his ship from the first place of rendezvous, would entirely frustrate the whole squadron in the first object of their attack, and possibly decide upon the fortune of the whole expedition. For the better understanding the force of his reasoning, it is necessary to explain, that the island of Socoro is in the neighbourhood of Baldivia; the capture of which place could not be effected without the junction of that ship which carried the ordnance and military stores.

The knowledge of the great importance of giving so early and unexpected a blow to the Spaniards, determined the captain to make the shortest way to the point in view; and that rigid adherence to orders from which he thought himself in no case at liberty to depart, begot in him a stubborn defiance of all difficulties, and took away from him those apprehensions, which so justly alarmed all such as, from ignorance of the orders, had nothing present to their minds but the dangers of a lee-shore.

We had for some time been sensible of our approach to the land, from no other tokens than those of weeds and birds, which are the usual indications of nearing the coast; but at length we had an imperfect view of an eminence, which we conjectured to be one of the mountains of the Cordilleras. This, however, was not so distinctly seen but that many conceived it to be the effect of imagination: but if the captain was persuaded of the nearness of our danger, it was now too late to remedy it; for at this time the straps of the fore-jeer blocks breaking, the fore-yard came down; and the greatest part of the men being disabled through fatigue and sickness, it was some time before it could be got up again. The few hands who were employed in this business now plainly saw the land on the larboard beam, bearing NW upon which the ship was driving bodily. Orders were then given immediately by the captain to sway the fore-yard up, and set the foresail; which done, we wore ship with her head to the southward, and endeavoured to crowd her off from the land; but the weather, from being exceedingly tempestuous, blowing now a perfect hurricane, and right in upon the shore, rendered our endeavours (for we were now only twelve hands fit for duty) entirely fruitless. The night came on, dreadful beyond description, in which, attempting to throw out our topsails to claw off the shore, they were immediately blown from the yards.

In the morning, about four o'clock, the ship struck. The shock we received upon this occasion, though very great, being not unlike a blow of a heavy sea, such as in the series of preceding storms we had often experienced, was taken for the same; but we were soon undeceived by her striking again more violently than before, which laid her upon her beam-ends, the sea making a fair breach over her. Every person that now could stir was presently upon the quarter-deck; and many even of those were alert upon this occasion, that had not shewed their faces upon deck for above two months before: several poor wretches, who were in the last stage of the scurvy, and who could not get out of their hammocks, were immediately drowned.

In this dreadful situation she lay for some little time, every soul on board looking upon the present minute as his last; for there was nothing to be seen but breakers all around us. However, a mountainous sea hove her off from thence; but she presently struck again, and broke her tiller. In this terrifying and critical juncture, to have observed all the various modes of horror operating according to the several characters and complexions amongst us, it was necessary that the observer himself should have been free from all impressions of danger. Instances there were, however, of behaviour so very remarkable, they could not escape the notice of any one who was not entirely bereaved of his senses; for some were in this condition to all intents and purposes; particularly one, in the ravings despair brought upon him, was seen stalking about the deck, flourishing a cutless over his head, and calling himself king of the country, and striking every body he came near, till his companions, seeing no other security against his tyranny, knocked him down. Some, reduced before, by long sickness and the scurvy, became on this occasion as it were petrified and bereaved of all sense, like inanimate logs, and were bandied to and fro by the jerks and rolls of the ship, without exerting any efforts to help themselves. So terrible was the scene of foaming breakers around us, that one of the bravest men we had could not help expressing his dismay at it, saying, it was too shocking a sight to bear! and would have thrown himself over the rails of the quarter-deck into the sea, had he not been prevented: but at the same time there were not wanting those who preserved a presence of mind truly heroic. The man at the helm, though both rudder and tiller were gone, kept his station; and being asked by one of the officers if the ship would steer or not, first took his time to make trial by the wheel, and then answered with as much respect and coolness as if the ship had been in the greatest safety; and immediately after applied himself with his usual serenity to his duty, persuaded it did not become him to desert it as long as the ship kept together. Mr Jones, mate, who now survives not only this wreck, but that of the Litchfield man-of-war upon the coast of Barbary, at the time when the ship was in the most imminent danger, not only shewed himself undaunted, but endeavoured to inspire the same resolution in the men; saying, 'My friends, let us not be discouraged: did you never see a ship amongst breakers before? Let us endeavour to push her thro' them. Come, lend a hand; here is a sheet, and here is a brace; lay hold; I don't doubt but we may stick her yet near enough to the land to save our lives.' This had so good an effect, that many who before were half dead seemed active again, and now went to work in earnest. This Mr Jones did purely to keep up the spirits of the people as long as possible; for he often said afterwards, he thought there was not the least chance of a single man's being saved. We now run in between an opening of the breakers, steering by the sheets and braces, when providentially we stuck fast between two great rocks; that to windward sheltering us in some measure from the violence of the sea. We immediately cut away the main and foremast; but the ship kept beating in such a manner, that we imagined she could hold together but a very little while. The day now broke, and the weather, that had been extremely thick, cleared away for a few moments, and gave us a glimpse of the land not far from us. We now thought of nothing but saving our lives. To get the boats out, as our masts were gone, was a work of some time; which when accomplished, many were ready to jump into the first, by which means they narrowly escaped perishing before they reached the shore. I now went to Captain Cheap (who had the misfortune to dislocate his shoulder by a fall the day before, as he was going forward to get the foreyard swayed up,) and asked him if he would not go on shore; but he told me, as he had done before, that he would be the last to leave the ship; and he ordered me to assist in getting the men out as soon as possible. I had been with him very often from the time the ship first struck, as he desired I would, to acquaint him with every thing that passed; and I particularly remarked, that he gave his orders at that time with as much coolness as ever he had done during the former part of the voyage.

The scene was now greatly changed; for many who but a few minutes before had shewn the strongest signs of despair, and were on their knees praying for mercy, imagining they were now not in that immediate danger grew very riotous, broke open every chest and box that was at hand, stove in the heads of casks of brandy and wine, as they were borne up to the hatchways, and got so drunk, that some of them were drowned on board, and lay floating about the decks for some days after. Before I left the ship, I went down to my chest, which was at the bulk-head of the ward-room, in order to save some little matters, if possible; but whilst I was there the ship thumped with such violence, and the water came in so fast, that I was forced to get upon the quarter-deck again, without saving a single rag but what was upon my back. The boatswain, and some of the people, would not leave the ship so long as there was any liquor to be got at; upon which Captain Cheap suffered himself to be helped out of his bed, put into the boat, and carried on shore.

It is natural to think that, to men thus upon the point of perishing by shipwreck, the getting to land was the highest attainment of their wishes; undoubtedly it was a desirable event; yet, all things considered, our condition was but little mended by the change. Which ever way we looked, a scene of horror presented itself; on one side, the wreck (in which was all we had in the world to support and subsist us) together with a boisterous sea, presented us with the most dreary prospect; on the other, the land did not wear a much more favourable appearance: desolate and barren, without sign of culture, we could hope to receive little other benefit from it than the preservation it afforded us from the sea. It must be confessed this was a great and merciful deliverance from immediate destruction; but then we had wet, cold, and hunger to struggle with, and no visible remedy against any of these evils. Exerting ourselves, however, though faint, benumbed, and almost helpless, to find some wretched covert against the extreme inclemency of the weather, we discovered an Indian hut, at a small distance from the beach, within a wood, in which as many as possible, without distinction, crouded themselves, the night coming on exceedingly tempestuous and rainy. But here our situation was such as to exclude all rest and refreshment by sleep from most of us; for besides that we pressed upon one another extremely, we were not without our alarms and apprehensions of being attacked by the Indians, from a discovery we made of some of their lances and other arms in our hut; and our uncertainty of their strength and disposition gave alarm to our imagination, and kept us in continual anxiety.

In this miserable hovel, one of our company, a lieutenant of invalids, died this night; and of those who for want of room took shelter under a great tree, which stood them in very little stead, two more perished by the severity of that cold and rainy night. In the morning, the calls of hunger, which had been hitherto suppressed by our attention to more immediate dangers and difficulties, were now become too importunate to be resisted. We had most of us fasted eight and forty hours, some more; it was time, therefore, to make inquiry among ourselves what store of sustenance had been brought from the wreck by the providence of some, and what could be procured on the island by the industry of others: but the produce of the one amounted to no more than two or three pounds of biscuit-dust reserved in a bag, and all the success of those who ventured abroad, the weather being still exceedingly bad, was to kill one seagull, and pick some wild sellery. These, therefore, were immediately put into a pot, with the addition of a large quantity of water, and made into a kind of soup, of which each partook as far as it would go; but we had no sooner thrown this down than we were seized with the most painful sickness at our stomachs, violent reachings, swoonings, and other symptoms of being poisoned. This was imputed to various causes, but in general to the herbs we made use of, in the nature and quality of which we fancied ourselves mistaken; but a little further inquiry let us into the real occasion of it, which was no other than this: the biscuit-dust was the sweepings of the bread-room, but the bag in which they were put had been a tobacco-bag; the contents of which not being entirely taken out, what remained mixed with the biscuit-dust, and proved a strong emetic.

We were in all about a hundred and forty who had got to shore; but some few remained still on board, detained either by drunkenness, or a view of pillaging the wreck, among which was the boatswain. These were visited by an officer in the yawl, who was to endeavour to prevail upon them to join the rest; but finding them in the greatest disorder, and disposed to mutiny, he was obliged to desist from his purpose, and return without them. Though we were very desirous, and our necessities required that we should take some survey of the land we were upon; yet being strongly prepossessed that the savages were retired but some little distance from us, and waited to see us divided, our parties did not make this day any great excursions from the hut; but as far as we went, we found it morassy and unpromising. The spot which we occupied was a bay formed by hilly promontories; that to the north so exceeding steep, that in order to ascend it (for there was no going round, the bottom being washed by the sea) we were at the labour of cutting steps. This, which we called Mount Misery, was of use to us in taking some observations afterwards, when the weather would permit: the southern promontory was not so inaccessible. Beyond this I, with some others, having reached another bay, found driven ashore some parts of the wreck, but no kind of provision: nor did we meet with any shellfish, which we were chiefly in search of. We therefore returned to the rest, and for that day made no other repast than what the wild sellery afforded us. The ensuing night proved exceedingly tempestuous; and the sea running very high, threatened those on board with immediate destruction by the parting of the wreck. They then were as solicitous to get ashore, as they were before obstinate in refusing the assistance we sent them; and when they found the boat did not come to their relief at the instant they expected it, without considering how impracticable a thing it was to send it them in such a sea, they fired one of the quarter-deck guns at the hut; the ball of which did but just pass over the covering of it, and was plainly heard by the captain and us who were within. Another attempt, therefore, was made to bring these madmen to land; which, however, by the violence of the sea, and other impediments, occasioned by the mast that lay alongside, proved ineffectual. This unavoidable delay made the people on board outrageous: they fell to beating every thing to pieces that fell in the way; and, carrying their intemperance to the greatest excess, broke open chests and cabins for plunder that could be of no use to them; and so earnest were they in this wantonness of theft, that one man had evidently been murdered on account of some division of the spoil, or for the sake of the share that fell to him, having all the marks of a strangled corpse. One thing in this outrage they seemed particularly attentive to, which was to provide themselves with arms and ammunition, in order to support them in putting their mutinous designs in execution, and asserting their claim to a lawless exemption from the authority of their officers, which they pretended must cease with the loss of the ship. But of these arms, which we stood in great need of, they were soon bereaved, upon coming ashore, by the resolution of Captain Cheap and Lieutenant Hamilton of the marines. Among these mutineers which had been left on board, as I observed before, was the boatswain; who, instead of exerting the authority he had over the rest, to keep them within bounds as much as possible, was himself a ringleader in their riot: him, without respect to the figure he then made (for he was in laced cloaths) Captain Cheap, by a blow well laid on with his cane, felled to the ground. It was scarce possible to refrain from laughter at the whimsical appearance these fellows made, who, having rifled the chests of the officers best suits, had put them on over their greasy trowsers and dirty checked shirts. They were soon stripped of their finery, as they had before been obliged to resign their arms.

The incessant rains, and exceeding cold weather in this climate, rendered it impossible for us to subsist long without shelter; and the hut being much too little to receive us all, it was necessary to fall upon some expedient, without delay, which might serve our purpose: accordingly the gunner, carpenter, and some more, turning the cutter keel upwards, and fixing it upon props, made no dispicable habitation. Having thus established some sort of settlement, we had the more leisure to look about us, and to make our researches with greater accuracy than we had before, after such supplies as the most desolate coasts are seldom unfurnished with. Accordingly we soon provided ourselves with some sea-fowl, and found limpets, mussles, and other shellfish in tolerable abundance; but this rummaging of the shore was now becoming exceedingly irksome to those who had any feeling, by the bodies of our drowned people thrown among the rocks, some of which were hideous spectacles, from the mangled condition they were in by the violent surf that drove in upon the coast. Those horrors were overcome by the distresses of our people, who were even glad of the occasion of killing the gallinazo (the carrion crow of that country) while preying on these carcases, in order to make a meal of them. But a provision by no means proportionable to the number of mouths to be fed could, by our utmost industry, be acquired from that part of the island we had hitherto traversed: therefore, till we were in a capacity of making more distant excursions, the wreck was to be applied to, as often as possible, for such supplies as could be got out of her. But as this was a very precarious fund in its present situation, and at best could not last us long; considering too that it was very uncertain how long we might be detained upon this island; the stores and provision we were so fortunate as to retrieve, were not only to be dealt out with the most frugal economy, but a sufficient quantity, if possible, laid by, to fit us out, whenever we could agree upon any method of transporting ourselves from this dreary spot. The difficulties we had to encounter in these visits to the wreck, cannot be easily described; for no part of it being above water except the quarter-deck and part of the forecastle, we were usually obliged to purchase such things as were within reach, by large hooks fastened to poles, in which business we were much incommoded by the dead bodies floating between decks.

In order to secure what we thus got in a manner to answer the ends and purposes above-mentioned, Captain Cheap ordered a store-tent to be erected near his hut, as a repository, from which nothing was to be dealt out, but in the measure and proportion agreed upon by the officers; and though it was very hard upon us petty officers, who were fatigued with hunting all day in quest of food, to defend this tent from invasion by night, no other means could be devised for this purpose so effectual as the committing this charge to our care; and we were accordingly ordered to divide the task equally between us. Yet, notwithstanding our utmost vigilance and care, frequent robberies were committed upon our trust, the tent being accessible in more than one place. And one night, when I had the watch, hearing a stir within, I came unawares upon the thief, and presenting a pistol to his breast, obliged him to submit to be tied up to a post, till I had an opportunity of securing him more effectually. Depredations continued to be made on our reserved stock, notwithstanding the great hazard attending such attempts; for our common safety made it necessary to punish them with the utmost rigour. This will not be wondered at, when it is known how little the allowance which might consistently be dispensed from thence, was proportionable to our common exigencies; so that our daily and nightly task of roving after food, was not in the least relaxed thereby; and all put together was so far from answering our necessities, that many at this time perished with hunger. A boy, when no other eatables could be found, having picked up the liver of one of the drowned men (whose carcass had been torn to pieces by the force with which the sea drove it among the rocks) was with much difficulty withheld from making a meal of it. The men were so assiduous in their research after the few things which drove from the wreck, that in order to have no sharers of their good fortune, they examined the shore no less by night than by day; so that many of those who were less alert, or not so fortunate as their neighbours, perished with hunger, or were driven to the last extremity. It must be observed that on the 14th of May we were cast away, and it was not till the 25th of this month, that provision was served regularly from the store tent.

The land we were now settled upon was about 90 leagues to the northward of the western mouth of the Streights of Magellan, in the latitude of between 47 and 48° south, from whence we could plainly see the Cordilleras; and by two lagoons on the north and south of us, stretching towards those mountains, we conjectured it was an island. But as yet we had no means of informing ourselves perfectly, whether it was an island or the main; for besides that the inland parts at little distance from us seemed impracticable, from the exceeding great thickness of the wood, we had hitherto been in such confusion and want (each finding full employment for his time, in scraping together a wretched subsistence, and providing shelter against the cold and rain) that no party could be formed to go upon discoveries. The climate and season too were utterly unfavourable to adventures, and the coast, as far as our eye could stretch seaward, a scene of such dismal breakers as would discourage the most daring from making attempts in small boats. Nor were we assisted in our inquiries by any observation that could be made from that eminence we called Mount Misery, toward land, our prospect that way being intercepted by still higher hills and lofty woods: we had therefore no other expedient, by means of which to come at this knowledge, but by fitting out one of our ship's boats upon some discovery, to inform us of our situation. Our long-boat was still on board the wreck; therefore a number of hands were now dispatched to cut the gunwale of the ship, in order to get her out. Whilst we were employed in this business, there appeared three canoes of Indians paddling towards us: they had come round the point from the southern lagoons. It was some time before we could prevail upon them to lay aside their fears and approach us; which at length they were induced to do by the signs of friendship we made them, and by shewing some bale-goods, which they accepted, and suffered themselves to be conducted to the captain, who made them, likewise, some presents. They were strangely affected with the novelty thereof; but chiefly when shewn the looking-glass, in which the beholder could not conceive it to be his own face that was represented, but that of some other behind it, which he therefore went round to the back of the glass to find out.

These people were of a small stature, very swarthy, having long, black, course hair, hanging over their faces. It was evident, from their great surprise, and every part of their behaviour, as well as their not having one thing in their possession which could be derived from white people, that they had never seen such. Their cloathing was nothing but a bit of some beast's skin about their waists, and something woven from feathers over the shoulders; and as they uttered no word of any language we had ever heard, nor had any method of making themselves understood, we presumed they could have no intercourse with Europeans. These savages, who, upon their departure, left us a few mussles, returned in two days, and surprised us by bringing three sheep. From whence they could procure these animals in a part of the world so distant from any Spanish settlement, cut off from all communication with the Spaniards by an inaccessible coast and unprofitable country, is difficult to conceive. Certain it is, that we saw no such creatures, nor ever heard of any such, from the Streights of Magellan, till we got into the neighbourhood of Chiloe: it must be by some strange accident that these creatures came into their possession; but what that was we never could learn from them. At this interview we bartered with them for a dog or two, which we roasted and eat. In a few days after, they made us another visit, and, bringing their wives with them, took up their abode with us for some days; then again left us.

Whenever the weather permitted, which was now grown something drier, but exceeding cold, we employed ourselves about the wreck, from which we had, at sundry times, recovered several articles of provision and liquor: these were deposited in the store tent. Ill-humour and discontent, from the difficulties we laboured under in procuring subsistence, and the little prospect there was of any amendment in our condition, was now breaking out apace. In some it shewed itself by a separation of settlement and habitation; in others, by a resolution of leaving the captain entirely, and making a wild journey by themselves, without determining upon any plan whatever. For my own part, seeing it was the fashion, and liking none of their parties, I built a little hut just big enough for myself and a poor Indian dog I found in the woods, who could shift for himself along shore, at low water, by getting limpets. This creature grew so fond of me and faithful, that he would suffer nobody to come near the hut without biting them. Besides those seceders I mentioned, some laid a scheme of deserting us entirely: these were in number ten; the greatest part of them a most desperate and abandoned crew, who, to strike a notable stroke before they went off, placed half a barrel of gunpowder close to the captain's hut, laid a train to it, and were just preparing to perpetrate their wicked design of blowing up their commander, when they were with difficulty dissuaded from it by one who had some bowels and remorse of conscience left in him. These wretches, after rambling some time in the woods, and finding it impracticable to get off, for they were then convinced that we were not upon the main, as they had imagined when they first left us, but upon an island within four or five leagues of it, returned and settled about a league from us; however, they were still determined, as soon as they could procure craft fit for their purpose, to get to the main. But before they could effect this, we found means to prevail upon the armourer, and one of the carpenter's crew, two very useful men to us, who had imprudently joined them, to come over again to their duty. The rest (one or two excepted) having built a punt, and converted the hull of one of the ship's masts into a canoe, went away up one of the lagoons, and never were heard of more.

These being a desperate and factious set, did not distress us much by their departure, but rather added to our future security: one in particular, James Mitchell by name, we had all the reason in the world to think, had committed no less than two murders since the loss of our ship; one on the person found strangled on board, another on the body of a man whom we discovered among some bushes upon Mount Misery, stabbed in several places, and shockingly mangled. This diminution of our number was succeeded by an unfavourable accident much more affecting in its consequences, I mean the death of Mr Cozens, midshipman; in relating which, with the necessary impartiality and exactness, I think myself obliged to be more than ordinary particular. Having one day, among other things, got a cask of pease out of the wreck, about which I was almost constantly employed, I brought it to shore in the yawl, when, having landed it, the captain came down upon the beach, and bid me to go up to some of the tents, and order hands to come down and roll it up; but finding none except Mr Cozens, I delivered him the orders, who immediately came down to the captain, where I left them when I returned to the wreck. Upon my coming on shore again, I found that Mr Cozens was put under confinement by the captain, for being drunk and giving him abusive language; however, he was soon after released. A day or two after, he had some dispute with the surgeon, and came to blows: all these things incensed the captain greatly against him. I believe this unfortunate man was kept warm with liquor, and set on by some ill-designed persons; for, when sober, I never knew a better natured man, or more inoffensive. Some little time after, at the hour of serving provisions, Mr Cozens was at the store-tent; and having, it seems, lately had a quarrel with the purser, and now some words arising between them, the latter told him he was come to mutiny; and without any further ceremony, fired a pistol at his head, which narrowly missed him. The captain, hearing the report of the pistol, and perhaps the purser's words, that Cozens was come to mutiny, ran out of his hut with a cocked pistol, and, without asking any questions, immediately shot him through the head. I was at this time in my hut, as the weather was extremely bad; but running out upon the alarm of this firing, the first thing I saw was Mr Cozens on the ground weltering in his blood: he was sensible, and took me by the hand, as he did several others, shaking his head, as if he meant to take leave of us. If Mr Cozens' behaviour to the captain was indecent and provoking, the captain's, on the other hand, was rash and hasty: if the first was wanting in that respect and observance which is due from a petty officer to his commander, the latter was still more unadvised in the method he took for the enforcement of his authority; of which, indeed, he was jealous to the last degree, and which he saw daily declining, and ready to be trampled upon. His mistaken apprehension of a mutinous design in Mr Cozens, the sole motive of his rash action, was so far from answering the end he proposed by it, that the men, who before were much dissatisfied and uneasy, were by this unfortunate step, thrown almost into open sedition and revolt. It was evident that the people, who ran out of their tents, alarmed by the report of fire-arms, though they disguised their real sentiments for the present, were extremely affected with this catastrophe of Mr Cozens (for he was greatly beloved by them) their minds were now exasperated, and it was to be apprehended, that their resentment, which was smothered for the present, would shortly shew itself in some desperate enterprise. The unhappy victim, who lay weltering in his blood before them, seemed to absorb their whole attention; the eyes of all were fixed upon him; and visible marks of the deepest concern appeared in the countenances of the spectators. The persuasion the captain was under, at the time he shot Mr Cozens, that his intentions were mutinous, together with a jealousy of the diminution of this authority, occasioned also his behaving with less compassion and tenderness towards him afterwards, than was consistent with the unhappy condition of the poor sufferer: for when it was begged as a favour by his mess-mates, that Mr Cozens might be removed to their tent, though a necessary thing in his dangerous situation, yet it was not permitted; but the poor wretch was suffered to languish on the ground some days, with no other covering than a bit of canvass, thrown over some bushes, where he died. But to return to our story: the captain, addressing himself to the people thus assembled, told them, that it was his resolution to maintain his command over them as usual, which still remained in as much force as ever; and then ordered them all to return to their respective tents, with which order they instantly complied. Now we had saved the long-boat from the wreck, and got it in our possession, there was nothing that seemed so necessary towards the advancing our delivery from this desolate place, as the new modelling this vessel so as to have room for all those who were inclined to go off in her, and to put her in a condition to bear the stormy seas we must of course encounter. We, therefore, halled her up, and having placed her upon blocks, sawed her in two, in order to lengthen her about twelve feet by the keel. For this purpose, all those who could be spared from the more immediate task of procuring subsistence, were employed in fitting and shaping timber as the carpenter directed them; I say, in procuring subsistence, because the weather lately having been very tempestuous, and the wreck working much, had disgorged a great part of her contents, which were every where dispersed about the shore.

We now sent frequent parties up the lagoons, which sometimes succeeded in getting some sea-fowl for us. The Indians appearing again in the offing, we put off our yawl, in order to frustrate any design they might have of going up the lagoon towards the deserters, who would have availed themselves of some of their canoes to have got upon the main. Having conducted them in, we found that their intention was to settle among us, for they had brought their wives and children with them, in all about fifty persons, who immediately set about building themselves wigwams, and seemed much reconciled to our company; and, could we have entertained them as we ought, they would have been of great assistance to us, who were extremely put to it to subsist ourselves, being a hundred in number; but the men, now subject to little or no controul, endeavoured to seduce their wives, which gave the Indians such offence, that in a short time they found means to depart, taking every thing along with them; and we being sensible of the cause, never expected to see them return again. The carpenter having made some progress in his work upon the long-boat, in which he was enabled to proceed tolerably, by the tools and other articles of his business retrieved from the wreck, the men began to think of the course they should take to get home; or rather, having borrowed Sir John Narborough's *Voyage* of Captain Cheap, by the application of Mr Bulkeley, which book he saw me reading one day in my tent, they immediately upon perusing it, concluded upon making their voyage home by the Streights of Magellan. This plan was proposed to the captain, who by no means approved of it, his design being to go northwards, with a view of seizing a ship of the enemy's, by which means he might join the commodore: at present, therefore, here it rested. But the men were in high spirits from the prospect they had of getting off in the long-boat, overlooking all the difficulties and hazards of a voyage almost impracticable, and caressing the carpenter, who indeed was an excellent workman, and deserved all the encouragement they could give him. The Indians having left us, and the weather continuing tempestuous and rainy, the distresses of the people for want of food, became insupportable. Our number, which was at first 145, was now reduced to 100, and chiefly by famine, which put the rest upon all shifts and devices to support themselves. One day when I was at home in my hut with my Indian dog, a party came to my door, and told me their necessities were such, that they must eat the creature or starve. Though their plea was urgent, I could not help using some arguments to endeavour to dissuade them from killing him, as his faithful services and fondness deserved it at my hands; but, without weighing any arguments, they took him away by force and killed him; upon which, thinking that I had at least as good a right to share as the rest, I sat down with them, and partook of their repast. Three weeks after that

I was glad to make a meal of his paws and skin, which, upon recollecting the spot where they had killed him, I found thrown aside and rotten. The pressing calls of hunger drove our men to their wits end, and put them upon a variety of devices to satisfy it. Among the ingenious this way, one Phips, a boatswain's mate, having got a water puncheon, scuttled it; then lashing two logs, one on each side, set out in quest of adventures in this extraordinary and original piece of imbarkation. By this means, he would frequently, when all the rest were starving, provide himself with wild-fowl; and it must have been very bad weather indeed which could deter him from putting out to sea when his occasions required. Sometimes he would venture far out in the offing, and be absent the whole day: at last it was his misfortune, at a great distance from shore, to be overset by a heavy sea: but being near a rock, tho' no swimmer, he managed so as to scramble to it, and, with great difficulty, ascended it: there he remained two days with very little hopes of any relief, for he was too far off to be seen from shore; but fortunately a boat, having put off and gone in quest of wild-fowl that way, discovered him making such signals as he was able, and brought him back to the island. But this accident did not so discourage him, but that soon after, having procured an ox's hide, used on board for sifting powder, and called a gunner's hide, by the assistance of some hoops he form'd something like a canoe, in which he made several successful voyages. When the weather would permit us, we seldom failed of getting some wild-fowl, though never in any plenty, by putting off with our boats; but this most inhospitable climate is not only deprived of the sun for the most part, by a thick, rainy atmosphere, but is also visited by almost incessant tempests. It must be confessed, we reaped some benefit from these hard gales and overgrown seas, which drove several things ashore; but there was no dependence on such accidental relief; and we were always alert to avail ourselves of every interval of fair weather, though so little to be depended on, that we were often unexpectedly, and to our peril, overtaken by a sudden change. In one of our excursions I, with two more, in a wretched punt of our own making, had no sooner landed at our station upon a high rock, than the punt was driven loose by a sudden squall; and had not one of the men, at the risk of his life, jumped into the sea, and swam on board her, we must in all probability have perished; for we were more than three leagues from the island at the time. Among the birds we generally shot, was the painted goose, whose plumage is variegated with the most lively colours; and a bird much larger than a goose, which we called the race-horse, from the velocity with which it moved upon the face of the water, in a sort of half flying, half running motion. But we were not so successful in our endeavours by land; for though we sometimes got pretty far into the woods, we met with very few birds in all our walks. We never saw but three woodcocks, two of which were killed by Mr Hamilton, and one by myself. These, with some humming birds, and a large kind of robin redbreast, were the only feathered inhabitants of this island, excepting a small bird, with two very long feathers in his tail, which was generally seen amongst the rocks, and was so tame that I have had them rest upon my shoulders whilst I have been gathering shellfish. Indeed, we were visited by many birds of prey, some very large; but these only occasionally, and, as we imagined, allured by some dead whale in the neighbourhood, which was once seen. However, if we were so fortunate as to kill one of them, we thought ourselves very well off. In one of my walks, seeing a bird of this latter kind upon an eminence, I endeavoured to come upon it unperceived with my gun, by means of the woods which lay at the back of that eminence; but when I had proceeded so far in the wood as to think I was in a line with it, I heard a growling close by me, which made me think it advisable to retire as soon as possible: the woods were so gloomy I could see nothing; but as I retired, the noise followed me close till I had got out of them. Some of our men did assure me, that they had seen a very large beast in the woods; but their description of it was too imperfect to be relied upon. The wood here is chiefly of the aromatic kind; the iron wood, a wood of a very deep red hue, and another of an exceeding bright yellow. All the low spots are very swampy; but what we thought strange, upon the summits of the highest hills were found beds of shells, a foot or two thick.

The long-boat being near finished, some of our company were selected to go out in the barge, in order to reconnoitre the coast to the southward, which might assist us in the navigation we were going upon. This party consisted of Mr Bulkely, Mr Jones, the purser, myself, and ten men. The first night we put into a good harbour, a few leagues to the southward of Wager's Island; where finding a large bitch big with puppies, we regaled upon them. In this expedition we had our usual bad weather, and breaking seas, which were grown to such a height the third day, that we were obliged, through distress, to push in at the first inlet we saw at hand. This we had no sooner entered, than we were presented with a view of a fine bay, in which, having secured the barge, we went ashore; but the weather being very rainy, and finding nothing to subsist upon, we pitched a bell tent, which we had brought with us, in the wood opposite to where the barge lay. As this tent was not large enough to contain us all, I proposed to four of the people, to go to the end of the bay, about two miles distant from the bell tent, to occupy the skeleton of an old Indian wigwam, which I had discovered in a walk that way upon our first landing. This we covered to windward with seaweed; and, lighting a fire, laid ourselves down, in hopes of finding a remedy for our hunger in sleep; but we had not long composed ourselves before one of our company was disturbed by the blowing of some animal at his face, and, upon opening his eyes, was not a little astonished to see, by the glimmering of the fire, a large beast standing over him. He had presence of mind enough to snatch a brand from the fire, which was now very low, and thrust it at the nose of the animal, who thereupon made off: this done, the man awoke us, and related, with horror in his countenance, the narrow escape he had of being devoured. But though we were under no small apprehensions of another visit from this animal, yet our fatigue and heaviness was greater than our fears; and we once more composed ourselves to rest, and slept the remainder of the night without any further disturbance. In the morning, we were not a little anxious to know how our companions had fared; and this anxiety was increased, upon tracing the footsteps of the beast in the sand, in a direction towards the bell tent. The impression was deep and plain, of a large round foot well furnished with claws. Upon our acquainting the people in the tent with the circumstances of our story, we found that they too, had been visited by the same unwelcome guest, which they had driven away by much the same expedient. We now returned from this cruise, with a strong gale, to Wager's Island, having found it impracticable to make farther discoveries in the barge, on so dangerous a coast, and in such heavy seas. Here we soon discovered, by the quarters of dogs hanging up, that the Indians had brought a fresh supply to our market. Upon inquiry, we found that there had been six canoes of them, who, among other methods of taking fish, had taught their dogs to drive the fish into a corner of some pond, or lake, from whence they were easily taken out, by the skill and address of these savages. The old cabal, during our absence, had been frequently revived; the debates of which generally ended in riot and drunkenness. This cabal was chiefly held in a large tent, which the people belonging to it had taken some pains to make snug and convenient, and lined with bales of broad cloth driven from the wreck. Eighteen of the stoutest fellows of the ship's company had possession of this tent, from whence were dispatched committees to the captain, with the resolutions they had taken with regard to their departure; but oftener for liquor. Their determination was to go in the long-boat to the southward by the Streights of Magellan; and the point they were labouring, was to prevail upon the captain to accompany them. But though he had fixed upon a quite different plan, which was to go to the northward, yet he thought it politic, at present seemingly to acquiesce with them, in order to keep them quiet. When they began to stipulate with him, that he should be under some restrictions in point of command, and should do nothing without consulting his officers, he insisted upon the full exercise of his authority, as before. This broke all measures between them, and they were from this time determined he should go with them, whether he would or no. A better pretence they could not have for effecting this design, than the unfortunate affair of Mr Cozens; which they therefore made use of for seizing his person, and putting him under confinement, in order to bring him to his trial in England. The long-boat was now launched, and ready for sailing, and all the men imbarked, except Captain Pemberton, with a party of marines, who drew them up upon the beach with intent to conduct Captain Cheap on board; but he was at length persuaded to desist from this resolution by Mr Bulkely. The men too, finding they were straitened for room, and that their stock of provision would not admit of taking supernumeraries aboard, were now no less strenuous for his enlargement, and being left to his option of staying behind. Therefore, after having distributed their share in the reserved stock of provision, which was very small, we departed, leaving Captain Cheap, Mr Hamilton of the marines, and the surgeon upon the island. I had all along been in the dark as to the turn this matter would take; and not in the least suspecting but that it was determined Captain Cheap should be taken with us, readily imbarked under that persuasion; but when I found that this design, which was so seriously carried on to the last, was suddenly dropped, I was determined, upon the first opportunity, to leave them, which was at that instant impossible for me to do, the long-boat lying some distance off shore, at anchor. We were in all eighty-one, when we left the island, distributed into the long-boat, cutter, and barge; fifty-nine on board the first; twelve in the second; in the last, ten. It was our purpose to put into some harbour, if possible, every evening, as we were in no condition to keep those terrible seas long; for without other assistance our stock of provisions was no more than might have been consumed in a few days; our water was chiefly contained in a few powder-barrels; our flour was to be lengthened out by a mixture of seaweed; and our other supplies depended upon the success of our guns, and industry among the rocks. Captain Pemberton having brought on board his men, we weighed; but by a sudden squall of wind having split our foresail, we with difficulty cleared the rocks, by means of our boats, bore away for a sandy bay, on the south side of the lagoon, and anchored in ten fathom. The next morning we got under weigh; but it blowing hard at W by N with a great swell, put into a small bay again, well sheltered by a ledge of rocks without us. At this time, it was thought necessary to send the barge away back to Cheap's Bay, for some spare canvas, which was imagined would be soon wanted. I thought this a good opportunity of returning, and therefore made one with those who went upon the business in the barge. We were no sooner clear of the long-boat, than all those in the barge with me declared they had the same intention. When we arrived at the island, we were extremely welcome to Captain Cheap. The next day, I asked him leave to try if I could prevail upon those in the long-boat to give us our share of provision: this he granted; but said, if we went in the barge, they would certainly take her from us. I told him my design was to walk it, and only desired the barge might land me upon the main, and wait for me till I came back. I had the most dreadful journey of it imaginable, through thick woods and swamps all the way; but I might as well have spared myself that trouble, as it was to no manner of purpose; for they would not give me, nor any one of us that left them, a single ounce of provisions of any kind. I therefore returned, and after that made a second attempt; but all in vain. They even threatened, if we did not return with the barge, they would fetch her by force. It was impossible to conceive the distressed situation we were now in, at the time of the long-boat's departure. I don't mention this event as the occasion of it; by which, if we who were left on the island experienced any alteration at all, it was for the better; and which, in all probability, had it been deferred, might have been fatal to the greatest part of us; but, at this time, the subsistence on which we had hitherto depended chiefly, which was the shellfish, were every where, along shore, eat up; and as to stock saved from the wreck, it may be guessed what the amount of that might be, when the share allotted to the captain, Lieutenant Hamilton, and the surgeon, was no more than six pieces of beef, as many of pork, and ninety pounds of flour. As to myself, and those that left the long-boat, it was the least revenge they thought they could take of us to withhold our provision from us, though, at the same time, it was hard and unjust. For a day or two after our return, there was some little pittance dealt out to us, yet it was upon the foot of favour; and we were soon left to our usual industry for a farther supply. This was now exerted to very little purpose, for the reason before assigned: to which may be added, the wreck was now blown up, all her upper works gone, and no hopes of any valuable driftage from her for the future. A weed, called slaugh, fried in the tallow of some candles we have saved, and wild sellery, were our only fare; by which our strength was so much impaired, that we could scarcely crawl. It was my misfortune too to labour under a severe flux, by which I was reduced to a very feeble state; so that in attempting to traverse the rocks in search of shellfish, I fell from one into very deep water, and with difficulty saved my life by swimming. As the captain was now freed, by the departure of the long boat, from the riotous applications, menaces, and disturbance of an unruly crew, and left at liberty to follow the plan he had resolved upon, of going northward, he began to think seriously of putting it in execution; in order to which, a message was sent to the deserters, who had seated themselves on the other side of the neighbouring lagoon, to sound them, whether they were inclined to join the captain in his undertaking; and if they were, to bring them over to him. For this sett, the party gone off in the long-boat, had left an half allowance proportion of the common stock of provision. These men, under the proposal, readily agreed to join their commander; and being conducted to him, increased our number to twenty. The boats which remained in our possession to carry off all these people were only the barge and yawl, two very creazy bottoms; the broadside of the last was entirely out, and the first had suffered much in a variety of bad weather she had gone through, and was much out of repair. And now as our carpenter was gone from us, we had no remedy for these misfortunes, but the little skill we had gained from him. However, we made tolerable shifts to patch up the boats for our purpose. In the height of our distresses, when hunger, which seems to include and absorb all others, was most prevailing, we were cheared with the appearance, once more, of our friendly Indians, as we thought, from whom we hoped for some relief; but as the consideration was wanting, for which alone they would part with their commodities, we were not at all benefited by their stay, which was very short. The little reserve too of flour made by the captain for our sea-stock when we should leave the island, was now diminished by theft: the thieves, who were three of our men, were however soon discovered, and two of them apprehended; but the third made his escape to the woods. Considering the pressing state of our necessities, this theft was looked upon as a most heinous crime, and therefore required an extraordinary punishment: accordingly the captain ordered these delinquents to be severely whipped, and then to be banished to an island at some distance from us; but before this latter part of the sentence could be put in execution, one of them fled; but the other was put alone upon a barren island, which afforded not the least shelter; however, we, in compassion, and contrary to order, patched him up a bit of a hut, and kindled him a fire, and then left the poor wretch to shift for himself. In two or three days after, going to the island in our boat with some little refreshment, such as our miserable circumstances would admit of, and with an intent of bringing him back, we found him dead and stiff. I was now reduced to the lowest condition by my illness, which was increased by the vile stuff I eat. When we were favoured by a fair day, a thing very extraordinary in this climate, we instantly took the advantage of it, and once more visited the last remains of the wreck, her bottom. Here our pains were repaid with great good fortune of hooking up three casks of beef, which were brought safe to shore. This providential supply could not have happened at a more seasonable time than now, when we were afflicted with the greatest dearth we had ever experienced, and the little strength we had remaining was to be exerted in our endeavours to leave the island. Accordingly we soon found a remedy for our sickness, which was nothing but the effects of famine, and were greatly restored by food. The provision was equally distributed among us all, and served us for the remainder of our stay here.

14

The ORDEAL *of the* PEGGY

From *An Extraordinary Famine in the American Ship* Peggy

1765

Keith Huntress prints this brief account, taken from the much longer story written by the captain of the Peggy, *David Harrison, that was published in London in 1766. This summary comes from an anthology published in 1833. Its interest lies not only in the key element in the story, the drawing of lots, but also in the fact that Byron used the story in* Don Juan *and Edgar Allan Poe used it in his shipwreck novel,* The Narrative of Arthur Gordon Pym. *It's amazing how much resonance some of these stories have. The difference between life and death lies in a roll of the dice. It's a compelling reminder of just how chancy life is.*

FAMINE FREQUENTLY LEADS MEN TO THE COMMISSION OF THE MOST horrible excesses: insensible, on such occasions, to the appeals of nature and reason, man assumes the character of a beast of prey; he is deaf to every representation, and coolly mediates the death of his fellow-creature.

One of these scenes, so afflicting to humanity, was, in the year 1765, exhibited in the brigantine the *Peggy*, David Harrison, commander, freighted by certain merchants of New York, and bound to the Azores. She arrived without accident at Fayal, one of those islands, and having disposed of her cargo, took on board a lading of wine and spirits. On the 24th of October, of the same year, she set sail on her return to New York.

On the 29th, the wind, which had till then been favorable, suddenly shifted. Violent storms, which succeeded each other, almost without interruption, during the month of November, did much damage to the vessel. In spite of all the exertions of the crew, and the experience of the captain, the masts went by the board, and all the sails, excepting one, were torn to rags: and, to add to their distress, several leaks were discovered in the hold.

At the beginning of December, the wind abated a little, but the vessel was driven out of her course; and, destitute of masts, sails, and rigging, she was perfectly unmanageable, and drifted to and fro, at the mercy of the waves. This, however, was the smallest evil; another of a much more alarming nature soon manifested itself. Upon examining the state of the provisions, they were found to be almost totally exhausted. In this deplorable situation, the crew had no hope of relief, but from chance.

A few days after this unpleasant discovery, two vessels were descried early one morning, and a transient ray of hope cheered the unfortunate crew of the *Peggy*. The sea ran so high as to prevent captain Harrison from approaching the ships, which were soon out of sight. The disappointed seamen, who were in want of every thing, then fell upon the wine and brandy, with which the ship was laden. They allotted to the captain two small jars of water, each containing about a gallon, being the remainder of their stock. Some days elapsed, during which the men, in some measure, appeased the painful cravings of hunger, by incessant intoxication.

On the fourth day, a ship was observed bearing towards them, in full sail: no time was lost in making signals of distress, and the crew had the inexpressible satisfaction to perceive that they were answered. The sea was sufficiently calm to permit the two vessels to approach each other. The strangers seemed much affected by the account of their sufferings and misfortunes, and promised them a certain quantity of biscuit; but it was not immediately sent on board, the captain alleging, as an excuse for the delay, that he had just begun a nautical observation, which he was desirous to finish. However unreasonable such a pretext appeared, under the present circumstances, the famished crew of the Peggy was obliged to submit. The time mentioned by the captain had nearly expired, when, to their extreme mortification, the latter regardless of his promise, crowded all his sails and bore away. No language is adequate to describe the despair and consternation which then overwhelmed the crew. Enraged, and destitute of hope they fell upon whatever they had spared till then. The only animals that remained on board were a couple of pigeons and a cat, which were devoured in an instant. The only favor they showed the captain was, to reserve for him the head of the cat.

He afterwards declared, that however disgusting it would have been on any other occasion, he thought it, at that moment, a treat exquisitely delicious. The unfortunate men then supported their existence by living on oil, candles, and leather, and these were entirely consumed by the 28th of December.

From that day until the 13th of January, it is impossible to tell, in what manner they subsisted. Captain Harrison had been for some time unable to leave his cabin, being confined to his bed by a severe fit of the gout. On the last mentioned day, the sailors went to him in a body, with the mate at their head; the latter acted as spokesman, and after an affecting representation of the deplorable state to which they were reduced, declared that it was necessary to sacrifice one, in order to save the rest; adding, that their resolution was irrevocably fixed, and that they intended to cast lots for the victim.

The captain, a tender and humane man, could not hear such a proposition without shuddering; he represented to them that they were men, and ought to regard each other as brethren; that by such an assassination, they would forever consign themselves to universal execration, and commanded them, with all his authority, to relinquish the idea of committing such an atrocious crime. The captain was silent; but he had spoken to deaf men. They all with one voice replied, that it was indifferent to them, whether he approved of their resolution or not; that they had only acquainted him with it, out of respect, and because he would run the same risk as themselves; adding that, in the general misfortune, all command and distinction were at an end. With these words, they left him, and went upon deck, where the lots were drawn.

A negro, who was on board and belonged to Captain Harrison, was the victim. It is more than probable, that the lot had been consulted only for the sake of form, and that the wretched black was proscribed, the moment the sailors first formed their resolution. They instantly sacrified him. One of the crew tore out his liver and devoured it, without having the patience to dress it by broiling, or in any other manner. He was soon afterwards taken ill, and died the following day in convulsions, and with all the symptoms of madness. Some of his comrades proposed to keep his body to live upon, after the negro was consumed; but this advice was rejected by the majority, doubtless on account of the malady which had carried him off. He was, therefore, thrown overboard, and consigned to the deep.

The captain, in the intervals, when he was least tormented by the gout, was not more exempt from the attacks of hunger, than the rest of the crew, but he resisted all the persuasions of his men to partake of their horrid repast. He contented himself with the water which had been assigned to him, mixing it with a small quantity of spirits, and this was the only sustenance he took during the whole period of his distress.

The body of the negro, equally divided, and eaten with the greatest economy, lasted till the 26th of January. On the 29th the famished crew deliberated upon selecting a second victim. They again came to inform the captain of their intention, and he appeared to give his consent, fearing lest the enraged sailors might have recourse to the lot without him. They left it with him to fix upon any method that he should think proper. The captain, summoning all his strength, wrote upon small pieces of paper, the name of each man who was then on board the brigantine, folded them up, put them into a hat, and shook them well together. The crew, meanwhile, preserved an awful silence; each eye was fixed, and each mouth was open, while terror was strongly impressed upon every countenance. With a trembling hand, one of them drew, from the hat, the fatal billet, which he delivered to the captain, who opened it and read aloud the name of DAVID FLATT. The unfortunate man, on whom the lot had fallen, appeared perfectly resigned to his fate:—"My friends, (said he to his companions,) the only favor I request of you, is, not to keep me long in pain; dispatch me as speedily as you did the negro." Then turning to the man who had performed the first execution, he added:—"It is you, I choose to give me the mortal blow." He requested an hour to prepare himself for death, to which his comrades could only reply with tears. Meanwhile, compassion, and the remonstrances of the captain, prevailed over the hunger of the most hard-hearted. They unanimously resolved to defer the sacrifice till eleven o'clock the following morning. Such a short reprieve afforded very little consolation to FLATT. The certainty of dying the next day made such a deep impression upon the mind, that his body, which, for above a month, had withstood the almost total privation of nourishment, sank beneath it. He was seized with a violent fever, and his state was so much aggravated by a delirium, with which it was accompanied, that some of the sailors proposed to kill him immediately, in order to terminate his sufferings. The majority, however, adhered to the resolution which had been taken, of waiting till the following morning.

At ten o'clock in the morning of the 30th of January, a large fire was already made to dress the limbs of the unfortunate victim, when a sail was descried, at a distance. A favorable wind drove her towards the *Peggy*, and she proved to be the *Susan*, returning from Virginia, and bound to London.

The captain could not refrain from tears at the affecting account of the sufferings endured by the famished crew. He lost no time in affording them relief, supplying them immediately with provisions and rigging, and offered to convoy the *Peggy* to London. The distance from New York, their proximity to the English coast, together with the miserable state of the brigantine, induced the two captains to proceed to England. The voyage was prosperous; only two men died; all the others gradually recovered their strength. Flatt himself was restored to perfect health, after having been so near the gates of death.

15

The LOSS *of the* HALSEWELL

From *The Loss of the Halsewell East Indiaman*

1786

The English Channel was an especially dangerous area for ships. Subject to frequent storms and powerful currents, it was not at all uncommon for ships to come to grief within sight of England or even on its shores. The Halsewell *was one such, an East Indiaman on its way to the Far East that died on the rocks near Portsmouth in a winter gale. Huntress prints this story, too, out of the same collection of 1835 from which he reprinted a number of other stories. It is in fact a canonical story, much beloved of editors like myself. It is based on the original account, published in London in 1786, written by two surviving officers of the ship.*

It is worth noting that it was not always the case that people on shore helped shipwreck victims, as they do here. In England there had been laws against plundering shipwrecks as early as Edward I, a sure sign that the practice was common. In 1713 a new law made it clear that no ship wrecked on the shore in which there were survivors could be considered as a wreck. This act, writes English historian John Rule, "was ordered to be read four times a year in all the churches and chapels on the sea coast." The new law was no more effective, apparently, than the old law had been. People living along the coast seem to have regarded it as their right to plunder a wreck. Or worse. In 1774 the only survivors of the Charming Jenny, *its captain and his wife, washed up on the coast of Anglesey: "Nearly exhausted," according to one contemporary account, "they lay for some time, till the savages of the adjacent places rushed down upon the devoted victims. The lady was just able to lift a handkerchief up to her head, when her husband was torn from her side. They cut his buckles from his shoes, and deprived him of every covering. Happy to escape with his life, he hastened to the beach in search of his wife, when horrible to tell! her half-naked, and plundered corpse presented itself to his view." She had cash on her person; it was, of course, gone.*

Nineteen years after the wreck of the Halsewell, *another East Indiaman, the* Earl of Abergavenny, *came ashore in almost the same place, this time caught in the strong incoming tide when the wind died. Again people were saved, 150 out of about 400, but not the captain. He was John Wordsworth, brother to William, and he drowned. The two men were close; it was in fact one of John Wordsworth's ambitions to make enough money to be able to subsidize his brother's poetry. One or two critics have advanced the theory, says Huntress, that Wordsworth's sorrow over his brother's death was partly responsible for the great falling off in quality of Wordsworth's poetry after this event.*

THE HALSEWELL EAST INDIAMAN, OF SEVEN HUNDRED AND FIFTY-EIGHT tons burthen, Richard Pierce, Esq. commander, having been taken up the Directors to make her third voyage to coast and bay, fell down to Gravesend the 16th of November, 1785, and there completed her lading. Having taken the ladies and other passengers on board at the Hope, she sailed through the Downs on Sunday, January the 1st, 1786, and the next morning, being abreast of Dunnose, it fell calm.

The ship was one of the finest in the service, and supposed to be in the most perfect condition for her voyage; and the commander a man of distinguished ability and exemplary character. His officers possessed unquestionable knowledge in their profession; the crew, composed of the best seamen that could be collected, was as numerous as the establishment admits. The vessel likewise contained a considerable body of soldiers, destined to recruit the forces of the company in Asia.

The passengers were Miss Eliza Pierce, and Miss Mary Anne Pierce, daughters of the commander; Miss Amy Paul, and Miss Mary Paul, daughters of Mr. Paul, of Somersetshire, and relations of captain Pierce; Miss Elizabeth Blackburne, daughter of captain B. likewise in the service of the East India company; Miss Mary Haggard, sister to an officer on the Madras establishment; Miss Ann Mansell, a native of Madras, but of European parents, who had received her education in England; and John George Schutz, Esq. returning to Asia, where he had long resided, to collect a part of his fortune which he had left behind.

On Monday, the 2d of January, at three P.M. a breeze springing up from the south, they ran in shore to land the pilot. The weather coming on very thick in the evening, and the wind baffling, at nine they were obliged to anchor in eighteen fathoms water. They furled their top-sails, but were unable to furl their courses, the snow falling thick and freezing as it fell.

Tuesday, the 3d, at four o'clock A.M. a violent gale came on from E.N.E. and the ship driving, they were obliged to cut their cables and run out to sea. At noon, they spoke with a brig to Dublin, and having put their pilot on board of her, bore down channel immediately. At eight in the evening, the wind freshening, and coming to the southward, they reefed such sails as were judged necessary. At ten, it blew a violent gale at south, and they were obliged to carry a press of sail to keep the ship off the shore. In this situation, the hause-plugs, which, according to a recent improvement, were put inside, were washed in, and the hause-bags washed away, in consequence of which they shipped a great quantity of water on the gun-deck.

Upon sounding the well, they found that the vessel had sprung a leak, and had five feet of water in her hold; they clued up the main top-sail, and immediately attempted to furl both, but failed in the attempt. All the pumps were set to work, on the discovery of the leak.

Wednesday the 4th, at two A.M. they endeavored to wear the ship, but without success. The mizzen-mast was instantly cut away, and a second attempt made to wear, which succeeded no better than the former. The ship having now seven feet of water in her hold, and the leak gaining fast on the pumps, it was thought expedient for the preservation of the ship, which appeared to be in immediate danger of foundering, to cut away the main-mast. In its fall, Jonathan Moreton, coxswain, and four men, were carried overboard by the wreck and drowned. By eight o'clock, the wreck was cleared, and the ship got before the wind. In this position she was kept about two hours, during which the pumps reduced the water in the hold two feet.

At ten in the morning the wind abated considerably, and the ship laboured extremely, rolled the fore top-mast over on the larboard side, which, in the fall, tore the fore-sail to pieces. At eleven, the wind came to the westward, and the weather clearing up, the Berry-Head was distinguished, at the distance of four or five leagues. Having erected a jury main-mast, and set a top-gallant-sail for a main-sail, they bore up for Portsmouth, and employed the remainder of the day in getting up a jury mizzen-mast.

On Thursday the 5th, at two in the morning, the wind came to the southward, blew fresh, and the weather was very thick. At noon, Portland was seen bearing north by east, distant about two or three leagues. At eight at night, it blew a strong gale at south; the Portland lights were seen bearing north-west, distant four or five leagues, when they wore ship and got her head to the westward. Finding they lost ground on that tack, they wore her again, and kept stretching to the eastward, in the hope of weathering Peverel Point, in which case they intended to have anchored in Studland bay. At eleven, they saw St. Alban's Head, a mile and a half to the leeward, upon which they took in sail immediately, and let go the small bower anchor, which brought up the ship at a whole cable, and she rode for about an hour, and then drove. They now let go the sheet anchor, and wore away a whole cable; the ship rode about two hours longer when she drove again.

In this situation the captain sent for Mr. Meriton, the chief officer, and asked his opinion concerning the probability of saving their lives. He replied with equal candor and calmness, that he apprehended there was very little hope, as they were then driving fast on shore, and might expect every moment to strike. It was agreed that the boats could not then be of any use, but it was proposed that the officers should be confidentially requested, in case an opportunity presented itself, of making it serviceable, to reserve the long boat for the ladies and themselves, and this precaution was accordingly taken.

About two, in the morning of Friday the 6th, the ship still driving, approaching the shore very fast, the same officer again went into the cuddy where the captain then was. Captain Pierce expressed extreme anxiety for the preservation of his beloved daughters, and earnestly asked Mr. Meriton, if he could devise any means of saving them. The latter expressed his fears that it would be impossible, adding, that their only chance would be to wait for the morning upon which the captain lifted up his hands in silent distress.

At this moment the ship struck with such violence, as to dash the heads of those who were standing in the cuddy against the deck above them, and the fatal blow was accompanied by a shriek of horror, which burst at the same instant from every quarter of the ship.

The seamen, many of whom had been remarkably inattentive and remiss in their duty during a great part of the storm, and had actually skulked into their hammocks, leaving the working of the pump, and the other labors required by their situation, to the officers, roused to a sense of their danger, now poured upon the deck, to which the utmost endeavors of their officers could not keep them while their assistance might have been useful. But it was now too late; the ship continued to beat upon the rocks, and soon bilged, falling with her broadside towards the shore. When the ship struck, several of the men caught hold of the ensign staff, under the apprehension of her going to pieces immediately.

At this critical juncture, Mr. Meriton offered his unhappy companions the best advice that could possibly be given. He recommended that they should all repair to that side of the ship which lay lowest on the rocks, and take the opportunities that might then present themselves of escaping singly to the shore. He then returned to the round-house, where all the passengers and most of the officers were assembled. The latter were employed in affording consolation to the unfortunate ladies, and with unparalleled magnanimity, suffering their compassion for the amiable companions of their own danger, and the dread of almost inevitable destruction. At this moment what must have been the feelings of a father—of such a father as captain Pierce?

The ship had struck on the rocks near Seacombe, on the island of Purbeck, between Peverel-point and St. Alban's Head. On this part of the shore the cliff is of immense height, and rises almost perpendicularly. In this particular spot the cliff is excavated at the base, presenting a cavern ten or twelve yards in depth, and equal in breadth to the length of a large ship. The sides of the cavern are so nearly upright as to be extremely difficult of access, and the bottom of it is strewed with sharp and uneven rocks which appear to have been rent from above by some convulsion of nature. It was at the mouth of this cavern that the unfortunate vessel lay stretched almost from side to side, and presented her broadside to the horrid chasm. But, at the time the ship struck it was too dark to discover the extent of their danger, and the extreme horror of their situation.

The number in the round-house was now increased to nearly fifty, by the admission of three black women and two soldier's wives, with the husband of one of the latter, though the sailors, who had demanded entrance to get a light, had been opposed and kept out by the officers. Captain Pierce was seated on a chair, or some other movable, between his two daughters, whom he pressed alternately to his affectionate bosom. The rest of the melancholy assembly were seated on the deck, which was strewed with musical instruments, and the wreck of furniture, boxes, and packages.

Here Mr. Meriton, after having lighted several wax candles, and all the glass lanthorns he could find, likewise took his seat, intending to wait till daylight, in the hope that it would afford him an opportunity of effecting his own escape, and also rendering assistance to the partners of his danger. But, observing that the ladies appeared parched and exhausted, he fetched a basket of oranges from some part of the round-house, with which he prevailed on some of them to refresh themselves.

On his return he perceived a considerable alteration in the appearance of the ship. The sides were visibly giving away, the deck seemed to heave, and he discovered other evident symptoms that she could not hold together much longer. Attempting to go forward to look out, he instantly perceived that the ship had separated in the middle and that the fore-part had changed its position, and lay rather farther out towards the sea. In this emergency he determined to seize the present moment, as the next might have been charged with his fate, and to follow the example of the crew and the soldiers, who were leaving the ship in numbers, and making their way to a shore, with the horrors of which they were yet unacquainted.

To favor their escape an attempt had been made to lay the ensign-staff from the ship's side to the rocks, but without success, for it snapped to pieces before it reached them. By the light of a lanthorn, however, Mr. Meriton discovered a spar, which appeared to be laid from the ship's side to the rocks, and upon which he determined to attempt his escape. He accordingly lay down upon it, and thrust himself forward, but soon found that the spar had no communication with the rock. He reached the end and then slipped off, receiving a violent contusion in his fall. Before he could recover his legs, he was washed off by the surge, in which he supported himself by swimming till the returning wave dashed him against the back of the cavern. Here he lay hold of a small projection of the rock, but was so benumbed that he was on the point of quitting it, when a seaman, who had already gained a footing, extended his hand and assisted him till he could secure himself on a little shelf of the rock, from which he clambered still higher till he was out of the reach of the surf.

Mr. Rogers, the third mate, remained with the captain and the ladies nearly twenty minutes after Mr. Meriton had left the ship. The latter had not long quitted the round house, before the captain inquired what was become of him, and Mr. Rogers replied, that he had gone upon deck to see what could be done. A heavy sea soon afterwards broke over the ship, upon which the ladies expressed great concern at the apprehension of his loss. Mr. Rogers proposed to go and call him, but this they opposed, fearful lest he might share the same fate.

The sea now broke in at the fore part of the ship, and reached as far as the main-mast. Captain Pierce and Mr. Rogers then went together, with a lamp, to the stern gallery, where, after viewing the rocks, the captain asked Mr. Rogers if he thought there was any possibility of saving the girls. He replied, he feared not; for they could discover nothing but the black surface of the perpendicular rock, and not the cavern which afforded shelter to those who had escaped. They then returned to the round house, where captain Pierce again seated himself between his two daughters, struggling to suppress the parental tear which then started into his eye.

The sea continuing to break in very fast, Mr. Rogers, Mr. Schutz, and Mr. M'Manus, a midshipman, with a view to attempt their escape, made their way to the poop. They had scarcely reached it, when a heavy sea breaking over the wreck, the round house gave way, and they heard the ladies shriek at intervals, as if the water had reach them; the noise of the sea at other times drowned their voices.

Mr. Brimer had followed Mr. Rogers to the poop, where, on the coming of the fatal sea, they jointly seized a hen-coop, and the same wave which whelmed those who remained below in destruction, carried him and his companion to the rock, on which they were dashed with great violence, and miserably bruised.

On this rock were twenty-seven men; but it was low water, and being convinced that, upon the flowing of the tide, they must all be washed off, many endeavored to get to the back or sides of the cavern beyond the reach of the returning sea. Excepting Mr. Rogers and Mr. Brimer, scarcely more than six succeeded in this attempt. Of the remainder, some experienced the fate they sought to avoid, others perished in endeavoring to get into the cavern.

Mr. Rogers and Mr. Brimer, however, having reached the cavern, climbed up the rock, on the narrow shelves of which they fixed themselves. The former got so near to his friend, Mr. Meriton, as to exchange congratulations with him; but between these gentlemen, there were about twenty men, none of whom could stir but at the most imminent hazard of his life. When Mr. Rogers reached this station, his strength was so nearly exhausted, that had the struggle continued a few minutes longer he must inevitably have perished.

They soon found that though many who had reached the rocks below, had perished in attempting to ascend, yet that a considerable number of the crew, seamen, soldiers, and some of the inferior officers, were in the same situation with themselves. What that situation was, they had still to learn. They had escaped immediate death; but they were yet to encounter a thousand hardships for the precarious chance of escape. Some part of the ship was still discernible, and they cheered themselves in this dreary situation, with the hope that it would hold together till day break. Amidst their own misfortunes, the sufferings of the females filled their minds with the acutest anguish; every returning sea increased their apprehensions for the safety of their amiable and helpless companions.

But, alas! Too soon were these apprehensions realized. A few minutes after Mr. Rogers had gained the rock, a general shriek, in which the voice of female distress was lamentably distinguishable, announced the dreadful catastrophe! In a few moments, all was hushed, excepting the warring winds and the dashing waves. The wreck was whelmed in the bosom of the deep, and not an atom of it was ever discovered. Thus perished the *Halsewell*, and with her, worth, honor, skill, beauty, and accomplishments!

This stroke was a dreadful aggravation of woe to the trembling and scarcely half-saved wretches, who were clinging about the sides of the horrid cavern. They felt for themselves, but they wept for wives, parents, fathers, brothers, sisters,—perhaps lovers!—all cut off from their dearest, fondest hopes!

Their feelings were not less agonized by the subsequent events of that ill-fated night. Many who had gained the precarious stations on the rocks, exhausted with fatigue, weakened by bruises, and benumbed with cold, quitted their hold, and falling headlong, either upon the rocks below, or into the surf, perished beneath the feet of their wretched associates, and by their dying groans and loud acclamations, awakened terrific apprehensions of a similar fate in the survivors.

At length, after three hours of the keenest misery, the day broke on them, but far from bringing with it the expected relief, it served only to discover to them all the horrors of their situation. They were convinced, that had the country been alarmed by the guns of distress, which they continued to fire several hours before the ship struck, but, which, from the violence of the storm, were unheard, they could neither be observed by the people above, as they were completely ingulphed in the cavern, and overhung by the cliff; nor was any part of the wreck remaining to indicate their probable place of refuge. Below, no boat could live to search them out, and had it been possible to acquaint those who were willing to assist them, with their exact situation, they were at a loss to conceive how any ropes could be conveyed into the cavern to facilitate their escape.

The only method, that afforded any prospect of success, was to creep along the side to its outer extremity, to turn the corner on a ledge scarcely as broad as a man's hand, and to climb up the almost perpendicular precipices, nearly two hundred feet in height. In this desperate attempt, some succeeded, while others, trembling with terror, and exhausted with bodily and mental fatigue, lost their precarious footing, and perished.

The first men who gained the summit of the cliff were the cook, and James Thompson, a quarter-master. By their individual exertions they reached the top, and instantly hastened to the nearest house, to make known the situation of their fellow-sufferers. Eastington, the habitation of Mr. Garland, steward, or agent, to the proprietors to the Purbeck quarries, was the house at which they first arrived. That gentleman immediately assembled the workmen under his direction, and with the most zealous humanity exerted every effort for the preservation of the surviving part of the crew of the unfortunate ship.

Mr. Meriton had, by this time, almost reached the edge of the precipice. A soldier, who preceded him, stood upon a small projecting rock, or stone, and upon the same stone Mr. Meriton had fastened his hands to assist his progress. Just at this moment the quarrymen arrived, and seeing a man so nearly within their reach they dropped a rope, of which he immediately laid hold. By a vigorous effort to avail himself of the advantage, he loosened the stone, which giving way, Mr. Meriton must have been precipitated to the bottom, had not a rope been lowered to him at the instant, which he seized, while in the act of falling, and was safely drawn to the summit.

The fate of Mr. Brimer was peculiarly severe. He had been married only nine days before the ship sailed, to the daughter of Captain Norman, of the Royal Navy, came on shore, as it has been observed, with Mr. Rogers, and, like him, got up the side of the cavern. Here he remained till the morning, when he crawled out; a rope was thrown him, but he was either so benumbed with the cold as to fasten it about him improperly, or so agitated as to neglect to fasten it at all. Whatever the cause, the effect proved fatal; at the moment of his supposed preservation he fell from his stand, and was unfortunately dashed to pieces, in sight of those who could only lament the deplorable fate of an amiable man and skillful officer.

The method of affording help was remarkable, and does honor to the humanity and intrepidity of the quarrymen. The distance from the top of the rock to the cavern, over which it projected, was at least one hundred feet; ten of these formed a declivity to the edge, and the remainder was perpendicular. On the very brink of this precipice stood two daring fellows, with a rope tied round them, and fastened above to a strong iron bar fixed into the ground. Behind these, in like manner, stood others, two and two. A strong rope, likewise properly secured, passed between them, by which they might hold, and support themselves from falling. Another rope, with a noose ready fixed, was then let down below the cavern, and the wind blowing hard, it was sometimes forced under the projecting rock, so that the sufferers could reach it without crawling to the edge. Whoever laid hold of it, put the noose around his waist, and was drawn up with the utmost care and caution by their intrepid deliverers.

In this attempt, however, many shared the fate of the unfortunate Mr. Brimer. Unable, through cold, perturbation of mind, weakness, or the inconvenience of the stations they occupied, to avail themselves of the succor that was offered them, they were precipitated from the stupendous cliff, and wether dashed to pieces on the rocks, or falling into the surge, perished in the waves.

Among these unhappy sufferers, the death of a drummer was attended with circumstances of peculiar distress. Being either washed off the rocks by the sea, or falling into the surf, he was carried by the returning waves beyond the breakers. His utmost efforts to regain them were ineffectual, he was drawn further out to sea, and being a remarkably good swimmer, continued to struggle with the waves, in the view of his commiserating companions, till his strength was exhausted, and he sank,—to rise no more!

It was late in the day when all the survivors were carried to a place of safety, excepting William Trenton, a soldier, who remained on his perilous stand till the morning of Saturday, the 7th, exposed to the united horrors of extreme personal danger, and the most acute disquietude of mind.

The surviving officers, seamen, and soldiers, being assembled at the house of their benevolent deliverer, Mr. Garland, they were mustered, and found to amount to 74, out of more than 240, which was nearly the number of the crew and passengers when she sailed through the Downs. Of the rest, it is supposed that fifty or more sank with the captain and the ladies in the round house, and that upwards of seventy reached the rocks, but were washed off, or perished in falling from the cliffs. All those who reached the summit survived, excepting two or three, who expired while being drawn up, and a black who died a few hours after he was brought to the house. Many, however, were so miserably bruised, that their lives were doubtful, and it was a considerable time before they perfectly recovered their strength.

The benevolence and generosity of the master of the Crown Inn, at Blanford, deserves the highest praise. When the distressed seamen arrived at that town he sent for them all to his house, and having given them the refreshment of a comfortable dinner, he presented each man with half a crown to help him on his journey.

16

LOSS *of the* LADY HOBART

From *Perils of the Sea*

BY WILLIAM DORSET FELLOWES

1803

The narrator of this tale is the ship's captain, whose name was William Dorset Fellowes, of a family that seems to have been known for its bad luck. The story first appeared in the Gentleman's Magazine *in 1805. I have it from* Perils of the Sea: Being Authentic Narratives of Remarkable and Affecting Disasters Upon the Deep, *published in New York in 1844 as no. XIV of the "Boy's and Girl's Library," and surrounded by the pious text of the editor, who attests here to the power of prayer. The people on this wreck do seem to have been unusually well-behaved—the captain remarks on the refusal of the seamen to break into the rum; in many shipwrecks that's the first thing they do, thinking apparently that dying drunk is preferable to dying sober—but people suspected at the time that the French captive on board the boat did not actually jump overboard in a fit of madness and vanish beneath the surface, but died and was eaten. We shall never know.*

"A NARRATIVE OF THE LOSS OF HIS MAJESTY'S PACKET THE LADY HOBART, on an Island of Ice in the Atlantic Ocean, on the 28th of June 1803; with a particular Account of the providential Escape of the Crew in two open Boats," has been published by William Dorset Fellowes, Esq., her commander. Of this highly interesting narrative, interesting not only on account of the intensity of suffering endured by Captain Fellowes, and his associates in danger, but of the extraordinary heroism displayed by the sufferers, we shall gratify our readers with an abstract. "It cannot fail," we use the words of his majesty's postmasters-general (prefixed to the account), which reflect no less honour on the character and principles of these distinguished noblemen, than on the captain and crew of the Lady Hobart,— "it cannot fail to impress on the minds of all who may read it, the benefit of religion and the consolation of prayer under the pressure of calamity; and also an awful sense of the interposition and mercies of Providence, in a case of extreme peril and distress. To seamen it will more especially show that discipline, order, generosity of mind, good temper, mutual benevolence, and patient exertion are, under the favour of Heaven, the best safeguards in all their difficulties."

On the 22d of June 1803, we sailed from Halifax for England, steering a course to the southward and eastward, to clear Sable Island. On the 26th, took a French schooner, the captain of which, with the mate and one boy, was retained on board the packet.

Tuesday, 28th June.—About one in the morning, the ship then going by the log at the rate of seven miles an hour, struck against an island of ice, with such violence that several of the crew were pitched out of their hammocks. *Being roused out of my sleep by the suddenness of the shock,* I instantly ran upon deck. The helm being put hard a-port, the ship struck again about the chest-tree, and then swung round on her heel, her stern-post being stove in, and her rudder carried away, before we could succeed in our attempts to haul her off. At this time the island of ice appeared to hang quite over the ship, forming a high peak, which must have been at least twice the height of our mast-head; and we suppose the length of the island to have been from a quarter to half a mile.

The sea was now breaking over the ice in a dreadful manner, the water rushing in so fast as to fill the hold in a few minutes. Made every possible exertion to prevent the vessel from sinking; but in less than a quarter of an hour she settled down to her fore-chains in the water.

Our situation was now become most perilous. Aware of the danger of a moment's delay in hoisting out the boats, I consulted Captain Thomas of the navy, and Mr. Bargus, my master, as to the propriety of making any further efforts to save the ship, or any attempt to preserve the mail. These gentlemen agreed with me that no time was to be lost in hoisting it out; and that, as the vessel was then settling fast, our first and only consideration was to endeavour to preserve the crew.

And here I must pay that tribute of praise which the steady discipline and good conduct of every one on board so justly merit. From the first moment of the ship's striking, not a word was uttered expressive of a desire to leave the wreck: my orders were promptly obeyed; and though the danger of perishing was every instant increasing, each man waited for his turn to get into the boats with a coolness and composure that could not be surpassed.

Having fortunately succeeded in hoisting out the cutter and jolly-boat, the sea then running high, we placed the ladies in the former. One of them, Miss Cotenham, was so terrified, that she sprang from the gunwale, and pitched into the bottom of the boat with considerable violence. This accident, which might have been productive of fatal consequences to herself, as well as to us all, was unattended by any bad effects. The few provisions which had been saved from the men's berths were then put into the boats. By this time the main deck forward was under water, and nothing but the quarter-deck appeared: I then ordered my men into the boats, and having lashed iron pigs of ballast to the mail, it was thrown overboard.

I now perceived that the ship was sinking fast, and called out to the men to haul up and receive me, intending to drop myself into the cutter from the end of the trysail boom; and I desired Mr. Bargus, who continued with me on the wreck, to go over first. In this instance, he replied that he begged leave to disobey my orders; that he must see me safe over before he attempted to go himself. Such conduct, and at such a moment, requires no comment.

The sea was running so high at the time we hoisted out the boats, that I scarcely flattered myself we should get them out in safety; and, indeed, nothing but the steady and orderly conduct of the crew could have enabled us to effect so difficult and hazardous an undertaking: and it is but justice to them to observe, that not a man in the ship attempted to make use of the liquor, which every one had in his power. While the cutter was getting out, I perceived one of the seamen (John Tipper) emptying a demijohn, or bottle, containing five gallons, which, on inquiry, I found to be rum. He said that he was emptying it for the purpose of filling it with water from the scuttle-cask on the quarter-deck, which had been generally filled overnight, and which was then the only fresh water to be got at: it became afterward our principal supply. I relate this circumstance as highly creditable to the character of a British sailor.

We had scarcely quitted the ship, when she suddenly gave a heavy lurch to port, and then went down head foremost. I had ordered the colours to be hoisted at the main top-gallantmast-head, with the union downwards, as a signal of distress, in case any vessel should happen to be near to us at the dawn of day.

At this awful crisis of the ship sinking, when it is natural to suppose that fear would be the predominant principle of the human mind, the coolness of a British seaman (John Andrews) was very conspicuously manifested by his exclaiming, "There, my brave fellows, there goes the pride of Old England!"

I cannot attempt to describe my own feelings, or the sensations of my people. Exposed as we were in two small open boats upon the great Atlantic Ocean, bereft of all assistance but that which our own exertions, under Providence, could afford us, we narrowly escaped being swallowed up in the vortex. Men used to vicissitudes are not easily dejected; but there are trials which human nature alone cannot surmount. The consciousness of having done our duty, and a reliance upon a good Providence, enabled us to endure our calamity; and we animated each other with the hope of a better fate.

While we were employed in deliberating about our future arrangements, at the moment the ship was sinking, she was surrounded by an incalculable number of whales. We were extremely apprehensive, from their near approach to the boats, that they might strike and materially damage them; we therefore shouted, and used every effort to drive them away, but without effect; they continued to pursue us, and remained about the boats for the space of half an hour, when, thank God! they disappeared, without having done us any injury.

Having at length surmounted dangers and difficulties which baffle all description, we rigged the foremast, and prepared to shape our course in the best manner that circumstances would admit of, the wind blowing from the precise point on which it was necessary to sail to reach the nearest land. An hour had scarcely elapsed from the time the ship struck till she foundered. The distribution of the crew was made in the following order: in the cutter, twenty feet long, six feet four inches broad, and two feet six inches deep, were embarked, including three ladies (Mrs. Fellowes, Mrs. Scott, and Miss Cotenham), Capt. Thomas, and myself, eighteen people; which, together with the provisions, brought the boat's gunwale down to within six or seven inches of the water. From this confined space, some idea may be formed of our crowded state; but it is scarcely possible for the imagination to conceive the extent of our sufferings in consequence of it. In the jolly-boat, fourteen feet long, five feet three inches broad, and two feet deep, were embarked Mr. Bargus, Lieutenant-colonel Cook of the guards, and nine others.

The only provisions we were enabled to save consisted of about fifty pounds of biscuit, five or six gallons of water, part of a barrel of spruce beer, one demijohn of rum, a few bottles of port wine, with two compasses, a quadrant, a spy-glass, a small tin mug, and a wineglass. The deck lantern, with a few spare candles, had been thrown into the boat, and the cook having secured his tinder-box and some matches, we were afterward enabled to steer by night.

The wind was now blowing strong from the westward, with a heavy sea, and the day had just dawned. Estimating ourselves to be at the distance of 350 miles from St. John's in Newfoundland, I represented to my companions in distress that we must begin by suffering privations, which I foresaw would be greater than I ventured to explain. To each person, therefore, were served out half a biscuit, and a glass of wine, which was the only allowance for the ensuing twenty-four hours, all agreeing to leave the water untouched as long as possible. Soon after daylight we made sail, with the jolly-boat in tow, and stood close hauled to the northward and westward. We now said prayers, and returned thanks to God for our deliverance.

Wednesday, June 29.—This day was ushered in with light variable winds from the southward and eastward. We had passed a long and sleepless night, and I found myself, at the dawn of day, with twenty-eight persons looking up to me with anxiety for the direction of our course, as well as for the distribution of their scanty allowance. On examining our provisions, we found the bag of biscuit much damaged by salt-water; it therefore become necessary to curtail the allowance, to which precaution all cheerfully assented.—We all returned thanks for our past mercies, and offered up prayers for our safety.

A thick fog soon after came on, with heavy rain, which we had no means of collecting. Our crowded and exposed situation was now rendered more distressing from being thoroughly wet. At noon served a quarter of a biscuit and a glass of rum to each person. One of the ladies again read prayers to us, particularly those for delivery after a storm, and those for safety at sea.

Thursday, June 30.—At daybreak we were all so benumbed with wet and extreme cold, that half a glass of rum and a mouthful of biscuit were served out to each person; the ladies, who had hitherto refused to taste the spirits, were now prevailed upon to take the stated allowance, which afforded them immediate relief. The sea was mostly calm, with thick fog and sleet; the air raw and cold: we had kept at our oars all night, and we continued to row during the whole of this day. At noon we judged ourselves to be distant 246 miles from St. John's. Performed divine service.

Friday, July 1.—During the greater part of the last twenty-four hours it blew a hard gale of wind from the west-south-west, with a heavy sea; thick fog and sleet; the weather excessively cold, for the spray, freezing as it flew over us, rendered our situation truly deplorable. We all felt a most painful depression of spirits; the want of nourishment, and the continued cold and wet weather, had rendered us almost incapable of exertion. The very confined space in the boat would not allow of our stretching our limbs, and several of the men, whose feet were considerably swelled, repeatedly called for water. On my reminding them of the resolution we had made, and of the absolute necessity of our persevering in it, they acknowledged the justice and propriety of my refusal, and the water remained untouched.

At the commencement of the gale we stood to the northward and westward; but the cutter was so low in the water, and had shipped so much sea that we were obliged to cast off the jolly-boat's tow-rope, and we very soon lost sight of her in the fog. This unlucky circumstance was productive of the utmost distress to us all. To add to the misery of our situation, we lost with the boat not only a considerable part of our stores, but with them our quadrant and spy-glass.

In the course of this day there were repeated exclamations of a strange sail, although I knew it was next to an impossibility to discern any thing, owing to the thickness of the fog; yet they were urged from the several seamen with such apparent certainty of their object, that I was induced to put the boat before the wind to convince them of their error; and as I then saw in a strong point of view the consequence of such deviations, I represented with all the force of which I was capable, that the depression arising from disappointment infinitely overbalanced the momentary relief proceeding from such delusive expectation, and I exhorted them not to allow such fancies to break out into expression. Under all these circumstances, the ladies particularly, with a heroism that no words can describe, afforded to us the best examples of patience and fortitude.

We all joined in prayers, which tranquillized our minds, and afforded us the consolatory hope of bettering our condition; on these occasions we were all bare-headed, notwithstanding the incessant showers. At noon St. John's distant 148 miles.

Saturday, July 2.—It rained hard during the night, and the cold became so severe that almost every one in the boat was unable to move. At day-break I served out about the third of a wineglass of rum to each person, with a quarter of a biscuit, and before noon a small quantity of spruce beer which afforded us great relief.

At half-past eleven A.M., a sail was discovered to the eastward, standing to the north-west. Our joy at such a sight, with the immediate hope of deliverance, gave us all new life. Having hauled close to the wind, we neared each other fast, and in less than a quarter of an hour we perceived the jolly-boat.

I cannot attempt to describe the various sensations of joy and disappointment which were, by turns, expressed on all our countenances. As soon as we approached the jolly-boat we threw out to her a tow-rope, and bore away to the north-west. The most singular circumstance was, their having steered two nights without any light; and our meeting again after such tempestuous weather could not have happened but from the interposition of Providence.

Our hopes of deliverance had now been buoyed up to the highest pitch. The excitement arising from our joy began perceptibly to lose its effect; and to a state of artificial strength succeeded such a despondency, that no entreaty nor argument could rouse some of the men even to the common exertions of making sail.

To the French captain, and several of the people who appeared to have suffered most, I now, for the first time, served out a wineglass full of water. I had earnestly cautioned the crew not to taste the salt-water, but some of the unhappy men had, nevertheless, taken large draughts of it, and became delirious; some were seized with violent cramps and twitching of the stomach and bowels. I again took occasion to point out to the rest of them the extreme danger of such indiscretion.

Performed divine service. At noon St. John's distant 110 miles.

Sunday, 3.—The cold, wet, hunger, and thirst which we now experienced are not to be described, and made our situation very deplorable. At eight P.M., having a strong breeze from the southward, we stood on under all the canvass we could spread. The French captain, who for some days had laboured under a despondency which admitted of no consolation, jumped overboard in a fit of delirium, and instantly sank. One of the other prisoners in the jolly-boat became so outrageous that it was found necessary to lash him to the bottom of the boat.

The melancholy fate of the poor captain, whom I had learned to esteem, affected me at first more sensibly, perhaps, than any other person; for on the day on which I was making the distribution in the boats, and was considering in which I should place him, he came to me with tears in his eyes, to implore me not to leave him to perish with the wreck; I assured him that I never had entertained such an idea; that, as I had been the accidental cause of his misfortunes, I would endeavour to make his situation as easy as I could, and that, as we were all exposed to the same danger, we would survive or perish together.

We were all deeply affected by this circumstance; the most trifling accident or disappointment was sufficient to render our irritable state more painful; and I was seized with such melancholy, that I lost all recollection of my situation for many hours; a violent shivering had seized me, which returned at intervals; and as I had refused all sustenance, my state was very alarming: towards night I enjoyed, for the first time, three or four hours' sound sleep, a perspiration came on, and I awoke as from a dream, free from delirium, but painfully alive to all the horrors that surrounded me.

The sea continued to break over the boats so much, that those who had strength enough were obliged to bale without intermission. Those who sat in the stern of the cutter were so confined, that it was difficult for any one to put his hand into his pocket, and the greater part of the crew lay in water upon the boat's bottom.

The return of dawn brought us no relief but its light. The sun had never cheered us but once during the whole of our perilous voyage; and those who had a few hours of interrupted sleep awoke to all the consciousness of wretchedness and misery.

A very heavy gale of wind came on from the south ward, with so tremendous a sea, that the greatest vigilance was necessary in managing the helm. We scudded before it, expecting every returning wave to overwhelm us; but, through the providence of Almighty God, we weathered the storm, which began to abate towards night. We had nearly run our distance from St. John's; but owing to the thickness of the fog, we were prevented from discerning to any great extent.

About this time a beautiful white bird hovered over the masthead of the cutter, and continued fluttering there until dark. Trifling as this circumstance may appear, it was considered by us all as a propitious omen. We indulged ourselves on this occasion with the most consolatory assurances, that the same Hand which had provided this solace to our distresses would extricate us from the danger that surrounded us.

There being every reason to conclude ourselves well in with the land, the few that were able to move were now called upon to make a last effort to save their lives by rowing, and taking advantage of the little breeze we then had. We had now been six days and nights, constantly wet and cold, without any other sustenance than a quarter of a biscuit and one wineglass of fluid for twenty-four hours. The men, who had appeared totally indifferent as to their fate, summoned up resolution, and as many as were capable of moving from the bottom of the boats applied to the oars.

Monday, 4.—As the day dawned, the fog became so thick that we could not see very far from the boat. During the night we had been under the necessity of casting off the jolly-boat's tow-rope, to induce her crew to exert themselves by rowing. We again lost sight of her, and I perceived that this unlucky accident was beginning to excite great uneasiness among us. We were now so reduced, that the most trifling remark or exclamation agitated us very much. I therefore found it necessary to caution the people against being deceived by the appearance of land, or calling out till we were quite convinced of its reality, more especially as fog-banks are often mistaken for land. Several of the poor fellows, however, repeatedly exclaimed they heard breakers, others the firing of guns; and the sounds we did hear resembled the latter so much, that I concluded some vessel had got on shore, and was making signals of distress: the noise afterward proved to be the blowing of whales, of which we saw a great number.

Soon after daylight the sun rose in view for the second time since we quitted the wreck. It is worthy of remark, that during the period of seven days that we were in the boats, we never had an opportunity of taking an observation, either of the sun, moon, or stars, nor of drying our clothes. The fog at length beginning to disappear, we instantly caught a glimpse of the land, within a mile distance, between Kettle Cove and Island Cove, in Conception Bay, fourteen leagues from the harbour of St. John's. Almost at the same moment we had the inexpressible satisfaction to discover the jolly-boat, and a schooner in shore standing off towards us.

I wish it were possible for me to describe our sensations at this interesting moment. From the constant watching and fatigue, and from the languor and depression arising from our exhausted state, such accumulated irritability was brought on, that the joy of a speedy relief affected us all in a most remarkable way: many burst into tears, some looked at each other with a stupid stare, as if doubtful of the reality of what they saw; several were in such a lethargic state that no consolation, no animating language, could rouse them to exertion.

At this affecting period, though overpowered by my own feelings, and impressed with the recollection of our sufferings, and the sight of so many deplorable objects, I proposed to offer up our solemn thanks to Heaven for our miraculous deliverance. Every one cheerfully assented;

and as soon as I opened the prayer-book (which I had secured the last time I went down to my cabin), there was a universal silence; a spirit of devotion was so singularly manifested on this occasion, that to the benefits of a religious sense in uncultivated minds, must be ascribed that discipline, good order, and exertion, which even the sight of land could scarcely produce.

The schooner being now within hail, and having made our situation known, she hove-to, and received us on board, our boats being taken in tow.

The wind having blown with great violence from off the coast, we did not reach the landing-place at Island Cove till four o'clock in the evening. All the women and children in the village, with two or three fishermen (the rest of the men being absent), came down to the beach, and appearing deeply affected at our wretched situation, assisted in lifting us out of the vessel, and afterward in carrying us up the craggy rocks, over which we were obliged to pass to get to their habitations. This small village afforded neither medical aid nor fresh provisions, of which we stood so much in need; potatoes and salt fish being the only food of the inhabitants. I determined, therefore, to lose no time in proceeding to St. John's, where we arrived on the 8th of July. Thence I proceeded to England, where I arrived on the 3d of August.

17

The LOSS *of the* POLLY

From R. Thomas, ed., *Interesting and authentic narratives of the most remarkable shipwrecks, fires, famines, calamites, providential deliverances, and disasters in the seas in most parts of the world.*

1811

Huntress reprints this from the same 1835 anthology that he reprinted many of his other accounts from, and I am reprinting it here for the same reason he did. This is one of the stories that Edgar Allan Poe used to put together his shipwreck novel, The Narrative of Arthur Gordon Pym. *Poe thought so much of the story that he actually reproduced a good part of it as a footnote. Poe knew nothing about the sea himself, but he certainly knew a sensational story when he saw one. Poe's biographer, Kenneth Silverman, points out that Poe emphasized the sensational in the book's subtitle, a list of what the reader will find within: "Incredible Adventures"; "Capture"; "Massacre"; "Mutiny and Atrocious Butchery;" "Shipwreck and Subsequent Horrible Sufferings From Famine." The reviewers of Poe's book, not surprisingly, loved it.*

THE BRIG *POLLY*, OF ONE HUNDRED AND THIRTY TONS BURTHEN, SAILED from Boston, with a cargo of lumber and provisions, on a voyage to Santa Croix, on the 12th of December 1811, under the command of Capt. W. L. Cazneau—with a mate, four seamen and a cook; Mr. I. S. Hunt, and a negro girl of nine years of age, passengers. Nothing material happened, until the 15th, when they had cleared Cape Cod, the shoal of Georges, and nearly, as they supposed, crossed the gulf stream, when there came on a violent gale from the southeast, in which the brig labored very hard, which produced a leak that so gained on the pumps as to sound nearly six feet,—when about midnight she was upset, and Mr. Hunt washed overboard! Not having any reason to hope for her righting, by much exertion the weather-lanyards were cut away, the deck load having been before thrown over, and the lashings all gone; in about half an hour, the mainmast went by the board, and soon after, the foremast, when she righted, though full of water, a dreadful sea making a fair breach over her from stem to stern.—In this situation the night wore away, and daylight found all alive except the passengers, and upon close search, the little girl was found clinging to the skylight, and so saved from drowning in the cabin. The glass and grating of the skylight having gone away, while on her beam ends, the little girl was drawn through the openings, but so much chilled that she survived but a few hours. In this situation they remained, without fire, as near as the captain can recollect, twelve days, when the cook, an Indian from Canton, near Boston, suggested the operation of rubbing two sticks together, which succeeded. Very fortunately, the caboose did not go overboard with the deck load; this was got to windward, a fire kindled, and some provisions cooked, which was the first they had tasted, except raw pork, for the whole time. They now got up a barrel of pork, part of a barrel of beef, and one half barrel of beef. A small pig had been saved alive, which they now dressed, not having any thing to feed it with. But at this time no apprehension was entertained of suffering for meat, there being several barrels stowed in the run, and upwards of one hundred under deck. With this impression, the people used the provisions very imprudently, till they discovered that the stern-post was gone, and the gale continuing for a long time, the barrels had stove, and their contents were all lost forever.

There happened to be a cask of water lashed on the quarterdeck, which was saved, containing about thirty gallons; all the rest was lost. This lasted about eighteen days, when the crew were reduced to the necessity of catching what rain they could, and having no more. At the end of forty days, the meat was all gone, and absolute famine stared them in the face. The first victim to this destroyer was Mr. Paddock, the mate, whose exquisite distress seemed to redouble the sufferings of his companions. He was a man of a robust constitution, who had spent his life in the Bank fishing, had suffered many hardships and appeared the most capable of standing the shocks of misfortune of any of the crew. In the meridian of life, being about thirty-five years old, it was reasonable to suppose that, instead of the first, he would have been the last to have fallen a sacrifice to cold and hunger: but Heaven ordered it otherwise—he became delirious, and death relieved him from his sufferings the fiftieth day of his shipwreck. During all this time, the storms continued, and would often overwhelm them so as to keep them always drenched with seawater, having nothing to screen them, except a temporary kind of cabin which they built up of boards between the windlass and night-head on the larboard side of the forecastle. The next who sunk under this horrid press of disasters was Howes, a young man of about thirty, who likewise was a fisherman by profession, and tall, spare, and as smart and active a seaman as any aboard. He likewise died delirious and in dreadful distress, six days after Paddock, being the fifty-sixth day of the wreck. It was soon perceived that this must evidently be the fate of all the survivors in a short time, if something was not done to procure water. About this time, good luck, or more probably, kind Providence, enabled them to fish up the tea-kettle, and one of the captain's pistols; and necessity, the mother of invention, suggested the plan of distillation. Accordingly, a piece of board was very nicely fitted to the mouth of the boiler, a small hole made in it, and the tea-kettle, bottom-upwards, fixed to the upper side of the board, the pistol-barrel was fixed to the nose of the kettle and kept cool by the constant application of cold water. This completely succeeded, and the survivors, without a doubt, owe their preservation to this simple experiment. But all that could be obtained by this very imperfect distillation, was a scanty allowance of water for five men; yet it would sustain life and that was all. The impression that there was meat enough under the deck, induced them to use every exertion to obtain it; but by getting up pieces of bone, entirely bare of meat and in a putrid state, they found that nothing was left for them but to rely on Heaven for food, and be contented with whatever came to hand, till relief should come. Their only sustenance now, was barnacles gathered from the sides of the vessel which were eaten raw that the distilling might not be interrupted, which would give them no more than four wine glasses of water each, per day. The next food which they obtained was a large shark caught by means of a running bow-line. This was a very great relief and lasted some time. Two advantages arose from this signal interposition of kind Providence; for while they lived upon their shark, the barnacles were growing larger and more nutritive. They likewise found many small crabs among the seaweed which often floated around the wreck, which were very pleasant food. But from the necessity of chewing them raw and sucking out the nourishment, they brought on an obstinate costiveness, which became extremely painful and probably much exasperated by the want of water.

On the 15th of March, according to their computation, poor Moho, the cook, expired, evidently from want of water, though with much less distress than the others and in the full exercise of his reason: he very devoutly prayed and appeared perfectly resigned to the will of the God who afflicted him. Their constant study was directed to the improvement of their still, which was made much better by the addition of the other pistol barrel, which was found by fishing with the grain they made by fixing nails into a piece of a stave. With this barrel they so far perfected the still as to obtain eight junk bottles full of water in twenty-four hours. But from the death of Moho to the death of Johnson, which happened about the middle of April, they seemed to be denied every kind of food. The barnacles were all gone, and no friendly gale wafted to their side the seaweed from which they could obtain crabs or insects. It seemed as if all hope was gone forever, and they had nothing before them but death, or the horrid alternative of eating the flesh of their dead companion. One expedient was left, that was to try to decoy a shark, if happily there might be one about the wreck, by part of the corpse of their shipmate! This succeeded, and they caught a large shark, and from that time had many fish, till their happy deliverance. Very fortunately, a cask of nails which was on deck, lodged in the lea-scuppers while on their beam ends: with these they were enabled to fasten the shingles on their cabin, which by constant improvement, had become much more commodious, and when reduced to two only, they had a better supply of water.

They had now drifted above two thousand miles, and were in latitude 28 North, and longitude 13 West, when to their unspeakable joy they saw three ships bearing down upon them. The ships came as near as was convenient, and then hailed, which captain Cazneau answered with all the force of his lungs. The ship which hailed, proved to be the Fame, of Hull, captain Featherstone, bound from Rio Janeiro home. It so happened that the three captains had dined together that day and were all on board the Fame. Humanity immediately sent a boat, which put an end to the dreadful thraldom of captain Cazneau and Samuel Badger, the only surviving persons who were received by these humane Englishmen with exalted sensibility. Thus was ended the most shocking catastrophe which our naval history has recorded for many years, after a series of distresses from December 15th to the 20th of June, a period of one hundred and ninety-one days! Every attention was paid to the sufferers that generosity warmed with pity and fellow-feeling could dictate, on board the Fame. They were cherished, comforted, fed, clothed and nursed until the 9th of July, when they fell in with captain Perkins, of the brig *Dromo*, in the chops of the channel of England, who generously took them on board and carefully perfected the work of goodness begun by the generous Englishmen, and safely landed them in Kennebunk.

It is natural to inquire how they could float such a vast distance upon the most frequented part of the Atlantic and not be discovered all this time? They were passed by more than a dozen sail, one of which came so nigh them that they could distinctly see the people on deck and on the rigging looking at them: but to the inexpressible disappointment of the starving and freezing men, they stifled the dictates of compassion, hoisted sail and cruelly abandoned them to their fate.

18

The TREACHERY

From A *Narrative of the Sufferings and Adventures of Capt. Charles H. Barnard*

BY CHARLES H. BARNARD

1813

Charles H. Barnard was the captain of an American sealer named the Nanina *that had gone to the Falklands in 1812 to take seals and seal skins. It was toward the middle of the great rush to harvest seals in Antarctic waters that eventually led to the discovery of the continent of Antarctica in 1820 by another American sealer. But in 1812 the more accessible Falklands were the target; during the southern summer as many as 40 ships might be found there wiping out seal populations. The skins were then taken to the Far East, where they brought very high prices and made fortunes, for as long as the seals lasted. Eventually sealers came close to wiping out the entire population of fur seals in Antarctica and the surrounding waters. It is a shameful episode in sealing history.*

Barnard and his crew of 11 had been there about six months when he found out that the United States had declared war on England. Shortly thereafter he was sailing in the western Falklands looking for promising seal beaches when he noticed smoke rising from a nearby island and went to investigate, thinking he might find shipwrecked sailors who needed help. Indeed he did. The Isabella, *a British ship with some 45 people aboard, on its way from Australia to England, had run aground in the islands and was a total loss. The people aboard had all survived, but they had no provisions and were dreading the coming winter. Barnard offered to interrupt his work, take them aboard, and deposit them in the nearest South American port. The United States and Britain were at war, he told them, which they did not know, so he asked them to sign an agreement that they would make no attempt to seize his ship. Of course, they said. They signed the agreement, all of them.*

Then one day, when Barnard was off in the ship's boat with four other men hunting pigs, which had been let loose on the islands years before to breed in order to provide fresh meat to sealers and whalers, the British officers Barnard had just rescued from a winter stranded in one of the harshest climates on Earth stole Barnard's boat and sailed away to South America with all aboard. Barnard and his four men, one a black whaler from Sag Harbor, Long Island, the other three British sailors, were left with the clothes on their back, Barnard's dog, the little ship's boat, and nothing more.

We print the chapter from Barnard's book that describes the discovery of this treachery and how Barnard coped with it. In all, he and the four other men spent 18 months in the Falklands before they were rescued by a couple of British whaling ships and made their way home. The first months were the hardest, and Barnard's direct, plain prose gives a vivid picture of this time. Justice, again, does not necessarily triumph. Despite the protests of the Americans who were taken as prisoners when the British seized the ship, Barnard's ship was registered in England as a "good and lawful" prize of war. Barnard went back to sea.

THE TREACHERY.

Not faster yonder rowers' might
Flings from their oars the spray;
Not faster yonder rippling bright
That tracks the shallop's course in light
Melts in the lake away;
Than men from memory erase
The benefits of former days.—*W. Scott.*

Life is indeed filled with vicissitudes. The changes of a natural day are a striking picture of the bright and gloomy circumstances in which we may be placed. Who can, after all his calculations, expect unclouded success, and promise himself hopes without clouds of disappointment? Our situation had been cheerless, but not without its comforts; but we little dreamed of the singular reverses that were to happen, and blight so soon our few remaining hopes.

Being in want of fresh provisions on the 10th for the supply of the passengers and crew, I proceeded to Beaver, one of the adjacent Islands, with four men who had volunteered their services, viz. Jacob Green, one of my crew, and an American citizen; and Sam. Ansel, Jos. Albrook, and James

Louder, British subjects, late of the *Isabella*. Having procured a sufficient number of wild hogs to load the boat, we departed, and about ten o'clock arrived at New Island Harbour, when we discovered, to our inexpressible surprise, that the vessel was gone! —but where? We instantly landed, hauled up the boat, and awaited the approach of day-light in the most impatient and tormenting anxiety, but still cherishing a hope, that we might discover a letter, which would inform us of the reason. But in vain did we search, for although they might have deposited one in a bottle, and buried or suspended it in some conspicuous place, yet, after a long and fruitless search, we were reluctantly compelled to abandon all expectation of finding any communication from the vessel. We were so confused and irritated that we could hardly persuade ourselves that we had been thus barbarously deserted, until we were constrained, by the certainty of the fact, to turn our thoughts to ourselves, and to devise means for prolonging our existence.

To be reduced to this deplorable and almost hopeless state of wretchedness, by the treachery and ingratitude of those for whose relief I had long been labouring, and who, by our unremitted exertions were raised from the lowest depths of despair, to a prospect of restoration to all the endearments of country and home, was dreadful in the extreme, and what was my return? To be betrayed and abandoned; and at the very time when I was actually engaged in providing subsistence for them, to cowardly avail themselves of my absence in procuring additions to their comfort, and plunge me into a situation at which humanity revolts, without scarcely any garments but those on our backs, and those considerably worn, to withstand, without shelter, the severity of a winter on this barren island, without stores or bread, or any thing that would answer as a substitute, and under the apprehension that the island would not afford game sufficient for us to exist upon. Wild hogs and game there were; but of the former we depended only on our faithful dog; and of the latter we had no prospect, as our ammunition was expended.

While reflecting on these circumstances, it occurred to me, that possibly the brig had gone into Beaver Island Harbour to take us off; and she could have entered it without being perceived by us, as we were engaged in hunting on the opposite side of it. The longer I meditated, the more improbable it appeared, that the crew and passengers could have so entirely divested themselves of every spark of humanity, as to leave us exposed to all the horrors and sufferings we must necessarily endure in this inhospitable climate. The weather being moderate, we went to the lee side of Beaver Island, whereas yesterday we were on the weather side; and cheered by the hope that we should find the brig there, we entered the harbour, preferring to be considered, and even treated as prisoners of war, and deprived of all our property, to being abandoned here; for in that case I would have nothing to cheer me, but every thing to fill me with the most gloomy forebodings. But on our arrival at Beaver Island Harbour, we were fated to endure, alas! the almost insupportable anguish of neither finding the brig nor discovering any trace that she had been in the harbour; thus our last gleam of hope, died away, like most of those favorite pursuits on which we place our hearts. Yet we trusted that Heaven had not abandoned us poor forlorn wretches, thus cruelly abandoned of men. We concluded, notwithstanding the dangers we must encounter, and which, under any other circumstances, we should have deemed insurmountable in an open boat, on account of the sudden changes in the weather, and the great tide rips which we must unavoidably pass, that we would attempt to effect a passage to Eagle Island, where the wreck was distant, about eighty miles.

The dread of remaining on these desolate islands, and a new, but faint hope, that possibly the pirates might have stopped there, to take on board the brig what they could of the wreck and cargo, and have left a written communication and some necessaries for us, inspired us with courage to face the dangers of the attempt. We therefore lightened the boat by throwing over four hogs, in order to make the passage in her with more safety, and retained four, which, in addition to the provisions we could procure at places where we might stop on account of bad weather, etc. would supply us during the passage, which we commenced at M. taking our course by the safest routes. After rowing the greatest part of the night, we landed on Island Harbour, the E. side of Swan Island, completely fatigued, by our exertions at the oar. Having been unavoidably compelled to fast all the time of our passage to this place, our sufferings were great, and we were necessitated to pass the remainder of the night on the open beach. The weather was so excessively cold, as to freeze that part of the beach which had been covered with the tide, to a considerable depth. Our clothes were wet, and the men frequently exclaimed that they must perish; this harrowed up my already agitated feelings, since they looked to me for relief although suffering equally with themselves. What a blessed thing it is that captains and commanders are often supported, sometimes with almost superhuman fortitude to soothe down the murmurs and complaints, and unite the jarring tempers and interests of the men who are placed under them. It is a fortunate circumstance, when an individual thus situated feels himself thus sustained, and still more fortunate when those whom he directs are willing to listen to and obey his instructions.

The next morning, after considerable difficulty, we succeeded in kindling a fire, and cooking some of the pork for breakfast; which was the first food we had taken for the last twenty-four hours; after our meal we launched the boat and proceeded on our passage. The wind being ahead and fresh, the sail was consequently of no use; we rowed down for Barnard's Island against a heavy head sea, which frequently broke over the boat's bows; but having a favourable tide we soon got under the lee of Barnard's Island, being distant twelve miles. We avoided going round Cape Orford, from its being an inaccessible iron-bound shore, almost the whole distance from the commencement of the cape to Port Stephens, extending ten or twelve miles, and lying open to the prevailing winds, which throw in a heavy sea, and at all times dangerous tide rips; and there was no place within the whole space, where we could land with safety, or haul the boat up so as to prevent her from being injured, if not dashed into pieces; forming altogether the most perilous cape in this part of the world. We might have avoided the dangers of Cape Orford, by hauling our boat over a neck of land about two miles across, which would bring us into Port Stephens, without any dangerous places to pass, except Cape Meridith, where the distance from one landing to the other was but short, and the tide rips not so great. Having effected this, we thought that by waiting for a favourable day to pass the sound, we could prosecute the remainder of the passage to the wreck, liable only to sudden gales, frequently occurring at this inclement season of the year. We therefore proceeded directly towards the mouth of Mc. Cockling's Lagoon, which is headed near the bay of Port Stephens, but separated by a strip of land about two miles wide, across which we intended to carry or drag the boat; but the wind blowing fresh and ahead, we could not reach it, but put into a small bay about one mile this side of the lagoon; the sun being down, we hauled up the boat and turned her over for a shelter. The night was very cold, with a light fall of snow.

This bay or cove is formed at the mouth of a valley, which lies between the mountains, with a gentle ascent of about a mile; and then gently tapers off with a gradual descent nearly the same distance; there we discovered that it was entered by water, which we had no doubt was the head of a lagoon that communicated with Port Stevens. We therefore decided to carry the boat across from thence, instead of proceeding to Mc. Cockling's Lagoon, as the distance from the two waters appeared to be less than at the latter place, and the saving of time and labour was very important to us: we therefore carried the oars, masts, sail, and other articles across, which occupied us till night, which we passed in the same manner as the last. In the morning we undertook the task, and a severe one it was, to get the boat to the water on the other side, and succeeded, after much fatigue and difficulty. We attempted to carry her, but were too much exhausted by our many privations to accomplish so much: about sunset she was floating in her proper element.

We proceeded down the lagoon, and if our conjecture of its communicating with Port Stephens were correct, there could, notwithstanding the darkness of the night and the falling snow, be no danger in proceeding down the bay. After running about three or four miles from the entrance of it, we were much surprised at finding ourselves in an open sea. The wind blowing fresh and fair, we kept before it to make a landing, as we had seen land in the direction we were steering previous to its becoming so hazy and dark; but to my astonishment, I found that we had run more than twice the distance of the breadth of Port Stephen's Bay, yet made no land, and the sea rose so as to break into the boat at times, which greatly alarmed us all. I began to fear and suspect that, in taking the boat across, we had mistaken the course, and that we were now running out to sea, and as unfortunately we had no compass, we could not ascertain the course we were steering, nor those we had steered in following the windings of the lagoon. All was conjecture: we were soon agreeably surprised to find breakers to the leeward; our next care on approaching the shore, which was lined with low flat rocks that were bare at low water, was to effect a landing without staving the boat; which, after much difficulty, we accomplished. It being low water, we were forced to haul the boat a considerable distance to reach high water mark, which at full tides was against a clay bank, intermixed with sand, fifteen or twenty feet perpendicular: on account of the darkness of the night, we could not find a safer situation. We removed the snow, which had fallen to the depth of six or eight inches, and turned up the boat, with her gunnel against the bank, for shelter: the four men not being provided with a change of dry clothes or stockings, suffered severely from the cold, as their clothing was worn threadbare, merely covering their nakedness, but affording very little warmth or yielding much protection from the severity of the weather. As soon as the boat was turned up, the poor fellows crept under it. As it afforded but a slight shelter from the wind and snow, they took their only blanket and wrapped their naked feet in it, weeping bitterly. If the authors of our extreme suffering could have beheld them for only a moment, it might perhaps have touched even their flinty hearts with pity, although they must have known the consequences that would ensue from their inhuman desertion. The dog laid down amongst them, alternately licking their feet and legs, appearing sensible of their distress, and desirous of relieving it. After changing my stockings, I made a hole with my knife in that part of the bank which the boat rested, built a fire under it, by breaking up a few pieces of drift wood which we had brought with us, suspended the pot by a string from the gunnel and boiled some pork for our supper and breakfast; for we supposed it now to be near day-light. While satisfying the cravings of hunger with the half-boiled pork, we were dreadfully alarmed by hearing the tide rapidly approaching, as in that case we would be obliged to turn up the boat, and remain in her till day-light, and at the same time be exposed to the fury of the surf, which might dash the boat against the bank, and stave her to pieces: but these apprehensions were soon quieted, by observing that it was neap tide, and would not reach us.

On June the 17th, strong gales from the S. and severe cold were endured. At daybreak we crawled out from under the boat, and looked round, to ascertain, if possible, on what land we were; but all appeared strange, and our suspicions, that we had in our haste hauled the boat to the wrong place, were confirmed; and, taking our departure in the dusk of the evening, without a compass to take the bearings of Port Stephens, and the courses we had steered, I was completely at a loss to tell where or on what island we landed. I set to work, and broke up the remainder of the wood, for the purpose of cooking our breakfast of pork. As I knew that we should soon be in great want of wood and water, and as the preparing of this meal would consume the whole of both articles, I sent Jacob Green and Samuel Ansel along shore in search of a supply of both; but they returned almost frozen, without having been so fortunate as to procure either. We were now almost in a state of despair, but as I knew that despairing would not relieve us, after eating of the par-boiled pork, and melting some snow in the cooking pot for drink, I took Joseph Albrook with me, and went along shore in the other direction for wood and water. Having travelled about a mile, we came to a frozen pond, and on breaking the ice we found the water both fresh and good; we filled our boat keg, and left it on the beach, and continued to proceed along shore, in hopes to find some drift wood, when we fortunately fell in with four sea elephants. We immediately killed the smallest with our clubs, cut off the blubber, and carried it to the boat for fuel. By this successful attempt in procuring water, which we had almost despaired of, and the means of continuing our fire; and knowing that without these two indispensable articles we could not long have existed, our spirits and hopes were renewed.

The tender providence of Heaven is never known to leave us so destitute, without sending counterbalancing blessings to keep us from sinking. Where is the wretch that will deny that he enjoys some soothing hope, some lingering joy, that enable him to encounter the miseries of life, and encourage him to prepare for a brighter reward hereafter? They who talk most about their sufferings, are little aware of the numerous blessings which are left behind, which far outbalance, if they would think aright, all the miseries they complain of.

The gale still continuing, with flurries of snow from the S. and generally lasting several days, and not uncommonly weeks at this season, we returned and killed the other three elephants, and secured the blubber for fuel, in case we should be detained here by foul weather.

Strong gales kept us close as possible on the 18th, under the boat, over a small blubber fire, the smoke of which turned the skin on all our faces pretty much of a colour. We began to consider what course to take, when the weather should become settled: I resolved to leave this shore as soon as it could be done with safety, and go over to the nearest land, which lay in an easterly direction, distant about ten or twelve miles, hoping when there I might discover whence we had come, or where we had first landed after hauling the boat over the neck. As I had visited almost every part of the shores of these islands in search of seal, I was confident that if I could reach any other landings or harbours, I should not long remain without recognising something with which I had been familiar.

The weather being fine and calm on the 20th of June, we launched our boat, and proceeded towards the land before mentioned. After rowing several hours, we found a safe place, where we landed, on a rocky shore, under the lee of a head land, about an hour before sun-set; hauled up the boat, and prepared her for shelter for the night. I attentively looked round, but observed nothing that reminded me that I had ever been here, but I was almost satisfied that we were now on some part of the Great Maloon, and what strengthened this opinion was the appearance of a fox, for this animal is not found on any other island; I knocked him down with the pole of my lance, and one of the men took off the skin, of which he made a cap. The weather continuing fine, and our pork being nearly expended, there being only sufficient for one meal, we formed ourselves into two parties, and went in search of provisions, and to ascertain, if possible, on what part of the island we were. I and my company returned at night, without having made any discoveries, and with only three wild fowls, which we killed with stones.

We launched our boat on the 22nd, with a strong wind from the W. and ran across to the eastern shore, distant about two leagues, and there made a strict search for any thing which might lead to any opinion of the place we were at; but all was new to my sight, and our provisions being entirely expended, I, with one man, coursed along the shore, and two others went in an opposite direction, in search of seal or wild fowl, or anything that might allay the cravings of hunger. The wild fowl that frequent this island are so unaccustomed to man, and the danger which generally attends his approach, that they take little or no notice of him. We returned about the middle of the afternoon, without having seen a single seal or fowl, or procuring the least morsel of food; being almost in a state of starvation, our want of success greatly depressed our spirits. As a last resource to prolong our wretched existence, we pulled up tushook, grass, and all the roots. It was nearly night, and the other two men not having arrived, I experienced the most alarming apprehensions for their safety; fearful lest they had gone to a considerable distance, and not finding any thing to eat, they had not, from want of sustenance, sufficient strength to return. However, about dusk they came back to the boat, but so completely exhausted by hunger and fatigue that they could hardly stand; but they had had better success than I and my companion, for they brought in seven carrion hawks, which they killed while they were feeding, with a large number of others, on the putrid carcase of an elephant, which, from its offensive state, must have been dead a long time.

On the 23d of June, Jacob Green and Sam. Ansel went for more carrion crows, Joseph Albrook and myself chose a course in a different direction, from the one they had taken; we had not proceeded far on our route, when we fortunately encountered a young sea-elephant, which was a cheering sight; we killed him, and having loaded ourselves with as much of the flesh and blubber as we could carry, returned speedily to the boat, and then went back for the remainder. The lean was allotted for present use, the blubber we reserved for our future necessities, as it will remain good a considerable time. Green and Ansel brought in four or five rooks. I now thought it best to retrace our way to the carrying place, and get our boat across without delay, apprehensive that our fatigue and scanty fare would so reduce our strength, that an attempt to accomplish it would prove unavailing. A strong head wind prevailing, we remained here a whole day, watching with the most intense anxiety for a favourable change of the wind, to enable us to return to Swan Island, where our dog could provide us with food which would be luxurious compared with our present scanty diet of sea-elephant meat and blubber. But what was that luxurious food our dog could procure for us? Why, a poor, miserable, half-starved wild hog, without bread or vegetables, or a substitute for either.

We launched the boat on the 24th, and left this place of famine to which I gave the name of "Pinch-gut Camp." The cravings of our stomachs most painfully acquiesced in the propriety of this name, which may sound indelicately to polite ears and delicate palates. We landed at Hook Camp which derived its name from one or more of the piratical rooks stealing and actually flying away with the only seal hook we had left. We landed with some difficulty on a shelving rock, on which the surf was breaking with considerable violence. We were soon visited by more than one hundred rook, which had been attracted by the smell of the elephant blubber, which constituted the whole of our unpalatable stock of provisions; indeed it could not be eaten by any one without disgust, except he was a Greenlander, Esquimaux, savage, or piratical rook, or unfortunately like ourselves, on the verge of starvation. On the attempt of the rooks to possess themselves of our pittance, we pelted them so heartily with stones, that they were compelled to abandon their object, leaving eighteen of their number dead on the field of battle; so that their attempts instead of diminishing, added to our stock. This night the wind blew a gale from the westward, and which, to our distress continued several days.

In this forlorn situation, exposed to every hardship that man could sustain without sinking under the pressure, with scarcely provisions sufficient to sustain our sinking frames, our bodily strength and mental energy daily declined, and most of us despaired of ever being relieved except by a lingering death. We were now compelled, and almost without hope, to separate in quest of something to eat; and each chose and pursued his solitary route with feelings that cannot be described, and not easily to be imagined. So heart-rending was our situation, cut off from all intercourse with the rest of mankind, on this cold inhospitable island, that it appeared allotted to be the place where all our relations with the world must close, and where we would not be even "by strangers honoured and by strangers mourned." Even now memory sickens at the recollection.

On assembling, we found that the whole amount of what we collected was one hair seal and two rooks; on which we subsisted, with very trifling addition, although constantly engaged in the pursuit, until the 26th, when we consumed the last morsel; yet all our endeavours to procure more were unavailing, and we were compelled by extreme hunger, to feed upon the roots of the tushook grass. The eating of those roots occasioned vomitings and dizziness in each of us, but more particularly in Louder and Green, who were reduced to the greatest extremity. In this deplorable state we continued until July the 1st, when the weather being more moderate, we, with the greatest difficulty, owing to our emaciation and loss of strength, launched the boat and got our things into her; but in effecting this we had the additional misfortune to split one of her bottom planks against the rocks, which caused the boat to leak badly. Jacob Green, on getting to her, was, by his extreme weakness, washed from the rocks, and was just saved from drowning. We now put off and ran along shore eight or ten miles, with strong wind and high sea. This shore is what is generally termed an iron-bound shore, formed of high perpendicular cliffs, against which the sea dashed with such violence as to render a landing almost impracticable, and even when effected, it would be impossible to climb the stupendous rocks. The sea running high, frequently broke into the boat, which, with the leak, caused her to make so much water, that it required the greatest exertions to keep her afloat. I wished to land, and on reaching the end of this rocky chain of cliffs, and coming to a sand beach partly sheltered from the sea by a point of rocks, we succeeded—hauled up the boat—then separated, and went in search of something to eat, and luckily procured some seal's flesh, two foxes, and three geese. The foxes here are such strangers to man, and his means and power of destruction, that they view him with the greatest indifference, unless he is carrying a goose or some other kind of fowl, when they will, without hesitation, attempt to seize, and convert it to their own use; but they generally paid dear for their temerity, being knocked down and killed with our seal clubs. I ate some of their flesh, but it is so very strong that nothing but the sauce of extreme hunger could force it down.

On the 2d of July we had hazy weather, with the wind from the N. and not so excessively cold as to prevent our being constantly on the forage for eatables. This day Samuel Ansel, in a state of despair, cried like a child, exclaiming that "we should never be released; and what a great fool he had been to volunteer to go with me in the boat, as at that time he was concerned in a plan to capture the brig, and which had been in agitation some time. In fact, from the time they were made acquainted with the war, he said he was to use his influence to induce the sailors to join in the conspiracy; and they were only waiting for a fair opportunity to execute their treacherous design; and that my leaving the brig to procure fresh provisions was the set time to accomplish their traiterous design." I was greatly agitated on hearing this, and told him "you are just where you ought to be; your guilty conscience troubles you, and you are tormented in mind, which renders your sufferings greater than ours, whose consciences are clear of having plotted against the property or happiness of any of our fellow-creatures."

The character of this man is as bad as it was represented; he is about twenty-six years of age, and has passed the greater part of his life on board a man-of-war: there he was known by the name of John Stone, but his real name was Samuel Stone, which he divulged yesterday in the boat, which we expected every moment would fill with water; when apprehensive of the consequences, and being no swimmer, he gave himself up for lost, and entreated that if any of us reached the shore, and should ever return home, that we would send information to his mother, who was known by the name of the widow Stone, living at Lutondon, near London, of the untimely death of her son Samuel. This was promised; but the moment we had safely landed, and his fears of immediate death had left him, he resumed his old habits, and began to domineer over and abuse Louder and Albrook, both excellent young men. And what was very singular about him, and what illustrates the excellence of real virtue and courage is, that though this fellow was the greatest bully breathing, and had domineered over the men and made them all afraid of him; yet, when we were in real difficulties and dangers, he was the very first to shrink back and despair; while they would bravely face them without a murmur or a tear. A striking proof this is that cowardice and guilt are only confident and brave when their cause is a bad one; but true, undaunted courage and goodness, like the main-mast, stands fast amidst the tempests, while the smaller spars are shivered and blown away.

We remained here until the 5th of July, waiting for a favourable opportunity to return to the place over which we were to haul the boat; but every moment added to my fears, that, in consequence of our increasing weakness, we should not be able to regain either Swan or Beaver Island, the places where hogs could be procured by our dog; and on this faithful and to us invaluable animal, was our sole dependence to procure them. As our lives depended upon our reaching those islands, as swine are not found on any others in this cluster, we re-launched our boat, and after severe agony of body and mind, arrived at the neck of land where we had before hauled over. To perform the same task again was much more difficult than it was before; the hope which then cheered us, that perhaps we might find our brig at Eagle Island, and be taken on board, was completely wrecked; our bodily infirmities were great and increasing; our spirits were so depressed as caused us at times to be almost indifferent whether we kept afloat or sunk in this whirlpool of adversity to rise no more. But the love of life prevailed, and at the expiration of two days' severe labour we succeeded in getting the boat, with all that belonged to her, on the opposite side of the neck of land, and immediately proceeded to Swan Island.

Now I knew where I was, I was astonished that I should lose myself in the neighbourhood of so many places with which I was so well acquainted; but the recent and unexpected flight of the brig, must at that time have impaired my recollection and firmness of mind. We landed on Swan Island about three P.M. where our faithful hunter soon procured for us a plentiful meal, furnished by a hog that he caught: we had for a long time been destitute of so good and full a supply of animal food, and nothing was required but bread or vegetables to render it truly delicious; although our impatience was so great, that, urged by hunger, it required more self-command than we possessed to permit it to remain over the fire long enough to cook. We were now engaged in hunting hogs—got six tolerable ones—and we determined to make another effort to arrive at the wreck.

We left Swan Island at about two A.M. on the 8th, steered in the direction of Mc. Cockling's Lagoon, in order, if it were possible, to find the place that communicated with Port Stephens; and if we found it, endeavour to get the boat across and proceed to Eagle Island; but we were so reduced in strength, as to render the attempt hazardous and doubtful. We arrived at the head of the lagoon about sun-rise; at the same time the wind came from the S. and blew tremendously heavy, attended with thick snow; we took our things out of the boat and hauled her up as quick as possible; turned her over for a shelter; scraped away the snow; made a fire under her, to obviate the piercing cold and heavy snow that was falling. But our anxiety to know whether we had now found the right place was so great, as to induce Jacob Green, accompanied by Sam. Ansel, to travel across the neck; when they arrived on the opposite side, Green immediately recognised it to be Port Stephen's Bay; for he had been repeatedly there in the shallop, and could not be deceived. They found the width of the neck of land, from the head of the lagoon to the bay, much greater than they had expected it, being, according to their estimation, about four miles. On their return they found great difficulty in wading through the high grass and deep snow, which continued to fall very fast. Night overtook them, and getting confused by the darkness and drifting snow, they mistook the direction, and went down the side of the lagoon opposite to the boat; when abreast of us, they accidentally saw the light of the fire that was under the boat; to get to us they had to return to the head of the lagoon, and from there travel down to us. It was near midnight when they returned much exhausted, and almost perishing with hunger and cold. They were gladly received, and all in our power was done by us poor mortals for their relief and comfort; for their long absence had greatly alarmed us, as we were apprehensive that, overcome by fatigue and the excessive cold, they might have been so unguarded as to rest themselves, when drowsiness overcame them, and they had fallen asleep in the icy arms of death, to wake no more.

Conversing about our voyage to the wreck, Green, Louder, and Albrook declared that their strength was not equal to the severe labour requisite to get the boat to the other side, and entreated me to relinquish the design of going to the wreck, and return to Beaver Island. Knowing that it would be impossible for me, without the assistance of all, to accomplish the object of the expedition; and that if we succeeded in getting the boat across, and should then be prevented, by adverse wind and weather, from proceeding to the wreck; or should we, on our arrival, find that the wreck had been carried off to sea, or destroyed by the treacherous barbarians, we most certainly would perish with hunger, cold, and fatigue, before we could get back to Beaver Island, I left the question to be decided by vote. On taking the vote, it appeared that Ansel was the only one for proceeding; but as I knew that he possessed neither resources nor firmness, I voted with the others. On this decision, and by such a majority, I thought that the sooner we commenced our return the better: it was therefore proposed and determined to start in the morning for Beaver Island, provided the weather would permit.

The storm still continued, and we suffered severely from its effects; all our fuel was consumed, and we had no fire to cook our scanty portion, nor to warm our shivering bodies and almost frozen limbs: it lasted all the next day. The piercing cold penetrated our emaciated bodies with the keenness of a dagger. With great labour we procured some withered grass and cranberry vines from under the cliffs, and half cooked some pork.

The weather having moderated on the following day, we steered for Swan Island, where we arrived in the course of a few hours. Thus ended this attempt to arrive at the wreck; a termination very different from that we had anticipated, as we commenced it with the hope of acquiring some information of the brig, either by letters that might be left for us, or the expectation of obtaining from the wreck articles which would benefit us. We were dreadfully disappointed, but we still hoped to renew the attempt when more favourable prospects presented. We run along the east side of the island until nearly up with Loop's Head, where we landed, and made the customary preparations to resist the inclemency of the night.

On the 12th we rowed round Loop's Head, and up the west side of Swan Island as far as Quaker Harbour, landed, and prepared for the approaching night by pulling up tushook grass for beds, and making ourselves as comfortable as we could. We were still employed in procuring hogs, as it was our intention to visit New Island, to examine if there were any appearances of a search having been made for us there. We got our boat afloat at daybreak of the 14th, and rowed over to New Island, and examined very closely to discover any tracks or other marks of persons having been on the island since we had left it; but after the strictest inspection we saw nothing to buoy up our hopes. We remained on the island several days, often deploring our wretchedness, which would cause us to vent invectives against those worse than savages, who had cruelly abandoned us to this cruel climate, less cruel than they; to the society of beasts—but less merciless than they; with scanty food and clothing, and this scarcely able by its raggedness to protect us from the cold; with no home but what our boat afforded—and all this we were encountering in the high latitude of 52° south. "Oh! for a whip of scorpions, to lash the rascals naked through the world."—We busied ourselves through the short day in wandering along shore, or going in-land seeking for food, as the supply of hogs that we had brought with us from Swan Island had been consumed some days since; and the wind having blown heavily from south to S. W. we had not been able to cross to Swan or Beaver Island to procure more.

The weather having moderated, and appearing settled on the 25th, we launched the boat and proceeded for, and landed on that part of Swan Island nearest to, and in full view of the harbour of New Island, as it was our intention to pass the remainder of the winter there; it being a good place to procure hogs, and only about one mile from the place which we had chosen for our camp was a small seal rookery. This rookery was formed among a great number of loose rocks, that had fallen from the adjacent cliffs: the tops of these high cliffs project far beyond the base, having the terrifying appearance of being on the point of falling, and crushing into atoms any of us who might be passing beneath, or any where within the range of the rocky fragments. Among these broken masses the seals, on being disturbed, seek for safety, and disappear in the caverns below; one of us then crawls in after them, and when near enough to reach them with a boat-hook, drags them from their concealment, and they are immediately despatched by a blow on the head, and skinned; this is performed as expeditiously as possible, from the threatening appearance of the overhanging cliffs.

The men's clothing, which was in a very indifferent state when they left the brig, was now so far worn out, that it was falling from their backs; and as food and clothing were indispensable to the preservation of our lives, we so arranged as to have two departments for procuring these in full activity at the same time. A strict look-out was to be likewise kept up for any boat or vessel that might be approaching or passing New Island Harbour. Indeed, no kind of craft could enter without our immediate notice, it being only seven miles distant, and open to our full view; for though often deceived by hope, she yet flattered us, by representing that perhaps the shallop would return to the harbour to search for us. Our duties and employments were therefore so ordered, that one should cook, and at the same time keep watch, as the harbour, its entrance, and all its parts were fully exposed to his view from the place where he had his fire. Two, with the dog, were to procure provisions; and the other two to procure fur seals, to make clothing of their skins.

The wild hogs had become very scarce and shy on this part of the island, the most of them resorting to the other end, and consequently to obtain food we were obliged to follow them to their haunts, and had to travel seven or eight miles through the wintry storms and frosts. After killing our game, we returned to the camp, carrying it on our backs; having to pass over hills, across valleys, floundering through high snow-banks, wading deep creeks or runs of water, and neither our feet or legs were a single moment dry. On these hunting excursions what did we not endure? These hogs in size, appearance, and habits, resemble the common or domestic hogs of the United States; the old boars are large and generally fierce, sometimes inflicting severe wounds on our dog; they are very thin and run fast; their flesh is sweet, but lean, not having an ounce of fat on their carcase, and has more the flavour of veal than of common pork. It is a very light diet, easy of digestion, which leaves a vacancy in the stomach that gives rise to unpleasant feelings, which it requires another meal to remove.

When obliged to bring hogs from the other end of the island, we made them light enough for a single man to carry, by taking out all the entrails except the liver, cutting off the head, and leaving the whole of these behind. We tied the fore and hinder legs together, put our head between them, and by this management the hog laid firmly on the shoulders, and we then commenced our march for the camp; such were the arduous and severe duties of the swine hunter—the other two were in close attendance on the rookery, and more than fifty seals were obtained.

We daily exchanged duties, so that each man performed his full share of all the labours. The seal skins were prepared by us in our best manner for clothing; first by drying, and then rubbing them until they were limber; they were then made up into full suits, consisting of jacket, trowsers, vest, and cap;

to sew them we were fortunate enough to have sail-needles, and a ball of twine, and when that was expended, we took a cloth out of our main-sail, which was new light duck, ravelled it, and thus procured a good substitute for twine. When the suits were completed and worn, the men found them so comfortable, in comparison with their old ones, that I was induced, after a while, to try a suit myself, although I had other clothes sufficient to make necessary changes; having always been accustomed, in every excursion in the boat, to carry with me a requisite supply.

The seals we particularly valued not only on account of their skins, but also for their blubber, which we used as fuel; when destitute of it, we had recourse to the dry tushook grass, which, having little substance, we could not keep up a fire with it that would more than parboil our pork, which caused it to be very unpalatable. During our stay at this place, which we called "Rat Camp," we were intolerably plundered and annoyed by the almost incredible number of rats with which it was infested. To prevent their ruinous and extensive depredations on our provisions, when we were so rich as to have much on hand, we were compelled to adopt several plans to prevent their piracies; but, in general, their sagacity in committing their felonies was greater than ours in preventing them. At length we made trial of raising a pair of shears, by lashing three oars together, and, with the boat's painter, hoisting the provisions as high as the shears would permit; we then greased the oars with seal's blubber, and this prevented the rats from mounting to the top of the shears, descending the rope, and nearly destroying a whole hog in the course of the night.

One day, while performing our customary tour in pursuit of necessaries, we fell in with a very large, old sea lion, asleep, at a distance from the shore; we were desirous to kill him to have his blubber for fuel, and his skin for mockasons; but we were without our lance, which, owing to the great difficulty in landing and getting our things into the boat, we had unfortunately left behind at Hook Camp. We thought it impossible to kill him without the lance, yet as his skin and blubber would be so valuable to us, and his being asleep so far from the shore, seemed almost to promise success to my attack, after lashing a skinning knife firmly to the end of my club, I directed the men to provide themselves with as many stones as they could carry in their caps and pockets. We then reconnoitered him. My plan of attack was, to stab him under one of his fore flippers, being the nearest to his heart, and if the knife were only long enough to reach it, we might succeed in killing him. The moment I made the assault, the others were to throw stones at his eyes, and blind him so that he should not be able to see his way to the water, and this would afford me an opportunity to repeat the stabs. Accordingly I very cautiously approached him, and when I was sufficiently near him, being still asleep, I gave him a deep stab under one of his fore flippers; but the knife was not long enough to reach the seat of life, and on receiving the wound he furously sprang up, and dashed about, bit and rooted up the tushooks from pain and madness, and attempted to fight his way to the water; but the stones were so effectually thrown against his eyes, that he could neither see the water, nor in what direction we were. I repeated the thrusts, until having fallen from loss of blood, we despatched him, and took off his skin and blubber.

The killing of an old sea lion, without a lance, may appear almost incredible, to those who have seen or attacked one of the largest size, and witnessed his desperate and determined manner of defence and attack. A blow on the head has little or no effect, even if a man has a fair opportunity to inflict it, which very seldom occurs, unless accompanied with great danger. The sea resembles the land lion in the head, shoulders, and breast; there is a difference in the mouth, their jaw bones being larger and their teeth nearly double the size; their neck and breast are covered with a mane, about four or five inches in length; their skin is very thick, particularly on the neck and shoulders. I have measured skins that were on these parts an inch thick. They have heavy and clumsy bodies, which generally weigh from five to 700 lbs.

Having now resigned all hope of being sought for, by either the shallop or brig, we decided to return to New Island, as whaling ships sometimes put in there for water: we therefore left Beaver, and crossed over to New Island. Having hauled up the boat, and made the usual preparations, I told the men that it was about the season when the albatross began to lay her eggs, and that they had better go up to the rookery, and see if the birds had commenced; they accordingly went and found five or six eggs. Having lost the run or account of time, I concluded, from the circumstance of finding eggs, that it was now about the 10th of October, and as the albatross begins laying in the first week of that month, I consequently began to reckon from this period as the 10th.

The weather continuing pleasant, each man was provided with a seal skin bag and repaired to the rookery, to collect eggs from the nests of the albatrosses; and as they never leave their eggs from the time they begin to cover them until they are hatched, they soon become unfit to eat. Every one obtained and carried to the boat two loads of these fresh eggs, which afforded us a noble feast. This bird never leaves her young until they are half-grown, for the rooks are always upon the alert, watching for an opportunity to dive down on the nest – break the eggs, or kill and devour the young. The albatross is almost as large again as a goose, and their eggs are of a proportionate size; their wings, when extended, measure from tip to tip thirteen or fourteen feet; their bills are large and strong, they bite severely and desperately wound the hands of those who disturb their nests.

I proposed to some of the men to go down to Sea Lion Point, at the south end, for a hair seal skin, to make mockasons of, as they were more lasting than those made of the fur seal skin. Green and Albrook said it was their turn to go for vines; Louder, that was his cook day; and Ansel, that he wanted to mend his trowsers. I went under the boat, and having sharpened my knife, took my club, and called the dog, but he did not come: I inquired where he was; Louder replied, that he supposed the dog had followed Green and Albrook, who had gone for vines. As they had taken an opposite direction to that which I intended, I resolved to wait for their return. Ansel then sprung up from where he was sitting, and said, "Capt. Barnard, I will go with you." I replied, "if you will go, we ought to have the dog to hunt the seals in the tushooks." "O, if there is any there," said he, "I will hunt them up." I agreed to his proposal, and set off: we passed round the mountain which makes the S. W. part of Hooker's Harbour, and then descended, engaged in conversation, to cross the valley. This valley is full of tushooks, which are higher than a man's head, and through which, as we walked, we continued our conversation, although we could not discern each other. After I had got out of the valley, upon the plain, I stood still, waited for and expected every moment to see Sam make his appearance from the tushooks; but as he did not come I called, and after waiting several minutes, I called again as loud as I could, but no answer was returned. A suspicion now darted through my mind, that he had returned to the boat, and that they were all acting upon some preconcerted plan. Their first declining to accompany me—the absence of my dog—the clandestine disappearance of Ansell, all added strength to the suspicion that some improper scheme was in agitation, the knowledge of which had been withheld from me.

Although I was far removed from the busy world and its distractions, yet I found that there was no spot of earth, however distant or concealed, which is free from the trials and disappointments incident to human nature; and that go where we will, we can never fly from ourselves. But there is one consolation left to support us as we tread life's journey—that every situation, however trying, has its peculiar antidote to bear it up; and that however deserted and cheerless the heart may be, there is a Being that "compasseth our path, and our lying down, and is acquainted with all our ways."

19

The RAFT *of the* MEDUSA

From *Narrative of a Voyage to Senegal*

BY J.–B. HENRY SAVIGNY AND ALEXANDER CORRÉARD

1816

The shipwreck of the Medusa *is perhaps as well known a story, at least in Europe, as the sinking of the* Titanic, *but it is far more gothic in its level of horror. The behavior of the survivors and the incredible indifference of the officers of the* Medusa *to those they abandoned on the raft became a national scandal in France after it became known; and Gericault's extraordinary painting* The Raft of the Medusa, *dominating the gallery in the Louvre devoted to heroic French painting of the 19th century, keeps that scandal perpetually in mind.*

We are excerpting those pages from the original English translation of the story, written by two of the raft's survivors, that describe what happened on the raft after it was abandoned by those who were supposed to be towing it to land. The ship, the Medusa, *was a French frigate, one of a small squadron carrying the new French governor of Senegal, various private citizens, and several hundred soldiers to Africa. All told there were 365 people on the four ships in the squadron, 240 of them on the* Medusa. *France had only just reacquired its West African territories in the treaty that finally ended the Napoleonic Wars. France itself was a defeated, dispirited country with the Bourbons restored to power, but with a strong left-leaning political opposition that was essentially Bonapartist. It was entering upon a half-century of political uncertainty and weakness. The squadron carried twenty women and eight children. The* Medusa *ran aground on a well-known reef, the so-called "bank of Arguin," according to the text, west of Cape Blanco in what is now Mauritania. The cause? Incompetence and stupidity. The captain listened to the wrong people. He should have known himself exactly where he was.*

Thanks to the same incompetence all measures to free the Medusa *failed. It was never clear who was in charge, the new governor or the captain of the ship, and in the end high winds doomed the ship. It had six small boats aboard, not nearly enough to carry the hundreds on board. The crew constructed a raft that was supposed to hold most of them; the idea was that the smaller boats would tow this raft to shore. The soldiers, many of them mercenaries from foreign countries, not native French, were convinced that the crew was going to leave them behind on the raft and came close to mutiny even while they were still on the ship. As it turned out, they were right. The raft was large, about 24 feet wide and 75 long, but when the 150 people who were consigned to it got on board, they found themselves standing in three feet of water. To lighten the load they threw most of the provisions overboard. The excerpt begins at this point.*

When it was all over and the survivors were rescued, the powers-that-be made every effort to suppress this story. That was not to be. The two authors of the book, J.-B. Henry Savigny and Alexander Correard, were determined to reveal the truth about how supposedly responsible people—the governor, the captain, the ship's crew—had behaved in a crisis. The book, which bore the bland title Narrative of a Voyage to Senegal *when it was published in 1817, caused an uproar. Not just human beings but the honor of the French nation had been betrayed. The honor of the French nation had already been badly damaged by the wars. Gericault's painting underlined the scandal.*

Which is a story in itself. Gericault, then in his late twenties, had just come back from Italy when the book was published, and he decided to use the raft as a subject about that time. He began working on the painting the following spring. His own life was in a state of turmoil then; he had been having an affair with his maternal uncle's wife and she became pregnant with his child. The affair had to be broken off. He threw himself into work on the painting as an escape, most likely, from his private troubles. Threw himself understates the case. It took him 18 months of intense work to finish it. He made endless studies. He made sketches in hospitals, where he could find "models who did not have to grimace to show every nuance of physical or mental suffering, the ravages of sickness, and the terror of death," according to one of his friends. From medical friends he obtained dead bodies, severed heads, severed arms and legs, kept them in his studio, "and insisted on working in this charnel house atmosphere, the infection of which only his most devoted friends and the most intrepid models were bold enough to risk." The finished painting catches a moment when the survivors on the raft spy a sail in the distance, and think it is a ship sent to rescue them. From the text, we know that the survivors did see a sail in the dis-

tance, and that it did not come. The painting capped Gericault's brief career. He died five years after finishing it of spinal tuberculosis. I have seen his death mask. He died in agony. It was as if he had lived only to paint this painting, which still draws crowds in the Louvre, a monument to the great paradox of human nature, its capacity for heroic endurance, its predilection for treachery and betrayal.

BEFORE WE PROCEED, WE WILL DESCRIBE THE CONSTRUCTION OF THIS raft, to which a hundred and fifty persons were entrusted.

It was composed of the top-masts of the frigate, yards, fishes, boom, &c. These different pieces joined together by very strong ropes, were perfectly solid; the two principal pieces were two top-masts, which were placed at the extremity of the two sides; four other masts, two of which were of the same length and strength as the first, joined two by two, at the center of the machine, added to its solidity. The other pieces were placed within these four first but were not equal to them in length. Boards were nailed on this first foundation, and formed a kind of parapet, which would have been of great service to us if it had been higher. To render our raft still more solid, long pieces of wood had been placed across, which projected at least three metres: on the sides, there was a kind of railing, but it was not above forty centimetres in height: it would have been easy to add some crotches to it, which would have formed a breast-work of sufficient height; but it was not done, probably because those who had the machine built, were not to be exposed upon it. To the ends of the top-masts, two top-gallant yards were lashed, the farther ends of which were bound by a very strong cord, and thus formed the front part of the raft. The angular space, formed by the two yards, was filled with pieces of wood laid across, and planks ill adjusted. This fore part, which was at least two metres in length, had very little solidity, and was continually submerged. The hinder part did not terminate in a point like the fore part, but a considerable length of this part was not more solid, so that in fact, there was only the center which was really to be depended upon: an example will enable the reader to judge of its dimensions. When we were no more than fifteen in it, we had not space enough to lie down, and yet we were extremely close together. The raft, from one extremity to the other was at least twenty metres in length, and above seven in breadth; this length might induce one to think, at the first sight, that it was able to carry two hundred men, but we soon had cruel proofs of its weakness. It was without sails or mast. As we left the frigate they threw us the fore-top-gallant and the main-top-gallant sails; but they did it with such precipitation, that, some persons who were at their post, were in danger of being wounded by the fall of these sails, which were bent to the yards. They did not give us any ropes to set up our mast.

There was on board the raft a great quantity of barrels of flour, which had been deposited there the preceding day, not to serve for provisions during the passage from the frigate to the coast, but because the raft, formed of the barrels, not having succeeded, they were deposited on the machine, that they might not be carried away by the sea; there were also six barrels of wine and two small casks of water, which had been put there for the use of the people.

Scarcely fifty men had got upon the raft, when it sunk at least seventy centimetres under water; so that to facilitate the embarkation of the other soldiers it was necessary to throw into the sea all the flour barrels, which lifted by the waves, began to float and were violently driven against the men who were at their post; if they had been fixed, perhaps some of them might have been saved: as it was, we saved only the wine and the water, because several persons united to preserve them, and had much difficulty to hinder them from being thrown into the sea like the flour barrels. The raft, lightened by throwing away these barrels, was able to receive more men; we were at length a hundred and fifty. The machine was submerged at least a metre: we were so crowded together that it was impossible to take a single step; at the back and the front, we were in water up to the middle. At the moment that we were putting off from the frigate, a bag with twenty-five pounds of biscuit was thrown us, which fell into the sea; we got it up with difficulty; it was converted into a paste, but we preserved it in that condition. Several considerate persons fastened the casks of wine and water to the cross pieces of the raft, and we kept a strict watch over them. Thus we have faithfully described the nature of our situation when we put off from the vessel.

The Commander of the raft was named Coudin who was, what is called in the French marine an *Aspirant* of the first class. Some days before our departure from the roads of the Isle of Aix, he had received a severe contusion on the fore part of the right leg, which was not approaching to its cure when we stranded and wholly incapacitated him from moving. One of his comrades, moved by his situation, offered to take his place, but Mr. Coudin, though wounded, preferred repairing to the dangerous post which was assigned him, because he was the oldest officer of his class on board. He was hardly on board the raft, when the sea water so increased the pain in his leg, that he nearly fainted; we gave notice of his situation to the nearest boat, we were answered that a boat would come and fetch this officer. I do not know whether the order was given, but it is certain the Mr. Coudin was obliged to remain on the fatal raft.

The long-boat, which we have been forced to lose sight of for a moment, in order to give these necessary details, at length rallied; it was, as we have stated, the last that left the frigate. The lieutenant who commanded her, justly fearing that he should not be able to keep the sea, in a crazy boat destitute of oars, badly rigged, and making much water, ran along-side of the first boat, begging it to take in some men; they refused. This long-boat was to leave us some ropes to fix our mast; which an instant before had been hauled to us, by the first boat, which we had before us: we do not know what reason hindered it from leaving us these ropes, but it passed on, and ran along-side the second boat, which equally refused to take anybody on board. The officer, who commanded the long-boat, seeing that they refused to take any of his men, and falling more and more under the wind, because his sails were badly trimmed, and the currents drove him, made up to the third boat, commanded by a sub-lieutenant named Maudet; this officer, commanding a slight boat which the day before had a plank beat in, by one of the cross pieces of the raft (an accident which had been remedied by covering the hole with a large piece of lead), and being besides heavily laden, in order to avoid the shock of the long-boat, which might have been fatal to him, was forced to let loose the towrope, which held him to the barge, and thus broke in two the line formed by the boats before the raft, by separating himself from it with the captains boat which was at the head: when the captain and Mr. Maudet had disengaged themselves they hauled the wind, and then put about to come and take their post; Mr. Maudet, even hailed M. de Chaumareys, "*Captain take your towrope again*," he received for answer, *yes my friend*. Two boats were still at their post, but before the other two were able to rejoin them, the barge separated itself; the officer who commanded it, expressed himself as follows respecting his thus abandoning us. "The towrope was not let go from my boat, but from that behind me." This second desertion was the forerunner of another still more cruel; for the officer who commanded the last boat in which was the governor, after having towed us alone, for a moment, caused the rope to be loosened which held it to the raft. When the towropes were let go, we were two leagues from the frigate; the breeze came from the sea, which was as favorable as could be desired. This last towrope did not break, as the governor has tried to persuade the minister of the marine, and several persons who escaped from the raft. Walking on the terrace of a French merchant at Senegal, in the presence of Messrs. Savigny and Coudin, the governor explained the affair as follows: "Some men were on the front of the raft, at the place where the towrope was fixed, which they pulled so as to draw the boat nearer to them; they had already pulled several fathoms of it to them, but a wave coming, gave a violent shock; these men were obliged to let go: the boats then proceeded more rapidly, till the rope was stretched; at the moment when the boats effected this tension the effort was such, that the rope broke." This manner of explaining this last desertion is very adroit, and might easily deceive those who were not on the spot, but it is not possible for us to accede to it, since we could even name the person who loosened it.

Some persons belonging to the other boats have assured us, that all the boats were coming to resume their post, when a cry of "*we forsake them*" was heard: we have this fact from many of our companions in misfortune. The whole line was thrown into disorder, and no measures were taken to remedy it: it is probable, that if one of the first officers had set the example, order would have been restored; but everyone was left to himself; hence there was no concert in the little division; everyone thought of escaping from personal danger.

Let us here do justice to the courage of Mr. Clanet, pay-master of the frigate, who was on board the governor's boat; if he had been listened to, this towrope would not have been let go; every moment an officer who was in the governor's boat cried out aloud, "*shall I let go?*" Mr. Clanet opposed it, answering with firmness, "*No, no!*" Some persons joined him, but could obtain nothing, the towrope was let go: we considered it as certain, that the commander of the other boats, on seeing the chief of the expedition courageously devote himself, would have come and resumed their posts: but it may be said that each individual boat was abandoned by all the others: there was wanting, on this occasion, a man of great coolness: and ought not this man to have been found among the chief officers? How shall their conduct be justified? There are, certainly, some reasons to be alleged. Impartial judges of events, we will describe them, not as unhappy victims of the consequences of this desertion, but as men free from all personal resentment, and who listen only to the voice of truth.

The raft, drawn by all the boats united, dragged them a little back; it is true that we just had the ebb, and the currents set from shore. To be in the open sea with undecked vessels, might well inspire some apprehensions: but, in a few hours, the currents would change and favor us; we ought to have waited for this moment, which would have infallibly demonstrated the possibility of drawing us to the coast, which was not above twelve or fifteen leagues distant: this is so true that the boats discovered the coast, the same evening, before sunset. Perhaps they would have been forced to forsake us the second night after our departure, if indeed more than thirty-six hours had been required to tow us to land; for the weather was very bad; but we should then have been very near to the coast, and it would have been very easy to save us: at least we should have had only the elements to accuse!— We are persuaded that a short time would have sufficed to tow us within sight of land, for, the evening of our being deserted, the raft was precisely in the direction which the boats had followed between the frigates and the coast, and, at least, five leagues from the former. The next morning, at daybreak, we could no longer see the Medusa.

At the first moment we did not really believe that we had been so cruelly abandoned. We imagined that the boats had let loose, because they had perceived a vessel, and hastened towards it to ask assistance. The long-boat was pretty near us to leeward on the starboard. She lowered her fore-sail halfway down: her manœuvre made us think that she was going to take the first towrope: she remained so a moment, lowered her foresail entirely, set up her main-mast, hoisted her sails, and followed the rest of the division. Some men in this boat, seeing that the others deserted us, threatened to fire upon them, but were stopped by Lieutenant Espiau. Many persons have assured us that it was the intention of this officer to come and take the towrope; but his crew opposed it; had he done so, he would certainly have acted with great imprudence. His efforts would have been of little use to us, and his devotedness would but have increased the number of victims. As soon as this boat was gone, we had no doubt but that we were abandoned; yet we were not fully convinced of it till the boats had disappeared.

It was now that we had need of all our courage, which, however, forsook us more than once: we really believed that we were sacrificed, and with one accord, we cried that this desertion was premeditated. We all swore to revenge ourselves if we had the good fortune to reach the shore, and there is no doubt but that, if we could have overtaken, the next day, those who had fled in the boats, an obstinate combat would have taken place between them and us.

It was then that some persons who had been marked out for the boats, deeply regretted that they had preferred the raft, because duty and honor had pointed out this post to them. We could mention some persons: for example, Mr. Corréard, among others, was to go in one of the boats; but twelve of the workmen, whom we commanded, had been set down for the raft; he thought that in his quality of commander of engineers, it was his duty not to separate from the majority of those who had been confided to him, and who had promised to follow him wherever the exigencies of the service might require; from that moment his fate became inseparable from theirs, and he exerted himself to the utmost to obtain the governor's permission to have his men embarked in the same boat as himself; but seeing that he could obtain nothing to ameliorate the fate of these brave men, he told the governor that he was incapable of committing an act of baseness: that since he would not put his workmen in the same boat with him, he begged him to allow him to go on the raft with them, which was granted.

Several military officers imitated their example; only two of those who were to command the troops did not think fit to place themselves upon the raft, the equipment of which, in truth, could not inspire much confidence.

One of them, Captain Beinière, placed himself in the long-boat with 36 of his soldiers. We had been told that these troops had been charged to superintend the proceedings of the other boats, and to fire upon those who should attempt to abandon the raft. It is true, as we have seen above, that some brave soldiers listening, perhaps, more to the voice of humanity and French honor, than to the strict maxims of discipline, were desirous of employing their arms against those who basely abandoned us, but, that their will and their actions were paralized by the passive obedience which they owed to their officers, who opposed this resolution.

The other, Mr. Danglas, a lieutenant, who had lately left the *gardes-du-corps*, had at first embarked with us upon the raft, where his post was assigned him, but when he saw the danger which he incurred on this unstable machine, he made haste to quit it, on the pretext that he had forgotten something on board the frigate, and did not return. It was he whom we saw, armed with a carbine, threaten to fire on the barge of the governor, when it began to move from the frigate. This movement, and some other actions which were taken for madness, nearly cost him his life; for while he was thus giving himself up to a kind of extravagance, the captain took flight, and abandoned him on board the frigate with the sixty-three men whom he left there. When M. Danglas saw himself treated in this manner, he gave marks of the most furious despair. They were obliged to hinder him from attempting his own life. With loud cries he invoked death, which he believed inevitable in the midst of perils so imminent. It is certain that if Mr. Espiau, who had his long-boat already full, had not returned to take from on board the frigate, the forty-six men, among whom, was Mr. Danglas, he and all his companions would not, perhaps, have experienced a better fate than the seventeen who were finally left on board the Medusa.

After the disappearance of the boats, the consternation was extreme: all the terrors of thirst and famine arose before our imaginations, and we had besides to contend with a perfidious element, which already covered the half of our bodies: when recovered from their stupefaction, the sailors and soldiers gave themselves up to despair; all saw inevitable destruction before them, and gave vent in lamentations to the gloomy thoughts which agitated them. All we said did not at first avail to calm their fears, in which we however participated, but which a greater degree of strength of mind enabled us to dissemble. At last, a firm countenance and consoling words succeeded in calming them by degrees, but could not wholly dispel the terror with which they were struck; for according to the judicious reflection, made after reading our deplorable story, by Mr. Jay, whose authority we quote with pleasure, "To support extreme misfortunes, and what is worthy of remark, to bear great fatigues, moral energy is much more necessary than corporeal strength, nay, than the habit of privations and hard labour. On this narrow theatre where so many sufferings are united, where the most cruel extremes of hunger and thirst are experienced, strong and indefatigable men who have been brought up to the most laborious professions, sink in succession under the weight of the common destiny, while men of weak constitution, and not inured to fatigue, find in their minds the strength which their bodies want, endure with courage unheard-of trials, and issue victorious from their struggle with the most horrible afflictions. It is to the education they have received, to the exercise of their intellectual faculties, that they owe this astonishing superiority and their deliverance." When tranquillity was a little restored, we began to look upon the raft for the charts, the compass and the anchor, which we presumed had been placed there, from what had been said to us at the time we quitted the frigate. These highly necessary articles had not been put upon our machine. The want of a compass in particular, greatly alarmed us, and we uttered cries of rage and vengeance. Mr. Corréard then recollected, that he had seen one in the hands of one of the chief workmen under his command, and enquired of this man about it: "Yes, yes," said he, "I have it with me." This news transported us with joy, and we thought that our safety depended on this feeble resource. This little compass was about the size of a crown-piece, and far from correct. He who has not been exposed to events, in which his existence was in imminent peril, can form but a faint idea of the value which one then sets upon the most common and simple objects, with what avidity one seizes the slightest means, that are capable of softening the rigour of the fate with which one has to contend. This compass was given to the commander of the raft; but an accident deprived us of it for ever: it fell, and was lost between the pieces of wood which composed our machine: we had kept it only for a few hours; after this loss, we had nothing to guide us but the rising and setting of the sun.

We had all left the frigate without taking any food: hunger began to be severely felt; we mixed our biscuit-paste (which had fallen into the sea) with a little wine, and we distributed it thus prepared: such was our first meal, and the best we had the whole time we were on the raft.

An order, according to numbers, was fixed for the distribution of our miserable provisions. The ration of wine was fixed at three quarters a day: we shall say no more of the biscuit: the first distribution consumed it entirely. The day passed over pretty quietly: we conversed on the means which we should employ to save ourselves; we spoke of it as a certainty, which animated our courage: and we kept up that of the soldiers, by cherishing the hope of being soon able to revenge ourselves upon those who had so basely abandoned us. This hope of vengeance inspired us all equally, and we uttered a thousand imprecations against those who had left us a prey to so many misfortunes and dangers. The officer who commanded the raft being unable to move, Mr. Savigny took on himself the care of setting up the mast; he caused the pole of one of the frigate's masts to be cut in two; we employed the main-top-gallant sail; the mast was kept up by the rope which had served to tow us, of which we made shrouds and stays: it was fixed on the anterior third of the raft. The sail trimmed very well, but the effect of it was of very little use to us; it served only when the wind came from behind, and to make the raft preserve this direction it was necessary to trim the sail, as if the wind came athwart. We think that the cross position which our raft always retained, may be attributed to the too great length of the pieces of wood which projected on each side.

In the evening, our hearts and our prayers, with the impulse natural to the unfortunate, were directed towards heaven; we invoked it with fervour, and we derived from our prayers the advantage of hoping in our safety: one must have experienced cruel situations, to imagine what a soothing charm, in the midst of misfortune, is afforded by the sublime idea of a God, the protector of the unfortunate. One consoling idea still pleased our imaginations; we presumed that the little division had sailed for the Isle of Arguin, and that after having landed there a part of its people, would return to our assistance: this idea, which we tried to inspire into our soldiers and sailors, checked their clamours. The night came, and our hopes were not yet fulfilled: the wind freshened, the sea rose considerably. What a dreadful night! Nothing but the idea of seeing the boats the next day, gave some consolation to our people, who being most of them unused to the motion of a vessel, at every shock of the sea, fell upon each other. Mr. Savigny, assisted by some persons, who, in the midst of this disorder, still retained their presence of mind, fastened some ropes to the pieces of the raft: the men took hold of them, and by means of this support, were better able to resist the force of the waves: some were obliged to fasten themselves. In the middle of the night the weather was very bad; very heavy waves rolled upon us, and often threw us down with great violence; the cries of the people were mingled with the roaring of the billows; a dreadful sea lifted us every moment from the raft, and threatened to carry us away. This scene was rendered still more awful by the horrors of a very dark night; for some moments we thought that we saw fires at a distance. We had taken the precaution to hang, at the top of the mast, some gun-powder and pistols, with which we had provided ourselves on board the frigate: we made signals by burning a great many charges of powder; we even fired some pistol-shot, but it seems that these fires were only an illusion of the eyesight, or perhaps they were nothing but the dashing of the breakers.

This whole night we contended against death, holding fast by the ropes which were strongly fastened. Rolled by the waves from the back to the front, and from the front to the back, and sometimes precipitated into the sea, suspended between life and death, lamenting our misfortune, certain to perish, yet still struggling for a fragment of existence with the cruel element which threatened to swallow us up. Such was our situation till day-break; every moment were heard the lamentable cries of the soldiers and sailors; they prepared themselves for death; they bid farewell to each other, imploring the protection of Heaven, and addressing fervent prayers to God: all made vows to him, notwithstanding the certainty that they should never be able to fulfil them. Dreadful situation! How is it possible to form an idea of it, which is not below the truth!

About seven o'clock, in the morning, the sea fell a little, the wind blew with less fury; but what a sight presented itself to our view! Ten or twelve unhappy wretches, having their lower extremities entangled in the openings between the pieces of the raft, had not been able to disengage themselves, and had lost their lives; several others had been carried off by the violence of the sea. At the hour of repast we took fresh numbers, in order to leave no break in the series: we missed twenty men: we will not affirm that this number is very exact, for we found that some soldiers, in order to have more than their ration, took two, and even three numbers. We were so many persons crowded together, that it was absolutely impossible to prevent these abuses.

Amidst these horrors, an affecting scene of filial piety forced us to shed tears: two young men raised and recognised, for their father, an unfortunate man who was stretched senseless under the feet of the people; at first, they thought he was dead, and their despair expressed itself by the most affecting lamentations; it was perceived, however, that this almost inanimate body still had breath; we lavished on him all the assistance in our power; he recovered by degrees, and was restored to life and to the prayers of his sons, who held him fast embraced in their arms. While the rights of nature resumed their empire in this affecting episode of our sad adventures, we had soon the afflicting sight of a melancholy contrast. Two young lads, and a baker, did not fear to seek death, by throwing themselves into the sea, after having taken leave of their companions in misfortune. Already the faculties of our men were singularly impaired; some fancied they saw the land; others, vessels which were coming to save us; all announced to us by their cries these fallacious visions.

We deplored the loss of our unhappy companions; we did not presage, at this moment, the still more terrible scene which was to take place the following night; far from that, we enjoyed a degree of satisfaction, so fully were we persuaded that the boats would come to our relief. The day was fine, and the most perfect tranquillity prevailed on our raft. The evening came, and the boats did not appear. Despondency began again to seize all our people, and a mutinous spirit manifested itself by cries of fury; the voice of the officers was wholly disregarded. When the night came, the sky was covered with thick clouds; the wind, which during the day had been rather high, now became furious, and agitated the sea, which, in an instant, grew very rough.

If the preceding night had been terrible, this was still more horrible. Mountains of water covered us every moment, and broke, with violence, in the midst of us; very happily we had the wind behind us, and the fury of the waves was a little checked by the rapidity of our progress; we drove towards the land. From the violence of the sea, the men passed rapidly from the back to the front of the raft, we were obliged to keep in the centre, the most solid part of the raft; those who could not get there, almost all perished. Before and behind the waves dashed with fury, and carried off the men in spite of all their resistance. At the centre, the crowd was such that some poor men were stifled by the weight of their comrades, who fell upon them every moment; the officers kept themselves at the foot of the little mast, obliged, every instant, to avoid the waves, to call to those who surrounded them to go on the one or the other side, for the waves which came upon us, nearly athwart, gave our raft a position almost perpendicular, so that, in order to counterbalance it, we were obliged to run to that side which was raised up by the sea.

The soldiers and sailors, terrified by the presence of an almost inevitable danger, gave themselves up for lost. Firmly believing that they were going to be swallowed up, they resolved to soothe their last moments by drinking till they lost the use of their reason; we had not strength to oppose this disorder; they fell upon a cask which was at the middle of the raft, made a large hole at one end, and with little tin cups which they had brought from on board the frigate, they each took a pretty large quantity, but they were soon obliged to desist, because the sea water entered by the hole which they had made.

The fumes of the wine soon disordered their brains, already affected by the presence of danger and want of food. Thus inflamed, these men, become deaf to the voice of reason, desired to implicate, in one common destruction, their companions in misfortune; they openly expressed their intention to rid themselves of the officers, who they said, wished to oppose their design, and then to destroy the raft by cutting the ropes which united the different parts that composed it. A moment after, they were proceeding to put this plan in execution. One of them advanced to the edge of the raft with a boarding-axe, and began to strike the cords: this was the signal for revolt: we advanced in order to stop these madmen: he who was armed with the axe, with which he even threatened an officer, was the first victim: a blow with a sabre put an end to his existence. This man was an Asiatic, and soldier in a colonial regiment: a colossal stature, short curled hair, an extremely large nose, an enormous mouth, a sallow complexion, gave him a hideous air. He had placed himself, at first, in the middle of the raft, and at every blow of his fist he overthrew those who stood in his way; he inspired the greatest terror, and nobody dared to approach him. If there had been half-a-dozen like him, our destruction would have been inevitable.

Some persons, desirous of prolonging their existence, joined those who wished to preserve the raft, and armed themselves: of this number were some subaltern officers and many passengers. The mutineers drew their sabres, and those who had none, armed themselves with knives: they advanced resolutely against us; we put ourselves on our defence: the attack was going to begin. Animated by despair, one of the mutineers lifted his sabre against an officer; he immediately fell, pierced with wounds. This firmness awed them a moment; but did not at all diminish their rage. They ceased to threaten us, and presenting a front bristling with sabres and bayonets, they retired to the back part, to execute their plan. One of them pretended to rest himself on the little railing which formed the sides of the raft, and with a knife began to cut the cords. Being informed by a servant, we rushed upon him—a soldier attempted to defend him—threatened an officer with his knife, and in attempting to strike him, only pierced his coat—the officer turned round—overpowered his adversary, and threw both him and his comrade into the sea!

After this there were no more partial affairs: the combat became general. Some cried lower the sail; a crowd of madmen instantly threw themselves on the yards and the shrouds, and cut the stays, and let the mast fall, and nearly broke the thigh of a captain of foot, who fell senseless. He was seized by the soldiers, who threw him into the sea: we perceived it—saved him, and placed him on a barrel, from which he was taken by the seditious; who were going to cut out his eyes with a pen-knife. Exasperated by so many cruelties, we no longer kept any measures, and charged them furiously. With our sabres drawn we traversed the lines which the soldiers formed, and many atoned with their lives for a moment of delusion. Several passengers displayed much courage and coolness in these cruel moments.

Mr. Corréard was fallen into a kind of trance, but hearing every moment cries of "*To arms! To us, comrades! We are undone!*" joined to the cries and imprecations of the wounded and the dying, he was soon roused from his lethargy. The increasing confusion made him sensible that it was necessary to be upon his guard. Armed with his sabre, he assembled some of his workmen on the front of the raft, and forbid them to hurt anyone unless they were attacked. He remained almost always with them, and they had several times to defend themselves against the attacks of the mutineers; who falling into the sea, returned by the front of the raft; which placed Mr. Corréard and his little troop between two dangers, and rendered their position very difficult to be defended. Every moment men presented themselves, armed with knives, sabres and bayonets; many had carbines, which they used as clubs. The workmen did their utmost to stop them, by presenting the point of their sabres; and, notwithstanding the repugnance they felt to combat their unhappy countrymen, they were however obliged to use their arms without reserve; because many of the mutineers attacked them with fury, it was necessary to repulse them in the same manner. In this action some of the workmen received large wounds; he who commanded them reckons a great number, which he received in the various combats they had to maintain. At last their united efforts succeeded in dispersing the masses that advanced furiously against them.

During this combat, Mr. Corréard was informed, by one of his workmen who remained faithful, that one of their comrades, named Dominique, had taken part with the mutineers, and that he had just been thrown into the sea. Immediately forgetting the fault and the treachery of this man, he threw himself in after him, at the place where the voice of the wretch had just been heard calling for assistance; he seized him by the hair, and had the good fortune to get him on board. Dominique had received, in a charge, several sabre wounds, one of which had laid open his head. Notwithstanding the darkness we found the wound, which appeared to us to be very considerable. One of the workmen gave his handkerchief to bind it up and stanch the blood. Our care revived this wretch; but as soon as he recovered his strength, the ungrateful Dominique, again forgetting his duty and the signal service that he had just received from us, went to rejoin the mutineers. So much baseness and fury did not go unpunished; and soon afterwards, while combating us anew, he met with his death, from which he, in fact, did not merit to be rescued, but which he would probably have avoided, if faithful to honor and to gratitude, he had remained among us.

Just when we had almost finished applying a kind of dressing to the wounds of Dominique, another voice was heard; it was that of the unfortunate woman who was on the raft with us, and whom the madmen had thrown into the sea, as well as her husband, who defended her with courage. Mr. Corréard, in despair at seeing two poor wretches perish, whose lamentable cries, especially those of the woman, pierced his heart, seized a large rope which was on the front of the raft, which he fastened round the middle of his body, and threw himself, a second time, into the sea, whence he was so happy as to rescue the woman, who invoked, with all her might, the aid of Our Lady of Laux, while her husband was likewise saved by the chief workman, Lavillette. We seated these two poor people upon dead bodies, with their backs leaning against a barrel. In a few minutes they had recovered their senses. The first thought of the woman was to enquire the name of him who had saved her, and to testify to him the warmest gratitude. Thinking, doubtless, that her words did not sufficiently express her sentiments, she recollected that she had, in her pocket, a little snuff, and immediately offered it to him—it was all she possessed. Touched by this present, but not making use of this antiscorbutic, Mr. Corréard, in turn, made a present of it to a poor sailor, who used it three or four days. But a more affecting scene, which it is impossible for us to describe, is the joy which this unfortunate couple displayed when they had sufficiently recovered their senses to see that they were saved.

The mutineers being repulsed, as we have said above, left us at this moment a little repose. The moon with her sad beams, illumined this fatal raft, this narrow space, in which were united so many heart-rending afflictions, so many cruel distresses, a fury so insensate, a courage so heroic, the most pleasing and generous sentiments of nature and humanity.

The man and his wife, who just before had seen themselves attacked with sabres and bayonets, and thrown at the same moment into the waves of a stormy sea, could hardly believe their senses when they found themselves in each others arms. They felt, they expressed, so fervently, the happiness which they were alas, to enjoy for so short a time, that this affecting sight might have drawn tears from the most insensible heart; but in this terrible moment, when we were but just breathing after the most furious attack, when we were forced to be constantly on our guard, not only against the attacks of the men, but also against the fury of the waves: few of us had time, if we may say so, to suffer ourselves to be moved by this scene of conjugal friendship.

Mr. Corréard, one of those whom it had most agreeably affected, hearing the woman still recommend herself, as she had done when in the sea, to our Lady of Laux, exclaiming every instant, "our good Lady of Laux do not forsake us," recollected that there was, in fact, in the Department of the Upper Alps, a place of devotion so called,* and asked her if she came from that country. She replied in the affirmative, and said she had quitted it 24 years before, and that since that time she had been in the Campaigns in Italy, &c. as a sutler; that she had never quitted our armies, "Therefore," said she, "preserve my life, you see that I am a useful woman." "Oh! if you knew how often I also have braved death on the field of battle, to carry assistance to our brave men." Then she amused herself with giving some account of her campaigns. She mentioned those she had assisted, the provisions which she had provided them, the brandy with which she had treated them. "Whether they had money or not," said she, "I always let them have my goods. Sometimes a battle made me lose some of my poor debtors; but then, after the victory, others paid me double or triple the value

* Our Lady of Laux is in the Department of the Upper Alps, not far from Gap. A church has been built there, the patroness of which is much celebrated, in the country, for her miracles. The lame, the gouty, the paralytic, found there relief, which it is said, never failed. Unfortunately, this miraculous power did not extend, it seems, to shipwrecked persons: at least the poor sutler drew but little advantage from it.

of the provisions which they had consumed before the battle. Thus I had a share in their victory." The idea of owing her life to Frenchmen, at this moment, seemed still to add to her happiness. Unfortunate woman! she did not foresee the dreadful fate that awaited her among us! Let us return to our raft.

After this second check, the fury of the soldiers suddenly abated, and gave place to extreme cowardice: many of them fell at our feet and asked pardon, which was instantly granted them. It is here, the place to observe and to proclaim aloud for the honour of the French army, which has shewn itself as great, as courageous, under reverses, as formidable in battle, that most of these wretches were not worthy to wear its uniform. They were the scum of all countries, the refuse of the prisons, where they had been collected to make up the force charged with the defence and the protection of the colony. When, for the sake of health, they were made to bathe in the sea, a ceremony from which some of them had the modesty to endeavour to excuse themselves, the whole crew had ocular demonstration that it was not upon the *breast* that these heroes wore the insignia of the exploits, which had led them to serve the state in the Ports of Toulon, Brest or Rochefort.

This is not the moment, and perhaps we are not competent to examine whether the penalty of branding, as it is re-established in our present code, is compatible with the true object of all good legislation, that of correcting while punishing, of striking only as far as is necessary to prevent and preserve; in short, of producing the greatest good to all, with the least possible evil to individuals. Reason at least seems to demonstrate, and what has passed before our own eyes authorises us to believe that it is as dangerous, as inconsistent, to entrust arms for the protection of society, to the hands of those whom society has itself rejected from its bosom; that it implies a contradiction to require courage, generosity, and that devotedness which commands a noble heart to sacrifice itself for its country and fellow creatures, from wretches branded, degraded by corruption, in whom every moral energy is destroyed, or eternally compressed by the weight of the indelible opprobrium which renders them aliens to their country, which separates them forever from the rest of mankind.

We soon had on board our raft a fresh proof of the impossibility of depending on the permanence of any honorable sentiment in the hearts of beings of this description.

Thinking that order was restored, we had returned to our post at the center of the raft, only we took the precaution to retain our arms. It was nearly midnight: after an hour's apparent tranquillity, the soldiers rose again: their senses were entirely deranged; they rushed upon us like madmen, with their knives or sabres in their hands. As they were in full possession of their bodily strength, and were also armed, we were forced again to put ourselves on our defence. Their revolt was the more dangerous, as in their delirium they were entirely deaf to the cries of reason. They attacked us; we charged them in our turn, and soon the raft was covered with their dead bodies. Those among our adversaries who had no arms, attempted to tear us with their teeth; several of us were cruelly bitten; Mr. Savigny was himself bitten in the legs and the shoulder; he received also a wound with a knife in his right arm which deprived him, for a long time, of the use of the fourth and little fingers of that hand; many others were wounded; our clothes were pierced in many places by knives and sabres. One of our workmen was also seized by four of the mutineers, who were going to throw him into the sea. One of them had seized him by the right leg, and was biting him cruelly in the sinew above the heel. The others were beating him severely with their sabres and the butt end of their carbines; his cries made us fly to his aid. On this occasion, the brave Lavillette, ex-serjeant of the artillery on foot, of the old guard, behaved with courage worthy of the highest praise: we rushed on these desperadoes, after the example of Mr. Corréard, and soon rescued the workman from the danger which threatened him. A few moments after, the mutineers, in another charge, seized on the sub-lieutenant Lozach, whom they took, in their delirium, for Lieutenant Danglas, of whom we have spoken above, and who had abandoned the raft when we were on the point of putting off from the frigate. The soldiers, in general, bore much ill will to this officer, who had seen little service, and whom they reproached with having treated them harshly while they were in garrison in the Isle of Rhé. It would have been a favorable opportunity for them to satiate their rage upon him, and the thirst of vengeance and destruction which animated them to fancy that they had found him in the person of Mr. Lozach, they were going to throw him into the sea. In truth, the soldiers almost equally disliked the latter, who had served only in the Vendean bands of Saint Pol de Leon. We believed this officer lost, when his voice being heard, informed us that it was still possible to save him. Immediately Messrs. Clairet, Savigny, l'Heureux, Lavillette, Coudin, Corréard, and some workmen, having formed themselves into little parties, fell upon the insurgents with so much impetuosity that they overthrew all who opposed them, recovered Mr. Lozach, and brought him back to the center of the raft.

The preservation of this officer cost us infinite trouble. Every moment the soldiers demanded that he should be given up to them, always calling him by the name of Danglas. It was in vain we attempted to make them sensible of their mistake, and to recall to their memory, that he, whom they demanded, had returned on board the frigate, as they had themselves seen; their cries drowned the voice of reason; every thing was in their eyes Danglas; they saw him every where, they furiously and unceasingly demanded his head, and it was only by force of arms, that we succeeded in repressing their rage, and in silencing their frightful cries.

On this occasion we had also reason to be alarmed for the safety of Mr. Coudin. Wounded and fatigued by the attacks which we had sustained with the disaffected, and in which he had displayed the most dauntless courage, he was reposing on a barrel, holding in his arms a sailor boy, of twelve years of age, to whom he had attached himself. The mutineers seized him with his barrel, and threw him into the sea with the boy, whom he still held fast; notwithstanding this burden, he had the presence of mind to catch hold of the raft, and to save himself from this extreme danger. Dreadful night! thy gloomy veil covered these cruel combats, instigated by the most terrible despair.

We cannot conceive how a handful of individuals could resist such a considerable number of madmen. There were, certainly, not more than twenty of us to resist all these furious wretches. Let it, however, not be imagined, that we preserved our reason unimpaired amidst all this disorder; terror, alarm, the most cruel privations had greatly affected our intellectual faculties; but being a little less deranged than the unfortunate soldiers, we energetically opposed their determination to cut the cords of the raft. Let us be allowed to make some reflections on the various sensations with which we were affected.

The very first day, Mr. Griffon lost his senses so entirely, that he threw himself into the sea, intending to drown himself. Mr. Savigny saved him with his own hand. His discourse was vague and unconnected. He threw himself into the water a second time, but by a kind of instinct he kept hold of one of the cross pieces of the raft: and was again rescued.

The following is an account of what Mr. Savigny experienced in the beginning of the night. His eyes closed in spite of himself, and he felt a general lethargy; in this situation the most agreeable images played before his fancy; he saw around him, a country covered with fine plantations, and he found himself in the presence of objects which delighted all his senses; yet he reasoned on his situation, and he felt that courage alone would recover him from this species of trance; he asked the master gunner of the frigate for some wine: who procured him a little; and he recovered in a degree from this state of torpor. If the unfortunate men, when they were attacked by these first symptoms, had not had resolution to struggle against them, their death was certain. Some became furious; others threw themselves into the sea, taking leave of their comrades with great coolness; some said "Fear nothing, I am going to fetch you assistance; in a short time you will see me again." In the midst of this general madness, some unfortunate wretches were seen to rush upon their comrades with their sabres drawn, demanding the *wing of a chicken*, or *bread* to appease the hunger which devoured them; others called for their hammocks, "*to go*," they said, "*between the decks of the frigate and take some moments' repose.*" Many fancied themselves still on board the Medusa, surrounded with the same objects which they saw there every day. Some saw ships, and called them to their assistance, or a harbour, in the background of which there was a magnificent city.

Mr. Corréard fancied he was travelling through the fine plains of Italy; one of the officers said to him, gravely, "I *remember that we have been deserted by the boats; but fear nothing;* I *have just written to the governor, and in a few hours we shall be saved.*" Mr. Corréard replied in the same tone, and as if he had been in an ordinary situation, "H*ave you a pigeon to carry your orders with as much celerity?*" The cries and the tumult soon roused us from the state in which we were plunged; but scarcely was tranquillity restored, when we sunk back into the same species of trance: so that the next day we seemed to awake from a painful dream, and asked our companions if, during their sleep, they had seen combats and heard cries of despair. Some of them replied that they had been continually disturbed by the same visions, and that they were exhausted with fatigue: all thought themselves deceived by the illusions of a frightful dream.

When we recall to our minds those terrible scenes, they present themselves to our imagination like those frightful dreams which sometimes make a profound impression on us; so that, when we awake, we remember the different circumstances which rendered our sleep so agitated. All these horrible events, from which we have escaped by a miracle, appear to us like a point in our existence: we compare them with the fits of a burning fever, which has been accompanied by a delirium: a thousand objects appear before the imagination of the patient: when restored to health, he sometimes recollects the visions that have tormented him during the fever which consumed him, and exalted his imagination. We were really seized with a fever on the brain, the consequence of a mental exaltation carried to the extreme. As soon as daylight beamed upon us, we were much more calm: darkness brought with it a renewal of the disorder in our weakened intellects. We observed in ourselves that the natural terror, inspired by the cruel situation in which we were, greatly increased in the silence of the night: then all objects seemed to us much more terrible.

After these different combats, worn out with fatigue, want of food and of sleep, we endeavoured to take a few moments' repose, at length daylight came, and disclosed all the horrors of the scene. A great number had, in their delirium, thrown themselves into the sea: we found that between sixty and sixty-five men had perished during the night; we calculated that, at least, a fourth part had drowned themselves in despair. We had lost only two on our side, neither of whom was an officer. The deepest despondency was painted on every face; every one, now that he was come to himself, was sensible of his situation; some of us, shedding tears of despair, bitterly deplored the rigour of our fate.

We soon discovered a new misfortune; the rebels, during the tumult, had thrown into the sea two barrels of wine, and the only two casks of water that we had on the raft.* As soon as Mr. Corréard perceived that they were going to throw the wine into the sea, and that the barrels were almost entirely made loose, he resolved to place himself on one of them; where he was continually thrown to and fro by the impulse of the waves; but he did not let go his hold. His example was followed by some others, who seized the second cask, and remained some hours at that dangerous post. After much trouble they had succeeded in saving these two casks; which being every moment violently driven against their legs had bruised them severely. Being unable to hold out any longer, they made some representations to those who, with Mr. Savigny, employed all their efforts to maintain order and preserve the raft. One of them took his (Mr. Corréard's) place; others relieved the rest: but finding this service too difficult, and being assaulted by the mutineers, they forsook this post. Then the barrels were thrown into the sea.

Two casks of wine had been consumed the preceding day; we had only one left, and we were above sixty in number; so that it was necessary to put ourselves on half allowance.

At daybreak the sea grew calm, which enabled us to put up our mast again; we then did our utmost to direct our course towards the coast. Whether it were an illusion or reality we thought we saw it, and that we distinguished the burning air of the Zaara Desert. It is, in fact, very probable that we were not very distant from it, for we had had winds from the sea which had blown violently. In the sequel we spread the sail indifferently to every wind that blew, so that one day we approached the coast, on the next ran into the open sea.

As soon as our mast was replaced, we made a distribution of wine; the unhappy soldiers murmured and accused us for privations, which we bore as well as they: they fell down with fatigue. For forty-eight hours we had taken nothing, and had been obliged to struggle incessantly against a stormy sea; like them we could hardly support ourselves; courage alone still made us act. We resolved to employ all possible means to procure fish. We collected all the tags from the soldiers, and made little hooks of them; we bent a bayonet to catch sharks: all this availed us nothing; the currents carried our hooks under the raft, where they got entangled. A shark bit at the bayonet, and straightened it. We gave up our project. But an extreme resource was necessary to preserve our wretched existence. We tremble with horror at being obliged to mention that which we made use of! we feel our pen drop from our hand; a deathlike chill pervades all our limbs; our hair stands erect on our heads!—Reader, we beseech you, do not feel indignation towards men who are already too unfortunate; but have compassion on them, and shed some tears of pity on their unhappy fate.

Those whom death had spared in the disastrous night which we have just described, fell upon the dead bodies with which the raft was covered, and cut off pieces, which some instantly devoured. Many did not touch them; almost all the officers were of this number. Seeing that this horrid nourishment had given strength to those who made use of it, it was proposed to dry it, in order to render it a little less disgusting. Those who had firmness enough to abstain from it took a larger quantity of wine. We tried to eat swordbelts and cartouch-boxes. We succeeded in swallowing some little morsels. Some eat linen. Others pieces of leather from the hats, on which there was a little grease, or rather dirt. We were obliged to give up these last means. A sailor attempted to eat excrements, but he could not succeed.

The day was calm and fine: a ray of hope allayed our uneasiness for a moment. We still expected to see the boats or some vessels; we addressed our prayers to the Eternal, and placed our confidence in him. The half of our men were very weak, and bore on all their features the stamp of approaching dissolution. The evening passed over, and no assistance came. The darkness of this third night increased our alarm; but the wind was slight, and the sea less agitated. We took some moment's repose: a repose which was still more terrible than our situation the preceding day; cruel dreams added to the horrors of our situation. Tormented by hunger and thirst, our plaintive cries sometimes awakened from his sleep, the wretch who was reposing close to us. We were even now up to our knees in the water, so that we could only repose standing, pressed against each other to form a solid mass. The fourth morning's sun, after our departure, at length rose on our disaster, and shewed us ten or twelve of our companions extended lifeless on the raft. This sight affected us the more as it announced to us that our bodies, deprived of existence, would soon be stretched on the same place. We gave their bodies to the sea for a grave; reserving only one, destined to feed those who, the day before, had clasped his trembling hands, vowing him an eternal friendship. This day was fine; our minds, longing for more agreeable sensations, were harmonized by the soothing aspect of nature, and admitted a ray of hope. About four in the afternoon a circumstance occurred which afforded us some consolation: a shoal of flying fish passed under the raft, and as the extremities left an infinite number of vacancies between the pieces which composed it, the fish got entangled in great numbers. We threw ourselves upon them, and caught a considerable quantity: we took near two hundred and put them in an empty cask;* as we caught them we opened them to take out what is called the milt. This food seemed delicious to us; but one man would have wanted a thousand. Our first impulse was to address new thanksgivings to God for this unexpected benefit.

An ounce of gunpowder had been found in the morning, and dried in the sun, during the day, which was very fine; a steel, some gun-flints and tinder were also found in the same parcel. After infinite trouble we succeeded in setting fire to some pieces of dry linen. We made a large hole in one side of an empty cask, and placed at the bottom of it several things which we wetted, and on this kind of scaffolding we made our fire: we placed it on a barrel that the seawater might not put out our fire. We dressed some fish, which we devoured with extreme avidity; but our hunger was so great and our portion of fish so small, that we added to it some human flesh, which dressing rendered less disgusting; it was this which the officers touched, for the first time. From this day we continued to use it; but we could not dress it any more, as we were entirely deprived of the means; our barrel catching fire we extinguished it without being able to save anything whereby to light it again next day. The powder and the tinder were entirely consumed. This repast gave us all fresh strength to bear new fatigues. The night was tolerable, and would have appeared happy had it not been signalised by a new massacre.

Some Spaniards, Italians, and Negroes, who had remained neuter in the first mutiny, and some of whom had even ranged themselves on our side, formed a plot to throw us all into the sea, hoping to execute their design by falling on us by surprise. These wretches suffered themselves to be persuaded by the negroes, who assured them that the coast was extremely near, and promised, that when they were once on shore, they would enable them to traverse Africa without danger. The desire of saving themselves, or perhaps the wish to seize on the money and valuables, which had been put into a bag, hung to the mast,† had inflamed the imagination of these unfortunate wretches. We were obliged to take our arms again; but how were we to discover the guilty? they were pointed out to us, by our sailors, who remained faithful, and ranged themselves near us; one of them had refused to engage in the plot. The first signal, for combat, was given by a Spaniard, who, placing himself behind the mast, laid fast hold of it, made the sign of the Cross with one hand, invoking the name of God, and held a knife in the other: the sailors seized him, and threw him into the sea. The servant of an officer of the troops on board was in the plot. He was an Italian from the light artillery of the Ex-King of his country. When he perceived that the plot was discovered, he armed himself with the last boarding-axe that there was on the raft, wrapped himself in a piece of drapery, which he wore folded over his breast, and, of his own accord, threw himself into the sea. The mutineers rushed forward to avenge their comrades, a terrible combat again ensued, and both sides fought with desperate fury. Soon the fatal raft was covered with dead bodies, and flowing with blood which ought to have been shed in another cause, and by other hands. In this tumult cries, with which we were familiar, were renewed, and we heard the imprecations of the horrid rage which demanded the head of Lieutenant Danglas! Our readers know that we could not satisfy this mad rage, because the victim, demanded, had fled the dangers to which we were exposed; but even if this officer had remained among us, we should most certainly have defended his life at the expence of our own, as we did that of Lieutenant Lozach. But it was not for him that we were reduced to exert, against these madmen, all the courage we possessed.

We again replied to the cries of the assailants, that he whom they demanded was not with us; but we had no more success in persuading them; nothing could make them recollect themselves; we were obliged to continue to combat them, and to oppose force to those over whom reason had lost all its influence. In this confusion the unfortunate woman was, a second time, thrown into the sea. We perceived it, and Mr. Coudin, assisted by some workmen, took her up again, to prolong, for a few moments, her torments and her existence.

In this horrible night, Lavillette gave further proofs of the rarest intrepidity. It was to him, and to some of those who have escaped the consequences of our misfortunes, that we are indebted for our safety. At length, after unheard-of efforts, the mutineers were again repulsed, and tranquillity restored. After we had escaped this new danger, we endeavoured to take some moment's repose. The day at length rose on us for the fifth time. We were now only thirty left; we had lost four or five of our faithful sailors; those who had survived were in the most deplorable state; the sea-water had almost entirely excoriated our lower extremities; we were covered with contusions or wounds, which, irritated by the salt-water, made us utter every moment piercing cries; so that there were not above twenty of us who were able to stand upright or walk. Almost our whole stock was exhausted; we had no more wine than was sufficient for four days, and we had not above a dozen fish left. In four days, said we, we shall be in want of everything, and death will be unavoidable. Thus arrived the seventh day since we had been abandoned; we calculated that, in case the boats had not stranded on the coast, they would want, at least, three or four times twenty-four hours to reach St. Louis. Time was further required to equip ships, and for these ships to find us; we resolved to hold out as long as possible. In the course of the day, two soldiers slipped behind the only barrel of wine we had left; they had bored a hole in it, and were drinking by means of a reed: we had all sworn, that he who should employ such means should be punished with death. This law was instantly put in execution, and the two trespassers were thrown into the sea.*

This same day terminated the existence of a child, twelve years of age, named Léon; he died away like a lamp which ceases to burn for want of aliment. Everything spoke in favor of this amiable young creature, who merited a better fate. His angelic countenance, his melodious voice, the interest inspired by his youth, which was increased by the courage he had shown, and the services he had performed, for he had already made, in the preceding year, a campaign in the East Indies, all this filled us with the tenderest interest for this young victim, devoted to a death so dreadful and premature. Our old soldiers, and our people in general, bestowed upon him all the care which they thought calculated to prolong his existence. It was in vain; his strength, at last, forsook him. Neither the wine, which we gave him without regret, nor all the means which could be employed, could rescue him from his sad fate; he expired in the arms of Mr. Coudin, who had not ceased to shew him the kindest attention. As long as the strength of this young marine had allowed him to move, he ran continually from one side to the other, calling, with loud cries, for his unhappy mother, water, and food. He walked, without discrimination, over the feet and legs of his companions in misfortune, who, in their turn, uttered cries of anguish, which were every moment repeated. But their complaints were very seldom accompanied by menaces; they pardoned everything in the poor youth, who had caused them. Besides, he was, in fact, in a state of mental derangement, and in his uninterrupted alienation he could not be expected to behave, as if he had still retained some use of reason.

We were now only twenty-seven remaining; of this number but fifteen seemed likely to live some days; all the rest, covered with large wounds, had almost entirely lost their reason; yet they had a share in the distribution of provisions, and might, before their death, consume thirty or forty bottles of wine, which were of inestimable value to us. We deliberated thus: to put the sick on half allowance would have been killing them by inches. So after a debate, at which the most dreadful despair presided, it was resolved to throw them into the sea. This measure, however repugnant it was to ourselves, procured the survivors wine for six days; when the decision was made, who would dare to execute it? The habit of seeing death ready to pounce upon us as his prey, the certainty of our infallible destruction, without this fatal expedient, everything in a word, had hardened our hearts, and rendered them callous to all feeling except that of self preservation. Three sailors and a soldier took on themselves this cruel execution: we turned our faces aside, and wept tears of blood over the fate of these unhappy men. Among them were the unfortunate woman and her husband. Both of them had been severely wounded in the various combats: the woman had a thigh broken between the pieces of wood composing the raft, and her husband had received a deep wound with a sabre on his head. Everything announced their speedy dissolution. We must seek to console ourselves, by the belief, that our cruel resolution shortened, but for a few moments only, the measure of their existence.

This French woman, to whom soldiers and Frenchmen gave the sea for a tomb, had partaken for twenty years in the glorious fatigues of our armies; for twenty years she had afforded to the brave, on the field of battle, either the assistance which they needed, or soothing consolations....It is in the midst of her friends; it is by the hands of her friends....Readers, who shudder at the cry of outraged humanity, recollect at least, that it was other men, fellow countrymen, comrades, who had placed us in this horrible situation.

This dreadful expedient saved the fifteen who remained; for, when we were found by the Argus, we had very little wine left, and it was the sixth day after the cruel sacrifice which we have just described: the victims, we repeat it, had not above forty-eight hours to live, and by keeping them on the raft, we should absolutely have been destitute of the means of existence two days before we were found. Weak as we were, we considered it as certain that it would have been impossible for us to hold out, even twenty-four hours, without taking some food. After this catastrophe, which inspired us with a degree of horror not to be overcome, we threw the arms into the sea; we reserved, however, one sabre in case it should be wanted to cut a rope or piece of wood.

After all this, we had scarcely sufficient food on the raft, to last for the six days, and they were the most wretched immaginable. Our dispositions had become soured: even in sleep, we figured to ourselves the sad end of all our unhappy companions, and we loudly invoked death.

A new event, for everything was an *event* for wretches for whom the universe was reduced to a flooring of a few toises in extent, who were the sport of the winds and waves, as they hung suspended over the abyss; an event then happened which happily diverted our attention from the horrors of our situation. All at once a white butterfly, of the species so common in France, appeared fluttering over our heads, and settled on our sail. The first idea which, as it were, inspired each of us made us consider this little animal as the harbinger, which brought us the news of a speedy approach to land, and we snatched at this hope with a kind of delirium of joy. But it was the ninth day that we passed upon the raft; the torments of hunger consumed our entrails; already some of the soldiers and sailors devoured, with haggard eyes, this wretched prey, and seemed ready to dispute it with each other. Others considered this butterfly as a messenger of heaven, declared that they took the poor insect under their protection, and hindered any injury being done to it. We turned our wishes and our eyes towards the land, which we so ardently longed for, and which we every moment fancied we saw rise before us. It is certain that we could not be far from it: for the butterflies continued, on the following days, to come and flutter about our sail, and the same day we had another sign equally positive: for we saw a (*goeland*) flying over our raft. This second visitor did not allow us to doubt of our being very near to the African shore, and we persuaded ourselves that we should soon be thrown upon the coast by the force of the currents. How often did we then, and in the following days, invoke a tempest to throw us on the coast, which, it seemed to us, we were on the point of touching.

The hope which had just penetrated the inmost recesses of our souls, revived our enfeebled strength, and inspired us with an ardour, an activity, of which we should not have thought ourselves capable. We again had recourse to all the means which we had before employed, to catch fish. Above all, we eagerly longed for the (goeland), which appeared several times tempted to settle on the end of our machine. The impatience of our desire increased, when we saw several of its companions join it, and keep following us till our deliverance; but all attempts to draw them to us were in vain; not one of them suffered itself to be taken by the snares we had laid for them. Thus our destiny, on the fatal raft, was to be incessantly tossed between transitory illusions and continued torments, and we never experienced an agreeable sensation without being, in a manner, condemned to atone for it, by the anguish of some new suffering, by the irritating pangs of hope always deceived.

Another care employed us this day; as soon as we were reduced to a small number, we collected the little strength we had remaining; we loosened some planks on the front of the raft, and with some pretty long pieces of wood, raised in the center a kind of platform, on which we reposed: all the effects which we had been able to collect, were placed upon it, and served to render it less hard; besides, they hindered the sea from passing with so much facility through the intervals between the different pieces of the raft; but the waves came across, and sometimes covered us entirely.

It was on this new theatre that we resolved to await death in a manner worthy of Frenchmen, and with perfect resignation. The most adroit among us, to divert our thoughts, and to make the time pass with more rapidity, got their comrades to relate to us their passed triumphs, and sometimes, to draw comparisons between the hardships they had undergone in their glorious campaigns, and the distresses we endured upon our raft. The following is what Lavillette the serjeant of artillery told us: "I have experienced, in my various naval campaigns, all the fatigues, all the privations and all the dangers, which it is possible to meet with at sea, but none of my past sufferings, is comparable to the extreme pain and privations which I endure here. In my last campaigns in 1813 and 1814, in Germany and France, I shared all the fatigues which were alternately caused us by victory and retreat. I was at the glorious days of Lutzen, Bautzen, Dresden, Leipzig, Hanau, Montmirail, Champaubert, Montereau," &c. "Yes," continued he, "all that I suffered in so many forced marches, and in the midst of the privations which were the consequences of them, was nothing in comparison with what I endure on this frightful machine. In those days, when the French valour shewed itself in all its lustre, and always worthy of a free people, I had hardly anything to fear, but during the battle; but here, I often have the same dangers, and what is more dreadful, I have to combat Frenchmen and comrades. I have to contend, besides, with hunger and thirst, with a tempestuous sea, full of dangerous monsters, and with the ardour of a burning sun, which is not the least of our enemies. Covered with ancient scars and fresh wounds, which I have no means of dressing, it is physically impossible for me to save myself from this extreme danger, if it should be prolonged for a few days."

The sad remembrance of the critical situation of our country also mingled with our grief; and certainly, of all the afflictions we experienced, this was not the least, to us, who had almost all of us left it, only that we might no longer be witnesses of the hard laws, of the afflicting dependence, under which it is bowed down by enemies jealous of our glory and of our power. These thoughts, we do not fear to say so, and to boast of it, afflicted us still more than the inevitable death which we were almost certain of meeting on our raft. Several of us regretted not having fallen in the defence of France. At least, said they, if it had been possible for us to measure our strength once more, with the enemies of our independence, and our liberty! Others found some consolation in the death which awaited us, because we should no longer have to groan under the shameful yoke which oppresses the country. Thus passed the last days of our abode on the raft. Our time was almost wholly employed in speaking of our unhappy country: all our wishes, our last prayers were for the happiness of France.

During the first days and nights of our being abandoned, the weather was very cold, but we bore the immersion pretty well; and during the last nights that we passed on the raft, every time that a wave rolled over us, it produced a very disagreeable sensation, and made us utter plaintive cries, so that each of us employed means to avoid it: some raised their heads, by means of pieces of wood, and made with whatever they could find a kind of parapet, against which the wave broke: others sheltered themselves behind empty casks which were placed across, along side each other; but these means often proved insufficient; it was only when the sea was very calm that it did not break over us.

A raging thirst, which was redoubled in the daytime by the beams of a burning sun, consumed us: it was such, that we eagerly moistened our lips with urine, which we cooled in little tin cups. We put the cup in a place where there was a little water, that the urine might cool the sooner; it often happened that these cups were stolen from those who had thus prepared them. The cup was returned, indeed, to him to whom it belonged, but not till the liquid which it contained was drank. Mr. Savigny observed that the urine of some of us was more agreeable than that of others. There was a passenger who could never prevail on himself to swallow it: in reality, it had not a disagreeable taste; but in some of us it became thick, and extraordinarily acrid: it produced an effect truly worthy of remark, namely, that it was scarcely swallowed, when it excited an inclination to urine anew. We also tried to quench our thirst by drinking sea-water. Mr. Griffon, the governor's secretary, used it continually, he drank ten or twelve glasses in succession. But all these means only diminished our thirst to render it more severe a moment afterwards.

An officer of the army found by chance a little lemon, and it may be imagined how valuable this fruit must be to him; he, in fact, reserved it entirely for himself; his comrades, notwithstanding the most pressing entreaties, could not obtain any of it; already emotions of rage were rising in every heart, and if he had not partly yielded to those who surrounded him, they would certainly have taken it from him by force, and he would have perished, the victim of his selfishness. We also disputed for about thirty cloves of garlic, which had been found accidentally in a little bag: all these disputes were generally accompanied with violent threats, and if they had been protracted we should, perhaps, have come to the last extremities.

We had found, also, two little phials which contained a spirituous liquor to clean the teeth; he who possessed them, kept them carefully, and made many difficulties to give one or two drops of this liquid in the hollow of the hand. This liquor, which we believe was an essence of guiacum, cinnamon, cloves, and other aromatic substances, produced on our tongues a delightful sensation, and removed for a few moments the thirst which consumed us. Some of us found pieces of pewter, which, being put into the mouth produced a kind of coolness.

One of the means generally employed, was to put some sea-water into a hat, with which we washed our faces for some time, recurring to it at intervals; we also moistened our hair with it, and held our hands plunged in the water.* Misfortune rendered us ingenious, and every one thought of a thousand means to alleviate his sufferings; extenuated by the most cruel privations, the smallest agreeable sensation was to us a supreme happiness; thus we eagerly sought a little empty phial, which one of us possessed, and which had formerly contained essence of roses: as soon as we could get hold of it we inhaled, with delight, the perfume which issued from it, and which communicated to our senses the most soothing impressions. Some of us reserved our portion of wine in little tin cups, and sucked up the wine with a quill; this manner of taking it was very beneficial to us, and quenched our thirst much more than if we had drunk if off at once. Even the smell of this liquor was extremely agreeable to us. Mr. Savigny observed that many of us, after having taken their small portion, fell into a state approaching to intoxication, and that there was always more discord among us after the distribution had been made.

The following is one instance, among many, which we could adduce. The tenth day of our being on the raft, after a distribution of wine, Messrs. Clairet, Coudin, Charlot, and one or two of our sailors, conceived the strange idea of destroying themselves, first intoxicating themselves with what remained in our barrel. In vain Captain Dupont, seconded by Messrs. Lavillette, Savigny, Lheureux, and all the others, opposed their purpose by urgent remonstrances, and by all the firmness of which they were capable—their disordered brains persisted in the mad idea which governed them, and a new combat was on the point of commencing; however, after infinite trouble, we were beginning to bring back Messrs. Clairet and Coudin to the use of their reason; or rather he who watched over us dispelled this fatal quarrel, by turning our attention to the new danger which threatened us, at the moment when cruel discord was, perhaps, about to break out among wretches already a prey to so many other evils—it was a number of sharks which came and surrounded our raft. They approached so near, that we were able to strike them with our sabre, but we could not subdue one of them, notwithstanding the goodness of the weapon we possessed, and the ardour with which the brave Lavillette made use of it. The blows which he struck these monsters, made them replunge into the sea; but a few seconds after, they reappeared upon the surface, and did not seem at all alarmed at our presence. Their backs rose about 30 centimetres above the water: several of them appeared to us to be at least 10 metres in length.

Three days passed in inexpressible anguish; we despised life to such a degree that many of us did not fear to bathe in sight of the sharks which surrounded our raft; others placed themselves naked on the front part of our machine which was still submerged: these means diminished, a little, their burning thirst. A kind of polypus (mollusques), known by seamen under the name of *galère*, was frequently driven in great numbers on our raft, and when their long arms clung to our naked bodies, they caused us the most cruel sufferings. Will it be believed, that amidst these dreadful scenes, struggling with inevitable death, some of us indulged in pleasantries which excited a smile, notwithstanding the horror of our situation? One, among others said, joking, "*If the brig is sent to look for us, let us pray to God that she may have the eyes of* Argus," alluding to the name of the vessel, which we presumed would be sent after us. This consolatory idea did not quit us an instant, and we spoke of it frequently.

During the day of the 16th, reckoning ourselves to be very near land, eight of the most determined of us, resolved to try to reach the coast: we unfastened a strong fish of a mast, which made part of the little parapet of which we have spoken, we fixed boards to it at intervals, transversely, by means of great nails, to hinder it from upsetting; a little mast and sail were fixed in the front; we intended to provide ourselves with oars made of barrel staves, cut out with the only sabre we had remaining: we cut pieces of rope, we split them, and made smaller ropes, that were more easy to manage: a hammock cloth, which was by chance on the raft, served for a sail; the dimensions of which, might be about 130 centimetres in breadth and 160 in length: the transverse diameter of the fish was 60 or 70 centimetres, and its length about 12 metres. A certain portion of wine was assigned to us, and our departure fixed for the next day, the 17th. When our machine was finished, it remained to make a trail of it: a sailor wanting to pass from the front to the back of it, finding the mast in his way, set his foot on one of the cross boards; the weight of his body made it upset, and this accident proved to us the temerity of our enterprise. It was then resolved that we should all await death in our present situation; the cable which fastened the machine to our raft, was made loose, and it drifted away. It is very certain that if we had ventured upon this second raft, weak as we were, we should not have been able to hold out six hours, with our legs in the water, and thus obliged continually to row.

Meantime the night came, and its gloomy shades revived in our minds the most afflicting thoughts; we were convinced that there were not above twelve or fifteen bottles of wine left in our barrel. We began to feel an invincible disgust at the flesh which had till then, scarcely supported us; and we may say that the sight of it inspired us with a sentiment of terror, which was doubtless produced by the idea of approaching destruction.

On the 17th, in the morning, the sun appeared entirely free from clouds; after having put up our prayers to the Almighty, we divided among us, a part of our wine; everyone was taking with delight his small portion, when a captain of infantry looking towards the horizon, descried a ship, and announced it to us by an exclamation of joy: we perceived that it was a brig; but it was at a very great distance; we could distinguish only the tops of the masts. The sight of this vessel excited in us a transport of joy which it would be difficult to describe; each of us believed his deliverance certain, and we gave a thousand thanks to God; yet, fears mingled with our hopes; we straitened some hoops of casks, to the end of which we tied handkerchiefs of different colours. A man, assisted by us all together, mounted to the top of the mast and waved these little flags.

For above half an hour, we were suspended between hope and fear; some thought they saw the ship become larger, and others affirmed that its course carried it from us: these latter were the only ones whose eyes were not fascinated by hope, for the brig disappeared. From the delirium of joy, we fell into profound despondency and grief; we envied the fate of those whom we had seen perish at our side, and we said to ourselves, when we shall be destitute of everything, and our strength begins to forsake us, we will wrap ourselves up as well as we can, we will lay ourselves down on this platform, the scene of so many sufferings, and there we will await death with resignation. At last, to calm our despair, we wished to seek some consolation in the arms of sleep; the day before we had been consumed by the fire of a burning sun; this day, to avoid the fierceness of his beams, we made a tent with the sails of the frigate: as soon as it was put up, we all lay down under it, so that we could not perceive what was passing around us. We then proposed to inscribe upon a board an account of our adventures, to write all our names at the bottom of the narrative, and to fasten it to the upper part of the mast, in the hope that it would reach the government and our families.

After we had passed two hours, absorbed in the most cruel reflections, the master gunner of the frigate wishing to go to the front of the raft, went out of our tent; scarcely had he put his head out, when he turned towards us, uttering a loud cry; joy was painted on his countenance, his hands were stretched towards the sea, he scarcely breathed: all that he could say was, "*Saved! see the brig close upon us.*" And in fact, it was, at the most, half a league distant, carrying a press of sail, and steering so as to come extremely close to us; we precipitately left the tent: even those whom enormous wounds, in the lower extremities, had confined for some days past, always to lie down, crawled to the back part of the raft, to enjoy the sight of this vessel, which was coming to deliver us from certain death. We all embraced each other with transports that looked like delirium, and tears of joy rolled down our cheeks, shrunk by the most cruel privations. Everyone seized handkerchiefs, or pieces of linen to make signals to the brig, which was approaching rapidly. Others prostrating themselves, fervently thanked Providence for our miraculous preservation. Our joy redoubled when we perceived a great white flag at the foremast head and we exclaimed "It is then to Frenchmen that we shall owe our deliverance." We almost immediately recognised the brig to be the Argus: it was then within two musket shot: we were extremely impatient to see her clue up her sails; she lowered them at length, and fresh cries of joy rose from our raft. The Argus came and lay-to on our starboard, within half a pistol shot. The crew, ranged on the deck and in the shrouds, shewed, by waving their hats and handkerchiefs, the pleasure they felt at coming to the assistance of their unhappy countrymen. A boat was immediately hoisted out; an officer belonging to the brig, whose name was Mr. Lemaigre, had embarked in it, in order to have the pleasure of taking us himself from this fatal machine. This officer, full of humanity and zeal, acquitted himself on his mission in the kindest manner, and took himself, those that were the weakest, to convey them into the boat. After all the others were placed in it, Mr. Lemaigre came and took in his arms Mr. Corréard, whose health was the worst, and who was the most excoriated: he placed him at his side in the boat, bestowed on him all imaginable cares, and spoke to him in the most consoling terms.

In a short time we were all removed on board the Argus, where we met with the lieutenant of the frigate, and some others of those who had been shipwrecked. Pity was painted on every face, and compassion drew tears from all who cast their eyes on us.

20

The LOSS *of The* ESSEX

From *Captain Pollard's Narrative*

1820

The story of the Essex *is famous and hardly needs an introduction. It is the only whaling ship ever known to have been attacked and sunk by a whale.* Melville *used it in* Moby Dick, *and* Nathaniel Philbrick's *book about the incident,* In the Heart of the Sea, *was a best-seller and won the* National Book Award *in 1998. There are three versions of what happened after the* Essex *sank. The longest is by* Owen Chase, *first mate of the* Essex, *who was on one of the three whale boats that left the scene after the disaster.* Chase *wrote a short book about the event that is still in print. The captain of the* Essex, George Pollard, *and* Thomas Chapple, *both of whom became separated from* Chase *and from each other, told their stories to missionaries; they survive in missionary tracts as instances of divine grace. We print the last two, complete. The* Chase *account is well enough known not to repeat it here, and the missionary overlay was so common to disaster stories in the 19th century that it seems worthwhile to let the reader see what they were like.*

I might add that whaling ships often suffered shipwreck, especially in the Arctic. *For the sheer scale of the disaster, probably nothing matches what happened in the* Bering Sea *in* September *1879, when the* Arctic *ice pack, grinding south on a powerful northwest wind, started crushing whaling ships like so much kindling. Nearly the entire fleet, thirty-nine ships, was caught by the ice, only seven escaping. Those seven had to take off the men on the other ships, all thirty-two of which were lost, and sail back, badly overloaded, to* Honolulu. *Yet not a single man died.*

What the ice did not do to the frozen ships the Inuit did. Seeing the ships as a source of wealth, they took whatever was usable from them. Anticipating this possibility, the captains had taken the precaution of destroying the liquor on board, so the Inuit drank what was in the medicine cabinets instead. That made them sick, but the Inuit believed that it was evil spirits on board the ships that had made them sick, so they burned most of the ships that had survived the ice. One ship did survive, however, and a lone seaman had decided to remain behind and spent the winter on it. There was plenty to eat, he knew he wouldn't starve, he must have thought he could somehow enrich himself with what was left behind. When he was picked up the following summer he said, "A hundred and fifty thousand dollars would not tempt me to try another winter in the Arctic." That amount of money would be perhaps ten million to fifteen million dollars today.

APRIL 16, [1823]. IN THE HARBOR HERE, WE FOUND THE AMERICAN brig *Pearl*, Captain Chandler, which had put in for repairs, having sprung a leak at sea; and on board of this vessel, to our great joy and surprise, we met with our friends, Mr. and Mrs. Chamberlain, from the Sandwich Islands. We never expected to have seen their faces again in this world. They were, however, for reasons which we had known and approved when we parted with them, on their return with their young family to America. They gave us the most gratifying account of the safe arrival and cordial reception of Mr. and Mrs. Ellis, at Oahu, by our American missionary friends there, by the king also, the chiefs, and the people—all of whom rejoiced to welcome them as servants of the Most High God, arrived among them to teach a nation, *without any religion*, the only doctrines under heaven worthy of that name.

There were three captains on board this brig, as passengers to America. The ships of two of these had been wrecked, and that of the third condemned. One of them was Captain George Pollard, whose singular and lamentable story, in the case of a *former* shipwreck (as nearly as can be recollected by Mr. Bennet), deserves to be recorded in his own manner. It was substantially as follows:—

"My first shipwreck was in open sea, on the 20th of November, 1820, near the equator, about 118° W. long. The vessel, a South Sea whaler, was called the *Essex*. On that day, as we were on the look out for sperm whales, and had actually struck two, which the boats' crews were following to secure, I perceived a very large one—it might be eighty or ninety feet long—rushing with great swifness through the water, right towards the ship. We hoped that she would turn aside, and dive under, when she perceived such a balk in her way. But no! the animal came full force against our stern-port: had any quarter less firm been struck, the vessel must have been burst; as it was, every plank and timber trembled throughout her whole bulk.

"The whale, as though hurt by a severe and unexpected concussion, shook its enormous head, and sheered off to so considerable a distance, that for some time we had lost sight of her from the starboard quarter; of which we were very glad, hoping that the worst was over. Nearly an hour afterwards, we saw the same fish—we had no doubt of this, from her size, and the direction in which she came—making again towards us. We were at once aware of our danger, but escape was impossible. She dashed her head this time against the ship's side, and so broke it in that the vessel filled rapidly, and soon became water-logged. At the second shock, expecting her to go down, we lowered our three boats with the utmost expedition, and all hands, twenty in the whole, got into them—seven, and seven, and six. In a little while, as she did not sink, we ventured on board again, and by scuttling the deck, were enabled to get out some biscuit, beef, water, rum, two sextants, a quadrant, and three compasses. These, together with some rigging, a few muskets, powder, etc., we brought away; and, dividing the stores among our three small crews, rigged the boats as well as we could; there being a compass for each, and a sextant for two, and a quadrant for one, but neither sextant nor quadrant for the third. Then, instead of pushing away for some port, so amazed and bewildered were we, that we continued sitting in our places, gazing upon the ship as though she had been an object of the tenderest affection. Our eyes could not leave her, till, at the end of many hours, she gave a slight reel, then down she sank. No words can tell our feelings. We looked at each other—we looked at the place where she had so lately been afloat—and we did not cease to look, till the terrible conviction of our abandoned and perilous situation roused us to exertion, if deliverance were yet possible.

"We now consulted about the course which it might be best to take—westward to India, eastward to South America, or south-westward to the Society Isles. We knew that we were at no great distance from Tahiti, but were so ignorant of the state and temper of the inhabitants, that we feared we should be devoured by cannibals, if we cast ourselves on their mercy. It was determined therefore to make for South America, which we computed to be more than two thousand miles distant. Accordingly we steered eastward, and though for several days harassed with squalls, we contrived to keep together. It was not long before we found that one of the boats had started a plank, which was no wonder, for whale-boats are all clinker-built, and very slight, being made of half-inch plank only, before planing. To remedy this alarming defect, we all turned to, and, having emptied the damaged boat into the two others, we raised her side as well as we could, and succeeded in restoring the plank at the bottom. Through this accident, some of our biscuit had become injured by the salt-water. This was equally divided among the several boats' crews. Food and water, meanwhile, with our utmost economy, rapidly failed. Our strength was exhausted, not by abstinence only, but by the labors which we were obliged to employ to keep our little vessels afloat, amidst the storms which repeatedly assailed us. One night we were parted in rough weather; but though the next day we fell in with one of our companion-boats, we never saw or heard any more of the other, which probably perished at sea being without sextant or quadrant.

"When we were reduced to the last pinch, and out of everything, having been more than three weeks abroad, we were cheered with the sight of a low uninhabited island, which we reached in hope, but were bitterly disappointed. There were some barren bushes, and many rocks on this forlorn spot. The only provisions that we could procure were a few birds and their eggs: this supply was soon reduced; the sea-fowls appeared to have been frightened away, and their nests were left empty after we had once or twice plundered them. What distressed us most was the utter want of fresh water; we could not find a drop anywhere, till, at the extreme verge of ebb tide, a small spring was discovered in the sand; but even that was too scanty to afford us sufficient to quench our thirst before it was covered by the waves at their turn.

"There being no prospect but that of starvation here, we determined to put to sea again. Three of our comrades, however, chose to remain, and we pledged ourselves to send a vessel to bring them off, if we ourselves should ever escape to a Christian port. With a very small morsel of biscuit for each, and a little water, we again ventured out on the wide ocean. In the course of a few days, our provisions were consumed. Two men died; we had no other alternative than to live upon their remains. These we roasted to dryness by means of fires kindled on the ballast-sand at the bottom of the boats. When this supply was spent, what could we do? We looked at each other with horrid thoughts in our minds, but we held our tongues. I am sure that we loved one another as brothers all the time; and yet our looks told plainly what must be done. We cast lots, and the fatal one fell on my poor cabin-boy. I started forward instantly, and cried out, 'My lad, my lad, *if you don't like your lot*, I'll shoot the first man that touches you.' The poor emaciated boy hesitated a moment or two; then, quietly laying his head down upon the gunnel of the boat, he said, 'I *like it as well as any other.*' He was soon dispatched, and nothing of him left. I think, then, another man died of himself, and him, too, we ate. But I can tell you no more—my head is on fire at the recollection; I hardly know what I say. I forgot to say, that we had parted company with the second boat before now. After some more days of horror and despair, when some were lying down at the bottom of the boat, not able to rise, and scarcely one of us could move a limb, a vessel hove in sight. We were taken on board, and treated with extreme kindness. The second lost boat was also picked up at sea, and the survivors saved. A ship afterwards sailed in search of our companions on the desolate island, and brought them away."

Captain Pollard closed his dreary narrative with saying, in a tone of despondency never to be forgotten by him who heard it—"After a time I found my way to the United States, to which I belonged, and got another ship. That, too, I have lost by a second wreck off the Sandwich Islands, and now I am utterly ruined. No owner will ever trust me with a whaler again, for all will say I am an *unlucky* man."

THOMAS CHAPPLE'S NARRATIVE

The ship *Essex*, George Pollard, Master, sailed from Nantucket, in North America, August 12, 1819, on a whaling voyage to the South Seas.

The *Essex* was for some months very successful, and procured 750 barrels of oil, in a shorter period than usual.

On the 20th November, 1820, she was on the equator, about 118° west longitude, when several whales were in sight, to the great joy of the crew, who thought they should soon complete their cargo.

The boats were soon lowered in pursuit of the whales: George Pollard, the master, and Thomas Chapple, the second mate, each succeeded in striking one, and were actively engaged in securing them, when a black man, who was in the mate's boat, exclaimed, "Massa, where ship?" The mate immediately looked round, and saw the *Essex* lying on her beam ends, and a large whale near her: he instantly cut his line and made towards the ship; the captain also saw what had happened and did the same. As soon as they got on board, to their great astonishment they found she had been struck by a whale of the largest size, which rose close to the ship and then darted under her, and knocked off a great part of the false keel. The whale appeared again, and went about a quarter of a mile off, then suddenly returned and struck the ship with great force. The shock was most violent, the bows were stove in, and the vessel driven astern a considerable distance; she filled with water and fell over on her beam ends. The crew exerted themselves to the utmost, the masts were cut away and the ship righted, but she was a mere wreck and entirely unmanageable; the quantity of oil on board alone kept her from foundering. They did not ascertain whether the whale received any injury, but it remained in sight for some hours without again coming near them.

When the captain found that it was impossible to save the ship, he directed the three boats to be got ready, and they succeeded in saving a small quantity of water, and some biscuit, which was in a very wet state.

As the *Essex* appeared likely to float for some days longer, the captain remained by her, hoping that some vessel might come in sight. After three days, finding these hopes were not realized, as the wind blew fresh from the east, he determined on attempting the Friendly [Tonga] Islands. They accordingly steered a south-westerly course, and proceeded rapidly for twenty-three days without seeing land. During this time they had only half a biscuit and a pint of water each man, per day; in that warm climate the scanty supply of water was particularly distressing, but they could not venture on a larger allowance; as on leaving the ship their whole stock of provisions was only about one hundred and fifty pounds of bread and fifty gallons of water; occasionally, however, some showers of rain fell, which gave them considerable relief.

On the twenty-fourth day after leaving the *Essex* they saw an island, discovered a few years since, and called Elizabeth's Isle [Henderson Island]. It is about eight or nine miles round, low and flat, nearly covered with trees and underwood.

The shore was rocky and the surf high; the crew were very weak, so that they did not land without considerable difficulty. Their first search was for water; and their joy was great at finding a spring of fresh water among the rocks; they were, however, disappointed on examining the island, as it was almost destitute of the necessaries of life, and no other fresh water could be discovered. These painful feelings were greatly increased the following day, for the sea had flowed over the rocks, and the spring of fresh water could not be seen, and did not again appear. In this extremity they endeavoured to dig wells, but without success; their only resource was a small quantity of water which they found in some holes among the rocks.

For six days they continued to examine the island, when finding their situation desperate, the captain and most of the crew determined to put to sea again. The continent of South America was seventeen hundred miles distant, and in their destitute condition they would scarcely expect to reach land: their hopes were rather directed to the possibility of falling in with some vessel.

Thomas Chapple, the second mate, being in a very weak state, thought he might as well remain on the island, as attempt such a voyage; William Wright and Seth Weeks also determined to remain with him.

On the 26th of December the boats left the island: this was indeed a trying moment to all: they separated with mutual prayers and good wishes, seventeen venturing to sea with almost certain death before them, while three remained on a rocky isle, destitute of water, and affording hardly any thing to support life. The prospects of these three poor men were gloomy: they again tried to dig a well but without success, and all hope seemed at an end, when providentially they were relieved by a shower of rain. They were thus delivered from the immediate apprehension of perishing by thirst. Their next care was to procure food, and their difficulties herein were also very great; their principal resource was small birds, about the size of a blackbird, which they caught while at roost. Every night they climbed the trees in search of them, and obtained, by severe exertions, a scanty supply, hardly enough to support life. Some of the trees bore a small berry which gave them a little relief, but these they found only in small quantities. Shell-fish they searched for in vain; and although from the rocks they saw at times a number of sharks, and also other sorts of fish, they were unable to catch any, as they had no fishing tackle. Once they saw several turtles, and succeeded in taking five, but they were then without water; at those times they had little inclination to eat, and before one of them was quite finished the others were become unfit for food.

Their sufferings from want of water were the most severe, their only support being from what remained in holes among the rocks after the showers which fell at intervals; and sometimes they were five or six days without any; on these occasions they were compelled to suck the blood of the birds they caught, which allayed their thirst in some degree; but they did so unwillingly, as they found themselves much disordered thereby.

Among the rocks were several caves formed by nature, which afforded a shelter from the wind and rain. In one of these caves they found eight human skeletons, in all probability the remains of some poor mariners who had been shipwrecked on the isle, and perished for want of food and water. They were side by side, as if they laid down, and died together! This sight deeply affected the mate and his companions; their case was similar, and they had every reason to expect ere long the same end; for many times they lay down at night, with their tongues swollen and their lips parched with thirst, scarcely hoping to see the morning sun; and it is impossible to form an idea of their feelings when the morning dawned, and they found their prayers had been heard and answered by a providential supply of rain.

In this state they continued till the 5th of April following; day after day hoping some vessel might touch at the island; but day after day, and week after week passed by, and they continued in that state of anxious expectation which always tends to cast down the mind and damp exertion, and which is so strongly expressed in the words of Scripture, "Hope deferred maketh the heart sick." The writer of this narrative says: "At this time I found religion not only useful but absolutely necessary to enable me to bear up under these severe trials. If any man wishes for happiness in this world or in the world to come, he can only find it by belief in God and trust in him: it is particularly important that seamen whose troubles and dangers are so numerous should bear this in mind. In this situation we prayed earnestly, morning, noon, and night, and found comfort and support from thus waiting upon the Lord."

This testimony of the benefits to be derived from religion is exceedingly valuable: hours of trial prove the vanity and uncertainty of all earthly enjoyments, and show the necessity of looking forward for another and a better world. The experience of believers of old taught them that they were but "strangers and pilgrims upon earth," and led them to earnest desires after another and a better country, that is, an heavenly. (See Heb. xi.) Prayer is the means which God has appointed whereby we may draw near to him, asking for the blessings we need. He has promised to hear and to answer us in such a manner as shall be for our good: but let us always remember, that prayer does not consist in merely kneeling down, and uttering our desires with our lips, but prayer should be the earnest expression of the feelings of the heart, filled with a sense of its own misery and wretchedness, not only as to the things of this life, but still more deeply affected as to the concerns of our souls. We may be miserable in this world and in the world to come also.—We may be happy in this life and miserable hereafter. The one does not depend upon the other, nor are they in any way connected with each other. The prayer of the poor publican (as related in the 18th of St. Luke) was, "God be merciful to me a sinner!" This will always be the first and principal desire of the soul, when awakened to a knowledge of its wretched and miserable state by nature and practice, and we would hope that such was the prayer of these poor men. Our Saviour himself has promised, that he will hear and answer such prayers: he graciously declares, "Come unto me all ye that labor and are heavy laden, and I will give you rest." He has also promised that he will give his Holy Spirit to those that ask him; and the soul that is led by the teaching of the Holy Spirit to draw near to the Saviour will find support under all the troubles of this life. It will find the peace which the world cannot give.

To return to these poor men. On the morning of April 5th, 1820, they were in the woods as usual, searching for food and water, as well as their weakness permitted, when their attention was aroused by a sound which they thought was distant thunder, but looking towards the sea, they saw a ship in the offing, which had just fired a gun. Their joy at this sight may be more easily imagined than described: they immediately fell on their knees and thanked God for his goodness, in thus sending deliverance when least expected; then hastening to the shore, they saw a boat coming towards them. As the boat could not approach the shore without great danger, the mate being a good swimmer, and stronger than his companions, plunged into the sea, and narrowly escaped a watery grave at the moment when deliverance was at hand; but the same Providence which had hitherto protected, now preserved him. His companions crawled out further on the rocks, and by the great exertions of the crew were taken into the boat, and soon found themselves on board the *Surry*, commanded by Captain Raine. They were treated in the kindest manner by him and his whole crew, and their health and strength were speedily restored, so that they were able to assist in the duties of the ship.

When on board the *Surry*, they were told the deplorable and painful history of their captain and shipmates. After leaving the isle, the boats parted company; the captain's boat was sixty days at sea, when it was picked up by an American whaler: only himself and a boy were then alive. Their scanty stock of provisions was soon exhausted, and life had only been sustained by the dead bodies of their companions. The particulars of their sufferings are too painful to relate, but they were confirmed by proofs which could not be doubted. The ship reached Valparaiso in a few days; when the particulars of the loss of the *Essex* and of the men left on the island were immediately communicated to the captain of an American frigate then in the port; who humanely endeavoured to procure a vessel to go to the island, as his own ship was not ready for sea. Captain Raine, of the *Surry*, engaged to do this, and sailed without loss of time: he had a quick passage; and, by the kind providence of God, the mate and his companions were preserved till thus unexpectedly relieved.

The sufferings of these men were great, and their preservation remarkable: such circumstances afford instruction to every one. If you are inclined to say, there is no probability of your being similarly situated, remember that although not placed in a desert island, or in a small boat, destitute of the means of subsistence, yet all are placed in the midst of many and great dangers, as to this life. But it is of infinitely more importance to remember that there is a great and awful danger, namely, of eternal death, to which we are all alike exposed, if ignorant of the Saviour and his salvation. The subject speaks *both* to seamen and landmen: are you aware of its importance? Pray earnestly to God for the knowledge of his truth: these men prayed earnestly for deliverance from their sufferings: and can you be less earnest respecting your soul? Again, remember that God has promised to give his Holy Spirit to those that ask, and it is only by his teaching that we can be led to a knowledge of our danger, and of the value of that salvation which is so fully and freely offered unto us, through Christ, who died for our sins, and rose again for our justification.

To return to our narrative. The mate and two survivors of his boat's crew were picked up by another ship, after sufferings similar to those of the captain; but the third boat was never heard of, and its crew are supposed to have perished for want, or to have found a watery grave.

The *Surry* proceeded to New South Wales and the mate, Mr. Chapple, returned to London, in June, 1823, and furnished the details from which this account has been drawn up. He says, "Before I was cast away, I was like most seamen, I never thought much about religion; but no man has seen more of the goodness of the Lord then I have, or had more reason to believe in Him. I trust I am enabled to do so." He also bears a strong testimony to the good resulting from the labors of the missionaries in the islands of the South Sea, and the great change effected in the natives; he says, "There are very many among the poor natives of those isles, who know more of religion, and show more of the effects of it in their conduct, than the greater part of our own countrymen."

We meet with many instances of unexpected dangers and remarkable preservations, but few are more worthy of notice than the one which has been related. May they lead the reader to a more earnest and constant attendance upon the means of Divine grace. Above all, remember, that it is not merely hearing of Divine truths, or bending the knees in prayer, that can save from the sentence of "Depart ye cursed"; which will be pronounced at the last day on all evil and wicked doers: nothing but feeling, deeply feeling, our lost and ruined state by nature, the evil of sin, and the necessity of a change of heart, can lead us to look to the Saviour, and to trust in him for pardon and salvation.

Again, remember that ALL, whether seamen or landsmen, are passing rapidly along and hastening to Eternity! ETERNITY! *solemn*, awful word! *Fearful* to those who are pursing a course of sin and folly, but *delightful* to the believer in the Lord Jesus Christ; who has been brought out of nature's darkness into marvellous light, and from the power of sin and Satan, to rejoice in the God of salvation; having obtained pardon and sanctification by the blood of the cross, through the influence of the Holy Spirit. And though the believer's course through life may be across a stormy and tempestuous ocean, yet he proceeds with confidence, assured that he shall reach his desired port in safety, because Christ is his pilot and Saviour.

21

The LOSS *of the* KENT

From *Perils of the Sea*

1825

The Kent *was a British East Indiaman, and the narrative of its loss takes up fully half of* Perils of the Sea, *the little 19th-century book that inspired this selection of shipwreck stories. The narrative is well written and very dramatic, and one would like to know who its author was. Following the narrative are 14 appendices, among them a note about what happened to the letter that one of the officers wrote to his father when the ship was on fire, enclosed in a bottle, and tossed overboard. It turned up a year later in Barbados, thousands of miles away. The letter reads in its entirety: "The ship Kent is on fire, Elizabeth, Joanna, and myself, commit our spirits into the hands of our blessed Redeemer; his grace enables us to be quite composed in the awful prospect of entering into eternity." It is signed D. McGregor. D. McGregor was one of those who survived.*

My Dear E——,

With the twofold view of gratifying the lively interest excited in the minds of our friends by the awful and afflicting calamity that has lately befallen the "Kent" East Indiaman, and of humbly recording the signal interposition of that God "who, in the midst of judgment, remembereth mercy," I am induced to transmit to you—to be disposed of as you may think fit—the following detailed account of the melancholy event, which has at once deprived the country of many valuable lives, and thereby plunged numerous families into the deepest distress, and involved, I fear, in pecuniary ruin, or reduced to extreme embarrassment, most of the gallant survivors.

You are aware that the *Kent*, Captain Henry Cobb, a fine new ship of 1350 tons, bound to Bengal and China, left the Downs on the 19th February, with 20 officers, 344 soldiers, 43 women, and 66 children, belonging to the 31st regiment: with 20 private passengers, and a crew (including officers) of 148 men on board.

The bustle attendant on a departure for India is undoubtedly calculated to subdue the force of those deeply painful sensations to which few men can refuse to yield, in the immediate prospect of a long and distant separation from the land of their fondest and earliest recollections. With my gallant shipmates, indeed, whose elasticity of spirits is remarkably characteristic of the professions to which they belonged, hope appeared greatly to predominate over sadness. Surrounded as they were by every circumstance that could render their voyage propitious, and in the ample enjoyment of every necessary that could contribute either to their health or comfort,—their hearts seemed to beat high with contentment and gratitude towards that country which they zealously served, and whose interests they were cheerfully going forth to defend.

With a fine fresh breeze from the north-east, the stately *Kent*, in bearing down the channel, speedily passed many a well-known spot on the coast, dear to our remembrance; and on the evening of the 23d, we took our last view of happy England, and entered the wide Atlantic, without the expectation of again seeing land until we reached the shores of India.

With slight interruptions of bad weather, we continued to make way until the night of Monday the 28th, when we were suddenly arrested in latitude 47° 30', longitude 10°, by a violent gale from the south-west, which gradually increased during the whole of the following morning.

To those who have never "gone down to the sea in ships, and seen the wonders of the Lord in the great deep," or even to such as have never been exposed in a westerly gale to the tremendous swell in the Bay of Biscay, I am sensible that the most sober description of the magnificent spectacle of "watery hills in full succession flowing," would appear sufficiently exaggerated. But it is impossible, I think, for the inexperienced mariner, however unreflecting he may try to be, to view the effects of the increasing storm, as he feels his solitary vessel reeling to and fro under his feet, without involuntarily raising his thoughts, with a secret confession of helplessness and veneration that he may never before have experienced, towards that mysterious Being whose power, under ordinary circumstances, we may entirely disregard, and whose incessant goodness we are too prone to requite with ingratitude.

The activity of the officers and seamen of the *Kent* appeared to keep ample pace with that of the gale. Our larger sails were speedily taken in, or closely reefed; and about ten o'clock on the morning of the 1st of March, after having struck our top-gallant yards, we were lying-to, under a triple-reefed main-topsail only, with our dead lights in, and with the whole watch of soldiers attached to the life-lines, that were run along the deck for this purpose.

The rolling of the ship, which was vastly increased by a dead weight of some hundred tons of shot and shells that formed a part of its lading, became so great about half-past eleven or twelve o'clock, that our main chains were thrown by every lurch considerably under water; and the best cleated articles of furniture in the cabins and the *cuddy** were dashed about with so much noise and violence, as to excite the liveliest apprehensions of individual danger.

It was a little before this period that one of the officers of the ship, with the well-meant intention of ascertaining that all was fast below, descended with two of the sailors into the hold, where they carried with them, for safety, a light in the patent lantern; and seeing that the lamp burned dimly, the officer took the precaution to hand it up to the orlop-deck to be trimmed. Having afterward discovered one of the spirit casks to be adrift, he sent the sailors for some billets of wood to secure it; but the ship, in their absence, having made a heavy lurch, the officer unfortunately dropped the light; and letting go his hold of the cask in his eagerness to recover the lantern, it suddenly stove, and the spirits communicating with the lamp, the whole place was instantly in a blaze.

I know not what steps were then taken. I myself had been engaged during the greater part of the morning in double-lashing and otherwise securing the furniture in my cabin, and in occasionally going to the cuddy, where the marine barometers were suspended, to mark their varying indications during the gale, in my journal; and it was on one of those occasions, after having read to Mrs. —, at her request, the 12th chapter of St. Luke, which so beautifully declares and illustrates the minute and tender providence of God, and so solemnly urges on all the necessity of continual watchfulness and readiness for the "coming of the Son of man," that I received from

*The *cuddy*, in an East Indiaman, is the large cabin or dining apartment, which is on a level with the quarter-deck.

Captain Spence, the captain of the day the alarming information that the ship was on fire in the after-hold; on hastening to the hatchway, whence smoke was slowly ascending, I found Captain Cobb and other officers already giving orders, which seemed to be promptly obeyed by the seamen and troops, who were using every exertion by means of the pumps, buckets of water, wet sails, hammocks, &c. to extinguish the flames.

With a view to excite among the ladies as little alarm as possible, in conveying this intelligence to Colonel Fearon, the commanding officer of the troops, I knocked gently at his cabin-door, and expressed a wish to speak with him, but whether my countenance betrayed the state of my feelings, or the increasing noise and confusion upon deck created apprehensions among them that the storm was assuming a more serious aspect, I found it difficult to pacify some of the ladies by repeated assurances that no danger whatever was to be apprehended from the gale. As long as the devouring element appeared to be confined to the spot where the fire originated, and which we were assured was surrounded on all sides by the water-casks, we ventured to cherish hopes that it might be subdued: but no sooner was the light blue vapour that at first arose succeeded by volumes of thick dingy smoke, which, speedily ascending through all the four hatchways, rolled over every part of the ship, than all further concealment became impossible, and almost all hope of preserving the vessel was abandoned. "The flames have reached the cable tier," was exclaimed by some individuals, and the strong pitchy smell that pervaded the deck confirmed the truth of the exclamation.

In these awful circumstances, Captain Cobb, with an ability and decision of character that seemed to increase with the imminence of the danger, resorted to the only alternative now left him, of ordering the lower decks to be scuttled, the combings of the hatches to be cut, and the lower ports to be opened, for the free admission of the waves.

These instructions were speedily executed by the united efforts of the troops and seamen: but not before some of the sick soldiers, one woman, and several children, unable to gain the upper deck, had perished. On descending to the gun-deck with Colonel Fearon, Captain Bray, and one or two other officers of the 31st regiment, to assist in opening the ports, I met, staggering towards the hatchway, in an exhausted and nearly senseless state, one of the mates, who informed us that he had just stumbled over the dead bodies of some individuals who must have died from suffocation, to which it was evident that he himself had almost fallen a victim. So dense and oppressive was the smoke, that it was with the utmost difficulty we could remain long enough below to fulfil Captain Cobb's wishes; which were no sooner accomplished than the sea rushed in with extraordinary force, carrying away, in its resistless progress to the hold, the largest chests, bulk-heads, &c.

Such a sight, under any other conceivable circumstances, was well calculated to have filled us with horror; but in our natural solicitude to avoid the more immediate peril of explosion, we endeavoured to cheer each other, as we stood up to our knees in water, with a faint hope that by these violent means we might be speedily restored to safety. The immense quantity of water that was thus introduced into the hold had indeed the effect, for a time, of checking the fury of the flames; but the danger of sinking having increased as the risk of explosion was diminished, the ship became water-logged, and presented other indications of settling, previous to her going down.

Death, in two of its most awful forms, now encompassed us, and we seemed left to choose the terrible alternative. But always preferring the more remote, though equally certain crisis, we tried to shut the ports again, to close the hatches, and to exclude the external air, in order, if possible, to prolong our existence, the near and certain termination of which appeared inevitable.

The scene of horror that now presented itself baffles all description—

> "Then rose from sea to sky the wild farewell; Then shriek'd the timid, and stood still the brave."

The upper deck was covered with between six and seven hundred human beings, many of whom, from previous sea-sickness, were forced on the first alarm to flee from below in a state of absolute nakedness, and were now running about in quest of husbands, children, or parents. While some were standing in silent resignation, or in stupid insensibility to their impending fate, others were yielding themselves up to the most frantic despair. Some on their knees were earnestly imploring, with significant gesticulations, and in noisy supplications, the mercy of Him whose arm, they exclaimed, was at length outstretched to smite them; others were to be seen hastily crossing themselves, and performing the various external acts required by their peculiar persuasion, while a number of the older and more stout-hearted soldiers and sailors sullenly took their seats directly over the magazine, hoping, as they stated, that by means of the explosion which they every instant expected, a speedier termination might thereby be put to their sufferings.* Several of the soldiers' wives and children, who had fled for temporary shelter into the after-cabins on the upper decks, were engaged in prayer and in reading the Scriptures with the ladies, some of whom were enabled, with wonderful self-possession, to offer to others those spiritual consolations which a firm and intelligent trust in the Redeemer of the world appeared at this awful hour to impart to their own breasts. The dignified deportment of two young ladies in particular formed a specimen of natural strength of mind, finely modified by Christian feeling, that failed not to attract the notice and admiration of every one who had an opportunity of witnessing it. On the melancholy announcement being made to them that all hope must be relinquished, and that death was rapidly and inevitably approaching, one of the ladies above referred to, calmly sinking down on her knees, and clasping her hands together, said, "Even so come, Lord Jesus," and immediately proposed to read a portion of the Scriptures to those around her; her sister, with nearly equal composure and collectedness of mind, selected the 46th and other appropriate Psalms, which were accordingly read, with intervals of prayer, by those ladies alternately, to the assembled females.

One young gentleman, of whose promising talents and piety I dare not now make further mention, having calmly asked me my opinion respecting the state of the ship, I told him that I thought we should be prepared to sleep that night in eternity; and I shall never forget the peculiar fervour with which he replied, as he pressed my hand in his, "My heart is filled with the peace of God:" adding, "yet, though I know it is foolish, I dread exceedingly the last struggle."

Among the numerous objects that struck my observation at this period, I was much affected with the appearance and conduct of some of the dear children, who, quite unconscious in the cuddy-cabins of the perils that surrounded them, continued to play as usual with their little toys in bed, or to put the most innocent and unseasonable questions to those around them. To some of the older children, who seemed fully alive to the reality of the danger, I whispered, now is the time to put in practice the instructions you used to receive at the regimental school, and to think of that Saviour of whom you have heard so much; they replied, as the tears ran down their cheeks, "O sir, we are trying to remember them, and we are praying to God."

* In addition to those who were naked on board the *Kent* at the moment the alarm of fire was heard, several individuals afterward threw off their clothes, to enable them the more easily to swim to the boats.

The passive condition to which we were all reduced, by the total failure of our most strenuous exertions, while it was well calculated, and probably designed, to convince us afterward that our deliverance was effected, not "by our own might or power, but by the Spirit of the Lord," afforded us ample room at the moment for deep and awful reflection, which, it is to be earnestly wished, may have been improved, as well by those who were eventually saved, as by those who perished.

It has been observed by the author of "The Retrospect," that "in the heat of battle, it is not only possible, but easy, to forget death, and cease to think; but in the cool and protracted hours of a shipwreck, where there is often nothing to engage the mind but the recollection of tried and unsuccessful labours, and the sight of unavoidable and increasing harbingers of destruction, it is not easy or possible to forget ourselves or a future state."

The general applicability of the latter part of this proposition I am disposed to doubt; for if I were to judge of the feelings of all on board by those of the number who were heard to express them, I should apprehend that a large majority of those men, whose previous attention has never been fairly and fully directed to the great subject of religion, approach the gates of death, it may be, with solemnity, or with terror, but without any definable or tangible conviction of the fact that "after death cometh the judgment."

Several there were, indeed, who vowed in loud and piteous cries, that if the Lord God would spare their lives, they would thenceforward dedicate all their powers to his service; and not a few were heard to exclaim, in the bitterness of remorse, that the judgments of the Most High were justly poured out upon them, for their neglected Sabbaths, and their profligate or profane lives; but the number of those was extremely small who appeared to dwell either with lively hope or dread on the view of an opening eternity. And as a further evidence of the truth of this observation, I may mention, that when I afterward had occasion to mount the mizen-shrouds, I there met with a young man who had brought me a letter of introduction from our excellent friend Dr. G——n, to whom I felt it my duty, while we were rocking on the mast, quietly to propose the great question, "What must we do to be saved?" and this young gentleman has since informed Mr. P., that though he was at that moment fully persuaded of the certainty of immediate death, yet the subject of eternity, in any form, had not once flashed upon his mind, previous to my conversation.

While we thus lay in a state of physical inertion, but with all our mental faculties in rapid and painful activity—with the waves lashing furiously against the side of our devoted ship, as if in anger with the hostile element for not more speedily performing its office of destruction,—the binnacle, by one of those many lurches which were driving every thing moveable from side to side of the vessel, was suddenly wrenched from its fastenings, and all the apparatus of the compass dashed to pieces upon the deck; on which one of the young mates, emphatically regarding it for a moment, cried out with the emotion so natural to a sailor under such circumstances, "What! Is the Kent's compass really gone?" leaving the bystanders to form, from that omen, their own conclusions. One promising young officer of the troops was seen thoughtfully removing from his writing-case a lock of hair, which he composedly deposited in his bosom; and another officer, procuring paper, &c., addressed a short communication to his father, which was afterward carefully enclosed in a bottle, in the hope that it might eventually reach its destination, with the view, as he stated, of relieving him from the long years of fruitless anxiety and suspense which our melancholy fate would awaken, and of bearing his humble testimony, at a moment when his sincerity could scarcely be questioned, to the faithfulness of that God in whose mercy he trusted, and whose peace he largely enjoyed in the tremendous prospect of immediate dissolution.

It was at this appalling instant, when "all hope that we should be saved was now taken away," and when the letter referred to was about being committed to the waves, that it occurred to Mr. Thomson, the fourth mate, to send a man to the foretop, rather with the ardent wish, than the expectation, that some friendly sail might be discovered on the face of the waters. The sailor, on mounting, threw his eyes round the horizon for a moment, —a moment of unutterable suspense, —and waving his hat, exclaimed, "A sail on the lee bow!" The joyful announcement was received with deep-felt thanksgivings, and with three cheers upon deck. Our flags of distress were instantly hoisted, and our minute guns fired; and we endeavoured to bear down under our three topsails and foresail upon the stranger, which afterward proved to be the Cambria, a small brig of 200 tons burden—Cook—bound to Vera Cruz, having on board twenty or thirty Cornish miners, and other agents of the Anglo-Mexican Company.

For ten or fifteen minutes we were left in doubt whether the brig perceived our signals, or, perceiving them, was either disposed or able to lend us any assistance. From the violence of the gale, it seems that the report of our guns was not heard; but the ascending volumes of smoke from the ship sufficiently announced the dreadful nature of our distress; and we had the satisfaction, after a short period of dark suspense, to see the brig hoist British colours, and crowd all sail to hasten to our relief.

Although it was impossible, and would have been improper, to repress the rising hopes that were pretty generally diffused among us by the unexpected sight of the Cambria, yet I confess that when I reflected on the long period our ship had been already burning—on the tremendous sea that was running—on the extreme smallness of the brig, and the immense number of human beings to be saved,—I could only venture to hope that a few might be spared; but I durst not for a moment contemplate the possibility of my own preservation.

While Captain Cobb, Colonel Fearon, and Major Macgregor, of the 31st regiment, were consulting together, as the brig was approaching us, on the necessary preparations for getting out the boats, &c., one of the officers asked Major M. in what order it was intended the officers should move off; to which the other replied, "Of course in funeral order;" which injunction was instantly confirmed by Colonel Fearon, who said, "Most undoubtedly the juniors first—but see that any man is cut down who presumes to enter the boats before the means of escape are presented to the women and children."

To prevent the rush to the boats, as they were being lowered, which, from certain symptoms of impatience manifested both by soldiers and sailors, there was reason to fear, some of the military officers were stationed over them with drawn swords. But from the firm determination which these exhibited, and the great subordination observed, with few exceptions, by the troops, this proper precaution was afterward rendered unnecessary.

Arrangements having been considerately made by Captain Cobb for placing in the first boat, previous to letting it down, all the ladies, and as many of the soldiers' wives as it could safely contain, they hurriedly wrapped themselves up in whatever articles of clothing could be most conveniently found; and I think about two, or half-past two o'clock, a most mournful procession advanced from the after-cabins to the starboard cuddy-port, outside of which the cutter was suspended. Scarcely a word was uttered—not a scream was heard—even the infants ceased to cry, as if conscious of the unspoken and unspeakable anguish that was at that instant rending the hearts of their parting parents—nor was the silence of voices in any way broken, except in one or two cases, where the ladies plaintively entreated permission to be left behind with their husbands. But on being assured that every moment's delay might occasion the sacrifice of a human life, they successively suffered themselves to be torn from the tender embrace, and with the fortitude which never fails to characterize and adorn their sex on occasions of overwhelming trial, were placed, without a murmur, in the boat, which was immediately lowered into a sea so tempestuous as to leave us only "to hope against hope" that it should live in it for a single moment. Twice the cry was heard from those on the chains that the boat was swamping. But He who enabled the apostle Peter to walk on the face of the deep, and was graciously attending to the silent but earnest aspirations of those on board, had decreed its safety.

Although Captain Cobb had used every precaution to diminish the danger of the boat's descent, and for this purpose stationed a man with an axe to cut away the tackle from either extremity, should the slightest difficulty occur in unhooking it; yet the peril attending the whole operation, which can only be adequately estimated by nautical men, had very nearly proved fatal to its numerous inmates.

After one or two unsuccessful attempts to place the little frail bark fairly upon the surface of the water, the command was at length given to unhook; the tackle at the stern was, in consequence, immediately cleared; but the ropes at the bow having got foul, the sailor there found it impossible to obey the order. In vain was the axe applied to the entangled tackle. The moment was inconceivably critical; as the boat, which necessarily followed the motion of the ship, was gradually rising out of the water, and must, in another instant, have been hanging perpendicularly by the bow, and its helpless passengers launched into the deep, had not a most providential wave suddenly struck and lifted up the stern, so as to enable the seamen to disengage the tackle; and the boat, being dexterously cleared from the ship, was seen, after a little while, from the poop, battling with the billows; now raised, in its progress to the brig, like a speck on their summit, and then disappearing for several seconds as if ingulfed "in the horrid vale" between them.

The Cambria having prudently lain-to at some distance from the *Kent*, lest she should be involved in her explosion, or exposed to the fire from our guns, which, being all shotted, afterward went off as the flames successively reached them, the men had a considerable way to row; and the success of this first experiment seeming to be the measure of our future hopes, the movements of this precious boat—incalculably precious, without doubt, to the agonized husbands and fathers immediately connected with it—were watched with intense anxiety by all on board. The better to balance the boat in the raging sea through which it had to pass, and to enable the seamen to ply their oars, the women and children were stowed promiscuously under the seats; and consequently exposed to the risk of being drowned by the continual dashing of the spray over their heads, which so filled the boat during the passage, that before their arrival at the brig the poor females were sitting up to the breast in water, and their children kept with the greatest difficulty above it.

However, in the course of twenty minutes, or half an hour, the little cutter was seen alongside the "ark of refuge;" and the first human being that happened to be admitted, out of the vast assemblage that ultimately found shelter there, was the infant son of Major Macgregor, a child of only a few weeks, who was caught from his mother's arms, and lifted into the brig, by Mr. Thomson, the fourth mate of the *Kent*, the officer who had been ordered to take the charge of the ladies' boat.

But the extreme difficulty and danger presented to the women and children in getting into the Cambria, seemed scarcely less imminent than that which they had previously encountered; for, to prevent the boat from swamping, or being stove against the side of the brig, while its passengers were disembarking from it, required no ordinary exercise of skill and perseverance on the part of the sailors, nor of self-possession and effort on that of the females themselves. On coming alongside the Cambria, Captain Cook very judiciously called out first for the children, who were successively thrown or handed up from the boat. The women were then urged to avail themselves of every favourable heave of the sea, by springing towards the many friendly arms that were extended from the vessel to receive them; and, notwithstanding the deplorable consequence of making a false step under such critical circumstances, not a single accident occurred to any individual belonging to the first boat. Indeed, the only one whose life appears to have been placed in extreme jeopardy alongside, was one of the ladies, who, in attempting to spring from the boat, came short of the hand that was held out to her, and would certainly have perished, had she not most happily caught hold, at the instant, of a rope that happened to be hanging over the Cambria's side, to which she clung for some moments, until she was dragged into the vessel.

I have reason to know, that the feelings of oppressive delight, gratitude, and praise, experienced by the married officers and soldiers, on being assured of the comparative safety of their wives and children, so entirely abstracted their minds from their own situation as to render them for a little while afterward totally insensible either to the storm that beat upon them, or to the active and gathering volcano that threatened every instant to explode under their feet.

It being impossible for the boats, after the first trip, to come alongside the *Kent*, a plan was adopted for lowering the women and children by ropes from the stern, by tying them two and two together. But from the heaving of the ship, and the extreme difficulty in dropping them at the instant the boat was underneath, many of the poor creatures were unavoidably plunged repeatedly under water; and much as humanity may rejoice that no woman was eventually lost by this process, yet it was as impossible to prevent, as it was deplorable to witness, the great sacrifice it occasioned of the younger children,—the same violent means which only reduced the parents to a state of exhaustion or insensibility having entirely extinguished the vital spark in the feeble frames of the infants that were fastened to them.

Amid the conflicting feelings and dispositions manifested by the numerous actors in this melancholy drama, many affecting proofs were elicited of parental and filial affection, or of disinterested friendship, that seemed to shed a momentary halo around the gloomy scene.

Two or three soldiers, to relieve their wives of a part of their families, sprang into the water with their children, and perished in their endeavours to save them. One young lady, who had resolutely refused to quit her father, whose sense of duty kept him at his post, was near falling a sacrifice to her filial devotion, not having been picked up by those in the boats until she had sunk five or six times. Another individual, who was reduced to the frightful alternative of losing his wife or his children, hastily decided in favour of his duty to the former. His wife was accordingly saved, but his four children, alas! were left to perish. A fine fellow, a solider, who had neither wife nor child of his own, but who evinced the greatest solicitude for the safety of those of others, insisted on having three children lashed to him, with whom he plunged into the water; not being able to reach the boat, he was again drawn into the ship with his charge, but not before two of the children had expired. One man fell down the hatchway into the flames, and another had his back so completely broken as to have been observed quite doubled falling overboard. These numerous spectacles of individual loss and suffering were not confined to the entrance upon the perilous voyage between the two ships. One man, who fell between the boat and the brig, had his head literally crushed to pieces; and some others were lost in their attempts to ascend the sides of the Cambria.

Seeing that the tardy means employed for the escape of the women and children necessarily consumed a great deal of time that might be partly devoted to the general preservation, orders were given, that, along with the females, each of the boats should also admit a certain portion of the soldiers; several of whom, in their impatience to take advantage of this permission, flung themselves overboard, and sunk in their ill-judged and premature efforts for deliverance.

One poor fellow of this number, a very respectable man, had actually reached the boat, and was raising his hand to lay hold on the gunnel, when the bow of the boat, by a sudden pitch, struck him on the head, and he instantly went down. There was a peculiarity attending this man's case that deserves notice. His wife, to whom he was warmly attached, not having been of the allotted number of women to accompany the regiment abroad, resolved, in her anxiety to follow her husband, to defeat this arrangement, and accordingly repaired with the detachment to Gravesend, where she ingeniously managed, by eluding the vigilance of the sentries, to get on board, and conceal herself for several days; and although she was discovered and sent ashore at Deal, she contrived a second time, with true feminine perseverance, to get within decks, where she continued to secrete herself until the morning of the fatal disaster.

While the men were thus bent in various ways on self-preservation, one of the sailors, who had taken his post with many others over the magazine, awaiting with great patience the dreadful explosion, at last cried out, as if in ill-humour that his expectation was likely to be disappointed, "Well! if she won't blow up, I'll see if I can't get away from her:" and instantly jumping up, he made the best of his way to one of the boats, which I understand he reached in safety.

I ought to state, that three out of the six boats we originally possessed were either completely stove or swamped in the course of the day, one of them with men in it, some of whom were seen floating in the water for a moment before they disappeared; and it is suspected that one or two of those who went down must have sunk under the weight of their spoils, the same individuals having been seen eagerly plundering the cuddy cabins.

As the day was rapidly drawing to a close, and the flames were slowly, but perceptibly extending, Colonel Fearon and Captain Cobb evinced an increasing anxiety to relieve the remainder of the gallant men under their charge.

To facilitate this object, a rope was suspended from the extremity of the spanker boom, along which the men were recommended to proceed, and thence slide down by the rope into the boats. But as, from the great swell of the sea, and the constant heaving of the ship, it was impossible for the boats to preserve their station for a moment, those who adopted this course incurred so great a risk of swinging for some time in the air, and of being repeatedly plunged under water, or dashed against the sides of the boats underneath, that many of the landsmen continued to throw themselves out of the stern windows on the upper deck, preferring what appeared to me the more precarious chance of reaching the boats by swimming. Rafts made of spars, hencoops, &c., were also ordered to be constructed, for the twofold purpose of forming an intermediate communication with the boats,—a purpose, by-the-by, which they very imperfectly answered,—and of serving as a last point of retreat, should the farther extension of the flames compel us to desert the vessel altogether: directions were at the same time given that every man should tie a rope round his waist, by which he might afterward attach himself to the rafts, should he be suddenly forced to take to the water. While the people were busily occupied in adopting this recommendation, I was surprised, I had almost said amused, by the singular delicacy of one of the Irish recruits, who, in searching for a rope in one of the cabins, called out to me that he could find none except the cordage belonging to an officer's cot, and wished to know whether there would be any harm in his appropriating it to his own use.

The gradual removal of the officers was at the same time commenced, and was marked by a discipline the most rigid and an intrepidity the most exemplary: none appearing to be influenced by a vain and ostentatious bravery, which in cases of extreme peril affords rather a presumptive proof of secret timidity than of fortitude; nor any betraying an unmanly or unsoldierlike impatience to quit the ship; but with the becoming deportment of men neither paralyzed by, nor profanely insensible to the accumulating dangers that encompassed them, they progressively departed in the different boats with their soldiers: they who happened to proceed first leaving behind them an example of coolness that could not be unprofitable to those who followed.

But the finest illustration of their conduct was displayed in that of their chief, whose ability and invincible presence of mind, under the complicated responsibility and anxiety of a commander, husband, and father, were eminently calculated, throughout this dismal day, to inspire all others with composure and fortitude. Never for a moment did Colonel Fearon seem to forget the authority with which his sovereign had invested him; nor did any of his officers, as far as my observation went, cease to remember the relative situations in which they were severally placed. Even in the gloomiest moments of that dark season, when the dissolution of every earthly distinction seemed near at hand, the decision and confidence with which orders were issued on the one hand, and the promptitude and respect with which they were obeyed on the other, afford the best proofs of the stability of the well-connected system of discipline established in the 31st regiment, and the most unquestionable ground for the high and flattering commendation which his royal highness the commander-in-chief has been pleased to bestow upon it.

I should, however, be guilty of injustice and unkindness, if I here omitted to bear my humble testimony to the manly behaviour of the East India Company's cadets, and other private passengers on board, who emulated the best conduct of the officers of the ship and of the troops, and equally participated with them in all the hardships and exertions of the day.

As an agreeable proof, too, of the subordination and good feeling that governed the poor soldiers in the midst of their sufferings, I ought to state, that towards evening, when the melancholy groups who were passively seated on the poop, exhausted by previous fatigue, anxiety, and fasting, were beginning to experience the pain of intolerable thirst, a box of oranges was accidentally discovered by some of the men, who, with a degree of mingled consideration, respect, and affection that could hardly have been expected at such a moment, refused to partake of the grateful beverage until they had offered a share of it to their officers.

I regret that the circumstances under which I write do not allow me sufficient time for recalling to my recollection all the busy thoughts that engaged my own mind on that eventful day, or the various conjectures which I ventured to form of what was passing in the minds of others.

But one idea, I remember, was forcibly suggested to me,—that instead of being able to trace, among my numerous associates, that diversity of fortitude which from my knowledge of their characters, I should have expected to mark their conduct,—forming, as it were, a descending series, from the decided heroism exhibited by some, down to the lowest degree of pusillanimity and phrensy discoverable in others,—I remarked that the mental condition of my fellow-sufferers was rather divided by a broad, but, as it afterward appeared, not impassable line; on the one side of which were ranged all whose minds were greatly elevated by the excitement above their ordinary standard; and on the other was to be seen the incalculably smaller, but more conspicuous group, whose powers of acting and thinking became absolutely paralyzed, or were driven into delirium, by the unusual character and pressure of the danger.

Nor was it uninteresting to observe the curious interchange, at least externally, of strength and weakness that obtained between those two discordant parties during the day. Some whose agitation and timidity had, in the earlier part of it, rendered them objects of pity or contempt, afterward rose, by some great internal effort, into positive distinction for the opposite qualities; while others, remarkable at first for calmness and courage, suddenly giving way, without any fresh cause of despair, seemed afterward to cast their minds, as they did their bodies, prostrate before the danger.

It were not difficult, perhaps, to account for these apparent anomalies; but I shall content myself with simply stating the facts, adding to them one of a similar description that sensibly affected my own mind.

Some of the soldiers near me having casually remarked that the sun was setting, I looked round, and never can I forget the intensity with which I regarded his declining rays. I had previously felt deeply impressed with the conviction, that that night the ocean was to be my bed; and had, I imagined, sufficiently realized to my mind both the last struggles and the consequences of death. But as I continued solemnly watching the departing beams of the sun, the thought that that was really the very last I should ever behold, gradually expanded into reflections, the most tremendous in their import. It was not, I am persuaded, either the retrospect of a most unprofitable life, or the direct fear of death or of judgment, that occupied my mind at the period I allude to; but a broad, illimitable view of eternity itself, altogether abstracted from the misery or felicity that flows through it,—a sort of painless, pleasureless, sleepless eternity. I know not whither the overwhelming thought would have hurried me, had I not speedily seized, as with the grasp of death, on some of those sweet promises of the gospel which give to an immortal existence its only charms; and that naturally enough led back my thoughts, by means of the brilliant object before me, to the contemplation of that "blessed city, which hath no need of the sun, neither of the moon to shine in it; for the glory of God doth lighten it, and the Lamb is the light thereof."

I have been the more particular in recording my precise feelings at the period in question, because they tend to confirm an opinion which I have long entertained,—in common, I believe, with yourself and others,—that we very rarely realize even those objects that seem, in our every-day speculations, to be the most interesting to our hearts. We are so much in the habit of uttering the awful words Almighty, heaven, hell, eternity, divine justice, holiness, &c., without attaching to them, in all their magnitude, the ideas of which such words are the symbols, that we become overwhelmed with much of the astonishment that accompanies a new and alarming discovery, if, at any time, the ideas themselves are suddenly and forcibly impressed upon us; and it is probably this vagueness of conception, experienced even by those whose minds are not altogether unexercised on the subject of religion, that enables others, devoid of all reflection whatever, to stand on the very brink of that precipice which divides the world of time from the regions of eternity, not only with apparent, but frequently, I am persuaded, with real tranquillity. How much is it to be lamented, that we do not keep in mind a truth which no one can pretend to dispute, that our indifference or blindness to danger, whether it be temporal or eternal, cannot possibly remove or diminish the extent of it.

Some time after the shades of night had enveloped us, I descended to the cuddy in quest of a blanket to shelter me from the increasing cold; and the scene of desolation that there presented itself was melancholy in the extreme. The place which, only a few short hours before, had been the seat of kindly intercourse and of social gayety, was now entirely deserted, save by a few miserable wretches, who were either stretched in irrecoverable intoxication on the floor, or prowling about like beasts of prey, in search of plunder. The sofas, drawers, and other articles of furniture, the due arrangement of which had cost so much thought and pains, were now broken into a thousand pieces, and scattered in confusion around me. Some of the geese and other poultry, escaped from their confinement, were cackling in the cuddy; while a solitary pig, wandering from its sty in the forecastle, was ranging at large in undisturbed possession of the Brussels carpet that covered one of the cabins. Glad to retire from a scene so cheerless and affecting, and rendered more dismal by the smoke which was oozing up from below, I returned to the poop, where I again found among the few officers that remained, Captain Cobb, Colonel Fearon, Lieutenants Ruxton, Booth, and Evans, superintending with unabated zeal the removal of the rapidly diminishing sufferers, as the boats successively arrived for their conveyance.

The alarm and impatience of the people increased in a high ratio as the night advanced; and our fears, amid the surrounding darkness, were fed as much by the groundless or exaggerated reports of the timid, as by the real and evident approach of the fatal crisis itself. With the view to ensure a greater probability of being discovered by those in the boats, some of the more collected and hardy soldiers (for I think almost all the sailors had already effected their escape) took the precaution to tie towels and such like articles round their heads previously to their committing themselves to the water.

As the boats were nearly three-quarters of an hour absent between each trip, which period was necessarily spent by those in the wreck in a state of fearful inactivity, abundant opportunity was afforded for collecting the sentiments of many of the unhappy men around me; some of whom, after remaining perhaps for a while in silent abstraction, would suddenly burst forth, as if awakened from some terrible dream to a still more frightful reality, into a long train of loud and desponding lamentation, that gradually subsided into its former stillness.

It was during those trying intervals of rest, that religious instruction and consolation appeared to be the most required and the most acceptable. Some there were, accordingly, who endeavoured to dispense it agreeably to the visible wants and feelings of the earnest hearers. On one of those occasions, especially, the officer to whom I have already alluded was entreated to pray. His prayer was short, but was frequently broken by the exclamations of assent to some of its confessions, that were wrung from the afflicted hearts of his honest auditors.

I know not in what manner, under those circumstances, spiritual hope or comfort could have been ministered to my afflicted companions by those who regard works, either wholly or partly, as the means of propitiating Divine justice, rather than the evidence and fruits of that faith which pacifies the conscience and purifies the heart. But in some few cases, at least, where the individuals deplored the want of time for repentance and good works, I well remember that no arguments tended to soothe their troubled minds but those which went directly to assure them of the freeness and fulness of that grace which is not refused, even in the eleventh hour, to the very chief of sinners. And if any of those to whom I now allude have been spared to read this record of their feelings in the prospect of death, it will be well for them to keep solemnly in mind the vows they then took upon them, and to seek to improve that season of probation which they so earnestly besought, and which has been so mercifully extended to them, by humbly and incessantly applying for accessions of that faith which they are sensible removed the terrors of their awakened consciences, and can alone enable them henceforward to live in a sober, righteous, and godly manner; and thereby give the only unquestionable proof of their love to God, and their interest in the great salvation of his Son Jesus Christ.

If, on reading this imperfect narrative, any persons beyond the immediate circle of my companions in misery (for within it I can safely declare that there were no indications of ridicule) should affect to despise, as contemptible or unsoldierlike, the humble devotional exercises to which I have now referred, I should like to assure them, that, although they were undoubtedly commenced and prosecuted much more with an eternal than a temporal object in view, yet they also subserved the important purpose of restoring order and composure among a certain limited class of the soldiers, at moments when mere military appeals had ceased to operate with their wonted influence.

I must state that, *in general*, it was not those most remarkable for their fortitude who evinced either a precipitancy to depart, or a desire to remain very long behind—the older and cooler soldiers appearing to possess too much regard for their officers, as well as for their individual credit, to take their hasty departure at a very early period of the day, and too much wisdom and resolution to hesitate to the very last.

But it was not till the close of this mournful tragedy that backwardness rather than impatience to adopt the perilous and only means of escape that offered, became generally discernible on the part of the unhappy remnant still on board; and that made it not only imperative on Captain Cobb to reiterate his threats, as well as his entreaties, that not an instant should be lost, but seemed to render it expedient for one of the officers of the troops, who had expressed his intention of remaining to the last, to limit in the hearing of those around him the period of his own stay. Seeing, however, between nine and ten o'clock, that some individuals were consuming the precious moments by obstinately hesitating to proceed, while others were making the inadmissible request to be lowered down as the women had been; learning from the boatmen, that the wreck, which was already nine or ten feet below the ordinary water mark, had sunk two feet lower since their last trip; and calculating, besides, that the two boats then under the stern, with that which was in sight on its return from the brig, would suffice for the conveyance of all who seemed in a condition to remove; the three remaining officers of the 31st regiment seriously prepared to take their departure.

As I cannot perhaps convey to you so correct an idea of the condition of others as by describing my own feelings and situation under the same circumstances, I shall make no apology for detailing the manner of my individual escape, which will sufficiently mark that of many hundreds that preceded it.

The spanker-boom of so large a ship as the *Kent*, which projects, I should think, 16 or 18 feet over the stern, rests on ordinary occasions about 19 or 20 feet above the water; but in the position in which we were placed, from the great height of the sea, and consequent pitching of the ship, it was frequently lifted to a height of not less than 30 or 40 feet from the surface.

To reach the rope, therefore, that hung from its extremity, was an operation that seemed to require the aid of as much dexterity of hand as steadiness of head. For it was not only the nervousness of creeping along the boom itself, or the extreme difficulty of afterward seizing on, and sliding down by the rope, that we had to dread, and that had occasioned the loss of some valuable lives, by deterring the men from adopting this mode of escape; but as the boat, which the one moment was probably close under the boom, might be carried the next, by the force of the waves, 15 or 20 yards away from it, the unhappy individual, whose best calculations were thus defeated, was generally left swinging for some time in mid-air, if he was not repeatedly plunged several feet under water, or dashed with dangerous violence against the sides of the returning boat, or what not unfrequently happened, was forced to let go his hold of the rope altogether. As there seemed, however, no alternative, I did not hesitate, notwithstanding my comparative inexperience and awkwardness in such a situation, to throw my leg across the perilous spar; and with a heart extremely grateful that such means of deliverance, dangerous as they appeared, were still extended to me; and more grateful still that I had been enabled, in common with others, to discharge my honest duty to my sovereign and to my fellow-soldiers; I proceeded, after confidently committing my spirit, the great object of my solicitude, into the keeping of Him who had formed and redeemed it, to creep slowly forward, feeling at every step the increasing difficulty of my situation. On getting nearly to the end of the boom, the young officer whom I followed and myself were met with a squall of wind and rain, so violent as to make us fain to embrace closely the slippery stick, without attempting for some minutes to make any progress, and to excite our apprehension that we must relinquish all hope of reaching the rope. But our fears were disappointed: and after resting for a while at the boom end, while my companion was descending to the boat, which he did not find until he had been plunged once or twice over head in the water, I prepared to follow; and instead of lowering myself, as many had imprudently done, at the moment when the boat was inclining towards us, and consequently being unable to descend the whole distance before it again receded, I calculated that while the boat was retiring I ought to commence my descent, which would probably be completed by the time the returning wave brought it underneath; by which means I was, I believe, almost the only officer or soldier who reached the boat without being either severely bruised or immersed in the water. But my friend Colonel Fearon had not been so fortunate: for after swinging for some time, and being repeatedly struck against the side of the boat, and at one time drawn completely under it, he was at last so utterly exhausted, that he must instantly have let go his hold of the rope and perished, had not some one in the boat seized him by the hair of the head and dragged him into it, almost senseless and alarmingly bruised.

Captain Cobb, in his immoveable resolution to be the last, if possible, to quit his ship, and in his generous anxiety for the preservation of every life intrusted to his charge, refused to seek the boat until he again endeavoured to urge onward the few still around him, who seemed struck dumb and powerless with dismay. But finding all his entreaties fruitless, and hearing the guns, whose tackle was burst asunder by the advancing flames, successively exploding in the hold into which they had fallen,—this gallant officer, after having nobly pursued, for the preservation of others, a course of exertion that has been rarely equalled either in its duration or difficulty, at last felt it right to provide for his own safety by laying hold on the topping lift, or rope that connects the driver boom with the mizen-top, and thereby getting over the heads of the infatuated men who occupied the boom, unable to go either backward or forward, and ultimately dropping himself into the water.

The means of escape, however, did not cease to be presented to the unfortunate individuals above referred to, long after Captain Cobb took his departure,—since one of the boats persevered in keeping its station under the Kent's stern, not only after all expostulation and entreaty with those on board had failed, but until the flames, bursting forth from the cabin windows, rendered it impossible to remain, without inflicting the greatest cruelty upon the individuals that manned it. But even on the return of the boat in question to the *Cambria*, with the single soldier who availed himself of it, did Captain Cook, with characteristic anxiety and caution, refuse to allow it to come alongside, until he learned that it was commanded by the spirited young officer, Mr. Thomson, whose indefatigable exertions during the whole day were to him a sufficient proof that all had been done that could be done for the deliverance of those individuals. But the same beneficent Providence which had been so wonderfully exerted for the preservation of hundreds was pleased, by a still more striking and unquestionable display of power and goodness, to avert the fate of a portion of those few who, we had all too much reason to fear, were doomed to destruction.

It would appear (for the poor men themselves give an extremely confused, though I am persuaded not a wilfully false, account of themselves) that shortly after the departure of the last boat, they were driven by the flames to seek shelter on the chains, where they stood until the masts fell overboard, to which they then clung for some hours, in a state of horror that no language can describe; until they were most providentially, I may say miraculously, discovered and picked up, by the humane master (Bibbey) of the *Caroline*, a vessel on its passage from Egypt to Liverpool, who happened to see the explosion at a great distance, and instantly made all sail in the direction whence it proceeded. Along with the fourteen men thus miraculously preserved were three others, who had expired before the arrival of the *Caroline* for their rescue.

The men, on their return to their regiment, expressed themselves in terms of the liveliest gratitude for the affectionate attentions they received on board the *Caroline*, from Captain Bibbey, who considerately remained till daylight close to the wreck, in the hope that some others might still be found clinging to it; an act of humanity which, it will appear on the slightest reflection, would have been madness in Captain Cook, in the peculiar situation of the *Cambria*, to have attempted.

In reference to this last most melancholy portion of my narrative, I feel it extremely painful to be obliged to hazard an opinion, that if the whole crew of the *Kent* had put forth, from the beginning, the same generous, and seamanlike efforts which several of them undoubtedly did, the few soldiers who were thus left behind would most probably have been safely disposed of before the advance of the flames or their own terror had incapacitated them, in the manner I have endeavoured to describe, from effecting their escape. But if, apart from this grievous consideration, I only recollect the lamentable state of exhaustion to which that portion of the crew were reduced, who unshrinkingly performed to the last their arduous and perilous duties, and that out of the three boats that remained afloat one was only prevented from sinking towards the close of the night, by having the hole in its bottom repeatedly stuffed with soldier's jackets; while the other two were rendered inefficient, the one by having its bow completely stove, and the second by being half filled with water, and the thwarts so torn as to make it necessary to lash the oars to the boat's ribs,—I must believe, that, independently of the counteracting circumstances formerly mentioned, all was done that humanity could possibly demand, or intrepidity effect, for the preservation of every individual.

Quitting, for a moment, the subject of the wreck, I would advert to what was in the mean time taking place on board the *Cambria*. I cannot, however, pretend to give you any adequate idea of the feelings of hope or despair that alternately flowed like a tide in the breasts of the unhappy females on board the brig, during the many hours of torturing suspense in which several of them were unavoidably held, respecting the fate of their husbands;—feelings which were inconceivably excited, rather than soothed, by the idle and erroneous rumours occasionally conveyed to them regarding the state of the Kent. But still less can I attempt to portray the alternate pictures of awful joy and of wild distraction exhibited by the sufferers (for both parties for the moment seemed equally to suffer) as the terrible truth was communicated that they and their children were indeed left husbandless and fatherless; or as the objects from whom they had feared they were for ever severed suddenly rushed into their arms.

But these feelings of delight, whatever may have been their intensity, were speedily chastened, and the attention of all arrested, by the last tremendous spectacle of destruction.

After the arrival of the last boat, the flames, which had spread along the upper deck and poop, ascended with the rapidity of lightning to the masts and rigging, forming one general conflagration, that illumined the heavens to an immense distance, and was strongly reflected upon several objects on board the brig. The flags of distress, hoisted in the morning, were seen for a considerable time waving amid the flames, until the masts to which they were suspended successively fell, like stately steeples, over the ship's side. At last, about half-past one o'clock in the morning, the devouring element having communicated to the magazine, the long-threatened explosion was seen, and the blazing fragments of the once magnificent Kent were instantly hurried, like so many rockets, high into the air; leaving, in the comparative darkness that succeeded, the deathful scene of that disastrous day floating before the mind like some feverish dream.

Shortly afterward the brig, which had been gradually making sail, was running at the rate of nine or ten miles an hour towards the nearest port. I would here endeavour to render my humble tribute of admiration and gratitude to that gallant and excellent individual who, under God, was undoubtedly the chief instrument of our deliverance; if I were not sensible that testimony has been already borne to his heroic and humane efforts, in a manner much more commensurate with, and from quarters reflecting infinitely greater honour upon his merits, than the feeble expressions of them which I should be able to record. I shall therefore content myself with appending to this letter some of the gratifying testimonials to which I refer. But I trust you will keep in mind, that Captain Cook's generous intentions and exertions must have proved utterly unavailing for the preservation of so many lives, had they not been most nobly and unremittingly supported by those of his mate and crew, as well as of the numerous passengers on board his brig. While the former, only eight in number, were usefully and necessarily employed in working the vessel, the sturdy Cornish miners and Yorkshire smelters, on the approach of the different boats, took their perilous station upon the chains, where they put forth the great muscular strength with which Heaven had endowed them, in dexterously seizing, at each successive heave of the sea, on some of the exhausted people, and dragging them upon deck. Nor did their kind anxieties terminate there. They and the gentlemen connected with them cheerfully opened their ample stores of clothes and provisions, which they liberally dispensed to the naked and famished sufferers;—they surrendered their beds to the helpless women and children, and seemed, in short, during the whole of our passage to England, to take no other delight than in ministering to all our wants.

Although, after the first burst of mutual gratulation, and of becoming acknowledgment of the Divine mercy on account of our unlooked-for deliverance, had subsided, none of us felt disposed to much interchange of thought, each being rather inclined to wrap himself up in his own reflections; yet we did not, during this first night, view with the alarm it warranted the extreme misery and danger to which we were still exposed, by being crowded together, in a gale of wind, with upwards of 600 human beings in a small brig of 200 tons, at a distance, too, of several hundred miles from any accessible port. Our little cabin, which was only calculated, under ordinary circumstances, for the accommodation of eight or ten persons, was now made to contain nearly eighty individuals, many of whom had no sitting room, and even some of the ladies no room to lie down. Owing to the continued violence of the gale, and to the bulwarks on one side of the brig having been driven in, the sea beat so incessantly over our deck, as to render it necessary that the hatches should only be lifted up between the returning waves to prevent absolute suffocation below, where the men were so closely packed together, that the steam arising from their respiration excited at one time an apprehension that the vessel was on fire; while the impurity of the air they were inhaling became so marked, that the lights occasionally carried down among them were almost instantly extinguished. Nor was the condition of the hundreds who covered the deck less wretched than that of their comrades below; since they were obliged, night and day, to stand shivering, in their wet and nearly naked state, ankle-deep in water. Some of the older children and females were thrown into fits, while the infants were pitifully crying for that nourishment which their nursing mothers were no longer able to give them.†

Our only hope amid these great and accumulating miseries was that the same compassionate Providence which had already so marvelously

† One of the soldier's wives was delivered of a child about an hour or two after her arrival on board the brig. Both she and the child, who has since received the appropriate name of Cambria, are doing well.

interposed on our behalf, would not permit the wind to abate or change until we reached some friendly port; for we were all convinced that a delay of a very few days longer at sea must inevitably involve us in famine, pestilence, and a complication of the most dreadful evils. Our hopes were not disappointed. The gale continued with even increasing violence; and our able captain, crowding all sail at the risk of carrying away his masts, so nobly urged his vessel onward, that in the afternoon of Thursday the 3d, the delightful exclamation from aloft was heard, "Land ahead!" In the evening we descried the Scilly lights; and running rapidly along the Cornish coast, we joyfully cast anchor in Falmouth harbour, about half-past 12 o'clock on the following morning.

On reviewing the various proximate causes to which so many human beings owed their deliverance from a combination of dangers as remarkable for their duration as they were appalling in their aspect, it is impossible, I think, not to discover, and gratefully acknowledge, in the beneficence of their arrangement, the overruling providence of that blessed Being, who is sometimes pleased in his mysterious operations to produce the same effects from causes apparently different; and on the other hand, as in our own case, to bring forth results the most opposite from one and the same cause. For there is no doubt that the heavy rolling of our ship, occasioned by the violent gale, which was the real origin of all our disasters, contributed also most essentially to our subsequent preservation; since, had not Captain Cobb been enabled, by the greatness of the swell, to introduce speedily through the gun ports the immense quantity of water that inundated the hold, and thereby checked for so long a time the fury of the flames, the Kent must unquestionably have been consumed before many, perhaps before any of those on board could have found shelter in the *Cambria*.

But it is unnecessary to dwell on an insulated fact like this, amid a concatenation of circumstances, all leading to the same conclusion, and so closely bound together as to force us to confess, that if a single link in the chain had been withdrawn or withheld, we must all most probably have perished.

The *Cambria*, which had been, it seems, unaccountably detained in port nearly a month after the period assigned for her departure, was, early on the morning of the fatal calamity, pursuing, at a great distance ahead of us, the same course with ourselves; but her bulwarks on the weather side having been suddenly driven in by a heavy sea breaking over her quarter, Captain Cook, in his anxiety to give ease to his labouring vessel, was induced to go completely out of his course, by throwing the brig on the opposite tack, by which means alone he was brought in sight of us. Not to dwell on the unexpected, but not unimportant facts, of the flames having been mercifully prevented, for eleven hours, from either communicating with the magazine forward, or the great spirit room abaft, or even coming into contact with the tiller ropes,—any of which circumstances would evidently have blasted all our hopes,—I would remark, that until the *Cambria* hove in sight, we had not discovered any vessel whatever for several days previous; nor did we afterward see another until we entered the chops of the channel. It is to be remembered, too, that had the *Cambria*, with her small crew, been homeward instead of outward bound, her scanty remainder of provisions, under such circumstances, would hardly have sufficed to form a single meal for our vast assemblage; or if, instead of having her lower deck completely clear, she had been carrying out a full cargo, there would not have been time, under the pressure of the danger and the violence of the gale, to throw the cargo overboard, and certainly with it, not sufficient space in the brig to contain one half of our number.

When I reflect, besides, on the disastrous consequences that must have followed if, during our passage home, which was performed in a period most unusually short, the wind had either veered round a few points, or even partially subsided, which must have produced a scene of horror on board more terrible if possible than that from which we had escaped; and, above all, when I recollect the extraordinary fact, and that which seems to have the most forcibly struck the whole of us, that we had not been above an hour in Falmouth harbour, when the wind, which had all along been blowing from the south-west, suddenly chopped round to the opposite quarter of the compass, and continued uninterruptedly for several days afterward to blow strongly from the north-east; —one cannot help concluding, that he who sees nothing of a Divine Providence in our preservation must be lamentably and wilfully blind "to the majesty of the Lord."

22

The SUFFERINGS *of* MISS ANN SAUNDERS

From *Narrative of the Shipwreck and Sufferings of Miss Ann Saunders*

1826

The Francis Mary *was laden with timber, which is why she did not sink. Even taking in large quantities of water, timber ships rarely sank. But she did just about everything else, losing various masts, various sails, the rear cabin, the jolly boat, the long boat, the tiller, whatever it took, in short, to get across the Atlantic Ocean. A heavy sea stove in the stern. Saltwater destroyed most of the ship's food supplies. They managed to save some cheese. The days went by. Passengers and crew started to die.*

Then the real horror begins. We will let Ann Saunders tell her own tale, but it should be said that another version of this story exists, an account by the captain, a man named Kendall, in which the details have not been quite so thoroughly purified by Miss Saunders' pen. I quote just a sentence or two from Kendall's story. "James Frier was working his passage home, under a promise of marriage to Ann Saunders, the female passenger, who attended on the master's wife, and who, when she heard of Frier's death, shrieked a loud yell, then snatching a cup from Clerk, the mate, cut her late intended husband's throat and drank his blood! insisting that she had the greatest right to it. A scuffle ensued, but the heroine got the better of her adversary, and then allowed him to drink one cup to her two."

The captain also remarked at the end of his brief account that "Ann Saunders had more strength in her calamity than most of the men. She performed the duty of cutting up and cleaning the dead bodies, keeping two knives for the purpose in her monkey jacket; and when the breath was announced to have flown, she would sharpen her knives, bleed the deceased in the neck, drink his blood, and cut him up as usual. From want of water, those who perished drank their own urine and salt water. They became foolish, and crawled upon their hands round the deck when they could, and died, generally, raving mad!"

What the survivors thought about what they had done we can only imagine. Cannibalism used to be called the "custom of the sea," and it was rare that anyone was prosecuted for it. Captain Pollard, in the Essex *shipwreck, was not charged with murder when it became known that they had drawn lots in his whaleboat and he had shot and they had eaten the cabin boy in order that some might live. In 1884 a case did come up in England, however, where survivors had killed a man, the weakest among them, and were tried for murder in England. The ship they were on was a yacht called the* Mignonette. *It came to grief on a voyage from England to Australia when it ran into a storm off the west coast of Africa, and four men escaped in a 13-foot boat that leaked and constantly had to be baled. They drifted without provisions except a couple of small tins of turnips for 19 days before the captain killed the cabin boy. Five days later a ship found and rescued them. The public fought for seats when the trial came up. Two of the men were convicted of murder, the third turning state's evidence, and sentenced to die. This was commuted, however, to six months in prison, when they were released. The trial ended official tolerance for the custom of the sea.*

One strange aspect of the case is that the young man they had killed to eat was named Richard Parker, and he was a cabin boy. The same thing happens in Poe's novel The Narrative of Arthur Gordon Pym, *written 47 years earlier. The survivors of Poe's shipwreck kill a cabin boy, and his name is Richard Parker.*

FOR THE INFORMATION OF SUCH OF MY READERS AS MAY BE UNACQUAINTED with the fact, it may not be unimportant that I commence the narrative of my recent unparalleled sufferings with stating that I am a native of Liverpool, where I was born in June, 1802, of reputable parents; who, although as regarding worldly riches were ranked with the poorer class, yet succeeded in bestowing on me what I now and ever shall conceive a legacy of more inestemable worth, to wit: an education sufficient to enable me to peruse the sacred Scriptures, whereby I was early taught the importance of attending to the concerns of my soul. At an early age I had the misfortune to lose my father—but, young as I was, the irreparable loss made a deep and lasting impression upon my mind. By this melancholy and unexpected event my poor mother was left a widow with five helpless children and without the means of contributing but a scanty pittance to their support. The three oldest were in consequence put out into respectable families in the neighborhood, where

I have reason to believe we were treated with as much tenderness as young children generally are who are bound out under similar circumstances. When I had arrived to the age of eighteen I was persuaded to take up my abode with a widowed aunt, with whom I remained until sometime in October, 1825. It was while with my aunt that I became first acquainted with that peculiarly unfortunate youth, James Frier, of whose wretched and untimely fate I shall hereafter have a sad occasion to speak.

While with my aunt I also became intimately acquainted with a Mrs. Kendall, the wife of Captain John Kendall, a lady of pious and amiable disposition and who, I believe, was very deservedly respected by all who had the pleasure of her acquaintance. It was by the very strong solicitations of this lady (and those of the unfortunate youth above mentioned) that I consented to accompany her with her husband on their passage from Liverpool to St. John, New Brunswick, in the fall of 1825.

It was early in the morning of the 10th November that I took an affectionate leave of my mother and sisters and embarked with Mrs. Kendall, whose companion I was to be, and bid adieu for the first time to the shores of my native land. The wind was favorable, but it being the first time in my life that I had ever adventured more than half a mile on the ocean, I was confined to my berth the first three days after we left port. But, becoming more accustomed to the motion of the vessel, I soon regained my health and spirits and from this moment enjoyed a pleasant passage, without any very remarkable occurrence attending us until we reached St. John, the port of our destination.

On the 18th January, 1826, Captain Kendall having obtained a cargo of timber and made every necessary preparation for our departure, we set sail for Liverpool with a favorable wind and with the prospect and joyful expectations of an expeditious passage. On board of the ship were twenty-one souls, including Mrs. Kendall and myself. Many of the seamen were married men and had left in Europe numerous families dependent on them for support. Alas! poor mortals, little did they probably think, when they bid their loving companions and their tender little ones the last adieu, that it was to be a final one and that they were to behold their faces no more in this frail world! But we must not charge an infinitely wise and good God foolishly, who cannot err, but orders every event for the best.

We enjoyed favorable weather until about the 1st February, when a severe gale was experienced, which blew away some of the yards and spars of our vessel and washed away one of the boats off the deck and severely wounded some of the seamen. Early in the morning ensuing, the gale having somewhat abated, Mrs. Kendall and myself employed ourselves in dressing the wounds of the poor fellows that were most injured while those who had escaped injury were employed in clearing the deck of the broken spars, splicing and disentangling the rigging. So that in a few hours they were enabled again to make sail, and with the pleasing hope that they should encounter no more boisterous and contrary winds to impede their passage. But in this they were soon sadly disappointed, for on the 5th they were visited with a still more severe gale from ESE, which indeed caused the sea to run mountains high. The captain gave orders to his men to do everything in their power to do, for the safety of our lives. All sails were clewed up and the ship hove to, but the gale still increasing, after noon our vessel was struck by a tremendous sea, which swept from her decks almost every moveable article and washed one of the seamen overboard, who was providentially saved. A few moments after, the whole of the ship's stern was stove in. This was only the beginning of a scene of horrid calamities, doubly horrible to me, who had never before witnessed anything so awful.

While the captain and officers of the ship were holding a consultation on deck what was best to be done for the preservation of our lives, Mrs. Kendall and myself were on our knees on the quarterdeck, engaged in earnest prayer.

The ensuing morning presented to our view an aspect the most dreary. The gale seemed to be increasing with redoubled vigor. Little else was now thought of but the preservation of our lives. Exertions were made by the crew to save as much of the ship's provisions as was possible, and by breaking out the bow port they succeeded in saving fifty or sixty pounds of bread and a few pounds of cheese, which were stowed in the main top; to which place Mrs. Kendall and myself were conveyed, it being impossible for us to remain below, the cabin being nearly filled with water and almost every sea breaking over us. The night approached with all its dismal horrors. The horizon was obscured by black and angry-looking clouds, and about midnight the rain commenced falling in torrents, attended with frightful peals of thunder and unremitting streams of lightning.

Daylight returned, but only to present to our view an additional scene of horror. One of the poor seamen, overcome by fatigue, was discovered hanging lifeless by some part of the rigging. His mortal remains were committed to the deep. As this was the first instance of entombing a human body in the ocean that I had ever witnessed, the melancholy scene made a deep impression on my mind, as I expected such eventually would be my own life.

At 6 A.M. our depressed spirits were a little revived by the appearance of a sail standing toward us; which proved to be an American, who remained in company with us until the next morning; when, in consequence of the roughness of the sea, being unable to afford us any assistance, they left us.

It would be impossible for me to attempt to describe the feelings of all on board at this moment, on seeing so unexpectedly vanish the pleasing hope of being rescued by this vessel from our perilous situation. As the only human means to prolong our miserable existence a tent of spare canvas was erected by the ship's crew on the forecastle, and all on board put on the short allowance of a quarter of a biscuit a day. On the 8th February, the gale still continuing, a brig was seen to leeward but at a great distance, and in the afternoon the same brig (as was supposed) was seen to the windward. Captain Kendall ordered a signal of distress to be made and we soon had the satisfaction to see the brig approach us within hail and inquire very distinctly how long we had been in that situation and what we intended to do. But night approaching and the gale still prevailing to that degree that no boat could have floated in the water, we saw no more of the brig.

All on board were now reduced to the most deplorable state imaginable. Our miserable bodies were gradually perishing and the disconsolate spirits of the poor sailors were overpowered by the horrible prospects of starving without any appearance of relief.

February the 11th another vessel was discovered at the northward and the signal of distress again made, but without any effect, as she did not alter her course and was soon out of sight. We had now arrived at an awful crisis. Our provisions were all consumed and hunger and thirst began to select their victims. On the 12th James Clarke, a seaman, died of no other complaint (as was judged) than the weakness caused by famine; whose body, after reading prayers, was committed to the deep. And on the 22nd John Wilson, another seaman, fell a victim of starvation.

As the calls of hunger had now become too importunate to be resisted, it is a fact, although shocking to relate, that we were reduced to the awful extremity to attempt to support our feeble bodies a while longer by subsisting on the dead body of the deceased. It was cut into slices, then washed in salt water and, after being exposed to and dried in the sun, was apportioned to each of the miserable survivors, who partook of it as a sweet morsel. From this revolting food I abstained for twenty-four hours, when I too was compelled by hunger to follow their example. We eyed each other with mournful and melancholy looks, as may be supposed of people perishing with hunger and thirst; by all of whom it was now perceived that we had nothing to hope from human aid but only from the mercy of the Almighty, whose ways are unsearchable.

On the 23rd J. Moore, another seaman, died, whose body was committed to the deep after taking therefrom the liver and heart, which was reserved for our subsistence. And in the course of twelve days after (during which our miseries continued without any alleviation) the following persons fell victims to fatigue and hunger, to wit: Henry Davis and John Jones, cabin boys; James Frier, cook; Alexander Kelly, Daniel Jones, John Hutchinson and John James, seamen. The heart-piercing lamentations of these poor creatures dying for the want of sustenance was distressing beyond conception. Some of them expired raving mad, crying out lamentably for water. Hutchinson, who, it appeared, had left a numerous family in Europe, talked to his wife and children as if they were present, repeating the names of the latter, and begged of them to be kind to their poor mother who, he represented, was about to be separated from him forever. Jones became delirious two or three days before his death and in his ravings reproached his wife and children as well as his dying companions present with being the authors of his extreme sufferings by depriving him of food and in refusing him even a single drop of water with which to moisten his parched lips. And, indeed, such now was the thirst of those who were but in a little better condition that they were driven to the melancholy distressful horrid act (to procure their blood) of cutting the throats of their deceased companions a moment after the breath of life had left their bodies!

In the untimely exit of no one of the unhappy sufferers was I so sensibly affected as in that of the unfortunate youth, James Frier—for in the welfare of none on board did I feel myself so immediately interested, as the reader may judge from the circumstances that I shall mention. I have already stated that with this ill-fated young man I became intimately acquainted in Liverpool. To me he had early made protestations of love and more than once intimated an inclination to select me as the partner of his bosom; and never had I any reason to doubt his sincerity. It was partly by his solicitations that I had been induced to comply with the wishes of Mrs. Kendall to accompany her in this unfortunate voyage, in the course of which, by frequent interviews, my attachment for this unfortunate youth was rather increased than diminished. And before this dreadful calamity befell us he had obtained my consent and we had mutually agreed and avowed to each other our determination to unite in marriage as soon as we should reach our destined port. Judge then, my female readers (for it is you that can best judge) what must have been my feelings, to see a youth for whom I had formed an indissoluble attachment—him with whom I expected so soon to be joined in wedlock and to spend the remainder of my days—expiring before my eyes for the want of that sustenance which nature requires for the support of life and which it was not in my power to afford him. And myself at the same moment so far reduced by hunger and thirst as to be driven to the horrid alternative to preserve my own life to plead my claim to the greater portion of his precious blood as it oozed half congealed from the wound inflicted upon his lifeless body! Oh, this was a bitter cup indeed! But it was God's will that it should not pass me—and God's will must be done. O, it was a chastening rod that has been the means, I trust, of weaning me forever from all the vain enjoyments of this frail world.

While almost every other person on board were rendered so weak by their extreme sufferings and deprivations as to be unable to stand upon their feet or even to detach from the lifeless bodies of their unfortunate companions that food which was now nature's only support, the Almighty, in mercy to me, endowed me with not only strength and ability to exhort the poor wretches to unite in prayer and to prepare their precious souls for eternity but to perform this office for them, for which purpose I constantly carried about with me a knife, with which I daily detached and presented each with a proportionable quantity of this their only food. My poor unfortunate female companion (Mrs. Kendall, who never failed to unite with me in prayer) seemed too to enjoy with me a share of God's great mercy. But the reader may judge to what extremity of want we all must have been driven when she, two days before we were relieved, was compelled by hunger to eat the brains of one of the seamen, declaring in the meantime that it was the most delicious thing she ever tasted. And, what is still more melancholy to relate, the unfortunate person whose brains she was thus compelled to subsist on had been three times wrecked before but providentially picked up by a vessel after being once twenty-two days on the wreck—but in the present instant he perished after surviving similar sufferings for the space of twenty-nine days and then became food for his surviving shipmates!

About the 26th February an English brig hove in sight, on which the usual signals of distress were made and, although the winds had become less boisterous and the sea more smooth, to our inexpressible grief she did not approach to afford us any assistance. Our longing eyes followed her until she was out of sight, leaving us in a situation doubly calamitous from our disappointment in not receiving the relief which appeared so near. Our hopes vanished with the brig and from the highest summit of expectation they now sunk into a state of the most dismal despair. Nature indeed seemed now to have abandoned her functions. Never could human beings be reduced to a more wretched situation. More than two thirds of the crew had already perished and the surviving few—weak, distracted, and destitute of almost everything—envied the fate of those whose lifeless corpses no longer wanted sustenance. The sense of hunger was almost lost, but a parching thirst consumed our vitals. Our mouths had become so dry for want of moisture for three or four days that we were obliged to wash them every few hours with salt water to prevent our lips glueing together.

Early in the morning of the 7th March a sail was discovered to windward. The ship's crew (with my assistance) made all the signals of distress that the little remaining strength of their bodies would enable them to do. They were indeed the last efforts of expiring nature. But, praised be God, the hour of our deliverance had now arrived. The ship was soon within hail, which proved to be His Majesty's Ship *Blonde*, Lord Byron, when her boat was manned and sent to our relief.

It would be in vain for me to attempt to describe our feelings at this moment or those manifested by our deliverers when they discovered who we were and what our miserable situation; and that they had arrived in season to rescue six of their fellow creatures from a most awful but certain death. My companions in misery, who for three or four of the preceding days had been only able to crawl about the deck upon their hands and knees, now became so animated at the prospect of relief as to raise themselves erect and with uplifted hands returned thanks to their Almighty preserver.

When relieved, but a small part of the body of the last person deceased remained, and this I had cut as usual into slices and spread on the quarterdeck; which being noticed by the lieutenant of the *Blonde* (who with others had been dispatched from the ship to our relief) and before we had time to state to him to what extremities we had been driven, he observed, "You have yet, I perceive, fresh meat." But his horror can be better conceived than described when he was informed that what he saw was the remains of the dead body of one of our unfortunate companions and that on this, our only remaining food, it was our intention to have put ourselves on an allowance the ensuing evening had not unerring Providence directed him to our relief.

When we reached the *Blonde* the narrative of our sufferings as well as a view of our weak and emaciated bodies caused tears to bedew those faces which probably are not used to turn pale at the approach of death. By Lord Byron and his officers and crew we were treated with all possible kindness and humanity; insomuch that we soon gained our strength to that degree as to be able in ten days after to go on board of a vessel bound to Europe. And it was on the 20th March following that I was landed in safety at Portsmouth, where for twelve days I was treated with that hospitality, by both sexes, as ought not, and I trust will not, pass without its merited reward. And on the 5th April following I was conveyed and restored to the arms of my dear mother, after an absence of nearly five months; in which time I think I can truly say I had witnessed and endured more of the heavy judgments and afflictions of this world than any other of its female inhabitants.

23

NARRATIVE *of a* SHIPWRECK, CAPTIVITY & SUFFERINGS

From *Narrative of the Shipwreck, Captivity & Sufferings of Horace Holden & Benj. H. Nute*

BY HORACE HOLDEN

1832

Some of the most interesting shipwreck accounts are those in which the survivors find themselves among native tribes in remote places. In many cases their accounts are the earliest ethnographic descriptions we have of those tribes, and that is the case with Horace Holden's little book. Holden and Nute were the sole survivors of a two-year captivity in the Palau Islands after their ship, the Mentor, *was wrecked on one of the reefs that surrounds the Palaus. They spent their first months with friendly natives who already had an Englishman living with them who had deserted his own ship some 29 years earlier in order to escape punishment for some offense. Wanting to escape, however, with these natives' permission and help they took their ship's boat back to sea, only to be wrecked again, this time falling in among natives on a small, desolate island with few resources, where they were treated cruelly. Some months after arriving there the captain of the* Mentor *was able to escape with one other man, leaving six men on the island. Holden describes what happened to them in the following pages.*

THE ISLAND, TO WHICH THEY WERE CARRIED, PROVES TO BE LORD North's Island, called by the natives To' bee.—Account of the island and its inhabitants.—Their manners and customs.

It may now be proper in this place to give some account of the place where our unhappy lot was cast, and of its rude and miserable inhabitants. It will be impossible to convey a correct idea of their ignorance, poverty, and degradation; but some conception may be formed, by imagining what the condition of beings must necessarily be, when wholly separated from the rest of their species, stripped of all the refinements of life, and deprived of all means and opportunities for improvement.

We were now upon the small piece of land called by the natives *To' bee*, but known to navigators by the name of Lord North's Island, situated between the third and fourth degrees of north latitude, and in longitude one hundred and thirty-one degrees twenty minutes east. It is also known by the name of Nevil's Island and Johnston's Island; and it has been hitherto considered by navigators and others as uninhabited. This is not surprising; as we were told by the natives that no white man had ever visited the place; though it seemed, from the pieces of iron in their possession, and from other circumstances, that they had had some communication with the Spaniards and Portuguese in that quarter of the world. Like many other islands in those seas, this is surrounded by a coral reef, which is from an eighth to one half of a mile wide; but outside of the reef the water is apparently fathomless, the water being as blue as it is in the middle of the ocean; and the largest vessels may in many places approach within a quarter of a mile of the beach. The whole island rises so little above the level of the sea, that the swell often rolls up to a considerable distance inland. It is about three-quarters of a mile in length, and not far from half a mile in width. There were upon it three villages, situated on the shores, and containing, in all, between three and four hundred souls, at the time when we were taken there; but the number was considerably diminished by famine and disease before we left.

The inhabitants are in a state of entire barbarism and ignorance. The men wear a sort of girdle or belt made of the bark of a tree. This is girded round the loins so as to leave one end to hang loose behind, the other is brought forward and fastened to the belt in front. This is their only clothing. The females, after arriving at the age of womanhood, wear an apron made of the leaves of a plant, by them called *Kurremung*, split into fine strips and plaited. This extends from the loins nearly to the knees. Some few wear rings upon their wrists made of white shell and some had this kind of ornament made of turtle-shell. In their ears, which are always bored, they sometimes wear a leaf; and round their necks a necklace made of the shell of the cocoanut, and a small white shell, called *keem* shell. The children go entirely naked. The complexion of these islanders is a light copper color; much lighter than the Maylays, or the Pelew islanders; which last, however, they resemble in the breadth of their faces, high cheekbones, and broad flattened noses. They do not color their teeth, by chewing anything, as many of those islanders do; but their teeth are so strong that they can husk a cocoa-nut with them instantly.

Their principal food is the cocoa-nut. They occasionally succeed in procuring fish, though the supply obtained during our residence there was exceeding small. Their fish-hooks are made of turtle-shell, and not well contrived for the purpose; but we could not induce them to use our hooks, till they had heated them and altered their form so that they would not hold the fish. They did this because they said that Yarris (God) would be angry with them, if they used our hooks without preparing them according to their fashion. Sometimes they are so fortunate as to obtain a sea-turtle; five only were taken during the two years we were there. The turtle, I may add, has something of a sacred character with them. They also raise small quantities of a vegetable somewhat resembling the yam; but while we were with them they were unsuccessful in cultivating it. These constitute the slender means of their support; and they are thus barely kept from actual death by famine, but on the very verge of starvation. When any one of them begins to fail, for want of food, so that his death is pretty certain, they inhumanly turn him off from among them, to starve to death.

Their religion is such as might be expected among a people in their condition. Their place of worship is a rudely constructed building, or hut, about fifty feet long and thirty wide. In the centre, suspended from the roof, is a sort of altar, into which they suppose their deity comes to hold converse with the priest. Rudely carved images are placed in different parts of the building, and are supposed to personate their divinity. As nearly as could be ascertained by us, they supposed that the object of their worship was of like passions with themselves capricious and revengeful. During the time we were with them, they attributed to his displeasure their want of success in taking fish as they had done in former times, and the unfruitfulness of their bread-fruit and cocoa trees.

Their religious ceremonies are singular. In the commencement the priest walks round the altar and takes from it a mat, devoted to the purpose, which is laid upon the ground. He then seats himself upon it, and begins to hoot, in the mean time throwing himself into a variety of attitudes, for the purpose of calling down the divinity into the altar. At intervals the congregation sing, but immediately stop when the priest breaks out in his devotions. By the side of the altar is always placed a large bowl, and six cocoa-nuts. After the incantation is gone through, and the divinity is supposed to be present, the bowl is turned up, and four of the nuts are broken and put in it, two being reserved for the exclusive use of a priest by them called also "*yarris.*" As soon as the nuts are broken, one of the company begins to shout, and, rushing to the centre, seizes the bowl, and drinks of the milk of the nut, generally spilling a considerable part of it upon the ground. After this a few pieces are thrown to the images, and the remainder are eaten by the priests. This closes the ceremony; after which they indulge in any recreations that chance to please them best.

While we were on the island several earthquakes happened, and some of them pretty severe. On those occasions the natives were much terrified; they would not let their children speak a word; and they said among themselves—*zahbee'too Yarris, To'bee yettah'men*, that is Yarris (God) is coming and *To'bee* (the name of the island) will sink. They were also very much alarmed at thunder and lightning; and used to say at such times, *Yarris tee'tree*, God is talking. I do not know how they would be affected by an eclipse, as none happened, that I noticed, while we remained there.

I will here mention some other things in respect to their customs and usages, as they now occur to me.

Their implements of war are spears and clubs; they have no bows and arrows. Their spears are made of the wood of the cocoa-nut trees; the points of them are set with rows of sharks' teeth; and, being at the same time very heavy and from ten to twenty feet long, are formidable weapons.

Their canoes are made of logs which drift to their island from other places, there being no trees on it large enough for that purpose; they are hollowed out with great labor, and are of very clumsy workmanship; to prevent their oversetting, they are fitted up with outriggers, like those of the Pelew islanders.

They kindle their fires, as they informed me, by rubbing two pieces of wood together, as is common in the islands of the Pacific Ocean; and they cook their turtle or other meat, (when they are so fortunate as to have any,) as well as their vegetables, by covering them with heated stones. I should state, however, that during the whole time we stayed among them, fire was always preserved in some part of the island, so that there was no necessity for kindling it in the manner here mentioned.

Like other savage people, they reckon time by moons; I could not learn that they ever reckoned by any other period, except, indeed, with speaking of two or three days.

They take pride in their hair, and are particularly careful about it, washing and cleansing it almost every day. They do not color it, however, as the natives of some islands are said to do; but they moisten it with the juice pressed out from the cocoa-nut, which gives it a very glossy appearance; and it is frequently so long as to reach down to their waist.

Their mode of salutation is to clasp each other in their arms, and touch their noses together, as is practised in many other islands.

We found no musical instruments of any kind among them. They sometimes, on particular occasions, would sing or bawl out something like a rude tune; but we could not understand it. We frequently tried to teach them to whistle, and their awkward attempts to do it amused us; but they never were able to learn how it was done.

In their names, I could not find that they had any thing like a family name, but only a single one, (corresponding to our Christian names,) as is the case, I believe, throughout the islands of the Pacific. I could not learn, that the names were significant either of animals or other objects, as the Indian names of America are, and I never found any two persons of the same name. The names of the members of the family with which I lived were as follows: —

Pahrahboo'ah, the father of the family.

Nah'kit, the mother.

Buhwur timar, the eldest child, a son, ten or twelve years old.

Kobaw'ut, the second, a daughter.

Kobahnoo'uk, the third, a daughter.

The children do not address their parents by any word corresponding to father or mother, papa or mamma, but by their names. Their parents treat them on the footing of equality; they are generally well behaved, and are never punished, except occasionally when impatient for their food.

Their language appears to be different from those of the other islands in that quarter; we found that the three natives of the Pelew Islands, that accompanied us, could not understand anything they said; though I observed afterwards, occasionally, a resemblance in two or three words. I may add, that the Pelew chiefs had never heard of Lord North's Island; but they are acquainted with the Caroline Islands.

A detail of all that befell us would serve only to give pain to the benevolent, or at most to show how much human beings can endure. I shall attempt but little more than to describe the sufferings of a day; observing once for all, that for the term of two long years we experienced the same privations, and were subjected to the same brutal treatment; life, during all that time, being no better than the constant succession of the most acute sufferings.

This island, unlike the Pelews, is one of the most horrible and wretched on the face of the globe. The only product of its soil worth mentioning is the cocoa-tree; and those are of so dwarfish and miserable a growth as to bear but very few nuts. These few, however, constitute the food of the inhabitants, with the exception of a species of fish caught occasionally near the shore. The only animals or creeping things known on the island are lizards and mice, and, during our stay there, scarcely a solitary sea-fowl was known to have alighted on the island, and but few fish were taken by the natives.

The character of the inhabitants much resembles that of the island itself. Cowardly and servile, yet most barbarous and cruel, they combine, in their habits, tempers, and dispositions, the most disgusting and loathsome features that disgrace humanity. And, what may be regarded as remarkable, the female portion of the inhabitants outstrip the men in cruelty and savage depravity; so much so, that we were frequently indebted to the tender mercies of the men for escapes from death at the hands of the women. The indolence of the natives, which not even the fear of starvation itself can rouse to exertion, prevents their undertaking the least toil, although a little labor, well applied, might be made to render them infinitely more comfortable.

Strange as it may appear, it is nevertheless true, that, notwithstanding they are in this miserable condition, with no prospect of its ever being improved, they are of the opinion that they are highly favored. This can be accounted for in no other way than by the fact, that they are entirely ignorant of all that lies beyond the narrow limits of their observation. They know nothing of any other portion of the globe, than the mere speck of barren land upon which by some accident they were thrown, and where they remain, to drag out a wretched existence. Their traditions do not extend further back than to about a hundred years; and, to their simple minds, it seems like a splendid effort of mind to be able to relate, with tolerable accuracy, the time-hallowed stories told them by their parents. Whether they could in any way be improved by instruction, is a question which it would be difficult to answer. They seem to be doomed to remain, as one of the last links in the chain that connects our race with the mere animal part of the creation.

A ship discovered at a small distance from the island.—The natives prepare to go on board of her.—Captain Barnard and Bartlet Rollins, after being severely beaten, are allowed to go with the natives in their canoes, and thus effect their escape; the rest of the Mentor's *people are still forcibly detained on the island.—Their hopes of being taken on board of the same ship are suddenly blasted.—Their despondency on that disappointment.—Return of the natives from the ship; their rage, and quarrels about the division of the articles procured on board of her.—They threaten to wreak their vengeance on the* Mentor's *people that remained with them.—Their cruel treatment of them.—A storm destroys the cocoa-nut trees and causes a scarcity of food.*

We were captured and taken to the island December 6, 1832; and on the third day of February 1833, two months wanting three days, Captain Barnard and Bartlet Rollins effected their escape. Compared with the remainder of our captivity, our privations and sufferings up to that time were less severe. But at no time did we have sufficient food to satisfy the cravings of hunger! The very crumbs that fall from an ordinary table would have been to us a luxury; the swine of America are better fed than we were, on the most fortunate day of our residence upon that island.

It was on the day above mentioned that a ship was discovered a short distance from the island, and the natives immediately collected, and prepared to go to it, in order to obtain iron, or some other articles of value. Hope once more visited us. To escape was, of course, our strong desire and intention. Accordingly, when the canoes put off we attempted to go. Our savage masters interposed their authority, and by menaces and blows prevented us. Many of us were severely beaten, and all but two were detained by the brutal force of the savages. At length Captain Barnard and Rollins, after being severely beaten, were allowed to accompany the natives to the ship, and succeeded in effecting their escape. Trusting to the humanity of the captain and crew, we for some time confidently expected, that they would contrive some way of enabling us to join them. They were in sight about three hours; at one time they were so near that we could distinctly see the hands on board; but judge of our feelings when we saw the vessel pursuing her course! Our expectations were all blasted in a moment, and our minds, which had been gladdened by the hope of once more enjoying the society of civilized beings, of once more reaching the shores of our beloved country, sunk back into a state of despair; we wept like children.

The natives, when they returned from the vessel, brought with them a small quantity of iron hoops, and a few articles of some little value, but they were highly dissatisfied with the amount received, and greatly enraged. The division of the property caused much difficulty, and they quarrelled about it for several days. Those of us who remained, though innocent, were the greatest sufferers. They held us accountable for the conduct of those who had left, and vented the malignity of their unfeeling hearts upon us. We were given to understand, that now our doom was fixed; that we should remain with them, and die the victims of our tormentors! Alas! it was but too true, that such was to be the fate of all but two of our number! We were destined to see one after another of our fellow-sufferers sink under the constantly increasing severity of the burdens imposed upon them, and perish either from actual starvation, or by the blows of the savages.

After the departure of the captain and Rollins, we were treated with much greater severity than we had been before. Generally we were aroused from our broken slumbers about sunrise, and compelled to go to work; we were usually employed in cultivating a species of vegetable somewhat resembling the yam, and called by them "*korei*." This root is raised in beds of mud, which are prepared by digging out the sand, and filling the place with mould. The whole of this labor was performed with the hands. We were compelled day after day to stand in the mud from morning till night, and to turn up the mud with our hands. Frequently we were required to do this without receiving a morsel of food till about noon, and sometimes we were left without anything to eat till night. At best we could get no more than a small piece of cocoa-nut, hardly a common-sized mouthful, at a time, and if, either from exhaustion or any other cause, we neglected to perform the required amount of labor, our pittance of food was withheld altogether.

From this plain and unexaggerated account it will be seen, that our condition at best was bad enough; but a misfortune befell us which rendered it still worse. About four months from the time of our landing on that dreary spot, there was a violent storm, which came very near sweeping away the whole of the means of support which remained for the miserable inhabitants. The wind blew down many of the best cocoa trees, and materially injured the fruit on such as were left standing. Besides this, the low places in which they raised the root, by them called "*korei*," were mostly filled with sand, and famine stared us all in the face.

They attributed this misfortune to the anger of their god, and did not fail to use such means as they thought best calculated to appease him; and the calamity greatly added to our sufferings. Besides subjecting us to still more severe deprivations, we were compelled (though hardly able to drag our limbs from place to place) to labor in repairing the damage done by the storm. We were employed for months in carrying in our arms and on our shoulders pieces of the coral rock, in order to form a sort of seawall to prevent the waves from washing away the trees; and this drudgery, considering that we were naked, under a burning sun, and reduced to nothing but skin and bones, was too severe to admit of anything like an adequate description. Our flesh, or, to speak more properly, our skin—for :

The natives compel the Mentor's *people to be tattooed.—Description of that painful operation.—They also oblige them to pluck their beards, &c.—Another vessel passes by the island; and, afterwards, a third comes in sight and remains for three days; the* Mentor's *people are closely guarded at these times.—The melancholy fate of* William Sedon; *and the barbarous murder of* Peter Andrews.*—Attack on* H. Holden, *who is protected by one of the natives, and escapes.—*B. Nute *and others are protected by the female natives from the fury of the men.—Death of one of the* Pelew *chiefs.—Another of the* Pelew *people is detected in stealing, and is punished in their manner.—Death of* Milton Hewlet *and* Charles C. Bouket; *leaving now only* B. Nute, H. Holden, *and the other* Pelew *chief, named* Kobak, *who all remained in a feeble and helpless condition.—Filthy practices of the natives.—Friendship of the surviving* Pelew *chief.*

A new trial now awaited us. The barbarous beings among whom our lot had been cast, deemed it important that we should be *tattooed*, and we were compelled to submit to the distressing operation. We expostulated against it—we entreated—we begged to be spared this additional affliction; but our entreaties were of no use. Those savages were not to be moved, and we were compelled to submit; and that the reader may form some idea of the painful process, I will here give a brief account of it.

We were in the first place securely bound down to the ground, and there held fast by our tormentors. They then proceeded to draw with a sharp stick the figures designed to be imprinted on the skin. This done, the skin was thickly punctured with a little instrument made of sharpened fish bones, and somewhat resembling a carpenter's adz in miniature, but having teeth, instead of a smooth, sharp edge. This instrument was held within an inch or two of the flesh, and struck into it rapidly with a piece of wood, applied to it in such a manner as to cause it to rebound at every stroke. In this way our breasts and arms were prepared; and subsequently the ink, which was made of a vegetable found on the island and called by them the "*savvan*," was applied. The operation caused such an inflammation of our bodies, that only a portion could be done at one time; and as soon as the inflammation abated another portion was done, as fast as we could bear it, till our bodies were covered. It was effectually done; for to this day the figures remain as distinct as they were when first imprinted, and the marks will be carried by us to the grave. They were exceedingly anxious to perform the operation upon our faces; but this we would not submit to, telling them that sooner than have it done we would die in resisting them. Among themselves, the oldest people had the greatest quantity of tattooing, and the younger class less.

Besides the operation of *tattooing,* they compelled us to pluck the hair from different parts of the body, and to pluck our beards about every ten days, which was extremely painful; and at every successive operation the beard grew out harder and stiffer.

About seventeen days after the captain and Rollins left, we saw a vessel to the windward; but the natives did not attempt to visit it. Five months afterward another came in sight, and remained for three days near the island. At one time we could distinctly see the men on board; but we were kept on shore and closely guarded. Several canoes visited the ship, and brought back a few pieces of iron, fish-hooks, glass bottles, &c. We tried, but in vain, to escape. It seemed to us, that we were doomed to remain on that dreary spot, to wear out our remaining strength in hopeless bondage, and to submit to the control of brutal masters whose tender mercies were cruelties. Death, in any form, would have been a relief and often did we see moments when it would have been welcomed as the best of friends! To some of our companions it did come, though dreadful in the manner yet as a not unwelcome alternative.

About a year after we first arrived at the island, William Sedon became so reduced as to deprive us of all hope of his recovery. He looked like a skeleton; and at last, was so entirely exhausted by hunger, as to be unable to walk, or even to rise from the ground. He continued, however, to crawl from place to place, until all his remaining strength was nearly gone, when the inhuman monsters placed him in an old canoe, and sent him adrift on the ocean! Gladly would his unhappy shipmates have extended to him the last sad offices of friendship; that poor consolation was denied both him and us! My heart bleeds at the recollection of our separation and his melancholy fate—when we saw him anxiously turn his languid eyes towards those who were doomed still to linger on the borders of the grave! Our sighs were breathed almost in silence, and our tears were shed in vain!

It may be observed here, that it is not their custom to deposit the bodies of any of their dead in the earth, except very young children. The bodies of grown people, after death, are laid in a canoe and committed to the ocean.

It was soon our lot to part with another of our companions, Peter Andrews. He was accused by the natives of some trifling offence, and put to death. The savages knocked him down with their clubs, and then despatched him in the most cruel and most shocking manner. I was at this time at a distance from the place where he was killed. My master was absent; and upon my hearing a noise in the direction of the place where the foul business was transacted, and suspecting that all was not right, I started to see what was going on. I was near the beach when I saw a number of the savages coming towards the spot where I stood, dragging along the lifeless and mangled body of our comrade! One of them approached me from behind, and knocked me down with his club. The body of Andrews was thrown into the sea, and it seemed to be their determination to destroy the whole of us. I warded off the blows aimed at me as well as I could, and recovering myself, ran towards the hut of my master. He had not yet returned; but, fortunately, an old man, who had previously shown some regard for me, and who was the particular friend of my master, happened at that moment to be passing; and seizing the man who had pursued me, held him fast. I escaped and ran into the hut, and crawled up through an aperture in the floor into the chamber under the roof. I seized an old box and covered up the hole through which I had ascended; but this was not sufficient to detain, for any great length of time, the wretches who were thirsting for my blood. They soon succeeded in displacing the box, and one of them seized me, but just as he was pulling me from my place of refuge, my master returned with several of his friends, and rescued me from the clutches of my enemies.

In the mean time Nute and the rest of our companions were at the "*Tahboo*," a place of public resort where, for the only time, the females rendered our people any assistance. They concealed the men under some mats, and kept them there till the fury of the natives had in a measure subsided.

We were next called upon to part with one of the Pelew chiefs who had come with us. He died of absolute starvation, and, according to custom, was committed to the waves in an old canoe. In a short time after this, the Pelew private (who had also come with us) was detected in the crime of taking a few cocoa-nuts without leave; for which offense he had his hands tied behind him, and was put into a canoe and sent adrift; which was their usual method of punishment for offenses of different kinds.

About a year and seven months from the commencement of our captivity Milton Hewlet died, and, like the others, was, according to the custom of the natives, committed to the ocean. A short time afterwards Charles C. Bouket, having become so reduced by his sufferings as to be unable to help himself, was (horrible to relate!) placed in a canoe, while still alive, and committed to the mercy of the ocean. Thus did one after another of our companions sink under the weight of their sufferings, and perish without any alleviation of their wretchedness. Nute and myself, with our friend *Kobac*, the other Pelew chief, were all that remained; and we were constantly expecting that the next hour would end our existence.

The idea of death, however, had now become familiar; and often did we desire the release from suffering which that alone could afford. Nothing, as it now appears to us, but the kind interposition of Providence, could have continued our lives, and have given us the power of endurance to hold out so long as we did. We were frequently so reduced as to be unable to walk, and were forced to drag ourselves on our hands and knees to some place where we could lie down under the shade of a bush, and take rest. But the small comfort to be obtained in this way was greatly lessened by the annoyance of musquetoes, which could attack us with impunity in our helpless and feeble condition. Besides this, our flesh had so fallen away, that on lying down, our bones would actually pierce through the skin, giving us the most severe pain. After we were tattooed, the parts operated upon were, for a long time, running sores; and when exposed to the sun, the pain was excruciating.

It has been already said, that the natives were indolent, filthy and degraded but the half has not been told; and some things which we witnessed cannot be related. The intercourse of the sexes was unrestrained by any law; and the decencies of life were almost entirely neglected. Instead of taking pains to keep clean, they seemed to be not unwilling to have their heads overrun with vermin and however incredible it may seem, it is a disgusting truth, that they are accustomed to eat them; and particular care seems to be taken to keep the loathsome animals in the heads of the children. But I forbear any further particulars.

I have already said, that only two of the crew of the *Mentor*, namely, Nute and myself, remained alive, with the exception of Captain Barnard and Rollins, who had fortunately escaped. The Pelew chief had become strongly attached to us, and we take pleasure in stating the fact, that his faithfulness and affection had greatly endured him to us. He seemed more like a brother than a barbarian; and most gladly would we have saved him from those sufferings which, no doubt before this time, have terminated his life. Alas! it was not in our power to administer to his relief; and when we last saw him he was but just alive.

The feeble and exhausted condition of the survivors, Nute *and* Holden.*–The natives consent to release them from labor, but refuse them food; and they obtain permission to leave the island in the first vessel, for a compensation to be made to the natives.–They crawl about from place to place, subsisting upon leaves, and occasionally begging a little food of the natives, for two months.–Their sudden joy at hearing of a vessel coming towards the island.–It proves to be the British barque* Britannia, *Captain Short, bound to Canton.–They are taken on board the* Britannia, *November 27, 1834, and treated with the kindest attention.–Their joy and gratitude at this happy termination of their sufferings.–They gradually recover their health so far as to take passage for* America, *in the ship* Morrison, *bound for* New York, *where they arrive May 5, 1835.–Acknowledgments for their kind reception at* New York *and* Boston.

Having thus briefly related the story of our captivity and sufferings, it only remains to give an account of our escape from this barbarous people. We continued to survive the horrible sufferings to which we were constantly subjected, and to serve our tyrannical masters, in despite of our agonies of body and mind, till the beginning of the autumn of 1834; at which time we had become so emaciated, feeble, and sickly, that we found it impossible any longer even to attempt to labor. By this time we had acquired a sufficient knowledge of their tongue to converse fluently with the natives, and we informed our masters, that our feeble condition rendered it impossible for us to attempt to do anything more. We also reasoned the matter with them, telling them that death was our inevitable doom, unless we were allowed to relax our labor; that if we died we could be of no service to them, but if allowed a respite, and we lived, and could be put on board a vessel, they should be generally rewarded.

With much difficulty we at length persuaded our masters to allow us to quit our labor and obtained from them a promise to be put on board the first vessel that would come to the island. But, at the same time, they informed us, that if we ceased to work, they should cease to furnish the miserable allowance of cocoa-nut on which we had before subsisted, and that we must either labor or starve. We deemed death as welcome in one shape as in another, and relinquished our labors and our pittance of food together.

We were thus literally turned out to die! We crawled from place to place, subsisting upon leaves, and now and then begging of the natives a morsel of cocoa-nut. In this way we contrived to live for about two months, when the joyful intelligence was brought to us that a vessel was in sight, and was coming near the island! Hope once more revisited our despairing hearts, and seemed to inspire us with renewed strength and animation.

After taxing our exhausted powers to the utmost, we persuaded the natives to prepare for visiting the vessel; and throwing our emaciated bodies into their canoes, we made for the ship with all possible despatch. The vessel proved to be the British barque *Britannia*, Captain Short, bound for Canton. Our reception on board is faithfully described in the following certificate given by Captain Short, the original of which is still in my possession:

"LINTIN, 29th December, 1834.

"This is to certify, that on the 27th day of November, 1834, off the small island commonly called Lord North's by the English, situated in latitude 3° 3' north, and longitude 131° 20' east, on board the British barque *Britannia*, bound to Canton River, we observed about ten or eleven canoes, containing upwards of one hundred men, approaching the vessel, in a calm, or nearly so, with the intention of coming alongside. But having the small complement of thirteen men, it was considered most prudent to keep them off, which was effected by firing a few six-pound shots in a contrary direction from the boats, some of which were then within pistol-shot. At the same time hearing cries in our own language, begging to be taken on board, the boat was despatched away to know the cause. The boat returned to the ship, and reported an American on board one of them. She was then sent back, having strict orders to act with caution, and the man got from the canoe into the sea, and was taken up by the ship's boat, and brought on board. He then stated in what manner he came there, and said he had another of his countrymen in another canoe. I said if we could get some of the boats dispersed, that every assistance should be rendered for the liberty of the other man. Accordingly they did so, all but three. The ship's boat was then despatched in search, and soon found the other man. He was brought on board, but in a most deplorable condition with fever, from the effects of a miserable subsistence. These two poor fellows were quite naked, under a burning sun. They appeared to bear all the marks of their long servitude, and I should suppose two or three days would have been the end of the last man taken on board, but from this act of Providence. It appears that these men were wrecked in the ship *Mentor*, on the Pelew Islands, and were proceeding with their commander to some Dutch settlement, in one of the Pelew Island canoes, when they got to the afore-mentioned island, and were detained by the natives; and that Captain Edward C. Barnard had got on board some ship, and reached Canton River shortly after their detention at the island; which has been confirmed by the different masters now at the port of Lintin.

"The statement given in to me by the two men runs thus:—That they were wrecked May 21st, 1832, on the Pelew Islands, and detained on Lord North's Island 6th December, 1832. The two men's names are Benjamin H. Nute and Horace Holden. I should thank any ship master now in port, acquainted with the circumstance, to confirm it by his signature, in order to make some provision for those men, should they require it. But from the disposition and liberality of those American gentlemen coming forward, that are already acquainted with the circumstance, perhaps it will be unnecessary. At the same time I shall be very willing to draw up any form, or in any other way that I may forward their views, according to the opinion of their American friends. I should hope that every vessel passing in the direction of the aforementioned island, passing any of their boats, will give them a trifle. I gave them what articles those two men thought most beneficial, and should have held a closer communication with them had I been better manned and armed.

"HENRY SHORT, Barque *Britannia*."

Never shall we find words to express our joy at once more finding ourselves in the company of civilized men! Nor can we be too grateful to Captain Short, and his officers and crew, for their kind attentions during our passage to Lintin. Every thing in their power was done to restore our health and strength, and to render us comfortable. On arriving at Lintin we found ourselves sufficiently recovered to be able to pass up the river to Canton. We remained there, at the factories, under medical treatment, until the ship *Morrison*, of New York, was ready to sail; when we took passage in her for our native country, and arrived in New York on the 5th day of May 1835.

In New York we found many kind friends who took a lively interest in our behalf. We would particularly acknowledge a debt of gratitude which we owe to Mr. John Munson, who opened his hospitable dwelling for our reception, and with whom we tarried for several weeks. Assisted by the humane and philanthropic citizens of New York, we have been enabled to reach Boston. Here Providence has raised us up warm friends, through whose assistance we have been rendered as comfortable as could under any circumstances have been expected.

In compliance with the solicitations of many respectable gentlemen, the foregoing narrative is submitted to the public, with the hope that it may not be entirely uninteresting, and not without use. Every statement may be relied upon as strictly true; and it is believed, that, simple and unadorned as is our story, it may serve to afford some information of a little spot hitherto supposed to be uninhabited, and to present to view of the curious and intelligent some knowledge of a portion of our race among whom no white man has ever before lived.

To Captain Barnard the author of the statements in this narrative is under great obligations for his uniformly kind treatment previous to the loss of the *Mentor*, and during the whole time we were together. We have no reason to doubt, that he did all in his power to obtain our release from captivity at the time when he was himself so fortunate as to escape; and not the least blame is to be imputed to him on account of the disasters that befell us.

Of the twenty-two persons who composed the ship's company of the Mentor when she sailed from New Bedford, only *four* have returned. It has been reported, that one of the three who was left at the Pelew Islands escaped a few months since. If such be the case only two remain there, and it is hoped that some measures will soon be adopted, either by the government or by humane individuals, to rescue them from their painful and distressing situation.

I cannot close this narrative without expressing the most heartfelt gratitude to that kind Providence which has sustained us under trials and sufferings the most severe, and returned us to our homes and friends. And may those who have been to us friends indeed, find an ample reward for their generosity, in the consciousness of having been influenced by those sentiments and feelings which best adorn and dignify the human character!

BOSTON, NOVEMBER 1835.

24

The SHIPWRECK

From *Cape Cod*

BY HENRY DAVID THOREAU

1855

Thoreau did not write Cape Cod *as a book; it was put together after his death by his friend* Ellery Channing *and his sister,* Sophia, *out of articles he had written for* Putnam's Magazine, *where three of them appeared, and other venues. The book did not receive good reviews when it appeared.* Henry James *did not like it. Later criticism has followed the line that it is the least of his books, and nothing so profound as* Walden. *As* Paul Theroux *pointed out, however, in his introduction to the* Penguin *edition of the book, it has been in print continuously since the early 1900s, and he credits* Thoreau *with insights about the sea comparable to* Melville's.

*The "*Shipwreck*" chapter is the first in the book, and among the most interesting; in it* Thoreau *catches something essential about disasters and the way we, as spectators, react to them. "About suffering they were never wrong, /* The Old Masters,*" wrote* W. H. Auden*; "how well they understood / Its human position; how it takes place / While someone else is eating or opening a window or just walking dully along..." So it is here in* Thoreau*; the men gathering seaweed from the shore continue their work, even as bodies wash up around them from the wreck of the* Irish *immigrant ship* St. John. *It is not we who have died, or any of ours. This has not happened to us. Says* Auden *again, "In* Brueghel's Icarus, *for instance: how everything turns away / Quite leisurely from the disaster; the ploughman may / Have heard the splash, the forsaken cry, / But for him it was not an important failure..." He continues his work. So do we. The world is a hard place; death is routine; this did not happen to us.*

Wishing to get a better view than I had yet had of the ocean, which, we are told, covers more than two-thirds of the globe, but of which a man who lives a few miles inland may never see any trace, more than of another world, I made a visit to Cape Cod in October 1849, another the succeeding June, and another to Truro in July 1855; the first and last time with a single companion, the second time alone. I have spent, in all, about three weeks on the Cape; walked from Eastham to Provincetown twice on the Atlantic side, and once on the Bay side also, excepting four or five miles, and crossed the Cape half a dozen times on my way; but having come so fresh to the sea, I have got but little salted. My readers must expect only so much saltness as the land breeze acquires from blowing over an arm of the sea, or is tasted on the windows and the bark of trees twenty miles inland, after September gales. I have been accustomed to make excursions to the ponds within ten miles of Concord, but latterly I have extended my excursions to the seashore.

I did not see why I might not make a book on Cape Cod, as well as my neighbor on "Human Culture." It is but another name for the same thing, and hardly a sandier phase of it. As for my title, I suppose that the word Cape is from the French *cap;* which is from the Latin *caput,* a head; which is, perhaps, from the verb *capere,* to take,—that being the part by which we take hold of a thing: —Take Time by the forelock. It is also the safest part to take a serpent by. And as for Cod, that was derived directly from that "great store of codfish" which Captain Bartholomew Gosnold caught there in 1602; which fish appears to have been so called from the Saxon word *codde,* "a case in which seeds are lodged," either from the form of the fish, or the quantity of spawn it contains; whence also, perhaps, *codling* (*pomum coctile?*) and coddle, —to cook green like peas. (V. Dic.)

Cape Cod is the bared and bended arm of Massachusetts: the shoulder is at Buzzard's Bay; the elbow, or crazy-bone, at Cape Mallebarre; the wrist at Truro; and the sandy fist at Provincetown, —behind which the State stands on her guard, with her back to the Green Mountains, and her feet planted on the floor of the ocean, like an athlete protecting her Bay,—boxing with northeast storms, and, ever and anon, heaving up her Atlantic adversary from the lap of earth,—ready to thrust forward her other fist, which keeps guard the while upon her breast at Cape Ann.

On studying the map, I saw that there must be an uninterrupted beach on the east or outside of the forearm of the Cape, more than thirty miles from the general line of the coast, which would afford a good sea view, but that, on account of an opening in the beach, forming the entrance to Nauset

Harbor, in Orleans, I must strike it in Eastham, if I approached it by land, and probably I could walk thence straight to Race Point, about twenty-eight miles, and not meet with any obstruction.

We left Concord, Massachusetts, on Tuesday, October 9th, 1849. On reaching Boston, we found that the Provincetown steamer, which should have got in the day before, had not yet arrived, on account of a violent storm; and, as we noticed in the streets a handbill headed, "Death! one hundred and forty-five lives lost at Cohasset," we decided to go by way of Cohasset. We found many Irish in the cars, going to identify bodies and to sympathize with the survivors, and also to attend the funeral which was to take place in the afternoon;—and when we arrived at Cohasset, it appeared that nearly all the passengers were bound for the beach, which was about a mile distant, and many other persons were flocking in from the neighboring country. There were several hundreds of them streaming off over Cohasset common in that direction, some on foot and some in wagons,—and among them were some sportsmen in their hunting-jackets, with their guns, and game-bags, and dogs. As we passed the graveyard we saw a large hole, like a cellar, freshly dug there, and, just before reaching the shore, by a pleasantly winding and rocky road, we met several hay-riggings and farm-wagons coming away toward the meeting-house, each loaded with three large, rough deal boxes. We did not need to ask what was in them. The owners of the wagons were made the undertakers. Many horses in carriages were fastened to the fences near the shore, and, for a mile or more, up and down, the beach was covered with people looking out for bodies, and examining the fragments of the wreck. There was a small island called Brook Island, with a hut on it, lying just off the shore. This is said to be the rockiest shore in Massachusetts from Nantasket to Scituate,—hard sienitic rocks, which the waves have laid bare, but have not been able to crumble. It has been the scene of many a shipwreck.

This brig *St. John*, from Galway, Ireland, laden with emigrants, was wrecked on Sunday morning; it was now Tuesday morning, and the sea was still breaking violently on the rocks. There were eighteen or twenty of the same large boxes that I have mentioned, lying on a green hillside, a few rods from the water, and surrounded by a crowd. The bodies which had been recovered, twenty-seven or eight in all, had been collected there. Some were rapidly nailing down the lids, others were carting the boxes away, and others were lifting the lids, which were yet loose, and peeping under the cloths, for each body, with such rags as still adhered to it, was covered loosely with a white sheet. I witnessed no signs of grief, but there was a sober despatch of business, which was affecting. One man was seeking to identify a particular body, and one undertaker or carpenter was calling to another to know in what box a certain child was put. I saw many marble feet and matted heads as the cloths were raised, and one livid, swollen, and mangled body of a drowned girl, —who probably had intended to go out to service in some American family,—to which some rags still adhered, with a string, half concealed by the flesh, about its swollen neck; the coiled-up wreck of a human hulk, gashed by the rocks or fishes, so that the bone and muscle were exposed, but quite bloodless,—merely red and white,—with wide-open and staring eyes, yet lustreless, dead-lights; or like the cabin windows of a stranded vessel, filled with sand. Sometimes there were two or more children, or a parent and child, in the same box, and on the lid would perhaps be written with red chalk, "Bridget such-a-one, and sister's child." The surrounding sward was covered with bits of sails and clothing. I have since heard, from one who lives by this beach, that a woman who had come over before, but had left her infant behind for her sister to bring, came and looked into these boxes and saw in one,—probably the same whose superscription I have quoted,—her child in her sister's arms, as if the sister had meant to be found thus; and within three days after, the mother died from the effect of that sight.

We turned from this and walked along the rocky shore. In the first cove were strewn what seemed the fragments of a vessel, in small pieces mixed with sand and seaweed, and great quantities of feathers; but it looked so old and rusty, that I at first took it to be some old wreck which had lain there many years. I even thought of Captain Kidd, and that the feathers were those which sea-fowl had cast there; and perhaps there might be some tradition about it in the neighborhood. I asked a sailor if that was the *St. John*. He said it was. I asked him where she struck. He pointed to a rock in front of us, a mile from the shore, called the Grampus Rock, and added:

"You can see a part of her now sticking up; it looks like a small boat."

I saw it. It was thought to be held by the chain-cables and the anchors. I asked if the bodies which I saw were all that were drowned.

"Not a quarter of them," said he.

"Where are the rest?"

"Most of them right underneath that piece you see."

It appeared to us that there was enough rubbish to make the wreck of a large vessel in this cove alone, and that it would take many days to cart it off. It was several feet deep, and here and there was a bonnet or a jacket on it. In the very midst of the crowd about this wreck, there were men with carts busily collecting the seaweed which the storm had cast up, and conveying it beyond the reach of the tide, though they were often obliged to separate fragments of clothing from it, and they might at any moment have found a human body under it. Drown who might, they did not forget that this weed was a valuable manure. This shipwreck had not produced a visible vibration in the fabric of society.

About a mile south we could see, rising above the rocks, the masts of the British brig which the *St. John* had endeavored to follow, which had slipped her cables and, by good luck, run into the mouth of Cohasset Harbor. A little further along the shore we saw a man's clothes on a rock; further, a woman's scarf, a gown, a straw bonnet, the brig's caboose, and one of her masts high and dry, broken into several pieces. In another rocky cove, several rods from the water, and behind rocks twenty feet high, lay a part of one side of the vessel, still hanging together. It was, perhaps, forty feet long, by fourteen wide. I was even more surprised at the power of the waves, exhibited on this shattered fragment, than I had been at the sight of the smaller fragments before. The largest timbers and iron braces were broken superfluously, and I saw that no material could withstand the power of the waves; that iron must go to pieces in such a case, and an iron vessel would be cracked up like an eggshell on the rocks. Some of these timbers, however, were so rotten that I could almost thrust my umbrella through them. They told us that some were saved on this piece, and also showed where the sea had heaved it into this cove, which was now dry. When I saw where it had come in, and in what condition, I wondered that any had been saved on it. A little further on a crowd of men was collected around the mate of the *St. John*, who was telling his story. He was a slim-looking youth, who spoke of the captain as the master, and seemed a little excited. He was saying that when they jumped into the boat, she filled, and, the vessel lurching, the weight of the water in the boat caused the painter to break, and so they were separated. Whereat one man came away, saying:—

"Well, I don't see but he tells a straight story enough. You see, the weight of the water in the boat broke the painter. A boat full of water is very heavy," —and so on, in a loud and impertinently earnest tone, as if he had a bet depending on it, but had no humane interest in the matter.

Another, a large man, stood near by upon a rock, gazing into the sea, and chewing large quids of tobacco, as if that habit were forever confirmed with him.

"Come," says another to his companion, "let's be off. We've seen the whole of it. It's no use to stay to the funeral."

Further, we saw one standing upon a rock, who, we were told, was one that was saved. He was a sober-looking man, dressed in a jacket and gray pantaloons, with his hands in the pockets. I asked him a few questions, which he answered; but he seemed unwilling to talk about it, and soon walked away. By his side stood one of the life-boatmen, in an oil-cloth jacket, who told us how they went to the relief of the British brig, thinking that the boat of the *St. John*, which they passed on the way, held all her crew,—for the waves prevented their seeing those who were on the vessel, though they might have saved some had they known there were any there. A little further was the flag of the *St. John* spread on a rock to dry, and held down by stones at the corners. This frail, but essential and significant portion of the vessel, which had so long been the sport of the winds, was sure to reach the shore. There were one or two houses visible from these rocks, in which were some of the survivors recovering from the shock which their bodies and minds had sustained. One was not expected to live.

We kept on down the shore as far as a promontory called Whitehead, that we might see more of the Cohasset Rocks. In a little cove, within half a mile, there were an old man and his son collecting, with their team, the seaweed which that fatal storm had cast up, as serenely employed as if there had never been a wreck in the world, though they were within sight of the Grampus Rock, on which the *St. John* had struck. The old man had heard that there was a wreck, and knew most of the particulars, but he said that he had not been up there since it happened. It was the wrecked weed that concerned him most, rock-weed, kelp and seaweed, as he named them, which he carted to his barnyard; and those bodies were to him but other weeds which the tide cast up, but which were of no use to him. We afterwards came to the life-boat in its harbor, waiting for another emergency,—and in the afternoon we saw the funeral procession at a distance, at the head of which walked the captain with the other survivors.

On the whole, it was not so impressive a scene as I might have expected. If I had found one body cast upon the beach in some lonely place, it would have affected me more. I sympathized rather with the winds and waves, as if to toss and mangle these poor human bodies was the order of the day. If this was the law of Nature, why waste any time in awe or pity? If the last day were come, we should not think so much about the separation of friends or the blighted prospects of individuals. I saw that corpses might be multiplied, as on the field of battle, till they no longer affected us in any degree, as exceptions to the common lot of humanity. Take all the graveyards together, they are always the majority. It is the individual and private that demands our sympathy. A man can attend but one funeral in the course of his life, can behold but one corpse. Yet I saw that the inhabitants of the shore would be not a little affected by this event. They would watch there many days and nights for the sea to give up its dead, and their imaginations and sympathies would supply the place of mourners far away, who as yet knew not of the wreck. Many days after this, something white was seen floating on the water by one who was sauntering on the beach. It was approached in a boat, and found to be the body of a woman, which had risen in an upright position, whose white cap was blown back with the wind. I saw that the beauty of the shore itself was wrecked for many a lonely walker there, until he could perceive, at last, how its beauty was enhanced by wrecks like this, and it acquired thus a rarer and sublimer beauty still.

Why care for these dead bodies? They really have no friends but the worms or fishes. Their owners were coming to the New World, as Columbus and the Pilgrims did,—they were within a mile of its shores; but, before they could reach it, they emigrated to a newer world than ever Columbus dreamed of, yet one of whose existence we believe that there is far more universal and convincing evidence—though it has not yet been discovered by science—than Columbus had of this; not merely mariners' tales and some paltry drift-wood and sea-weed, but a continual drift and instinct to all our shores. I saw their empty hulks that came to land; but they themselves, meanwhile, were cast upon some shore yet further west, toward which we are all tending, and which we shall reach at last, it may be through storm and darkness, as they did. No doubt, we have reason to thank God that they have not been "shipwrecked into life again." The mariner who makes the safest port in Heaven, perchance, seems to his friends on earth to be shipwrecked, for they deem Boston Harbor the better place; though perhaps invisible to them, a skilful pilot comes to meet him, and the fairest and balmiest gales blow off that coast, his good ship makes the land in halcyon days, and he kisses the shore in rapture there, while his old hulk tosses in the surf here. It is hard to part with one's body, but, no doubt, it is easy enough to do without it when once it is gone. All their plans and hopes burst like a bubble! Infants by the score dashed on the rocks by the enraged Atlantic Ocean! No, no! If the *St. John* did not make her port here, she has been telegraphed there. The strongest wind cannot stagger a Spirit; it is a Spirit's breath. A just man's purpose cannot be split on any Grampus or material rock, but itself will split rocks till it succeeds.

The verses addressed to Columbus, dying, may, with slight alterations, be applied to the passengers of the *St. John*: —

"Soon with them will all be over,
Soon the voyage will be begun
That shall bear them to discover,
Far away, a land unknown.

"Land that each, alone, must visit,
But no tidings bring to men;
For no sailor, once departed,
Ever hath returned again.

"No carved wood, no broken branches,
Ever drift from that far wild;
He who on that ocean launches
Meets no corse of angel child.

"Undismayed, my noble sailors,
Spread, then spread your canvas out;
Spirits! on a sea of ether
Soon shall ye serenely float!

"Where the deep no plummet soundeth,
Fear no hidden breakers there,
And the fanning wing of angels
Shall your bark right onward bear.

"Quit, now, full of heart and comfort,
These rude shores, they are of earth;
Where the rosy clouds are parting,
There the blessed isles loom forth."

One summer day, since this, I came this way, on foot, along the shore from Boston. It was so warm that some horses had climbed to the very top of the ramparts of the old fort at Hull, where there was hardly room to turn around, for the sake of the breeze. The *Datura stramonium*, or thorn-apple, was in full bloom along the beach; and, at sight of this cosmopolite,—this

Captain Cook among plants,—carried in ballast all over the world, I felt as if I were on the highway of nations. Say, rather, this Viking, king of the Bays, for it is not an innocent plant; it suggests not merely commerce, but its attendant vices, as if its fibres were the stuff of which pirates spin their yarns. I heard the voices of men shouting aboard a vessel, half a mile from the shore, which sounded as if they were in a barn in the country, they being between the sails. It was a purely rural sound. As I looked over the water, I saw the isles rapidly wasting away, the sea nibbling voraciously at the continent, the springing arch of a hill suddenly interrupted, as at Point Alderton, —what botanists might call premorse,—showing, by its curve against the sky, how much space it must have occupied, where now was water only. On the other hand, these wrecks of isles were being fancifully arranged into new shores, as at Hog Island, inside of Hull, where everything seemed to be gently lapsing into futurity. This isle had got the very form of a ripple,—and I thought that the inhabitants should bear a ripple for device on their shields, a wave passing over them, with the *datura*, which is said to produce mental alienation of long duration without affecting the bodily health, springing from its edge. The most interesting thing which I heard of, in this township of Hull, was an unfailing spring, whose locality was pointed out to me, on the side of a distant hill, as I was panting along the shore, though I did not visit it. Perhaps, if I should go through Rome, it would be some spring on the Capitoline Hill I should remember the longest. It is true, I was somewhat interested in the well at the old French fort, which was said to be ninety feet deep, with a cannon at the bottom of it. On Nantasket beach I counted a dozen chaises from the public-house. From time to time the riders turned their horses toward the sea, standing in the water for the coolness,—and I saw the value of beaches to cities for the sea breeze and the bath.

At Jerusalem village the inhabitants were collecting in haste, before a thunder-shower now approaching, the Irish moss which they had spread to dry. The shower passed on one side, and gave me a few drops only, which did not cool the air. I merely felt a puff upon my cheek, though, within sight, a vessel was capsized in the bay, and several others dragged their anchors, and were near going ashore. The sea-bathing at Cohasset Rocks was perfect. The water was purer and more transparent than any I had ever seen. There was not a particle of mud or slime about it. The bottom being sandy, I could see the sea-perch swimming about. The smooth and fantastically worn rocks, and the perfectly clean and tress-like rock-weeds falling over you, and attached so firmly to the rocks that you could pull yourself up by them, greatly enhanced the luxury of the bath. The stripe of barnacles just above the weeds reminded me of some vegetable growth,—the buds, and petals, and seed-vessels of flowers. They lay along the seams of the rock like buttons on a waistcoat. It was one of the hottest days in the year, yet I found the water so icy cold that I could swim but a stroke or two, and thought that, in case of shipwreck, there would be more danger of being chilled to death than simply drowned. One immersion was enough to make you forget the dog-days utterly. Though you were sweltering before, it will take you half an hour now to remember that it was ever warm. There were the tawny rocks, like lions couchant, defying the ocean, whose waves incessantly dashed against and scoured them with vast quantities of gravel. The water held in their little hollows, on the receding of the tide, was so crystalline that I could not believe it salt, but wished to drink it; and higher up were basins of fresh water left by the rain,—all which, being also of different depths and temperature, were convenient for different kinds of baths. Also, the larger hollows in the smoothed rocks formed the most convenient of seats and dressing-rooms. In these respects it was the most perfect seashore that I had seen.

I saw in Cohasset, separated from the sea only by a narrow beach, a handsome but shallow lake of some four hundred acres, which, I was told, the sea had tossed over the beach in a great storm in the spring, and, after the alewives had passed into it, it had stopped up its outlet, and now the alewives were dying by thousands, and the inhabitants were apprehending a pestilence as the water evaporated. It had five rocky islets in it.

This rocky shore is called Pleasant Cove, on some maps; on the map of Cohasset, that name appears to be confined to the particular cove where I saw the wreck of the *St. John*. The ocean did not look, now, as if any were ever shipwrecked in it; it was not grand and sublime, but beautiful as a lake. Not a vestige of a wreck was visible, nor could I believe that the bones of many a shipwrecked man were buried in that pure sand.

25

The RUNAWAYS

From *Arctic Researches, and Life Among the Esquimaux*

BY CHARLES FRANCIS HALL

1865

Hall was one of the first Americans to spend serious time in the Arctic, where he lived with the Inuit and learned from them how to survive Arctic conditions. He was a strange man who went north for the first time when he read about the disappearance of the British explorer Sir John Franklin in the late 1840s and the subsequent search for him. He persuaded himself that he knew where Franklin was, and that some of his crew might still be alive. While he was living with the Inuit he discovered—more accurately, they showed him—where Martin Frobisher had established his would-be gold mine, in what is now Frobisher Bay, 300 years earlier. Folk memory of that event had passed down among the Inuit, one generation to the next.

The tale he tells here comes early in the book, when he is on his way to Baffin Island on a whale ship and comes across the deserters from a whale ship farther north trying to make it to Newfoundland. As I have said before, Arctic whaling ships were subject to the most severe conditions and were often lost, and the men who manned them were never eager to winter over in the Arctic. These men blamed harsh conditions on board for their desertion, but their character appears from Hall's story not to have been of the best.

With this book Hall established himself as an Arctic explorer of the first rank, but he was a natural loner and came to grief when he persuaded the government in 1871 to put him in charge of a ship named the Polaris *and try for the North Pole. Hall managed to get his ship farther north than anyone else had sailed before, into Smith Sound, which divides northern Greenland from Ellesmere Island, and then beyond into*

Kennedy Channel. But Hall could not command men; the crew was contentious, the conditions appalling. Hall came back from a sledge trip north of Greenland in October and was poisoned. The following summer the remaining crew was able to get the ship out of the ice by the middle of August, after which pack ice swept them south. In October, beset by ice, they panicked and half abandoned the ship, putting ship's stores and 19 people onto the ice, only to have the ship break free suddenly and leave them stranded. As the months passed it was the Inuit hunters with them who enabled the party to survive. In the end these 19 people, nine of them Inuit, one of those an infant, had drifted 1,300 miles south, all the way to Labrador. On April 30 a ship finally saw them and picked them up. Hall's murder was discovered when two forensic experts exhumed his frozen corpse some 35 years ago and took samples of hair and fingernails. They found them loaded with arsenic.

AT THIS TIME A CIRCUMSTANCE OCCURRED THAT STARTLED MYSELF AND all on board beyond measure. I will relate it from my journal as I find it recorded at the time.

"*Tuesday, August 7th*. After dinner I had gone and perched myself up in one of the whale-boats hanging over the ship's side, for the purpose of viewing the mountain scenery as we passed along, and also sketching. I had my marine glass with me, and during an interval when the fog—which now and again settled upon us—disappeared, I swept the horizon all around. As I looked *easterly*, my eye caught a strange black sail. Directing the captain and mate's attention to it, they examined, but could not make out what it was. At length we decided that it was a whale-boat with dark-colored sails, and approaching us. Nearer and nearer it came, though yet far off; for when I had first seen it, refraction had made the small sails loom up higher even than those of a 300-ton vessel. By this time every one on board was anxiously looking to the strange boat, wondering what it was, coming from a direction seaward. After watching it more than an hour, we noticed that the sail was taken down, and soon afterward we lost sight of the boat entirely. In vain our glasses were pointed in the direction she was last seen. Nothing could be observed of her, and many began to think we had been deceived by refraction; but at length the captain exclaimed, 'I can now see the boat, though a mere speck. I should not wonder if it is one of my own left here on the last voyage, and manned by Esquimaux.' I looked long and attentively. At last I saw the flash of oars following each stroke, as the dazzling rays of a western sun fell upon the uplifted blades. I could see nothing else but these oars, and to me it seemed as if the rowers were pulling quickly—desperately. The excitement now became great among us, especially as the distance decreased between the boat and the ship. Captain B— thought it was an Esquimaux crew, and Mr. Rogers said the men were *white*.

"As they neared, it struck me that the rowers—now to be seen more clearly—might be some shipwrecked mariners pulling for dear life; and to ascertain this, the ship was deadened in her way. In a few moments more the strange boat was near enough to make her crew out for white men, nine in number; and directly they got alongside, a question was put by Captain B— as to who they were. The steersman promptly answered, 'Crew from the *Ansell Gibbs*, of New Bedford.' In reply to another question, he said, 'We are from the north, and bound to the south.' This was enough to satisfy us that they were *runaways*.

"In a few minutes a variety of questions was put as to the number of ships, the whaling, etc., in Northumberland Inlet, where we conjectured the *Ansell Gibbs* to be; and then the inquiry was made of them, 'You are runaways, are you not?' The response immediately was, 'Yes, we are!' They then told us that they had left *Kingaite*, in Northumberland Sound, on Saturday, August 2d, at 11 P.M., and had thus run the distance, 250 miles to where we met them; in less than three days. The reason they gave for deserting their ship was because of 'bad treatment on board,' and 'not having enough to eat.' They explained about this, and added much more, which may or may not be true. At all events, they made up their minds to start *for the United States* on the first chance, and this they did by taking a whale-boat, two tubs of whale-line, three harpoons and as many lances, a 'conjuror'—that is, a portable cooking apparatus—two guns and ammunition, a small quantity of provisions, a few blankets, and other trifling things; and this to go a voyage over a tempestuous sea, part of it often full of ice, and along an iron-bound coast, for a distance of say 1500 miles! However, there they were so far. One instrument—a compass—only for navigation; no sextant or quadrant; no one in the boat capable of taking observations had they possessed instruments, and without food enough to carry them on. The chief of this rash crew was John Giles, a 'boat-steerer,' which means, in whaling parlance, one who has charge of the boat and crew when out whaling. Only two of the company had ever been to sea before, and those two had been on whaling voyages to 'Desolation' Island in the South Seas. They were all young men—Americans belonging to various places in the Eastern States.

"When Captain B— had asked several questions, the chief of these unfortunate men modestly supplicated for some food, as they were all very hungry. This was immediately responded to by the captain saying 'Come and eat;' but at first they hesitated, fearing they might be arrested. But hunger prevailed, and, making secure their boat, they entered the ship, and fell to upon the salt junk and biscuit like hungry wolves. Never before did I see men eat with such avidity and relish. To them it was a feast, having had only half a biscuit each and one small duck among the whole number during the past day.

"I found that nothing would alter their purpose as to proceeding on their desperate voyage. They meant to strike for York Factory in Hudson's Bay; but on my showing them a chart and the course to Resolution Island, thence across Hudson's Strait to Labrador, this latter course was decided upon, with the hope that fishermen might pick them up.

"The captain kindly gave them some beef and pork, powder and shot, and a chart. To this I also added some ammunition and caps.

"They remained with us about two hours, and then, after deciding to go, instead of landing for the night (perhaps they were still fearful of being captured), they got into their boat, and, with many thanks to us, started on their perilous voyage.

"I watched them long as they passed away from us bending to their oars. It was 9 P.M. when they departed. The moon was shining brightly in the east—the alabaster mountains of ice were scattered about upon the darkening waters—the craggy rocks sharply cut their black profiles against the distant sky, and the winds were gently but coldly blowing in sad harmony with the occasion. As they vanished from my view I said to myself, 'Will the civilized world ever see these desperate men again? It is next to a miracle if so. And yet what lesson do they teach me? If these nine men can undertake such a voyage, and under such wretched circumstances, with so little preparation, why should not I, having far better means, be able to accomplish mine? For themselves, I added, 'God be with them!' I know not how just or unjust their cause may be, but I do know that human life is now at stake, and my sympathy goes with them.' "

Before I pass from this strange occurrence, it will be better to give the sequel of their history, so far as yet known, through three of the wretched crew who reached Indian Harbor, Labrador. The following particulars I gleaned at St. John's, Newfoundland, on my way home in the fall of 1862.

It seems that a Captain Nathan Norman, who does business in Labrador, and is also a magistrate, encountered the survivors of this boat's crew, and, hearing their tale, demanded from them a statement in writing; whereupon one of them, Sullivan by name, drew up an account, the original of which is in my possession. It was given to me by Robert Winton, Esq., editor and proprietor of the St. John's *Daily News*, through C.O. Leach, Esq.,

United States consul at that place. The following is a *verbatim* copy of Sullivan's written statement, made in the fall of 1861:

"My name is John F. Sullivan. I left my home in South Hadley Falls, Mass., about the 1st of March, 1860, for Boston. I remained in Boston until the 20th of the same month. I applied at different offices for a chance to ship; being a stranger in the place, and a green hand, I found it very difficult to get a berth to suit me. At last I got a little discouraged, and that day signed my name at No. 172 Commercial street, Boston, and left for New Bedford, Mass. Next morning I shipped to go aboard of the ship Daniel Webster, then laying at New Bedford, but to sail the same day on a whaling cruise to Davis's Straits, to be gone 18 months.

"I left New Bedford in the Daniel Webster on the 21st of March, 1860. There were forty of us in the crew, all told. We had very rough weather for many days after leaving, which caused many of us to be sea-sick; I suffered from it about three weeks; after that time I began to recruit. There was nothing happened of any consequence worth mentioning until we passed Cape Farewell, about the last of May. After that we had quite a hard time, working the ship through the ice; occasionally, however, we made out to get her through, and came to anchor, July 6, 1860.

"We spoke many vessels going in. I will name some of them: the *Hannibal*, of New London; the *Black Eagle* and *Antelope*, of New Bedford; the *Ansell Gibbs*, of Fairhaven; the *Pioneer*, of New London. These vessels were anchored very close to one another in the harbor; the crews were at liberty sometimes to pay visits to each other; each one would tell how he was treated; several complained of very bad treatment, especially the crew of the *Ansell Gibbs*; they were planning some way of running away for a long time, but they found no opportunity till the 4th of August.

"My shipmate, whose name was Warren Dutton, was aboard that day, and heard a little of the conversation, and he joined in with them, and said he would go, and perhaps one or two more of his crew. He immediately came aboard and informed me; and he pictured every thing out so nice, that I finally consented to go with him. We had no great reason for leaving our vessel; we could not complain of very bad treatment aboard; all we could complain of was that we were very badly fitted out for such a cold climate; and, after we arrived there, hearing of so many men that died there the last winter of scurvy, we were afraid to remain there, for fear that we might get it. We thought by running away, also, we would be all right; but we were sadly mistaken.

"After it was agreed upon to leave, each one was busy making preparations for a start. I, with my shipmate, packed what few things we thought would be necessary into a traveling-bag which belonged to me; we then crept into the hold, and filled a small bag and a pair of drawers with hard bread, and waited for an opportunity to hide it on deck, unknown to the watch. After we succeeded in that, we made a signal to the other crew that we were ready. It being boats' crew watches aboard the *Ansell Gibbs*, they every one of them left; they found no difficulty in lowering away the boat, which after they did so they lowered themselves easily into her, and soon paddled under our bows; we then dropped our traps into her, and, taking with us two guns and a little ammunition, got into her, and soon pulled around a small point out of sight of the vessels. The names of the crew that left the *Ansell Gibbs* are as follows: John Giles, boat-steerer, John Martin, Hiram J. Davis, Williard Hawkins, Thomas Colwell, Joseph Fisher, and Samuel J. Fisher.

"At 11 o'clock at night, on the 4th of August, we left the vessels in Cumberland Straits, latitude 65° 59', about five miles from Penny's Harbor. Although it being a little foggy, with a fair wind we stood across the Straits. When about half way across we dumped overboard a tub of towline to lighten the boat some. We had nothing but a small boat-compass to guide us; we had no opportunity of getting a chart before we left, and not much of any thing else.

"We made the other side of the Straits by morning; then, by taking the spyglass, we thought we could perceive a sail in chase of us, but we soon lost sight of her. The other crew were depending mostly on us for bread, as my shipmate informed them we had a better chance to get it out of the hold; their bread lay close to the cabin; so, what bread they had, with ours, would not exceed more than twenty pounds. We all saw that the bread would not last long, so each one desired to be put on allowance of one biscuit a day to each man. We hoped, by the time that was gone, to reach some place where we would find help. We made a very good run the first three days, sleeping at night in the boat; on the fourth day out we fell in with the barque George Henry, Captain Budington, of New London. He asked us aboard; the boat-steerer acted as spokesman. The captain told us we were very foolish to leave the vessels to undertake so long a trip. I believe he would have taken us all if we wished to stay; but as we had left a whaler, we did not like to go on board another, as he was also going to remain there through the winter; so we were determined to push along, as we had been foolish enough to start in the first place. However, before we left, he gave us a small bag of bread, a piece of salt pork, and some ammunition; also a chart. We then bade him good-by, and set off again. That night we made a 'lee,' found some moss, and made a fire; before we ran in we shot a small duck, which made a good stew for all hands. Two days after this we shot a white bear; he was in the water when we shot him, and there being a heavy sea on at the time, we could get no more than his hind quarters in; them we skinned—the rest we could not save. That night we managed between us to cook it, as we were divided into watches, two in each watch; by doing so, we could watch the boat and keep her with the tide. We kept on in this way, always tracking the shore, and at night going ashore to lay on the rocks, with our boat's sail over us for shelter.

"We had very rough weather in crossing the Straits. We were on Resolution Island four days, waiting for a fair wind; we got it at last, but so strong that it came very near swamping our little boat many times through the night. It kept two of us bailing water out all the time, and we were glad to reach the land, after being in the boat thirty hours, wet to the skin. What bear's meat and bread we had was most gone by this time; there was nothing left but a few crumbs in the bottom of the bag. There was nine parts made of the crumbs; then they were caked off, each man taking his share.

"On the 16th of August we made Cape Chidleigh; on the 20th we divided the last crumbs; after that we picked up what we could find to eat. We found a few berries and mushrooms; we suffered very much from the cold, very seldom having a dry rag upon us.

"We continued on in this condition until the 3d of September, when, to add to our misfortune, Williard Hawkins and Hiram J. Davis (who we called 'the doctor') ran away from us that night, and took with them everything that was of any use to us; they even took the boat's compass, and left us in a miserable condition, with our boat broadside on the beach. It being their watch, they made out to get off. We thought it was useless to make chase after them, so we let them go. It then commenced to rain, and there was a heavy sea rolling in, and, weak as we were, we found some difficulty in shoving the boat off. However, after a hard tug, we succeeded, and then pulled out some ways; we then up sail; it was not up long before it blew so strong that it carried away the mast. We then ran in under a jib, and made a lee. About half an hour after we landed my shipmate died of starvation. The evening he died, Samuel Fisher proposed to eat him; he took his knife, and cut a piece off the thigh, and held it over the fire until it was cooked. Then, next morning, each one followed his example; after that the meat was taken off the bones, and each man took a share. We stopped here three days. We then made a start; but the wind being ahead, we were obliged to put back. Here we stopped two more days. During that time the bones were broken up small, and boiled in a pot or kettle we had; also the skull was broken open, the brains taken out, and cooked. We then got a fair wind, but as we got around a point, we had the wind very fresh off shore; we could hardly manage the boat; at last we drove on to an island some ways out to sea; we got the boat under the lee of it; but the same night we had a large hole stove into her. Being unable to haul her up, we were obliged to remain here eight days: it was on this island they tried to murder me.

"The third day we stopped here, I was out as usual picking berries, or any thing I could find to eat. Coming in, I chanced to pick up a mushroom. I brought it in with me; also an armful of wood to keep. While kneeling down to cook the mushroom, I received a heavy blow of a club from Joseph Fisher, and before I could get on my feet I got three more blows. I then managed to get to my feet, when Samuel Fisher got hold of my right arm; then Joseph Fisher struck me three more blows on the arm. I somehow got away from them, and, being half crazy, I did not know what to do. They made for me again; I kept begging of them, for God's sake, to spare my life, but they would not listen to my cries. They said they wanted some meat, and were bound to kill me. I had nothing I could defend myself with but a small knife; this I held in my hand until they approached me. Samuel Fisher was the first to come toward me; he had a large dirk-knife in his hand; his cousin was coming from another direction with a club and a stone. Samuel came on and grasped me by the shoulder, and had his knife raised to stab me. I then raised my knife, and stabbed him in the throat; he immediately fell, and I then made a step for Joe; he dropped his club, and went up to where the rest was. I then stooped down to see if Samuel was dead; he was still alive. I did not know what to do. At this time I began to cry; after a little while the rest told me to come up; they would see there was nothing more done to me. I received four deep cuts on the head; one of the fellows dressed them for me, and washed the blood off my face. Next day Samuel Fisher died; his cousin was the first one to cut him up; his body was used up the same as my unfortunate shipmate's.

"After a while we managed to repair the boat, and left this island. We ran in where we thought was main land, but it proved to be an island; here we left the boat, and proceeded on foot, walking about one mile a day. At last we reached the other side of the island in four days; then put back again to the boat. It took us four days to get back again. When we got there, we found the boat was stove very bad since we left her. We tried to get around the island in her, but she sunk when we got into her; we then left her, and went back again to the other side of the island, to remain there until we would die or be picked up. We ate our boots, belts, and sheaths, and a number of bearskin and sealskin articles we had with us. To add to our misery, it commenced to rain, and kept up for three days; it then began to snow. In this miserable condition, we were picked up by a boat's crew of Esquimaux on the 29th of September, and brought to Okoke on the 3d of October. The missionaries did all that lay in their power to help us along, and provided us with food and clothing, then sent us on to Nain, where we met 'the doctor,' who was picked up three days before we were. He reported that his companion died, and told many false stories after he was picked up.

"The missionaries of Nain helped us on to Hopedale; from there we were sent on to Kibokok, where two of us remained through the winter. One stopped with a planter, named John Lane, between Nain and Hopedale; the doctor stopped with John Walker until March, when he left for Indian Harbor; the remaining two, Joseph Fisher and Thomas Colwell, also stopped with planters around Indian Harbor. Mr. Bell, the agent at Kibokok, kept two of us until we could find an opportunity of leaving the coast. We left his place about the 10th of July, and came to Macovic, waiting a chance to get off.

"Captain Duntan has been kind enough to give me a passage; my companion was taken by Captain Hamilton, of the Wild Rover. We have had a very pleasant passage so far, and I hope it will continue so.

"Sir, I hope you make it out; it is very poor writing, and was written in haste.

"JOHN F. SULLIVAN."

In addition to the above, Mr. Leach kindly furnished me with the following information in a letter dated Feb. 25th, 1863:

"Mr. Kenneth M'Lea, Jr., merchant of Newfoundland, informs me that he has had letters from the missionary settlements on the coast of Labrador, in which they say these men conducted themselves 'shamefully.' Instead of feeling grateful for the hospitality they received, they demanded to be supported with the privilege of doing as they pleased. I understand one of them still remained at Labrador. No doubt the rest have shipped under assumed names, feeling ashamed to return to their native country."

Soon after the boat, with its desperate crew, had left us, we were passing one of the channels leading to the long-sought bay. This bay is a very fine sheet of water, and is protected by "Sarah's" Island at the entrance. Its length is about fifty miles, and its width six miles. On entering it by the south channel we were becalmed, and the boats were set to work towing us in; but, though we were up all night, next morning saw us still at some ten miles' distance from our harbor. At this time a perfect flotilla of boats were discovered approaching us. They were six whale-boats, fully manned, five belonging to a ship called the *Black Eagle*, Captain Allen, and one to the *Rescue*. As soon as they arrived, quietly greeting us, they wheeled in line ahead of our own boats, and aided in towing us in. An interesting scene it was before and around us: eight boats in line, pulling the ship onward, with brawny arms at the oars, and merry voices pouring forth the sailor's songs as measured and uniform strokes gave even time to the movement; the still waters of the deep bay, the perpendicular rocks by our side, and the craggy mountains overhanging our heads, their peaks reaching up as if to kiss the clouds!

At noon, August 8th, 1860, we reached our anchorage, and at length were secure in the harbor we had so long been seeking. The *Rescue* had anchored before us.

26

The BURNING *of the* CLIPPER SHIP *HORNET* AT SEA

From *The Sacramento Daily Union*

BY MARK TWAIN

JULY 19, 1866

Mark Twain was a young journalist with a regional reputation when this story came his way. He was in the Hawaiian Islands at the time, sending letters back to the Sacramento paper as a travel correspondent. He had made friends with the American minister to China, Anson Burlingame, who was returning to China after a stretch in the United States and stopping over in Hawaii. Burlingame was a powerful, well-connected man, and it was he who got Twain his interviews with the survivors of the Hornet, *which enabled him to be first in the United States with the news of their wreck and their 43 days in an open boat. The story was a sensation, and Twain would later say that it launched his career. He wrote an expanded version of it, quoting from the diaries kept by several of the survivors, for* Harper's *magazine; it appeared in December 1866. It was his first national publication. A sketch derived from it appears in his first book,* The Celebrated Jumping Frog of Calaveras County. *The expanded version from* Harper's *appeared again in* The Man That Corrupted Hadleyburg, *published 34 years later.*

We print the original version, the piece for the Sacramento Daily Union. *It's a lovely piece of writing. When he returned to Sacramento not too long after the piece appeared, he asked for extra pay for it, and they were glad to pay him.* Harper's *got his name wrong, incidentally, when they ran the extended piece in December. They called him Mark Swain.*

HONOLULU, JUNE 25, 1866.

In the postscript to a letter which I wrote two or three days ago, and sent by the ship Live Yankee, I gave you the substance of a letter received here from Hilo by Walker, Allen & Co. informing them that a boat containing fifteen men, in a helpless and starving condition, had drifted ashore at Laupahoehoe, Island of Hawaii, and that they had belonged to the clipper ship *Hornet*, Mitchell master, and had been afloat on the ocean since the burning of that vessel, about one hundred miles north of the equator, on the 3d of May—forty-three days.

The third mate and ten of the seamen have arrived here and are now in the hospital. Captain Mitchell, one seaman named Antonio Passene, and two passengers (Samuel and Henry Ferguson, of New York City, young gentlemen, aged respectively 18 and 28) are still at Hilo, but are expected here within the week.

In the Captain's modest epitome of this terrible romance, which you have probably published, you detect the fine old hero through it. It reads like Grant.

THE THIRD MATE

I have talked with the seamen and with John S. Thomas, third mate, but their accounts are so nearly alike in all substantial points, that I will merely give the officer's statement and weave into it such matters as the men mentioned in the way of incidents, experiences, emotions, etc. Thomas is very intelligent and a very cool and self possessed young man, and seems to have kept a pretty accurate log of his remarkable voyage in his head. He told his story, of three hours length, in a plain, straightforward way, and with no attempt at display and no straining after effect. Wherever any incident may be noted in this paper where any individual has betrayed any emotion, or enthusiasm, or has departed from strict, stoical self-possession, or had a solitary thought that was not an utterly unpoetical and essentially practical one, remember that Thomas, the third mate, was not that person. He has been eleven days on shore, and already looks sufficiently sound and healthy to pass almost anywhere without being taken for an invalid. He has the marks of a hard experience about him though, when one looks closely. He is very much sunburned and weatherbeaten, and looks thirty-two years old. He is only twenty-four, however, and has been a sailor fifteen years. He was born in Richmond, Maine, and still considers that place his home.

SAILING OF THE *HORNET*—PACIFIC RAILROAD IRON

The following is the substance of what Thomas said: The *Hornet* left New York on the 15th of January last, unusually well manned, fitted and provisioned—as fast and as handsome a clipper ship as ever sailed out of that port. She had a general cargo—a little of everything; a large quantity of kerosene oil in barrels; several hundred cases of candles—also four hundred tons of Pacific Railroad iron and three engines. The third mate thinks they were dock engines, and one of the seamen thought they were locomotives. Had no gales and no bad weather—nothing but fine sailing weather and she went along steadily and well—fast, very fast, in fact. Had uncommonly good weather off Cape Horn; he had been around that Cape seven times—each way—and had never seen such fine weather there before. On the 12th of April, in latitude, say, 35 south and longitude 95 west, signaled a Prussian bark—she set Prussian ensign, and the *Hornet* responded with her name, expressed by means of Merritt's system of signals. She was sailing west—probably bound for Australia. This was the last vessel ever seen by the *Hornet's* people until they floated ashore at Hawaii in the long boat—a space of sixty-four days.

THE SHIP ON FIRE

At seven o'clock on the morning of the 3d of May, the chief mate and two men started down into the hold to draw some "bright varnish" from a cask. The captain told him to bring the cask on deck—that it was dangerous to have it where it was, in the hold. The mate, instead of obeying the order, proceeded to draw a can full of the varnish first. He had an "open light" in his hand, and the liquid took fire; the can was dropped, the officer in his consternation neglected to close the bung, and in a few seconds the fiery torrent had run in every direction, under bales of rope, cases of candles, barrels of kerosene, and all sorts of freight, and tongues of flame were shooting upward through every aperture and crevice toward the deck.

The ship was moving along under easy sail, the watch on duty were idling here and there in such shade as they could find, and the listlessness and repose of morning in the tropics was upon the vessel and her belongings. But as six bells chimed, the cry of "Fire!" rang through the ship, and woke every man to life and action. And following the fearful warning, and almost as fleetly, came the fire itself. It sprang through hatchways, seized upon chairs, table, cordage, anything, everything—and almost before the bewildered men could realize what the trouble was and what was to be done the cabin was a hell of angry flames. The mainmast was on fire—its rigging was burnt asunder! One man said all this had happened within eighteen or twenty minutes after the first alarm—two others say in ten minutes. All say that one hour after the alarm, the main and mizzenmasts were burned in two and fell overboard.

Captain Mitchell ordered the three boats to be launched instantly, which was done—and so hurriedly that the longboat (the one he left the vessel in himself) had a hole as large as a man's head stove in her bottom. A blanket was stuffed into the opening and fastened to its place. Not a single thing was saved, except such food and other articles as lay about the cabin and could be quickly seized and thrown on deck. Thomas was sent into the longboat to receive its proportion of these things, and, being barefooted at the time, and bareheaded, and having no clothing on save an undershirt and pantaloons, of course he never got a chance afterward to add to his dress. He lost everything he had, including his log-book, which he had faithfully kept from the first. Forty minutes after the fire alarm the provisions and passengers were on board the three boats, and they rowed away from the ship—and to some distance, too, for the heat was very great. Twenty minutes afterward the two masts I have mentioned, with their rigging and their broad sheets of canvas wreathed in flames, crashed into the sea.

All night long the thirty-one unfortunates sat in their frail boats and watched the gallant ship burn; and felt as men feel when they see a tried friend perishing and are powerless to help him. The sea was illuminated for miles around, and the clouds above were tinged with a ruddy hue; the faces of the men glowed in the strong light as they shaded their eyes with their hands and peered out anxiously upon the wild picture, and the gun wales of the boats and the idle oars shone like polished gold.

At five o'clock on the morning after the disaster, in latitude 2 degrees 20' north, longitude 112 degrees 8' west, the ship went down, and the crew of the Hornet were alone on the great deep, or, as one of the seamen expressed it, "We felt as if somebody or something had gone away—as if we hadn't any home any more."

Captain Mitchell divided his boat's crew into two watches and gave the third mate charge of one and took the other himself. He had saved a studding sail from the ship, and out of this the men fashioned a rude sail with their knives; they hoisted it, and taking the first and second mates' boats in tow, they bore away upon the ship's course (northwest) and kept in the track of vessels bound to or from San Francisco, in the hope of being picked up.

THEIR WATER, PROVISIONS, ETC.

I have said that in the few minutes time allowed him, Captain Mitchell was only able to seize upon the few articles of food and other necessaries that happened to lie about the cabin. Here is the list: Four hams, seven pieces of salt pork, (each piece weighed about four pounds), one box of raisins, 100 pounds of bread (about one barrel), twelve two-pound cans of oysters, clams and assorted meats; six buckets of raw potatoes (which rotted so fast they got but little benefit from them), a keg with four pounds of butter in it, twelve gallons of water in a forty-gallon tierce or "scuttle-butt," four one-gallon demijohns full of water, three bottles of brandy, the property of passengers; some pipes, matches and a hundred pounds of tobacco; had no medicines. That was all these poor fellows had to live on for forty-three days—the whole thirty one of them!

Each boat had a compass, a quadrant, a copy of *Bowditch's Navigator* and a nautical almanac, and the captain's and chief mate's boat had chronometers.

RATIONS

Of course, all hands were put on short allowance at once. The day they set sail from the ship each man was allowed a small morsel of salt pork—or a little piece of potato, if he preferred it—and half a sea biscuit three times a day. To understand how very light this ration of bread was, it is only necessary to know that it takes seven of these sea biscuits to weigh a pound. The first two days they only allowed one gill of water a day to each man; but for nearly a fortnight after that the weather was lowering and stormy, and frequent rain squalls occurred. The rain was caught in canvas, and whenever there was a shower the forty-gallon cask and every other vessel that would hold water was filled—even all the boots that were water tight were pressed into this service, except such as the matches and tobacco were deposited in to keep dry. So for fourteen days. There were luxurious occasions when there was plenty of water to drink. But after that how they suffered the agonies of thirst for four long weeks!

HOPING AGAINST HOPE

For seven days the boats sailed on, and the starving men eat their fragment of biscuit and their morsel of raw pork in the morning, and hungrily counted the tedious hours until noon and night should bring their repetitions of it. And in the long intervals they looked mutely into each other's faces, or turned their wistful eyes across the wild sea in search of the succoring sail that was never to come.

"Didn't you talk?" I asked one of the men.

"No; we were too down-hearted—that is, the first week or more. We didn't talk—we only looked at each other and over the ocean."

And thought, I suppose. Thought of home—of shelter from storms—of food and drink, and rest.

The hope of being picked up hung to them constantly—was ever present to them, and in their thoughts, like hunger. And in the Captain's mind was the hope of making the Clarion Islands, and he clung to it many a day.

The nights were very dark. They had no lantern and could not see the compass, and there were no stars to steer by. Thomas said, of the boat, "She handled easy, and we steered by the feel of the wind in our faces and the heave of the sea." Dark, and dismal, and lonesome work was that! Sometimes they got a fleeting glimpse of the sailor's friend, the north star, and then they lighted a match and hastened anxiously to see if their compass was faithful to them—for it had to be placed close to an iron ring-bolt in the stern, and they were afraid, during those first nights, that this might cause it to vary. It proved true to them, however.

SUMPTUOUS FARE

On the fifth day a notable incident occurred. They caught a dolphin! and while their enthusiasm was still at its highest over this stroke of good fortune, they captured another. They made a trifling fire in a tin plate and warmed the prizes—to cook them was not possible—and divided them equitably among all hands and eat them.

On the sixth day two more dolphins were caught.

Two more were caught on the seventh day, and also a small bonita, and they began to believe they were always going to live in this extravagant way, but it was not to be—these were their last dolphins, and they never could get another bonita, though they saw them and longed for them often afterward.

RATIONS REDUCED

On the eighth day the rations were reduced about one-half. Thus—breakfast, one-fourth of a biscuit, an ounce of ham and a gill of water to each man; dinner, same quantity of bread and water, and four oysters or clams; supper, water and bread the same, and twelve large raisins or fourteen small ones, to a man. Also, during the first twelve or fifteen days, each man had one spoonful of brandy a day, then it gave out.

This day, as one of the men was gazing across the dull waste of waters as usual, he saw a small, dark object rising and falling upon the waves. He called attention to it, and in a moment every eye was bent upon it in intense interest. When the boat had approached a little nearer, it was discovered that it was a small green turtle, fast asleep. Every noise was hushed as they crept upon the unconscious slumberer. Directions were given and hopes and fears expressed in guarded whispers. At the fateful moment—a moment of tremendous consequence to these famishing men—the expert selected for the high and responsible office stretched forth his hand, while his excited comrades bated their breath and trembled for the success of the enterprise, and seized the turtle by the hind leg and handed him aboard! His delicate flesh was carefully divided among the party and eagerly devoured—after being "warmed" like the dolphins which went before him.

THE BOATS SEPARATE

After the eighth day I have ten days unaccounted for—no notes of them save that the men say they had their two or three ounces of food and their gill of water three times a day—and then the same weary watching for a saving sail by day and by night, and the same sad "hope deferred that maketh the heart sick," was their monotonous experience. They talked more, however, and the Captain labored without ceasing to keep them cheerful. [They have always a word of praise for the "old man."]

The eighteenth day was a memorable one to the wanderers on the lonely sea. On that day the boats parted company. The Captain said that separate from each other there were three chances for the saving of some of the party where there could be but one chance if they kept together.

The magnanimity and utter unselfishness of Captain Mitchell (and through his example, the same conduct in his men) throughout this distressing voyage, are among its most amazing features. No disposition was ever shown by the strong to impose upon the weak, and no greediness, no desire on the part of any to get more than his just share of food, was ever evinced. On the contrary, they were thoughtful of each other and always ready to care for and assist each other to the utmost of their ability. When the time came to part company, Captain Mitchell and his crew, although theirs was much the more numerous party (fifteen men to nine and seven respectively in the other boats), took only one-third of the meager amount of provisions still left, and passed over the other two-thirds to be divided up between the other crews. These men could starve, if need be, but they seem not to have known how to be mean.

After the division the Captain had left for his boat's share two-thirds of the ham, one-fourth of a box of raisins, half a bucket of biscuit crumbs, fourteen gallons of water, three cans of "soup-and bully." [That last expression of the third mate's occurred frequently during his narrative, and bothered me so painfully with its mysterious incomprehensibility, that at length I begged him to explain to me what this dark and dreadful "soup and-bully" might be. With the Consul's assistance he finally made me understand the French dish known as "soup bouillon" is put up in cans like preserved meats, and the American sailor is under the impression that its name is a sort of general tide which describes any description of edible whatever which is hermetically sealed in a tin vessel, and with that high contempt for trifling conventionalities which distinguishes his class, he has seen fit to modify the pronunciation into soup-and-bully.—MARK.]

The Captain told the mates he was still going to try to make the Clarion Isles, and that they could imitate his example if they thought best, but he wished them to freely follow the dictates of their own judgment in the matter. At eleven o'clock in the forenoon the boats were all cast loose from each other, and then, as friends part from friends whom they expect to meet no more in life, all hands hailed with a fervent "God bless you, boys; Good-bye!" and the two cherished sails drifted away and disappeared from the longing gaze that followed them so sorrowfully.

ANOTHER CAPTURE

On the afternoon of this eventful eighteenth day two "boobies" were caught—a bird about as large as a duck, but all bone and feathers—not as much meat as there is on a pigeon—not nearly so much, the men say. They eat them raw—bones, entrails and everything—no single morsel was wasted; they were carefully apportioned among the fifteen men. No fire could be built for cooking purposes—the wind was so strong and the sea ran so high that it was all a man could do to light his pipe.

A GOOD FRIEND GONE

At even tide the wanderers missed a cheerful spirit—a plucky, strong-hearted fellow, who never drooped his head or lost his grip—a staunch and true good friend, who was always at his post in storm or calm, in rain or shine—who scorned to say die, and yet was never afraid to die—a little trim and taut old rooster, he was, who starved with the rest, but came on watch in the stern-sheets promptly every day at four in the morning and six in the evening for eighteen days and crowed like a maniac! Right well they named him Richard of the Lion Heart! One of the men said with honest feeling: "As true as I'm a man, Mr. Mark Twain, if that rooster was here to-day and any man dared to abuse the bird I'd break his neck!" Richard was esteemed by all and by all his rights were respected. He received his little ration of bread crumbs every time the men were fed, and, like them, he bore up bravely and never grumbled and never gave way to despair. As long as he was strong enough he stood in the stern-sheets or mounted the gunwale as regularly as his watch came round, and crowed his two-hour talk, and when at last he grew feeble in the legs and had to stay below, his heart was still stout and he slapped about in the water on the bottom of the boat and crowed as bravely as ever! He felt that under circumstances like these America expects every rooster to do his duty, and he did it. But is it not to the high honor of that boat's crew of starving men, that, tortured day and night by the pangs of hunger as they were, they refused to appease them with the blood of their humble comrade? Richard was transferred to the chief mate's boat and sailed away on the eighteenth day.

RELIGIOUS SERVICES

The third mate does not remember distinctly, but thinks morning and evening prayers were begun on the nineteenth day. They were conducted by one of the young Fergusons, because the Captain could not read the prayer book without his spectacles, and they had been burned with the ship. And ever after this date, at the rising and the setting of the sun, the storm tossed mariners reverently bowed their heads while prayers went up for "they that are helpless and far at sea."

AN INCIDENT

On the morning of the twenty-first day, while some of the crew were dozing on the thwarts and others were buried in reflection, one of the men suddenly sprang to his feet and cried, "A sail! a sail!" Of course, sluggish blood bounded then and eager eyes were turned to seek the welcome vision. But disappointment was their portion, as usual. It was only the chief mate's boat drifting across their path after three days' absence. In a short time the two parties were abreast each other and in hailing distance. They talked twenty minutes; the mate reported "all well" and then sailed away, and they never saw him afterward.

FURTHER REDUCTION OF RATIONS

On the twenty-fourth day Captain Mitchell took an observation and found that he was in latitude 16 degrees north and longitude 117 degrees west—about 1,000 miles from where his vessel was burned. The hope he had cherished so long that he would be able to make the Clarion Isles deserted him at last he could only go before the wind, and he was now obliged to attempt the best thing the southeast trades could do for him—blow him to the "American group" or to the Sandwich Islands—and therefore he reluctantly and with many misgivings turned his prow towards those distant archipelagoes. Not many mouthfuls of food were left, and these must be economized. The third mate said that under this new programme of proceedings "we could see that we were living too high; we had got to let up on them raisins, or the soup-and-bullies, one, because it stood to reason that we warn't going to make land soon, and so they wouldn't last." It was a matter which had few humorous features about it to them, and yet a smile is almost pardonable at this idea, so gravely expressed, of "living high" on fourteen raisins at a meal.

The rations remained the same as fixed on the eighth day, except that only two meals a day were allowed, and occasionally the raisins and oysters were left out.

What these men suffered during the next three weeks no mortal man may hope to describe. Their stomachs and intestines felt to the grasp like a couple of small tough balls, and the gnawing hunger pains and the dreadful thirst that was consuming them in those burning latitudes became almost insupportable. And yet, as the men say, the Captain said funny things and talked cheerful talk until he got them to conversing freely, and then they used to spend hours together describing delicious dinners they had eaten at home, and earnestly planning interminable and preposterous bills of fare for dinners they were going to eat on shore, if they ever lived through their troubles to do it, poor fellows. The Captain said plain bread and butter would be good enough for him all the days of his life, if he could only get it.

But the saddest things were the dreams they had. An unusually intelligent young sailor named Cox said: "In those long days and nights we dreamed all the time—not that we ever slept. I don't mean—no, we only sort of dozed—three-fourths of the faculties awake and the other fourth benumbed into the counterfeit of a slumber; oh, no—some of us never slept for twenty-three days, and no man ever saw the Captain asleep for upward of thirty. But we barely dozed that way and dreamed—and always of such feasts! bread, and fowls, and meat—everything a man could think of, piled upon long tables, and smoking hot! And we sat down and seized upon the first dish in our reach, like ravenous wolves, and carried it to our lips, and—and then we woke up and found the same starving comrades about us, and the vacant sky and the desolate sea!

These things are terrible even to think of.

RATIONS STILL FURTHER REDUCED

It even startles me to come across that significant heading so often in my notebook, notwithstanding I have grown so familiar with its sound by talking so much with these unfortunate men.

On the twenty-eighth day the rations were: One teaspoonful of bread crumbs and about an ounce of ham for the morning meal; a spoonful of bread crumbs alone for the evening meal, and one gill of water three times a day! A kitten would perish eventually under such sustenance.

At this point the third mate's mind reverted painfully to an incident of the early stages of their sufferings. He said there were two between decks, on board the *Hornet*, who had been lying there sick and helpless for he didn't know how long; but when the ship took fire they turned out as lively as any one under the spur of the excitement. One was a "Portyghee," he said, and always of a hungry disposition—when all the provisions that could be got had been brought aft and deposited near the wheel to be lowered into the boats, "that sick Portyghee watched his chance, and when nobody was looking he harnessed the provisions and eat up nearly a quarter of a bar'l of bread before the old man caught him, and he had more than two notions to put his lights out." The third mate dwelt up on this circumstance as upon a wrong he could not fully forgive, and intimated that the Portyghee stole bread enough, if economised in twenty eighth-day rations, to have run the long-boat party three months.

THEY CAPTURE A PRIZE

Four little flying fish, the size of the sardines of these latter days, flew into the boat on the night of the twenty eighth day. They were divided among all hands and devoured raw. On the twenty-ninth day they caught another, and divided it into fifteen pieces, less than a teaspoonful apiece.

On the thirtieth day they caught a third flying fish and gave it to the revered old Captain—a fish of the same poor little proportions as the others—four inches long—a present a king might be proud of under such circumstances—a present whose value, in the eyes of the men who offered it, was not to be found in the Bank of England—yea, whose vaults were notable to contain it! The old Captain refused to take it; the men insisted; the Captain said no—he would take his fifteenth—they must take the remainder. They said in substance, though not in words, that they would see him in Jericho first! So the Captain had to eat the fish.

I believe I have done the third mate some little wrong in the beginning of this letter. I have said he was as self-possessed as a statue that he never betrayed emotion or enthusiasm. He never did except when he spoke of "the old man." It always thawed through his ice then. The men were the same way; the Captain is their hero—their true and faithful friend, whom they delight to honor. I said to one of these infatuated skeletons, "But you wouldn't go quite so far as to die for him?" A snap of the finger— "As quick as that!—I wouldn't be alive now if it hadn't been for him." We pursued the subject no further.

RATIONS STILL FURTHER REDUCED

I still claim the public's indulgence and belief. At least Thomas and his men do through me. About the thirty-second day the bread gave entirely out. There was nothing left, now, but mere odds and ends of their stock of provisions. Five days afterward, on the thirty-seventh day—latitude 16 degrees 30' north, and longitude 170 degrees west—kept off for the "American group"—"which don't exist and never will, I suppose," said the third mate. Ran directly over the ground said to be occupied by these islands—that is between latitude 16 degrees and 17 degrees north and longitude 133 degrees to 136 degrees west. Ran over the imaginary islands and got into 136 degrees west, and then the Captain made a dash for Hawaii, resolving that he would go till he fetched land, or at any rate as long as he and his men survived.

THE LAST RATION!

On Monday, the thirty-eighth day after the disaster, "we had nothing left," said the third mate, "but a pound and a half of ham—the bone was a good deal the heaviest part of it—and one soup-and-bully tin." These things were divided among the fifteen men, and they ate it all—two ounces of food to each man. I do not count the ham bone, as that was saved for the next day. For some time, now, the poor wretches had been cutting their old boots into small pieces and eating them. They would also pound wet rags to a sort of pulp and eat them.

STARVATION FARE

On the thirty-ninth day the ham bone was divided up into rations, and scraped with knives and eaten. I said: "You say the two sick men remained sick all through, and after awhile two or three had to be relieved from standing watch; how did you get along without medicines!"

The reply was: "Oh, we couldn't have kept them if we'd had them, if we'd had boxes of pills, or anything like that, we'd have eaten them. It was just as well—we couldn't have kept them, and we couldn't have given them to the sick men alone—we'd have shared them around all alike, I guess." It was said rather in jest, but it was a pretty true jest, no doubt.

After apportioning the ham bone, the Captain cut the canvas cover that had been around the ham into fifteen equal pieces, and each man took his portion. This was the last division of food that the Captain made. The men broke up the small oaken butter tub and divided the staves among them selves, and gnawed them up. The shell of the little green turtle, heretofore mentioned, was scraped with knives and eaten to the last shaving. The third mate chewed pieces of boots and spit them out, but eat nothing except the soft straps of two pairs of boots—eat three on the thirty-ninth day and saved one for the fortieth.

THE AWFUL ALTERNATIVE

The men seem to have thought in their own minds of the shipwrecked mariner's last dreadful resort—cannibalism; but they do not appear to have conversed about it. They only thought of the casting lots and killing one of their number as a possibility; but even when they were eating rags, and bone, and boots, and shell, and hard oak wood, they seem to have still had a notion that it was remote. They felt that some one of the company must die soon—which one they well knew; and during the last three or four days of their terrible voyage they were patiently but hungrily waiting for him. I wonder if the subject of these anticipations knew what they were thinking of? He must have known it—he must have felt it. They had even calculated how long he would last; they said to themselves, but not to each other, I think they said, "He will die Saturday—and then!"

There was one exception to the spirit of delicacy I have mentioned—a Frenchman, who kept an eye of strong personal interest upon the sinking man and noted his failing strength with untiring care and some degree of cheerfulness. He frequently said to Thomas: "I think he will go off pretty soon, now, sir. And then we'll eat him!" This is very sad.

Thomas and also several of the men state that the sick "Portyghee," during the five days that they were entirely out of provisions, actually eat two silk handkerchiefs and a couple of cotton shirts, besides his share of the boots, and bones, and lumber.

THE CAPTAIN'S BIRTHDAY

Captain Mitchell was fifty-six years old on the 12th of June—the fortieth day after the burning of the ship and the third day before the boat's crew reached land. He said it looked somewhat as if it might be the last one he was going to enjoy. He had no birth day feast except some bits of ham canvas—no luxury but this, and no substantials save the leather and oaken bucket staves.

Speaking of the leather diet, one of the men told me he was obliged to eat a pair of boots which were so old and rotten that they were full of holes; and then he smiled gently and said he didn't know, though, but what the holes tasted about as good as the balance of the boot. This man was still very feeble, and after saying this he went to bed.

LAND HO!

At eleven o'clock on the 15th of June, after suffering all that men may suffer and live for forty-three days, in an open boat, on a scorching tropical sea, one of the men feebly shouted the glad tidings, "Land ho!" The "watch below" were lying in the bottom of the boat. What do you suppose they did? They said they had been cruelly disappointed over and over again, and they dreaded to risk another experience of the kind—they could not bear it—they lay still where they were. They said they would not trust to an appearance that might not be land after all. They would wait.

Shortly it was proven beyond question that they were almost to land. Then there was joy in the party. One man is said to have swooned away. Another said the sight of the green hills was better to him than a day's rations, a strange figure for a man to use who had been fasting for forty days and forty nights.

The land was the island of Hawaii, and they were off and could see nothing in shore but breakers. I was there a week or two ago and it is a very dangerous place. When they got pretty close to shore they saw cabins, but no human beings. They thought they would lower the sail and try to work in with the oars. They cut the ropes and the sail came down, and then they found they were not strong enough to ship the oars. They drifted helplessly toward the breakers, but looked listlessly on and cared not a straw for the violent death which seemed about to overtake them after all their manful struggles, their privations and their terrible sufferings. They said "it was good to see the green fields again." It was all they cared for. The "green fields" were a haven of rest for the weary wayfarers; it was sufficient; they were satisfied; it was nothing to them that death stood in their pathway; they had long been familiar to him; he had no terrors for them.

Two of Captain Spencer's natives saw the boat, knew by the appearance of things that it was in trouble, and dashed through the surf and swam out to it. When they climbed aboard there were only five yards of space between the poor sufferers and a sudden and violent death. Fifteen minutes afterward the boat was beached upon the shore and a crowd of natives (who are the very incarnation of generosity, unselfishness and hospitality) were around the strangers dumping bananas, melons, taro, poi—anything and everything they could scrape together that could be eaten—on the ground by the cart-load; and if Mr. Jones, of the station, had not hurried down with his steward, they would soon have killed the starving men with kindness. As it was, the sick "Portyghee" really ate six bananas before Jones could get hold of him and stop him. This is a fact. And so are the stories of his previous exploits. Jones and the Kanaka girls and men took the mariners in their arms like so many children and carried them up to the house, where they received kind and judicious attention until Sunday evening, when two whaleboats came from Hilo, Jones furnished a third, and they were taken in these to the town just named, arriving there at two o'clock Monday morning.

REMARKS

Each of the young Fergusons kept a journal from the day the ship sailed from New York until they got on land once more at Hawaii. The Captain also kept a log every day he was adrift. These logs, by the Captain's direction, were to be kept up faithfully as long as any of the crew were alive, and the last survivor was to put them in a bottle, when he succumbed, and lash the bottle to the inside of the boat. The Captain gave a bottle to each officer of the other boats, with orders to follow his example. The old gentleman was always thoughtful.

The hardest berth in that boat, I think, must have been that of provision-keeper. This office was performed by the Captain and the third mate; of course they were always hungry. They always had access to the food, and yet must not gratify their craving appetites.

The young Fergusons are very highly spoken of by all the boat's crew, as patient, enduring, manly and kind-hearted gentlemen. The Captain gave them a watch to themselves—it was the duty of each to bail the water out of the boat three hours a day. Their home is in Stamford, Connecticut, but their father's place of business is New York.

In the chief mate's boat was a passenger—a gentlemanly young fellow of twenty years, named William Lang, son of a stockbroker in New York.

The chief mate, Samuel Hardy, lived at Chatham, Massachusetts; second mate belonged in Shields, England; the cook, George Washington (negro), was in the chief mate's boat, and also the steward (negro); the carpenter was in the second mate's boat.

CAPTAIN MITCHELL

To this man's good sense, cool judgment, perfect discipline, close attention to the smallest particulars which could conduce to the welfare of his crew or render their ultimate rescue more probable, that boat's crew owe their lives. He has shown brain and ability that make him worthy to command the finest frigate in the United States, and a genuine unassuming heroism that [should] entitle him to a Congressional medal. I suppose some of the citizens of San Francisco who know how to appreciate this kind of a man will not let him go on hungry forever after he gets there. In the above remarks I am only echoing the expressed opinions of numbers of persons here who have never seen Captain Mitchell, but who judge him by his works—among others Hon. Anson Burlingame and our Minister to Japan, both of whom have called at the hospital several times and held long conversations with the men. Burlingame speaks in terms of the most unqualified praise of Captain Mitchell's high and distinguished abilities as evinced at every point throughout his wonderful voyage.

THE SICK

Captain Mitchell, one sailor, and the two Fergusons are still at Hilo. The two first mentioned are pretty feeble, from what I can learn. The Captain's sense of responsibility kept him strong and awake all through the voyage; but as soon as he landed, and that fearful strain upon his faculties was removed, he was prostrated—became the feeblest of the boat's company.

The seamen here are doing remarkably well, considering all things. They already walk about the hospital a little—and very stiff-legged, because of the long inaction their muscles have experienced.

When they came ashore at Hawaii no man in the party had had any movement of his bowels for eighteen days, several not for twenty-five or thirty, one not for thirty-seven, and one not for forty-four days. As soon as any of the men can travel they will be sent to San Francisco.

I have written this lengthy letter in a great hurry in order to get it off by the bark *Milton Badger*, if the thing be possible, and I may have made a good many mistakes, but I hardly think so. All the statistical information in it comes from Thomas, and he may have made mistakes, because he tells his story entirely from memory, and although he has naturally a most excellent one, it might well be pardoned for inaccuracies concerning events which transpired during a series of weeks that never saw his mind strongly fixed upon any thought save the weary longing for food and water. But the log-books of the Captain and the two passengers will tell the terrible romance from the first day to the last in faithful detail, and these I shall forward by the next mail if I am permitted to copy them.

MARK TWAIN.

27

A REPORT OF EVENTS ON THE COAST *of* PERU

From *Reports of the* USS Powhatan *and* USS Wateree *Concerning the Earthquake and* Tidal *Wave of 13 August 1868 at Arica,* Peru

U.S. NAVY

1868

Shipwrecks can occur and lives can be lost even in harbors, at a dead calm. The Roddam, *a British steamship, was resting at anchor in the harbor of St. Pierre, on Martinique, when Mount Pelee erupted in 1902, and the* nuee ardente, *the cloud of fire that sometimes rolls down the mountainsides of erupting volcanoes, swept over the ship and killed most of the crew. The* Roraima, *another British ship, at anchor nearby, was destroyed. One of the most notorious wrecks in United States history occurred when the* Eastland, *a passenger steamer, capsized while standing at a pier in the Chicago River on July 24, 1915. The ship was unstable to begin with, it had 3,500 people on board, 1,000 more than its capacity, and 852 people died.*

And then there are the tsunamis, like this one on the coast of Peru in 1868. We print the official U.S. Navy Department accounts, the first from the commander of the Powhatan, *flag-ship of the South Pacific Squadron, the second from an officer on board the* Wateree, *which wound up a third of a mile inland, saved from destruction only by the fact that it had a flat bottom. Most of the other ships in the harbor did not, so that when the water receded before the incoming tsunamis they were left on their sides. When the water returned, most of them were lost. Another American ship, the* Fredonia, *had her hull breached. Everyone on board died. The town was destroyed.*

UNITED STATES FLAG-SHIP *POWHATAN*, (1st rate,)
BAY OF CALLAO, PERU, SEPTEMBER 3, 1868.

SIR: The honorable Secretary may be desirous to learn from me the condition and appearance of the city of Arica, as I found it on my arrival, occasioned by the terrific earthquake of the 13th ultimo, which has devastated more or less of this whole coast.

The upper part of the city, which from its elevation escaped the encroachment of the sea, has not a single house or wall left standing—it is in one confused mass of ruins, more or less in every part prostate; whilst the lower part, which comprised chiefly the better and more substantial order of edifices, including a large custom-house of stone mason work, is literally as perfectly swept away, even the foundations, as though they had never existed, and present the appearance of a waste that had been ravaged by the waters of a mighty river, carrying everything before it in its irresistible volume.

The inhabitants of the city, destitute of everything but the clothes in which they stand, are dispersed upon the heights and crests overlooking the city, living under tents of canvas, those who were so fortunate as to obtain them, and under mats, the fabric of the country, without food and without the common necessaries of life, other than those which have been generously bestowed by the charities of sympathizing strangers.

Availing myself of the authority contained in paragraph 158 of the Regulations of the Navy, I directed for their relief a liberal distribution of provisions and clothing of the squadron, which was not only received by them with the most lively demonstrations of joy and gratitude, but has produced a most profound impression upon the minds and sensibilities of the population of Peru at large.

It is of some satisfaction to me to inform the honorable Secretary that three of the vessels of this command were the first of a national character on the spot—two French and one English vessel of war coming in afterwards—and that the officers and men of our ships emulated and vied with each other in administering to this suffering community, both publicly and privately, in a manner which has left a most memorable record to their lasting honor and reputation, as the citizens of a Christian country.

At the time of my departure it was affirmed that a number of the dead still remained under the ruins, who had not been sought for or removed; the people, crushed in spirit, stricken by grief and paralyzed by fright, seemed without hope, animation or object, and to have surrendered themselves to desperation and despondency, without either the expectation or desire to rebuild for themselves homes upon a spot which has been commemorated by so frightful a tragedy.

It may be a matter of interest to the honorable Secretary, as a physical fact, to be informed that the soundings in Arica bay have been materially changed, by this convulsion, the depth having decreased from the outside of the anchorage, seaward.

Very respectfully, your obedient servant,
T. Turner,
Rear-Admiral, Commanding South Pacific Squadron.

Hon. GIDEON WELLES,
Secretary of the Navy, Washington, D. C.

Source: *Report of the Secretary of the Navy, with an Appendix, Containing Bureau Reports, etc.* (Washington: Government Printing Office, 1868): 34–35.

Detailed report of the loss of *Wateree.*
UNITED STATES STEAMER *WATEREE,* (3d rate,)
Arica, Peru, August 20, 1868.

SIR: I respectfully submit the following detailed report of the circumstances attending the stranding of this vessel on the 13th instant:

At 5.05 P.M. on that day, a rumbling noise, accompanied by a tremulous motion of the ship, was observed. This increased in force rapidly until it was evident that an unusually severe shock of an earthquake was taking place, and I proceeded on deck, and, while standing there, looking at the city, I observed the buildings commence to crumble down, and in less than a minute the whole city was but a mass of ruins, scarcely a house being left standing.

I immediately gave orders to secure the battery, have the second anchor ready to let go, chain ready to veer, and the hatches battened down. I then had a boat called away, and, as there was no indications of the sea coming in, at 5.20 took the doctor and paymaster and proceeded on shore, ordering all boats to follow as soon as possible, for the purpose of rendering such assistance as might be needed. I met Captain Doty on the wharf, and he directed me to send on board for as many men as could be spared, to assist in extricating those who had been buried beneath the ruins; but it was impossible to get the boat to the wharf again, as the sea was by this time rapidly receding. I also met Lieutenant Commander M. L. Johnson, of this vessel, who requested me to give him assistance to extricate his wife from amongst the ruins. I took a party with me, and succeeded in recovering her remains before the water reached the place where she was buried. She was doubtless killed instantly, but it has been a great satisfaction to all of us to be able to give Christian burial at this time to a brother officer's wife.

At 5.32 the sea commenced to rise rapidly, and the ship, in a violent current, setting along the beach to northward and eastward, commenced dragging. I immediately let go the second anchor, and veered away chain, which brought her up. Four men were stationed at the wheel. About this time the mole was submerged, and the sea had come up to the houses nearest the beach, the people rushing to the Morro. After several minutes there was a sudden reflux, and the ship swung to seaward; sheering her with the helm to keep the chains clear, more chain was veered away, until there were ninety (90) fathoms on starboard, and seventy-five (75) fathoms on port anchor.

A bark and brig in shore of the *Wateree* were left aground; after a lapse of a few minutes the sea rushed in again, veered away to ninety-five (95) fathoms on port, and one hundred (100) on starboard chain. It was now near 6 o'clock. The brig was washed ashore, and the bark on her beam ends, a wreck. The United States ship Fredonia, Peruvian corvette *America*, English bark *Chanarcillo*, and this vessel, were still holding on.

There was an ebb and flow of the sea for some little time after this, the water being covered with floating debris. Several shore boats with people in them were picked up while drifting past us, and one boat with eight (8) men from the English bark *Chanarcillo*. A little before 6 o'clock Midshipman Taussig was sent in the first cutter to the relief of a drowning man floating past. Between 6 and 7 there was another tremendous rising of the sea, and as it receded the ship was swung violently seaward, and, after holding on for about a minute, the deck stoppers parted, the chain flew rapidly out of the hawse pipes, tearing away compartments between the lockers, and, being both shackled together, brought on the light underneath upper deck. The ship now commenced to drift rapidly seaward, passing very near Alacran island, but clear of it, when the sea very suddenly commenced to rush in again. The vessel swung violently around, and in doing so just cleared the English bark *Chanarcillo*; a severe strain came upon the chains, and the starboard one parted close to hawse pipes, and the ship drifted rapidly towards shore. About this time saw the *America* go on her beam ends, and heard terrible groans and cries proceeding from her. The English bark *Chanarcillo* was also on her beam ends. The sky was now completely overcast. About 6.55 the ship was among the breakers, and several heavy seas broke over her, but did no other injury than throwing the vessel nearly on her beam ends, (she quickly righted again,) breaking paddle-box, bending portion of rim and braces of starboard wheels, jamming the wheel itself against the side, and carrying away store-rooms on the guard forward, and part of starboard hammock netting.

Life lines were got up fore and aft. Shortly afterwards the wheel ropes parted. Several seas came in after this, and, about 7.20, vessel took to bottom, close up to a high bank, about four hundred and seventy (470) yards from, and twelve (12) feet above, high water mark.

Once or twice afterwards the sea came up, but not high enough to float the vessel.

When first beached the ship was lying about broadside to the sea coming in, but was finally washed around until her head lay west half south by compass, and head on to the beach.

During the ebb and flow of the sea the wheels turned very easily, and added but slightly to the strain on the chains. All boats except the "dinghy" were lost. The pumps were sounded frequently during time of being washed ashore, but not enough water was found to cause any apprehension of a leak.

Heavy shocks of earthquake were felt at short intervals from time of occurrence of first one, until the following morning. I cannot sufficiently express my appreciation of the conduct of the officers and men during this trying time, and my great regret is that I am not able to bear personal testimony to the same; but all speak in the highest terms of the officerlike bearing of the executive officer, Lieutenant Commander M. S. Stuyvesant, and from him I have the assurance that every officer and man did his duty faithfully, and that there was at no time the slightest confusion, and when I returned to the ship, at a little after 2 A.M., everything was in perfect order as it was possible to be under the circumstances, and no one would have supposed that the ship had passed through so terrible an ordeal.

I have had the height to which the solid sea wave rose measured, and find that it is 42 feet and 5 inches, and the wash is from 10 to 15 feet higher.

I would specially recommend to the consideration of the government for some suitable reward for gallant conduct and meritorious services during the earthquake, and while remaining at the wreck, the following named men, viz: Richard Fowle, signal quartermaster; Michael Burke, quartermaster; William Reed, quarter gunner; Henry Wilson, quarter gunner;

George Woodgate, painter; John Johnson, carpenter; Louis Rector, sail-maker's mate; Johan Kellner and Martin Green, 1st class firemen; John Cammerson, 2d class fireman; William Richards, George Pettit and William Stonebrink, seamen; John Murphy, 2d, ordinary seaman; George W. Reed, captain's steward; Louis Mussey, captain's cook; John Seeley, wardroom cook; Antonio Emanuel, steerage cook; and Charles Brown, cabin boy.

I would not forget to mention my appreciation of the conduct of Midshipman E. D. Taussig, who so gallantly volunteered to save the life of a drowning man, and when he found that he could not make the ship again, went on board the Peruvian corvette *America*, and there rendered material assistance in securing the battery.

Very respectfully, your obedient servant,
JAMES H. GILLIS,
Commander, United States Navy

Rear-Admiral T. Turner,
Commanding South Pacific Squadron,
Flag-ship Powhatan, *Arica, Peru.*

Source: *Report of the Secretary of the Navy, with an Appendix, Containing Bureau Reports, etc.* (Washington: Government Printing Office, 1868): 32–34.

28

STORY *of a* HOODOO SHIP

From the *New York Times*

JUNE 24, 1900

I *found this little item on a maritime history website and couldn't resist including it. "We were old in the business," one of the mariners here described says. Given the prevalence of shipwreck, how many sailors get old in the business? They say that sailors are a superstitious lot. Who can blame them?*

THE *BLENGFELL* WAS AN IRON FULL-RIGGED SHIP BUILT BY THE Whitehaven Shipbuilding Company and owned by J.Edgar & Co. of Liverpool. On the 17th October 1898 she was destroyed by an explosion of her naphtha cargo, her loss being reported in the New York Times the following day (see Blengfell ship history). Two years later the same newspaper printed the following report describing superstitions surrounding the ship.

THE NEW YORK TIMES, 24TH JUNE 1900, PAGE 6.
STORY OF A HOODOO SHIP
How the *Blengfell* of Liverpool Went Down
Nocturnal Visions and Madness Beseiged Her Sailors at Sea—A Cargo of Naphtha Her Doom.

As the British ship *Ellisland* was being made fast to one of the piers in the Erie Basin a few days ago, four sailors who stood leaning over the forward deck rail saw something that made them start suddenly and cross themselves superstitiously. What caused their uneasiness was a blurred inscription on the pier's string-piece. It was printed in half-illegible and badly formed letters and read like this:

BLENGFELL, LIVERPOOL

The names of the four sailors were R. Cochrane, John Johnson, Charles Walback, and H. Kimber. More than two years ago, in the early part of 1898, they came to this port in an English bark called the *Blengfell*, from Liverpool, and she had only been here two days when these four members of her crew left her on the ground that she was a " hoodoo ship." A month afterward she sailed homeward again, but she never reached port, for the evil fate that hung over her fulfilled its mission, and the battered remains of her big hulk have long lain many fathoms under the sea.

When Cochrane and his companions saw the name of their former ship written on the Erie Basin pier, their memories took a turn by no means pleasant. It seems that the ill-omened *Blengfell*'s disastrous experiences began three voyages before the one that brought her to America, though it was on that trip that all hands aboard became convinced of a hoodoo's presence among them.

During a trip she took about three years before that time, a seaman went mad because of "visions" in his cabin at night. He drowned himself at last in despair. On the next voyage a negro sailor, who had been sick and in delirium, suddenly arose from his bed, grasped a brace of pistols, and ran all the rest of the crew aft, where he kept them at bay for twenty-four hours. Finally he threw down his pistols, uttered a wild shriek, and jumped headlong over the railing, disappearing immediately under the water and never rising to the surface again.

During the trip that came next, another seaman saw nightly visions that drove him to madness. For weeks he muttered and groaned and shrieked, frightening all his companions half to death, and then he was found hanging by his neck on one of the yards. In a note which he left in his cabin he said that the hoodoo had commanded him to depart from life and that it had prophesied a horrible doom for the bark *Blengfell*.

It was after this that Cochrane, Johnson, Wallback, and Kimber shipped with the bark. They got aboard of her at Liverpool. Her commander was Capt. Johnston of Whitehaven, and with him sailed his wife and little girl. The bark sailed from Liverpool to Brisbane, Australia, and thence to New York, touching at Newcastle, Valparaiso, and Junin on the voyage. When she reached here, the Captain ordered some of his men to put a new coat of paint on the bark, and while they were doing the job, some of them scrawled the ragged inscription on the Erie Basin pier.

"It was while that painting was being done that we skipped," said Seaman Cochrane, in telling the story of the hoodoo. "And it's a good thing we did, for if we'd sailed away with the blasted bark, the fishes would have had us long before this. Do you know what happened to the *Blengfell* and how the hoodoo at last got in his work? No? Well, I'll tell you."

"Capt. Johnston, his wife and child; the two mates, and two apprentices were blown into so many little pieces that not a trace of them was ever found. And as for the bark, there wasn't anything left of her but driftwood. The Dover pilot was killed too, but they found his body later on.

"It was all the work of the hoodoo, wasn't it, boys?" added the seaman, turning to his companions. "But we were old in the business, so we knew what was coming and jumped the game. It's a good thing to know a little about hoodoos once in a while. You may live a bit longer for it, you know, and, besides, when you die you don't want to get a sure pass to hell. And that's what you get if a hoodoo sees your finish."

29

UNSINKABLE

From *Titanic Disaster: Hearings Before a Subcommittee of the Committee on Commerce, United States Senate*

APRIL 19—MAY 25, 1912

We have Senator William Smith of Michigan to thank for these hearings. He convened them as soon as the survivors began to reach New York, mainly in order to prevent J. Bruce Ismay, the managing director of the White Star Line, which owned the Titanic, *to escape back to England before he could be grilled in the United States. Sen. Smith knew nothing about ships and the sea, but he certainly knew this was one of the biggest stories of his time, and he wanted to find out how so many lives were lost, and why.*

The hearings were held first in New York, to make sure that Ismay could not simply transfer to another ship and set sail for London. President Taft authorized a revenue cutter to intercept the Carpathia, *the rescue ship, and subpoena Ismay before he could board a departing ship. It was hardly worth it. Ismay's testimony proved, to say the least, unrevealing. He seemed to know nothing of the ship it was his job to know a great deal about.*

We print instead the testimony of Maj. Arthur G. Peuchen, a Canadian military man and yachtsman who was familiar with ships and the sea and was also a sharp, cool observer. He was a gentleman as well. He only got into a lifeboat when he was ordered into it by one of the ship's officers. The tradition in the sea that women and children shall go first dates from the loss of the Birkenhead, *a British troopship, in 1852 off the coast of South Africa. The ship was carrying 680 people, most of them British troops; when the ship struck a rock and started to sink. Their commanding officer, a Maj. Alexander*

Seton, mustered the men on deck and ordered them to stand at attention until the women and children had been lowered into lifeboats. Soon after, the ship broke in half and the troops had to swim for it. Most of them, including Major Seton, drowned. But while the boats were being lowered not a single man broke ranks. The tradition of women and children first has been called, ever since, the Birkenhead Drill.

Whether the men and officers on board the Titanic followed this tradition of the sea was a big part of Sen. Smith's concern. One of the men who died in the Titanic was Maj. Archibald Butt, who was President Taft's personal aide; he was said to have threatened to shoot any man who boarded a lifeboat before the women and children had been taken care of. All kinds of remarkable personal stories have survived the loss. Some women refused to leave their husbands' sides and died with them. The Captain, Edward Smith, was seen leaping from the bridge at the last minute into the sea. He did not live. Second Officer Charles Lightoller was going down with the ship, sucked against the grate of a blower, when the boilers exploded and blew him clear. He did live. So much depends on luck. That's one of the lessons of shipwrecks. Luck rules. The Titanic might not have hit its iceberg if there had been binoculars in the crow's nest. If they had had binoculars, said Mr. Fleet, who was in the nest when they hit the iceberg, "We could have seen it a bit sooner." How much sooner? asked the senator. "Well," he replied, "enough to get out of the way." No one ever explained why there were no binoculars in the crow's nest.

Luck, then. Small things like binoculars. "Loose lips sink ships" was the motto used to warn American citizens during World War II not to tell anyone anything they knew about the movement of ships or troops or anything else relating to the war effort. The truth is that almost anything can sink a ship. The sea is a dangerous place, and it has a way of rewarding human carelessness, human arrogance–all the things we associate with the word hubris–with disaster, suffering, and death.

Witness: Maj. Arthur G. Peuchen, 53

...Senator Smith: Major, I wish you would tell the committee... as nearly as you can, in your own way, what took place from the time the *Titanic* sailed. You may proceed in your own way and take your own time, and you will not be interrupted until you finish.

Maj. Peuchen: ...The weather up to the time of Sunday was pleasant. There was very little wind; it was quite calm. Everything seemed to be running very smoothly on the steamer, and there was nothing that occurred. There was no mention of fire in any way. In fact, it was a very pleasant voyage up to Sunday evening. We were all pleased with the way the new steamer was progressing, and we had hopes of arriving in New York quite early on Wednesday morning.

Do you wish me to go on further?

SENATOR SMITH: Go right along. I wish you to complete your statement, in your own way, up to the time you went on board the *Carpathia*.

MAJ. PEUCHEN: It would be a rather long story.

SENATOR SMITH: Well, I want it in the record, Major.

MAJ. PEUCHEN: Sunday evening I dined with my friends, Markleham Molson, Mr. Allison, and Mrs. Allison; and their daughter was there for a short time. The dinner was an exceptionally good dinner. It seemed to be a better bill of fare than usual, although they are all good. After dinner my friends and I went to the sitting-out room and had some coffee. I left the friends I had dined with about 9 o'clock, I think, or a little later. I then went up to the smoking room and joined Mr. Beatty, Mr. McCaffery, and another English gentleman who was going to Canada. We sat chatting and smoking there until probably 20 minutes after 11, or it may have been a little later than that. I then bid them good night and went to my room. I probably stopped, going down, but I had only reached my room and was starting to undress when I felt as though a heavy wave had struck our ship. She quivered under it somewhat. If there had been a sea running I would simply have thought it was an unusual wave which had struck the boat; but knowing that it was a calm night and that it was an unusual thing to occur on a calm night, I immediately put my overcoat on and went up on deck. As I started to go through the grand stairway I met a friend, who said, "Why, we have struck an iceberg."

SENATOR SMITH: Give his name, if you can.

MAJ. PEUCHEN: I can not remember his name. He was simply a casual acquaintance I had met. He said, "If you will go up on the upper deck," or "If you will go up on A deck, you will see the ice on the fore part of the ship." So I did so. I went up there. I suppose the ice had fallen inside the rail, probably 4 to 4½ feet. It looked like shell ice, soft ice. But you could see it quite plainly along the bow of the boat. I stood on deck for a few minutes, talking to other friends, and then I went to see my friend, Mr. Hugo Ross, to tell him that it was not serious; that we had only struck an iceberg. I also called on Mr. Molson at his room, but he was out. I afterwards saw Mr. Molson on deck and we chatted over the matter, and I suppose 15 minutes after that I met Mr. Hays, his son-in-law, and I said to him, "Mr. Hays, have you seen the ice?" He said, "No." I said, "If you care to see it I will take you up on the deck and show it to you." So we proceeded from probably C deck to A deck and along forward, and I showed Mr. [Charles M.] Hays the ice forward. I happened to look and noticed the boat was listing, probably half an hour after my first visit to the upper deck. I said to Mr. Hays, "Why, she is listing; she should not do that, the water is perfectly calm, and the boat has stopped." I felt that looked rather serious. He said, "Oh, I don't know; you can not sink this boat." He had a good deal of confidence. He said, "No matter what we have struck, she is good for 8 or 10 hours."

I hardly got back in the grand staircase—I probably waited around there 10 minutes more—when I saw the ladies and gentlemen all coming in off the deck looking very serious, and I caught up to Mr. Beatty, and I said, "What is the matter?" He said, "Why the order is for life belts and boats." I could not believe it at first, it seemed so sudden. I said, "Will you tell Mr. Ross?"

He said, "Yes, I will go and see Mr. Ross." I then went to my cabin and changed as quickly as I could from evening dress to heavy clothes. As soon as I got my overcoat on I got my life preserver and I came out of my cabin.

In the hallway I met a great many people, ladies and gentlemen, with their life belts on, and the ladies were crying, principally, most of them. It was a very serious sight, and I commenced to realize how serious matters were. I then proceeded up to the boat deck, and I saw that they had cleared away—SENATOR SMITH (interposing): Pardon me one moment. Were you still on C deck?

MAJ. PEUCHEN: I was on C deck when I came out and saw the people standing in the corridor near the grand stairway. I then proceeded upstairs to the boat deck, which is the deck above A.

I saw the boats were all ready for action; that is, the covers had been taken off of them, and the ropes cleared, ready to lower. This was on the port side. I was standing near by the second officer, and the captain was standing there as well, at that time. The captain said—I do not know whether it was the captain or the second officer said—"We will have to get these masts out of these boats, and also the sail." He said, "You might give us a hand," and I jumped in the boat, and we got a knife and cut the lashings of the mast, which is a very heavy mast, and also the sail, and moved it out of the boat, saying it would not be required. Then there was a cry, as soon as that part was done, that they were ready to put the women in; so the women came forward one by one. A great many women came with their husbands....They would only allow women in that boat, and the men had to stand back.

SENATOR SMITH: Was there any order to that effect given?

MAJ. PEUCHEN: That was the order. The second officer stood there and he carried out that to the limit. He allowed no men except the sailors, who were manning the boat, but there were no passengers that I saw got into that boat.

SENATOR SMITH: How many sailors?

MAJ. PEUCHEN: I am not sure, but I imagine there were about four. As far as my memory serves me, there were about four. I was busy helping and assisting to get the ladies in. After a reasonable complement of ladies had got aboard, she was lowered, but I did not see one single passenger get in that first boat.

Senator Fleet: You mean male passenger.

MAJ. PEUCHEN: Yes, male passenger.

SENATOR SMITH: Did you see any attempt to get in?

MAJ. PEUCHEN: No, I never saw such order. It was perfect order. The discipline was splendid. The officers were carrying out their duty and I think the passengers behaved splendidly. I did not see a cowardly act by any man.

SENATOR SMITH: Was the boat safely lowered?

MAJ. PEUCHEN: The boat was loaded, but I think they could have taken more in that boat. They took, however, all the ladies that offered to get in at that point.

SENATOR SMITH: Was the boat safely lowered?

MAJ. PEUCHEN: Oh, very; the boat was safely lowered.

SENATOR SMITH: Who was in it that you know of?

MAJ. PEUCHEN I should say about—I do not know—I imagine about 26 or 27. There was room for more.

Then as soon as that boat was lowered, we turned our attention to the next.

I might say I was rather surprised that the sailors were not at their stations, as I have seen the fire drill very often on steamers where they all stand at attention, so many men at the bow and stern of these lifeboats. They seemed to be short of sailors around the lifeboats that were being lowered at this particular point. I do not know what was taking place in other parts of the steamer.

There was one act, sire, I would like to mention a little ahead of my story. When I came on deck first, on this upper deck, there were, it seems to me, about 100 stokers came up with their dunnage bags, and they seemed to crowd this whole deck in front of the boats. One of the officers—I do not know which one, but a very powerful one—came along and drove these men right off that deck. It was a splendid act.

SENATOR SMITH: Off the boat deck?

MAJ. PEUCHEN: Off the boat deck. He drove them, every man, like a lot of sheep, right off the deck.

SENATOR SMITH: Where did they go?

MAJ. PEUCHEN: I do not know. He drove them right ahead of him, and they disappeared. I do not know where they went, but it was a splendid act. They did not put up any resistance. I admired him for it.

I had finished with the lowering of the first boat from the port side. We then proceeded to boat No. 2 or No. 4 or No. 6; I do not know which it is called.

SENATOR SMITH: You had stepped into the boat to assist in lowering it?

MAJ. PEUCHEN: Yes; and then got out of it again.

SENATOR SMITH: And you stepped out of it?

MAJ. PEUCHEN: I only got into the boat to assist in taking out the mast and the sail.

SENATOR SMITH: I understand. Then you got out again?

MAJ. PEUCHEN: Then I got out again, and I assisted in putting the ladies into the boat. We then went to the next boat and we did the same thing – got the mast and sail out of that. There was a quartermaster in the boat, and one sailor, and we commenced to put the ladies in that boat. After that boat had got a full complement of ladies, there were no more ladies to get in, or if there were any other ladies to get in they did not wish to do so, because we were calling out for them—that is, speaking of the port side—but some would not leave their husbands.

SENATOR SMITH: Do you know who they were?

MAJ. PEUCHEN: I only saw one or two stand by who would not get in. Whether they afterwards left them I can not say, but I saw one or two women refuse to get in on that account.

SENATOR SMITH: Did you see any woman get in and then get out because her husband was not with her?

MAJ. PEUCHEN: No, I do not think I did. I saw one lady where they had to sort of pull her away from her husband, he insisting upon her going to the boat and she did not want to go.

This boat was then lowered down, and when it got—

SENATOR SMITH (interposing): Pardon me a moment. How many were put into this second boat?

MAJ. PEUCHEN: I did not know at the time of the lowering, but as I happened to be a passenger later on, they were counted and there were exactly 20 women, 1 quartermaster, 1 sailor, and 1 stowaway that made his appearance after we had been out about an hour.

SENATOR SMITH: Twenty-three all together?

MAJ. PEUCHEN: Twenty-three all together; before I was a passenger.

After that the boat was lowered down some distance, I should imagine probably parallel with C deck, when the quartermaster called up to the officer and said, "I can not manage this boat with only one seaman."

SENATOR SMITH: Where was this call from?

MAJ. PEUCHEN: As the boat was going down, I should think about the third deck. So he made this call for assistance, and the second officer leaned over and saw he was quite right in his statement, that he had only one man in the boat, so they said, "We will have to have some more seamen here," and I did not think they were just at hand, or they may have been getting the next boat ready. However, I was standing by the officer, and I said, "Can I be of any assistance? I am a yachtsman, and can handle a boat with an average man." He said, "Why, yes. I will order you to the boat in preference to a sailor."

SENATOR SMITH: Pardon me right there. Who was this man then in the boat?

MAJ. PEUCHEN: He was one of the quartermasters. The captain was standing still by him at that time, and I think, although the officer ordered me to the boat, the captain said, "You had better go down below and break a window and get in through a window, into the boat."

SENATOR SMITH: The captain said that?

MAJ. PEUCHEN: Yes. That was his suggestion; and I said I did not think it was feasible, and I said I could get in the boat if I could get hold of a rope. However, we got hold of a loose rope in some way that was hanging from the davit, near the block anyway, and by getting hold of this I swung myself off the ship, and lowered myself into the boat.

SENATOR SMITH: How far did you have to swing yourself?

MAJ. PEUCHEN: The danger was jumping off from the boat. It was not after I got the a straight line; it was very easy lowering. But I imagine it was opposite the C deck at the time. On getting into the boat I went aft in the lifeboat, and said to the quartermaster, "What do you want me to do?" He said, "Get down and put that plug in, " and I made a dive down for the plug, and the ladies were all sitting pretty well aft, and I could not see at all. It was dark down there. I felt with my hands, and I said it would be better for him to do it and me do his work, and I said, "Now, you get down and put in the plug, and I will undo the shackles," that is, take the blocks off. So he dropped the blocks, and he got down, and he came rushing back to assist me, and he said, "Hurry up." He said, "This boat is going to founder." I thought he meant our lifeboat is going to founder. I thought he had had some difficulty in finding the plug, or he had not gotten it in properly. But he meant the large boat was going to founder, and that we were to hurry up and get away from it. So we got the rudder in, and he told me to go forward and take an oar. I went forward and got an oar on the port side of the lifeboat; the sailor was on my left, on the starboard side. But we were just opposite each other in rowing.

SENATOR SMITH: Who was the sailor?

MAJ. PEUCHEN: He was the man who gave evidence just before me.

SENATOR SMITH: Mr. Fleet, from the lookout.

MAJ. PEUCHEN: From the lookout, yes; sitting next to me on my left. He told us to row as hard as possible away from the suction. Just as we got rowing out part of the way, this stowaway, an Italian—

SENATOR SMITH: Pardon me. Did the officer say to row away, so as to get away from the suction?

MAJ. PEUCHEN The quartermaster who was in charge of our boat told us to row as hard as we could to get away from this suction, and just as we got a short distance away this stowaway made his appearance. He was an Italian by birth, I should think, who had a broken wrist or arm, and he was of no use to us to row. He got an oar out, but he could not do much, so we got him to take the oar in.

SENATOR SMITH: Where did he make his appearance from, Major?

MAJ. PEUCHEN: Underneath; I think he was stowed away underneath. I should imagine if there was any room for him to get underneath the bow of the boat he would be there. I imagine that was where he came from. He was not visible when looking at the boat. There were only two men when she was lowered.

SENATOR SMITH: Would you know him if you should see him?

MAJ. PEUCHEN: No, it was dark. At daylight I was rowing very hard—in the morning—and I did not notice. As we rowed, pulled away from the *Titanic*, there was an officer's call of some kind. We stopped rowing.

SENATOR SMITH: A whistle?

MAJ. PEUCHEN: A sort of a whistle. Anyway, the quartermaster told us to stop rowing so he could hear it, and this was a call to come back to the boat. So we all thought we ought to go back to the boat. It was a call. But the quartermaster said, "No, we are not going back to the boat." He said, "It is our lives now, not theirs," and he insisted upon our rowing farther away.

SENATOR SMITH: Who made the rebellion against it?

MAJ. PEUCHEN: I think the rebellion was made by some of the married women that were leaving their husbands.

SENATOR SMITH: And did you join in that?

MAJ. PEUCHEN: I did not say anything. I knew I was perfectly powerless.

He was at the rudder. He was a very talkative man. He had been swearing a good deal, and was very disagreeable. I had had one row with him. I asked him to come and row, to assist us in rowing, and let some women steer the boat, as it was a perfectly calm night. It did not require any skill for steering. The stars were out. He refused to do it, and he told me he was in command of that boat, and I was to row.

SENATOR SMITH: Did he remain at the tiller?

MAJ. PEUCHEN: He remained at the tiller, and if we wanted to go back while he was in possession of the tiller, I do not think we could have done so. The women were in between the quartermaster and myself and the other seaman. The night was cold and we kept rowing on. Then he imagined he saw a light. I have done a good deal of yachting in my life, I have owned a yacht for six years and have been out on the Lakes, and I could not see these lights. I saw a reflection. He thought it was a boat of some kind. He thought probably it might be a buoy out there of some kind, and he called out to the next boat, which was within hearing, asking if he knew if there was any buoy around there. This struck me as being perfectly absurd, and showed me the man did not know anything about navigating, expecting to see a buoy in the middle of the Atlantic. However, he insisted upon us rowing. We kept on rowing toward this imaginary light and, after a while, after we had gone a long distance—I am ahead of my story. We commenced to hear signs of the breaking up of the boat.

SENATOR SMITH: Of the *Titanic*?

MAJ. PEUCHEN: Of the *Titanic*. At first I kept my eyes watching the lights, as long as possible.

SENATOR SMITH: From your position in the boat, did you face it?

MAJ. PEUCHEN: I was facing it at this time. I was rowing this way [indicating], and afterwards I changed to the other way. We heard a sort of a call for help after this whistle I described a few minutes ago. This was the officer calling us back. We heard a sort of a rumbling sound and the lights were still on at the rumbling sound, as far as my memory serves me; then a sort of an explosion, then another. It seemed to be one, two, or three rumbling sounds, then the lights went out. Then the dreadful calls and crys.

SENATOR SMITH: For help?

MAJ. PEUCHEN: We could not distinguish the exact cry for assistance; moaning and crying; frightful. It affected all the women in our boat whose husbands were among these; and this went on for some time, gradually getting fainter, fainter. At first it was horrible to listen to.

SENATOR SMITH: How far was it away?

MAJ. PEUCHEN: I think we must have been five-eighths of a mile, I should imagine, when this took place. It was very hard to guess the distance. There were only two of us rowing a very heavy boat with a good many people in it, and I do not think we covered very much ground.

SENATOR SMITH: While these cries of distress were going on, did anyone in the boat urge the quartermaster to return?

MAJ. PEUCHEN: Yes; some of the woman did. But, as a said before, I had had a row with him, and I said to the women, "It is no use you arguing with that man, at all. It is best not to discuss matters with him." He said it was no use going back there, there was only a lot of stiffs there, later on, which was very unkind, and the women resented it very much. I do not think he was qualified to be a quartermaster.

SENATOR SMITH: As a matter of fact, you did not return to the boat?

MAJ. PEUCHEN: We did not return to the boat.

SENATOR SMITH: After you left its side?

MAJ. PEUCHEN: No.

SENATOR SMITH: And when the boat went down, were you looking toward it?

MAJ. PEUCHEN: I was looking toward the boat; yes.

SENATOR SMITH: Did you see it.

MAJ. PEUCHEN: I saw it when the lights went out. You could not tell very much after the lights went out.

SENATOR SMITH: You were not close enough to recognize anyone aboard?

MAJ. PEUCHEN: Oh, no.

SENATOR SMITH: Could you see the outlines of the people on the deck?

MAJ. PEUCHEN: No; you could not. I could only see the outline of the boat; you might say.

SENATOR SMITH: Do you know how she went down?

MAJ. PEUCHEN: While the lights were burning, I saw her bow pointing down and the stern up; not in a perpendicular position, but considerable.

SENATOR SMITH: About what angle?

MAJ. PEUCHEN: I should think an angle of not as much as 45°.

SENATOR SMITH: From what you saw, do you think the boat was intact, or had it broken in two?

MAJ. PEUCHEN: It was intact at that time. I feel sure that an explosion had taken place in the boat, because in passing the wreck the next morning – we steamed past it – I just happened to think of this, which may be of some assistance to this inquiry—I was standing forward, looking to see if I could see any dead bodies, or any of my friends, and to my surprise I saw the barber's pole floating. The barber's pole was on the C deck, my recollection is —the barber shop—and that must have been a tremendous explosion to allow this pole to have broken from its fastenings and drift with the wood.

SENATOR SMITH: Did you hear the explosions?

MAJ. PEUCHEN: Yes, sir, I heard the explosions.

SENATOR SMITH: How loud were they?

MAJ. PEUCHEN: Oh, a sort of a rumbling sound. It was not a sharp sound —more of a rumbling kind of a sound, but still sharp at the same time. It would not be as loud as a clap of thunder, or anything that way, or like a boiler explosion, I should not think.

SENATOR SMITH: Were these explosions evidently from under the water?

MAJ. PEUCHEN: I should think they were from above. I imagined that the decks had blown up with the pressure, pulling the boat down, bow on, this heavy weight and the air between the decks; that is my theory of the explosion. I do not know whether it is correct or not, but I do not think it was the boilers. I think it was the pressure, that heavy weight shoving that down, the water rushing up, and the air coming in between the decks; something had to go.

SENATOR SMITH: How many explosions did you hear?

MAJ. PEUCHEN: I am not absolutely certain of this, because there was a good deal of excitement at the time, but I imagine there were three, one following the other very quickly.

SENATOR SMITH: Did you see the captain after he told you to go below and get through the window into the lifeboat?

MAJ. PEUCHEN: No; I never saw him after that.

SENATOR SMITH: From what you saw of the captain, was he alert and watchful?

MAJ. PEUCHEN: He was doing everything in his power to get women in these boats, and to see that they were lowered properly. I thought he was doing his duty in regard to the lowering of the boats, sir.

SENATOR SMITH: Did you see the officer of the watch that night?

MAJ. PEUCHEN: Whom do you mean? I hardly know what you mean.

SENATOR SMITH: Who was the officer with you on your side of the boat.

MAJ. PEUCHEN: The second officer.

SENATOR SMITH: Mr. Lightoller?

Maj. Peuchen: Yes, sir.

Senator Smith: Had you seen the captain before that night?

Maj. Peuchen: I passed him in one of the companionways some place, just about dinner time.

Senator Smith: What time?

Maj. Peuchen: I can not be very certain as to the hour, around 7 o'clock, I imagine. I generally come out to dress about 7 o'clock.

Senator Smith: What time did you dine that night?

Maj. Peuchen: I dined a little after 7; I think it was a quarter after.

Senator Smith: In the main dining room?

Maj. Peuchen: In the main dining room; yes.

Senator Smith: Did the captain dine in that room?

Maj. Peuchen: I do not think so. I think he dined in the other–in the restaurant.

Senator Smith: But you did not see him?

Maj. Peuchen: I did not see him dining.

Senator Smith: I wish you would say whether or not these lifeboats were equipped with food and water and lights.

Maj. Peuchen: As far as I could tell, our boat was equipped with everything in that respect. I heard some talk that there was not proper food in some of the boats, and when I was on the *Carpathia* I made it my business to go down and look at one or two, and I found hard-tack in this sealed box.

Senator Smith: In both of them?

Maj. Peuchen: On the boat. I did not go all around the fleet.

Senator Smith: You say you looked at one or two?

Maj. Peuchen: One or two.

Senator Smith: Did you find provisions and water in both?

Maj. Peuchen: I did not examine the kegs, but I was assured by the sailors there was water in them.

Senator Smith: Did you see lights in them?

Maj. Peuchen: We had lights in our boat, but some of the other boats did not. I know there was a boat that hung near us that had not lights. Whether it was on account of not being able to light their lights I do not know.

Senator Smith: You say there were 36 or 37 people in your boat?

Maj. Peuchen: No, sir.

Senator Smith: In the first boat that was lowered?

Maj. Peuchen: No; I said I thought about 26 or 27.

Senator Smith: In the first one?

Maj. Peuchen: Yes; I think so.

Senator Smith: And 23 in the second boat before you got in?

Maj. Peuchen: Including the stowaway there would be 23. I made the twenty-fourth.

Senator Smith: Twenty women?

Maj. Peuchen: Twenty women, yes; the quartermaster, one seaman, the stowaway, and then when I got in there were 24.

Senator Smith: Any children?

Maj. Peuchen: No; I do not think we had any children. Later on we tied up to another boat, toward morning, for a very short time—I think for about 15 minutes.

Senator Smith: What boat was that?

Maj. Peuchen: I do not know. Our quartermaster did not know the number of our boat. I do not know the other. I know they called out and asked the number of our boat and our quartermaster did not know which it was.

Senator Smith: Did you hear the testimony given this morning by the third officer?

Maj. Peuchen: I heard part of it, sir. I was out in the hall while he was giving some of it.

Senator Smith: Did you hear him say that a lifeboat was attached to his lifeboat for a while?

Maj. Peuchen: Yes; but, then, let me see; did he not say he took some people off of that boat?

Senator Smith: I was going to come to that.

Maj. Peuchen: No; that was not our boat.

Senator Smith: He said he took three people out of his lifeboat.

Maj. Peuchen: And put them into the one attached.

Senator Fletcher: On the starboard side of No. 7.

Senator Smith: That was not done in your boat?

Maj. Peuchen: No. The only thing that occurred with the boat we were tied up with was, we asked how many men they had in their boat, and this quartermaster said he had about seven sailors, or something like that—six or seven. Then we said, "Surely you can spare us one man, if you have so many," and we got a fireman.

Senator Smith: You got a fireman?

Maj. Peuchen: One more man out of that boat.

Senator Smith: They transferred one more man to you?

Maj. Peuchen: Yes; one more man.

Senator Smith: What did he do?

Maj. Peuchen: He assisted in rowing on the starboard side of the lifeboat, and I rowed on the port side.

Senator Smith: Did any of the women help with the oars?

Maj. Peuchen: Yes; they did, very pluckily, too. We got the oars. Before this occurred we got a couple of women rowing aft, on the starboard side of our boat, and I got two women to assist on our side; but of course the woman with me got sick with the heavy work, and she had to give it up. But I believe the others kept on rowing quite pluckily for a considerable time.

Senator Smith: Do you know who these women were at the oars?

Maj. Peuchen: I know one of them.

Senator Smith: Give the name.

Maj. Peuchen: If you will excuse me, I will have to look it up. [Referring to memorandum.] Miss M. E. A. Norton, Apaley Villa, Horn Lane, Acton, London.

Senator Smith: Is that the only one of the women who handled the oars that you know by name?

Maj. Peuchen: No; I think there is another.

Senator Smith: The other two women who handled the oars you do not know?

Maj. Peuchen: I do not know their names....

Senator Smith: Major, at any time between leaving the side of the *Titanic*, and reaching the *Carpathia*, did Mrs. Douglas [Mahala Douglas, first-class passenger] hold the tiller?

Maj. Peuchen: In our lifeboat?

Senator Smith: Yes.

Maj. Peuchen: I think the quartermaster was at the tiller all the time, with the exception probably of a couple of minutes. I know he asked one of the ladies for some brandy, and he also asked for one of her wraps, which he got.

Senator Smith: The officer did?

Maj. Peuchen: The quartermaster, not the officer....

Senator Smith: You say when the impact occurred, the ship shuddered?

Maj. Peuchen: When the impact occurred, describing it I would say it would be like a wave striking it, a very heavy wave.

Senator Smith: How soon after that did the boat begin to list?

Maj. Peuchen: I should think about 25 minutes afterwards.

SENATOR SMITH: So far as you could observe, did the passengers have on life belts?

MAJ. PEUCHEN: They had...

SENATOR SMITH: I believe you said you have had considerable experience as a mariner?

MAJ. PEUCHEN: Yes, sir.

SENATOR SMITH: Can you say whether the *Titanic* listed to the starboard or port side?

MAJ. PEUCHEN: She listed to the starboard side; the side she was struck on.

SENATOR SMITH: Did she go down by the bow or by the head?

MAJ. PEUCHEN: Eventually, you mean?

SENATOR SMITH: Yes.

MAJ. PEUCHEN: It is the same thing.

SENATOR SMITH: No; not exactly the same thing. Where was this impact on the bow of the ship?

MAJ. PEUCHEN: She was down by the bow. You mean the head by the bow, do you not?

SENATOR SMITH: Exactly.

MAJ. PEUCHEN: It was aft of the bow about 40 feet, I should imagine, on the starboard side—about 40 or 50 feet, I should imagine—from where the ice started to come off the iceberg.

SENATOR SMITH: You say you saw some ice on the deck?

MAJ. PEUCHEN: Yes, sir.

SENATOR SMITH: Do you know of anyone being injured by ice on the deck?

MAJ. PEUCHEN: No; but I know a great many of the passengers were made afraid by this iceberg passing their portholes. The ship shoved past this ice, and a great many of them told me afterwards they could not understand this thing moving past them—those that were awakened at the time. In fact, it left ice on some of the portholes, they told me.

SENATOR SMITH: Do you know of your own knowledge whether any alarm was sounded to arouse the passengers from their rooms after the impact?

MAJ. PEUCHEN: There was no alarm sounded whatever. In fact, I talked with two young ladies who claimed to have had a very narrow escape. They said their stateroom was right near the Astors, I think almost next to it, and they were not awakened.

SENATOR SMITH: They were not awakened?

MAJ. PEUCHEN: They slept through this crash, and they were awakened by Mrs. Astor. She was in rather an excited state, and their door being open—and I think the Astor door was open—they think that was the means of their being saved.

SENATOR SMITH: On what deck were they?

MAJ. PEUCHEN: I do not know, sir. It was only conversation told me on the *Carpathia.*

SENATOR SMITH: I think you said that from your judgment and from your own observation there was no general alarm given?

MAJ. PEUCHEN: No, I did not hear one. I was around the boat all the time...

SENATOR FLETCHER: Major, do you mean for us to understand that at the time lifeboat No. 4 and lifeboat No. 6 on the port side of the ship were loaded and lowered every woman in sight was given an opportunity?

MAJ. PEUCHEN: Every woman on the port side was given an opportunity. In fact, we had not enough women to put into the boats. We were looking for them. I can not understand why we did not take some men. The boats would have held more.

SENATOR FLETCHER: If there had been more women there they could have found room in those boats?

MAJ. PEUCHEN: Plenty of room....

SENATOR FLETCHER: Is it your idea that the water was so cold that a person could not live in it except for a short time?

MAJ. PEUCHEN: I feel quite sure that a person could not live in that water very long. Those who had been in the water had their feet frozen; that is, those who were standing up in a boat in the water. I happened to have the cabin with three of them who were rescued, and they said they sustained their life by punching each other during the two or three hours they stood up. The minute any one got tired and sat down in the water, or at least very shortly thereafter, he floated off the raft, dead, I believe.

SENATOR FLETCHER: What was the temperature of the water, if you know?

MAJ. PEUCHEN: I do not know, sir.

SENATOR FLETCHER: You say people were frozen?

MAJ. PEUCHEN: Their feet were frozen; yes, sir.

SENATOR FLETCHER: Was that by exposure, after being taken out of the water on the boat?

MAJ. PEUCHEN: Yes, sir. A number of them swam, I know of three cases, at least, where they jumped from the big boat and swam and got on to a raft which was partly submerged in the water, and they stood up in the raft, and those are the ones whose feet were badly swollen or frozen.

Senator Fletcher: You assume from that that the water was very cold?

Maj. Peuchen: I am sure it was.

Senator Fletcher: Was it below the freezing point?

Maj. Peuchen: It must have been very near the freezing point, anyway. It probably would not be quite freezing; but it being in salt water, of course it would not freeze very readily.

Senator Fletcher: Was there any floating ice, aside from these icebergs?

Maj. Peuchen: Oh, yes; when we started to steam away we passed a lot of floating ice, I suppose several miles long.

Senator Fletcher: You mean the *Carpathia* steamed through the ice?

Maj. Peuchen: Yes.

Senator Fletcher: Did you come into contact with floating ice while you were on the lifeboat?

Maj. Peuchen: No, sir; we did not.

Senator Fletcher: Have you any idea as to how long a person could live in water like that?

Maj. Peuchen: It depends on his constitution, but I should imagine that if a person could stay in the water a half an hour he would be doing very well.

Senator Fletcher: Would not the effort to swim, and exercise, prevent one getting numb for several hours?

Maj. Peuchen: Up to a certain point; yes. But I do not think a man could live an hour in that water....

Anthony Brandt is an expert in the history of travel and adventure and is the book review editor for *Adventure* magazine. He has edited more than 20 books for National Geographic, including a new edition of *The Journals of Lewis and Clark*. He is a contributor to GQ, *Esquire*, and the *New York Times Sunday Magazine* in addition to other publications. Anthony Brandt lives in Sag Harbor, New York.